A Maê

D1368082

The
ONLY WAY
to
Eternal
Life

Ma Tante d'amour

BY CHAIKOU BAH

2006/12/12

TRAFFORD
PUBLISHING

Note for Librarians: A cataloguing record for this book is available from Library and Archives Canada at www.collectionscanada.ca/amicus/index-e.html

ISBN 1-4120-6399-x

Printed in Victoria, BC, Canada. Printed on paper with minimum 30% recycled fibre. Trafford's print shop runs on "green energy" from solar, wind and other environmentally-friendly power sources.

TRAFFORD
PUBLISHING™

Offices in Canada, USA, Ireland and UK

This book was published on-demand in cooperation with Trafford Publishing. On-demand publishing is a unique process and service of making a book available for retail sale to the public taking advantage of on-demand manufacturing and Internet marketing. On-demand publishing includes promotions, retail sales, manufacturing, order fulfilment, accounting and collecting royalties on behalf of the author.

Book sales for North America and international:
Trafford Publishing, 6E–2333 Government St.,
Victoria, BC v8t 4p4 CANADA
phone 250 383 6864 (toll-free 1 888 232 4444)
fax 250 383 6804; email to orders@trafford.com

Book sales in Europe:
Trafford Publishing (uk) Limited, 9 Park End Street, 2nd Floor
Oxford, UK oxi 1hh UNITED KINGDOM
phone 44 (0)1865 722 113 (local rate 0845 230 9601)
facsimile 44 (0)1865 722 868; info.uk@trafford.com

Order online at:
trafford.com/05-1310

10 9 8 7 6 5 4 3

Acknowledgments

I thank my wife and children for their love.

I thank my parents, my in-laws and other members of my family for their support.

I thank all the acquaintances, friends and patients who have prayed for me and helped me and all the men and women who have taught and are teaching me the word of God.

I thank Jane Broderick for editing the book and sister Debbie Brown and brother John Garris for proofreading it.

I thank God for my salvation, for His love and for everything He has done and will do in my life. Finally, I thank the Most High for the privilege of writing about Him.

Introduction

"God hath chosen the foolish things of the world to confound the wise; and God hath chosen the weak things of the world to confound the things which are mighty; And base things of the world, and things which are despised, hath God chosen, yea, and things which are not, to bring to nought things that are: That no flesh should glory in his presence" (I Corinthians 1:27–29).

The story that follows is true. However, the names of certain people have been changed. The purpose of the book is not to insult or alienate, any person or group but to write about God and the Truth; if in the process I have offended or alienated any person or group, I sincerely apologize.

Dedication

To my unsaved family members, friends, and all the unsaved readers of this book, in the hope that they will come to know God and be saved.

Contents

Acknowledgments iii

Introduction iv

Dedication vi

1   The Phone Call 1

2   The Decision 8

3   The Move 23

4   Easter 1996 33

5   In Search of the Truth 41

6   To Mexico 57

7   "A Church in My Neighbourhood" 61

8   Looking for a Doctor 64

9   The Inquiry 72

10   The Case of Mr. D. 76

11   Negotiating with Dr. Trouts 79

12   Interview with the Subcommittee 83

13   The Contract 89

14   "Jungle House" 93

15   The "Witch Hunt" 101

16   The Case of Mrs. Aguilera 107

17   Blood Loss and Operating Room Problems 113

18   The Solution to Operating Room Problems 117

19   Problems on the Ward 123

20   Dr. Trouts' Guidelines 127

21   The Scientific Meeting 133

22   Summer 1997 139

23   End of the Agreement 143

24   A Review of the Orthopaedics Division 148

25   Witnesses 154

26   A Sheep Among Wolves 163

27   At the Discretion of the Minister 169

28	The Advocate!	174
29	The Review	178
30	The Klein Report	184
31	Meeting with the Board	189
32	Awaiting the Board's Decision	195
33	The Board's Decision	200
34	Working Again	206
35	The "Independent Review"	210
36	Pocket Stitching	217
37	Moving	222
38	Learning from the Bible	226
39	"The Way, the Truth and the Life"	250
40	November 9th	259
41	Applying for a Judicial Review	269
42	Help?	275
43	Fear	279
44	The Promise	288
45	The Tenth Attorney	291
46	Another Promise	296
47	The Court Hearing	299
48	Licence to Harm	305
49	To London!	314
50	The Network	322
51	Leaving Bermuda	330
52	Witnessing	334
53	"Many Patients Against You"	376
54	Conclusion	392
Appendix: Patients' Letters		410
Bibliography		419

CHAPTER ONE

The Phone Call

It was a Thursday evening in October 1993. I had finished work at seven o'clock and arrived home half an hour later. I had finished eating and was putting our baby to bed when the phone rang. I became apprehensive, fearing that it was the hospital calling and I would have to go back to work, for I was on duty. My wife answered the phone and told me that a Dr. Trouts wanted to speak to me.

I had not spoken to Dr. Trouts in four years. We had first met in January 1987 while doing our training in orthopaedic surgery. Dr. Trouts, who was training at the other medical school in the city, had come to do a rotation at the medical school where I was training. I had fond memories of the three months I worked with him. I remembered particularly his eating habits. Dr. Trouts always had tea and a snack around ten o'clock in the morning, then two hours later would be hungry again and impatient to eat. After the three months were up I ran into him on a few occasions while attending conferences. The last I heard, he was practising orthopaedic surgery somewhere in the United States.

My wife took the baby from me and handed me the phone. Dr. Trouts and I went through the usual salutation, after which he informed me that he was working in a town near Hartford, Connecticut. He was in Montreal to sit for the oral part of the Royal College examinations. He said he had failed the exam twice in the past and this would be his last chance to sit for it. Because of the exam situation, he said, he had been unable to go back and work in his native Bermuda and his two associates in Hartford were very unkind to him. Dr. Trouts said he had met some orthopaedic residents at one of the hospitals in town who told him I had a successful practice.

Finally, he explained why he was calling me. He wanted me to help him prepare for the exam. I was surprised that he was asking for my help, for other than the three months we trained together in 1987 Dr. Trouts and I had never socialized. I was also surprised that he had not sought help from his former classmates, most of whom were still living in Montreal. I told him I could not help much, given my busy schedule, but would try to find a few hours. I invited him to come to my home Saturday evening so we could discuss how I might help.

On Saturday evening Dr. Trouts and his wife, whom I had not met before, came to my home. I gave him my personal notes, books and other documents I had used to prepare for the same exam two years earlier. I instructed Dr. Trouts in what he should concentrate his studies on and suggested we meet again so that I could quiz him on the study materials I had given him.

On numerous occasions over the next two weeks, at the end of my work day, I would drive forty-five minutes to meet Dr. Trouts in a downtown library. At this stage he knew the exam material very well, but was disorganized, timid and hesitant, probably because of his negative experiences on the two previous occasions when he had sat for the exam. I spent hours giving Dr. Trouts a mock exam. We pretended that I was the examiner and he was the examinee. I pounced on him and asked questions in the ruthless manner of some examiners. With time, he became more structured and confident. We even met the evening before his exam and worked late into the night. As I drove him to his hotel that night, I kept on asking him questions until I dropped him at his hotel.

The next evening Dr. Trouts called to inform me that he had passed the exam. He told me that during the exam he was so direct and structured that the examiners could not believe they were dealing with the same person they had examined twice previously. The first questions they asked him concerned the case of spine pathology I had quizzed him about the night before as I drove him to his hotel – questions he would have been unable to answer before that. Dr. Trouts thanked me for my help and said he wanted to invite my wife and me to dinner. The following Saturday my wife and I met Dr. Trouts and his wife for dinner at a restaurant on Prince Arthur

Street. I paid for my wife's meal and my own. Dr. Trouts gave me back the study materials I had lent him.

Five months later, in March 1994, Dr. Trouts phoned me from Bermuda. He said he had moved back to Bermuda where he had opened an office and was running a very successful surgical practice (two years later I would learn that his practice was not nearly as successful at he had portrayed it to be). He said he was calling to ask me to join him in his practice. I told him I was not interested and suggested he call a former classmate of his who wished to move away from Montreal. Dr. Trouts said he was looking for a spine surgeon. I gave him the name of another former classmate of his who had spine training and suggested he call this person. Dr. Trouts said he would prefer to work with me. I thanked him for the job offer and said I was not interested in leaving my current practice.

Three months later, in June, Dr. Trouts and I met at a conference in the United States. Again he asked me to go and work with him in Bermuda. Again I told him I was not interested in leaving Montreal. During the conference Dr. Trouts asked me to join him in Bermuda so often that it became a nuisance. At one point I politely asked his wife, who was also at the conference, to tell Dr. Trouts to leave me alone.

Dr. Trouts was the second professional who had asked me to go and work in Bermuda. In 1990, when I finished my orthopaedic training, Dr. Fowler, my program director, had suggested that I called Dr. Jameson, a general surgeon practising in Bermuda, who wished to hire an orthopaedic surgeon. At first I did not call Dr. Jameson because I was not interested in moving to Bermuda and I thought Dr. Jameson should have been the one contacting me, but finally, at Dr. Fowler's insistence, I phoned him. Dr. Jameson was not warm at all. He told me he was looking to hire a black orthopaedic surgeon and would pay me an annual salary of $80,000 US. I was offended that after all my medical studies someone would choose to hire me because of the colour of my skin rather than because of my qualifications. I told Dr. Jameson that I was not interested in his job offer and that my plan for the next two years was to do a fellowship in spine surgery.

In July 1994, Dr. Trouts phoned and said he had patients with complicated spine pathologies and he needed my expertise. He suggested I go to Bermuda for a vacation and see his patients at the same time. I told him I would think about it.

In October 1994, I went to Bermuda, accompanied by my wife, to attend a conference and to see Dr. Trouts' patients.

The first patient I saw was Mr. J.T., a white male in his sixties who had had two back operations in England. The surgeon had inserted four screws in Mr. J.T.'s back; they were tied together with some chicken wire that was not holding at all. The patient told me the surgeon had billed him $30,000 US for the second procedure and suggested that he could benefit from a third, which would cost the same as the second. The patient was in severe pain, which was not relieved by medication or the strong liquor he was ingesting.

The second patient I saw was Mrs. L.R., a white woman in her sixties who presented with a scoliosis (curvature) and a spinal stenosis (narrowing of the spinal canal). A surgeon in Boston had performed an extensive laminectomy (removal of bone) on her back eight years before and told her that she would need further surgery in the future. When she went back to see the surgeon because of severe pain, he told her that her back condition had worsened and he could not operate on her.

The third patient I saw was Mr. G.L., a black male bus driver in his sixties who had severe back and leg pain and difficulty walking.

All three patients were very polite and I was impressed with their manners and behaviour. They rose when I entered the examining room, shook my hand, and sat down only when I told them to.

I explained to Mr. G.L. and the other two patients that they required back surgery to alleviate their suffering. Mr. G.L. told me he either would wait for me to come to Bermuda to perform the surgery or would travel to the United States to find a surgeon.

At the end of my visit, Dr. Trouts asked me if I could return to Bermuda to operate on the three patients. I told him I would not be available until January 1995, at which time I could perhaps travel back to the Island for a few days.

The conference lasted six days. The staff at the hotel, like most hotel staff everywhere, were very friendly. The only time we left the hotel to have dinner, the manager of the Italian restaurant would not let us take the carriage in which our son was sleeping into the restaurant. He suggested we wake our son and leave the carriage outside. Dr. Trouts said this was highly unusual as most people on the Island were very friendly. At the end of our dinner, Dr. Trouts drove us around the Island. He took us to Tucker Town, the wealthiest part of Bermuda, where a former U.S. presidential candidate and the current Italian president, a billionaire, owned homes. Dr. Trouts said I would be able to afford a house in that neighbourhood if I were to work in Bermuda. He told me that Dr. Fascioni, a Canadian orthopaedic surgeon, had bought a four-bedroom house with a swimming pool for $1.3 million US after having worked in Bermuda for only five years. I told him that my house in Montreal was bigger than Dr. Fascioni's and I had paid a fraction of the price for it, and that in any case I went home only to eat and sleep and thus needed only two rooms. Then Dr. Trouts said houses in Bermuda are built of limestone and can last three hundred years. I told him I did not intend to live that long.

The day my family and I were scheduled to leave Bermuda, Dr. Trouts invited us for brunch at the Floral Beach Club, a private club where he was a member. At the end of the meal he again asked me to come and work with him in Bermuda. He described to me the workings of the orthopaedic division at the hospital. There were four other orthopaedic surgeons practising on the Island. He explained that Dr. Cooperson, a white Bermudian in his mid-fifties, had been practising there for twenty-five years. Dr. Cooperson had hired Dr. Fascioni, the Canadian, who was in his early forties, six years earlier, as well as Dr. Chalvin, a surgeon from India who was in his mid-forties. Dr. Trouts estimated that Dr. Fascioni was billing $600,000 a year and said that he was paying twenty percent of his income, after office expenses, to Dr. Cooperson. Dr. Trouts estimated that Dr. Chalvin was billing the same amount as Dr. Fascioni. He said that Dr. Jameson paid Dr. Chalvin a salary of $90,000 a year and kept the balance of the money that Dr. Chalvin earned. Dr. Trouts said that in his first year in Bermuda he billed $400,000 US, without working hard. He said that if I were to move to Bermuda, with my specialization in spine surgery I could expect to bill at least $500,000 US the first year. He then said that I would need a work permit and that it would be mandatory for a Bermudian, such as Dr. Trouts, to hold my work permit. Because we were friends, he said, he would ask me to give him anywhere between zero and twenty percent of my income after expenses for holding my work permit.

I asked Dr. Trouts why he could not work with Dr. Cooperson. He said that Dr. Cooperson had promised him a position when his surgical training was complete, but when he approached Dr. Cooperson about work at the end of his training Dr. Cooperson ignored him. I suggested that he offer Dr. Chalvin a higher salary than he was receiving from Dr. Jameson. Dr. Trouts said he had considered that option. I strongly advised him to reconsider it because I was not interested in moving to Bermuda. My family and I flew back to Montreal that afternoon.

Over the next few weeks Dr. Trouts called me on a few occasions to discuss my trip to Bermuda to operate on the three patients I had seen in consultation during my visit. One of the things I wanted to know was whether the hospital had the necessary surgical instruments for the procedures. I asked Dr. Trouts to fax me a list of the hospital's surgical instruments. The list he faxed me showed that the hospital had less than ten percent of the instruments necessary for a spine case. The hospital did not even have an operating frame, a table essential for spine surgery. I suggested to Dr. Trouts that he ask the hospital administrator to purchase the instruments. He called me back to report that the head operating room nurse said that she was not going to buy surgical instruments for us to use on three spinal cases and that a visiting spine specialist from Boston, working with Dr. Cooperson, managed to operate on spine cases with the few instruments the hospital had; she would, however, purchase the .instruments if I were to move to Bermuda. To solve the problem of the lack of instruments and implants, I contacted a medical sales representative in Toronto, who agreed to bring temporarily to Bermuda the surgical implants necessary to operate on Dr. Trouts' three patients. I also borrowed some instruments from my hospital in Montreal.

In January 1995, I travelled to Bermuda to operate on the spinal cases. Assisted by Dr. Trouts, I operated on the three patients on three different days. The medical sales representative from Toronto was in the operating room at all times during the procedures to instruct the staff in the use of the implants. All the surgeries went well, but the whole process was long and tedious. They took an average of five hours. It was a free-for-all in the operating room. People walked in and out at random and talked loudly. Dr. Trouts tried to reassure me by explaining that the process had been long and difficult because the staff were not used to operating on such complex spine cases. At the end of the three days I had severe pain in my right wrist and developed a tendinitis because I had been using some very old instruments.

Dr. Trouts and I performed the last operation on Friday morning. The following day we went to the hospital to see the three patients. On Sunday afternoon I boarded the plane back to Montreal via Toronto. On the plane I met Kate, a Canadian woman who introduced herself as an interior designer. She told me she had been living in Bermuda for eight years and was travelling to Toronto to see her physician. Kate said she had to deal with a lot of professional jealousy the first years she lived in Bermuda, but was doing well now. She urged me to move to Bermuda, saying that the Island needed good doctors. She gave me her phone number and asked me to call her if I decided to move to Bermuda. She told me she was well connected and would help me to find accommodations and get settled. My plane to Montreal landed at ten o'clock in the evening and I arrived home an hour later.

At half past seven the next morning I was in the operating room at my hospital in Montreal ready to operate on six patients, including a complex spinal case similar to one of the cases I had operated on in Bermuda. It took less effort to operate on the six patients than to perform one surgery in Bermuda. In spite of having the wrist pain, I finished the six operations by four o'clock in the afternoon.

When I got home that evening I called Dr. Trouts to inquire about the status of the three patients. He said they were doing very well. He said he had been so exhausted by the three surgeries we had performed that on Sunday after I left he had gone to bed at six o'clock and slept like a log until eight the next morning.

Over the next few months Dr. Trouts phoned me and sent me X-rays to inform me about the progress of the three patients. Every time we spoke he asked me to come and work with him in Bermuda. My answer was always the same – that is, negative.

CHAPTER TWO

The Decision

One of the reasons why I did not want to leave Canada was that all of my family lived within an hour's drive from me. Another reason was that I was happy with my working conditions. My former classmates who had moved to the United States advised me that I too should consider moving there because they were billing more than $500,000 a year. One had bought a Porsche, another a Mercedes convertible, within years of moving there. Another told me that he had built a million-dollar mansion. I was not making as much money as my colleagues in the United States, but I was happy with my standard of living and my yearly income of over $300,000 CDN, which was far more than most people in Canada were earning. Neither was I impressed with the fact that my colleagues in the United States possessed luxurious cars. In my first year of practice in Montreal, I had bought the most popular 4x4 at the time because some of my colleagues drove that car. Two years later most of my colleagues in Montreal bought luxurious baby boomer cars. I decided that for the moment I was not going to follow their example, because there would be no end to the competition. And I was not impressed by my colleague's talk of the mansion he owned in the United States. We had a house that was satisfactory for me, which my wife said was too big to clean. One former classmate and friend who had moved to the States told me he was paying only thirty-eight percent of his income in income tax, while fifty-four percent of my income went to taxes. The friend told me that each year he invested $30,000 US towards his retirement, while I was allowed to invest only $13,500 CDN each year towards mine. I must admit that on this ground I envied my friend, but not enough to make me want to leave Canada. I envied him more when he told me that while he made twice as much money in the United States as he had in Canada, he worked significantly less and was able to spend more time with his family; however, this was still not a reason for me to move to the United States, at least for now.

I was content with my working conditions. I was practising in two hospitals in a Montreal suburb. The working environments were pleasant, the operating room staff were extremely efficient and the surgeons were extremely competent. The chief of staff at the main hospital and the head nurses at both hospitals went to great lengths to get me all the instruments and implants I needed in order to operate. I had double the instruments I required. I worked with seven other surgeons. We all met once a week for a scientific meeting. Once a month we had dinner together and twice a year we invited the office and hospital staff to dinner. We consulted each other, transferred patients back and forth from one to the other for the benefit of the patients, and assisted each other in the operating room whenever the need arose.

Though we all worked together, everyone took home the money he or she made. There was not a senior-junior or master-slave relationship. At one point the working relationship became poisoned when the associates invited their wives to become involved in a business they co-owned. As a result, two associates left the group and established a practice in a separate location. The hospital chief of staff met with all the associates and warned us that he would not tolerate any bickering at the hospital. He advised us to put aside our personal differences and work together for the benefit of the patients and the hospital. We followed his advice and continued working together at the hospital.

The first eighteen months I practised as a surgeon in Montreal, I was so enthusiastic that I didn't take a vacation. At one point the chief of orthopaedic asked me why I didn't take a vacation. I told him that for me a vacation was doing what I liked, and I liked working. He looked at me as if I were crazy. At the time I thought I was very smart, but now I realize I was off-track. In addition to running back and forth between the two hospitals, I saw patients in eight different clinics and once a month I drove three hours to see patients at one of the five federal prisons my group covered. At the end of two years, in spite of operating two or three days per week I had more than a one-year waiting list for surgery and a four-month waiting list for consultations in my office. People were coming from all corners of the province to see me. Former professors of mine working in teaching hospitals were referring patients to me. All of this only fed my ego, the ego of a surgeon.

For the first six months I worked all day without breaking for lunch and did not get home for dinner until nine in the evening. On one such gruelling day I had worked all morning and afternoon seeing patients in the clinic. At four o'clock I had seen eighty patients and had fifteen more to see. As I was making my way to the washroom, a patient who was sitting in the waiting room commented that he had been waiting more than two hours to be seen because I was wandering around. This comment upset me. When I returned from the washroom, I asked the clinic nurse to direct me to the cafeteria. She replied that the cafeteria was closed at that time of day. I said never mind and asked her again to direct me to the cafeteria, which she did. I exited the clinic again, leaving the fifteen patients in the waiting room. A few minutes later I returned to the clinic and saw all fifteen. From that day on, I took the time to have lunch and go to the washroom when the need arose, but worked with the same enthusiasm as before.

In my third year a series of events made me realize that perhaps I should change my work habits. The first event occurred in the clinic. I was running left and right, seeing patients, talking to the nurses, talking on the phone with my office staff, patients, patients' family members, physicians and workers' compensation agents. Then I got to a patient, a gentleman in his sixties who had been waiting patiently. He said, "Doctor, I have been watching you running around. Do you always work like this?" I answered yes.

"If you continue at this pace," he said, "you'll never make it to my age." The gentleman was right. In the previous fifty years, less than half a dozen orthopaedic surgeons in Quebec had been able to enjoy their retirement. All the others had died before or just after retiring. I thought of the gentleman's comment for a few days, but kept up my hectic pace.

The second event occurred in the operating room. One day I was scheduled to perform eight fairly significant operations. At noon, upon discovering that I was behind schedule, I started pressuring the staff to work faster. I told one of the nurses who was not keeping pace with me that she was not fast enough and urged her several times to hurry. A few moments later I noticed that the nurse was chubbier than usual. I asked the other nurses if she was pregnant, to which they answered yes. I felt very bad and apologized to the nurse. She accepted my apology so graciously that I felt even worse for having reprimanded her. I finished operating on the eight cases at four o'clock, on schedule. This event made me realize that in addition to pushing myself, I was stressing others, which I did not like at all.

If the first two events did not convince me to alter my work habits, the third left me no choice. Sometime in 1994 I developed a headache. It was not incapacitating and was relieved by Tylenol. A month later I had a second headache, no worse than the first. This was unusual for me. I had not had a headache since 1984, and that had lasted less than three hours. My first reaction was to see a dentist, because I remembered that, aside from the episode in 1984, my only previous headache occurred concurrently with a minor dental problem.

The dentist examined me, took x-rays of my mouth and said everything was fine. Next, I went to an eye specialist because I thought my headaches might be an indication that I needed glasses. The eye specialist told me nothing was wrong with my eyesight. Still curious about the source of my headache, I went to see a family physician, someone who worked at the same hospital I did. The physician said I was working too hard and my headaches might be related to my work habits. I disagreed completely with this assessment because, apart from the two episodes of headache, I had no complaints. My mood, sleep habits and energy level were unaltered. I ran an hour every second morning, bicycled every other morning and bicycled extensively on those weekends when I was not on duty. In addition, there were few places I felt more at ease than in the operating room. I nonetheless thought it would be wise to change my work habits.

The one part of my schedule that needed drastic change was the clinic, where I routinely saw a hundred patients a day. I informed my colleagues and the head nurse at the clinic that I wanted to see only fifty patients a day. I organized my schedule accordingly and for the next month rarely saw more than fifty patients in the clinic. There were times when I got bored seeing so few patients, but overall I enjoyed my work.

Then one day the chief of orthopaedic informed me that he and the other surgeons had discussed my seeing only fifty patients a day and they all agreed that I had to see at least eighty, as they did. He said their clinics were overflowing with patients since I had started seeing fewer. I suggested that he and the other surgeons follow my example and see fewer patients. This was what the Quebec Orthopaedic Association recommended to its members, because the more patients a doctor saw the less the government paid us per patient. When doctors saw an average of fifty patients per day the government paid us $50 per patient, but when we saw an average of sixty per day the government decreased our per-patient fee to $40 because it had a fixed budget for doctors' wages. The doctors who thought they were invincible and did not understand the system saw sixty, seventy, eighty or even ninety patients per day and the government paid them less and less for each patient. As a result doctors were being paid an average of less than $20 per patient. However, the chief of orthopaedic smiled at my suggestion and said they were not interested in seeing fewer patients, even though they often complained about seeing eighty to a hundred per day, because they were driven by economics and by an overburdened and sick health-care system. Furthermore, it was less demanding for them to see a large number of patients than it was for me. They all practised sports medicine and took an average of five minutes to see a patient with knee or hip pain, while as a spine specialist I needed at least thirty minutes to adequately evaluate a patient. I could have argued with the chief of orthopaedics and my other colleagues and held my ground, but it would have been a waste of time and energy because, first, I could not be present all the time to verify the number of patients who were scheduled in my clinic, and second, I could not have refused to see the fifty-first patient who had been scheduled, against my wishes, and who had waited hours to see me.

Soon, therefore, I was back to seeing more than eighty patients a day. I thought that since I had no say with regard to the number of patients I saw, I could limit the amount of time I spent with each. This led to a patient's complaining about me. A man in his late sixties complained that I had failed to address all his problems. I saw this man on a day when I had finished operating at one hospital at one o'clock in the afternoon, an hour later than scheduled. I rushed to the second hospital where I was supposed to start a clinic at one p.m. but arrived at 1:45. Upon my arrival, with dozens of patients already waiting impatiently in the waiting room, the clinic staff informed me that I had forty-seven patients scheduled in my clinics and a few others to see in the emergency room. In addition, I had to see a few patients on the surgical ward and be back at the other hospital by five o'clock to attend a surgical meeting.

The man in question was the third patient I saw in the clinic. He complained of pain in his neck and right arm. I examined him thoroughly and sent him for x-rays. When he returned, I explained that he had degenerative changes to his neck, suggested treatment for the condition and made appropriate arrangements for the prescribed treatment. When I rose to leave the examining room, the man told me he had a problem with his right shoulder and right arm. I told him that the degenerative changes in his neck were the source of his shoulder and arm pain. He said I had not looked at his right shoulder. Instead of arguing that I had already examined his shoulder, I proceeded to conduct another physical examination of his right shoulder and arm and showed him that his shoulder and arm pain were referred pain from the neck. I thought the gentleman was satisfied until I had my hand on the doorknob, about to leave the room. In an authoritative voice, he said, "Whoa, whoa." I said, "What?" The man said, "Don't leave so fast," and pointed to his feet dangling from the examining table. He said I had not examined his bunions. I told him that I had seen him for his neck problem, the reason for his visit, and would not have time to examine his bunions because, as he had seen, there were many other patients waiting and I was behind schedule. I suggested he take another appointment and left the room. The man was in no hurry. He sat and monopolized the examining room for few minutes, then finally left when he realized that I was not going to examine his bunions. He complained to the hospital that I had not treated him adequately. I spent more time responding to the man's complaint in front of a committee than it would have taken me to examine his bunions. The committee concluded that I had acted properly.

Since my colleagues would not allow me to see fewer patients in my clinic and I could not limit the amount of time I spent with each patient, I thought I would take some time off. In May 1995, I wrote to my colleagues and to the chief of orthopaedic requesting a six-month sabbatical. They turned down my request, on the basis that the hospital rules stated that one could take a sabbatical only after working for ten years. My colleagues were so upset that I had asked for time off that they refused to speak to me.

Under the circumstances, I felt that the only way to alleviate my recurring headaches was to relocate to an environment where the workload might be lighter.

In the midst of all this, in June 1995, I received a call from Dr. Trouts asking me once again to join him in Bermuda. He said I could replace him for part of the summer, as it was a very busy season at the hospital with all the tourists having motorbike accidents. I told him I could not replace him on such short notice because of my busy practice. He said that during our meeting at the Floral Beach Club in October 1994 he had suggested taking anywhere between zero and twenty percent of my income after expenses for holding my work permit. He said that now he would agree to withhold only ten percent of my income after expenses. I asked why he would withhold any part of my income if we were friends. He answered that he would have to complete a lot of paper work regarding immigration, the hospital and the doctors' association, and that to have only ten percent of my income withheld was a bargain. At the end of our conversation I asked Dr. Trouts to fax me the contract, including his new proposal to withhold only ten percent of my income after expenses, so that I could consider it and present it to my attorney. A few days later he faxed me an eight-page document that began as follows:

> "By way of introduction I would like to put down what I think the essence of our agreement is. In other words, an outline. I will send you also some more formal drafts. Our final version will have to be one we put together between ourselves."

I called Dr. Trouts and told him he was supposed to fax me a contract, not a summary of our discussion. He said legal fees were very high in Bermuda and it would cost $4,000 to prepare a service contract. He could not invest that amount of money, he said, when he was not sure I would move to Bermuda. He promised to have an attorney prepare a contract and have it ready for signing within one week of my arrival. I told Dr. Trouts that I did not trust people, especially surgeons, when it came to money. He said that he too had had a bad experience, as his former associates in Hartford had tried to rob him. He said he would not rob me because we were friends, because I had helped him with the exam and because of his bad experience. Dr. Trouts' speech did not reassure me, but I did not insist on a ready-made contract because I was not sure I wanted to move to Bermuda.

If I was not sure I wanted to move to Bermuda, my wife was certain she did not want to move anywhere. She was happy living close to her family and was content with her life. She adored her house and liked her brand-new car of the year. I had invested in a very lucrative business for her that gave her enough spending money. She was on maternity leave and spent most of her time shopping, or what she called "bargain hunting." So when I tried to discuss the virtues of moving to Bermuda or the United States, she was not enthusiastic. I complained that I worked too hard and was not often home with her and our son. She did not stay anything, but I could tell by the expression on her face that she did not have a problem with my not being home often.

One Friday in July 1995, I worked all day as a physician for the Montreal International Tennis Tournament. On the weekend I was on duty at the hospital. On Sunday I operated most of the day. Towards the end of the day I developed a headache. I went home, took analgesic tablets and lay down. The headache did not go away as it had in the past; in fact it became severe.

On Monday morning I cancelled my office hours and went to the clinic to have a CT scan of my head, which turned out to be normal. Late in the afternoon I called a colleague, who prescribed an injectable medication, which my wife administered. In the evening I went to the hospital emergency room because none of the medications had relieved my headache. The physician there prescribed an intravenous medication that relieved my headache completely after a few hours. I left the emergency room late at night and returned home.

The next day I went to work feeling unwell, but able to see all the patients that were scheduled at the clinic. Towards the end of the day my headache was back, and was even more severe. I went home, but had to return to the emergency room, where I received the same intravenous medication. Late at night I left to go home, against the advice of the emergency physician and the neurologist who had treated me (I have disliked being a patient ever since my youth, and I sometimes wonder how I ever became a doctor).

On Wednesday morning I went to work feeling slightly better and able to work, but towards evening my headache came back and was more severe than ever. I returned to the emergency room and this time had no choice, but to be admitted to hospital. The doctors prescribed two intravenous medications, the first to control my headache and the second, a cortisone derivative, to stabilize the first. The side effects were such that I could not read and was so weak that I needed to hold onto the intravenous pole to walk the length of the hospital corridor. It took me fifteen minutes to walk from one end of the corridor to the other, while normally I would zoom down it faster than Ben Johnson could run a hundred metres. For the first time, I really understood what it was like to be sick and had a grasp of the meaning of the words sympathy and empathy.

The next day I was feeling better, but still weak. I sat in a chair in my hospital room and watched the people outside walking and running to their cars. I envied them and thought that no amount of money or material goods could make me happier than to be able to walk and run as they did.

By Saturday I was feeling stronger and able to walk without the use of my friend, the IV pole. On Sunday morning I was discharged from the hospital with a prescription for medications for the next two weeks. The doctors did not know the cause of my headache. A male nurse carried the bag containing my belongings to the parking lot for me, as I was still very weak.

On Monday I stayed home and rested. I did not sleep at all that night because I was worried about the eighty patients scheduled in my clinic the next day.

On Tuesday morning I got up, washed, had breakfast and asked my wife to drive me to the hospital because I still felt too weak to drive. When I arrived at the clinic there were already more than a dozen patients waiting. A woman sent from the emergency room was the first patient I saw. I examined her, looked at her x-rays and made the diagnosis of a displaced wrist fracture requiring reduction. I discussed the condition with the patient and gave her an injection in order to anaesthetize her wrist. I proceeded to write in her chart while the anaesthesia took effect and realized that I could not read. My eyesight was blurry, probably because of the medications I was taking. I realized that, despite my best efforts, I was too sick to see the eighty patients. I called the operating room and left a message for the chief of orthopaedic, who was in surgery, explaining that I was sick and unable to run my clinic. I suggested to the chief of orthopaedic – a long-time friend and the best man at my wedding – that the colleague who was assisting him leaves the operating room and replace me in the clinic.

The answer I got from both was that they were operating together and I would have to manage on my own. I was upset at their reaction because, in my twelve years of surgical training and practice, I had missed only three hours' work. In all those years I had never asked a colleague to cover for me yet had often been very accommodating to my colleagues, including the two who were now refusing to help me. I was also frustrated because my body would not follow my commands. A week earlier I had been able to bicycle a hundred kilometres in one day and now I could barely lift a pen.

When my colleagues told me they would not replace me in the clinic I went back to the patient with the wrist fracture and tried to treat her. Again I realized that, despite my will, I could not properly treat this woman or the other patients who were by now flooding the clinic. I phoned the hospital chief of staff and asked him to come to the clinic. Within minutes he was there. I told him about my condition and my colleagues' refusal to help me. Under the circumstances, I explained, I had no choice, but to resign from the hospital in order to take care of my health. The chief of staff was very understanding. He did not argue with me or question my decision. He immediately called my two colleagues in the operating room and within minutes one of was there to replace me. I left the clinic and went to the hospital entrance to wait for my lift. Some patients who I was scheduled to see in the clinic followed me to the entrance to ask who was going to take care of them. They were all concerned with themselves and none expressed concern for my health.

I went home and tried to get some rest. Apparently the chief of orthopaedic felt that I had betrayed him by resigning. He did not wish to speak to me, but sent Dr. Mesri, a colleague and long-time friend, to my home to talk me out of resigning. Dr. Mesri began the conversation by blaming me. He said I was creating a mess at the hospital by resigning. I told him I was not in the mood to argue and he was entitled to his opinion. I asked Dr. Mesri if, having known me for many years, he could look me in the eye and say that I was faking my illness. He apologized for blaming me and offered to help if necessary. I thanked him for his offer and said I would be fine.

The chief of orthopaedic next sent Dr. Pierre, an orthopaedic surgeon working at a different hospital and also a friend, to talk me out of resigning. I was not in the mood to speak with Dr. Pierre, but listened to him since he had driven more than an hour to see me. He said I was foolish to resign without having secured another job. He suggested that I could lose the means to support my family. He looked at my house and said he would be the first to buy it if I were forced to sell. I told Dr. Pierre I was not worried about finding alternative work. I reminded him that he had called me two months earlier and implored me to work at his hospital. He now said that position had recently been filled. He said that at this stage he would prefer I work in the north end of Montreal and would not even give me a reference if it involved my working in a hospital in the south end, since I would be in direct competition with him. Dr. Pierre was unable to convince me to withdraw my resignation. Nine months later he and I would speak on the phone; the first thing he would ask was whether I had a position for him at my new place of work.

When I left the hospital, in addition to dealing with my health I had to respond to a letter from the government. It stated that my income tax returns for the previous three years were being audited and that, within 1 month, I had to submit all receipts and documents to support my returns for these years. Because I had already missed the one-month deadline, I obtained a letter from my family physician to justify my tardiness in responding. I gathered all the requested documents and went to meet a government agent. I met a relaxed, friendly young man who introduced himself as an accountant. He offered me get me a coffee, which I politely declined. He said he would get one for himself and bring along his supervisor for the interview.

A few minutes later the young accountant returned with another gentleman, also carrying a coffee. They sat across the desk from me and I submitted the documents I had been asked to provide. They looked at them briefly and the young accountant said that the $600, or fifty percent of the $1,200 in gas expenses, claimed for transportation to and from work was excessive, and that forty percent, or $500, would be more acceptable. I explained that

I had deducted fifty percent only because my accountant had suggested I do so, but in reality I used my car ninety percent of the time for work purposes. The agents said I would have to provide my work schedule for June 1993 (two years earlier) to back up this claim.

Next they said I had claimed $1,000 a year for meals and was not allowed to deduct restaurant meals as a professional expense. They showed me a 1987 court decision in which a doctor had lost against the government for doing so. I said that all the physicians I knew claimed meals with colleagues as a professional expense. I told them that the accountant who prepared my tax returns worked for the government; she was well acquainted with the rules and regulations of the revenue department and had always been extremely cautious in preparing my returns. If what they were telling me was true, I asked, why not send a notice to the doctors advising them of the rule, thus making it simple for us to complete our tax returns? One of the men asked who was my accountant was. I responded that she had advised me not to give her name since she was in a conflict of interest by preparing my tax return while working for the government. The two agents said they would accept a fraction of the $1,000 I had claimed for meals if I could provide them with the names of all the professionals with whom I had dined.

After speaking with the two agents for a while, I understood that the purpose of the audit was not to determine whether I had made a fraudulent tax return, nor to congratulate me for being a good, hard-working, taxpaying citizen, but, rather, to extract more money from me. A reliable source would later tell me that government auditors are expected to bring in $700 for every hour spent with a taxpayer. Although I found the experience upsetting, I did not express my frustration because I was too ill to do so and because I had been advised that to express any anger would only make matters worse.

A few days later I met with the agents to give them my work schedule for the month of June 1993 and the documents they had requested. The schedule showed that in June 1993 I had driven hundreds of kilometres in order to see patients in eleven different clinics and two government prisons and to operate at two hospitals. I received no accolades for working hard and being a good citizen. The agents said they would allow me to deduct $500 a year for transportation instead of the $600 I had claimed.

I wanted to tell them that every year I paid more than $100,000 in income tax and that for every hour I worked I gave the government more than the $100 they were trying to extract from me. But I did not.

I later learned that I could have hired an accountant to represent me at the interview with the government agents, something my accountant had not told me. So I hired an accountant to control the damage caused by my ignorance. By the time my accountant finished negotiating with the government I had paid in excess of $260,000 related to the audit and in income tax for the current year. One person commented sarcastically that I should be happy to have paid that much in income tax because it meant I had made a lot of money.

On Wednesday, four days after I had left the hospital and two days after I had had to abandon my clinic duties, a secretary from my office phoned to advise me that many of my patients had left messages. She added that my colleagues were becoming impatient and wanted to know when I would be returning to work. I told her I hoped to be back soon.

The next day the secretary phoned to say that my colleagues were very eager to know when I would be coming back. I told her I would inform her of the date of my return as soon as I got better. I explained that I was still very weak and unable to read because of the two medications I was taking.

The following day the phone rang many times, but I didn't answer since I knew it was the office. When I failed to answer the phone, the secretary sent me a fax advising me again that my colleagues were very impatient. When I realized I would not be able to get any rest at home because of all the phone calls and faxes, I went up north to a country house.

I stayed in the country for a few days, but had to return to the city because my wife was due to deliver. The delivery went well, but my wife was so happy in the hospital, not having to deal with my health problems, that she did not want to leave. I finally convinced the doctor to discharge her.

I went back to work as soon as my wife returned home. I learned that while I had been away none of my colleagues except Dr. Mesri would agree to see my patients. My patients told me they would come to the clinic for their scheduled appointment and wait two hours to be seen by a doctor, who would then rudely inform them that he was not seeing any of "Dr. Bah's patients." Furthermore, Dr. Mesri was the only orthopaedic colleague who would speak to me, the others apparently being too angry to do so. My non-orthopaedic colleagues, however, were very kind. The chief of surgery and Dr. McHugh, the chief of anaesthesia and a friend, asked if there was anything they could do to make me withdraw my resignation. I thanked them for their understanding, but said my decision was final. At first they refused to accept my resignation, but then reluctantly did so.

Hospital policy stated that I had to continue working for three months after submitting my resignation, in order to allow for the transfer of my patients to other physicians. My orthopaedic colleagues, still unhappy about my decision to resign, continued to refuse to see my patients. Thus I had to look elsewhere for a surgeon willing to treat them. I called Dr. Morais, a friend and former professor working at another hospital, who kindly agreed. During my last three months at the hospital, I operated on as many patients as I could in order to ease the burden on Dr. Morais, who himself had a one-year waiting list.

The last patient I operated on was a sixty-five-year-old prisoner who had been suffering from low back pain for more than eight years. He had difficulty with his bladder, erection and walking. In eight years he had not found a surgeon willing to operate on him. It took me more than five hours to complete the surgery because none of my colleagues would assist me and because the patient had severe spinal stenosis (narrowing of the spinal canal) and hard bones. The operation was a success, but my enthusiasm was dampened when, a few days later, a family physician told me that my patient was a recidivist child molester. I told the physician that it was my policy not to inquire about the reasons why my patients were in jail.

In October 1995, I took a week off and went to the United States to visit a former classmate, a spine surgeon who had offered me a position. He had a very successful practice, making a lot of money and living in a mansion. He invited me to share his office and said he could introduce me to an attorney who would help me get a green card. My practice would be completely independent of his and I would have to build up my own clientele. He said there were no strings attached to his offer apart from the fact that I would see his patients when he was on vacation and vice versa. He said he was confident I would not steal his patients. If at any point I was unhappy working with him, he explained, I could move my office to a building across the street, and he would be unable to do anything about it since I would have my own green card. He said I could sue him if I felt he cheated me – or, if I did not want to deal with lawyers, shoot him. He told me that wearing a concealed weapon was allowed in the state in which he lived. The thought of dealing with people who could carry a weapon at all times scared me. My colleague's offer seemed genuine, nevertheless, and I told him I would think about it.

When I returned to Montreal, a former professor of mine working in a teaching hospital called to offer me work with his group. I told him that one of the reasons I had resigned from the hospital where I had been working was that I found it exhausting and bad medicine to see more than fifty spine patients a day. He assured me that if I joined his group I would be free to see as many patients as I wished and to do research on the days when I did not feel like seeing patients.

In the end I chose to move to Bermuda because Dr. Trouts had said the work pace there was slower than what I was used to in Montreal and in other places where I had been offered work. My wife was still not keen to move. Dr. Trouts' wife suggested a book I might buy in order to motivate her. The author, a Canadian living in Bermuda with her husband, writes that, "Even in paradise, there is a price to be paid"[1] and suggests that the only problems one has to deal with in Bermuda are cockroaches and mildew. My wife read the book and remained unconvinced. However, in the end she agreed to move because I had been ill and had been told that my migraines were the result of my gruelling schedule.

In November I finished my work in Montreal. The hospital authorities wrote to thank me for my work at the hospital. On three separate occasions, anaesthesiologists, nurses, respiratory physiologists, surgeons and other hospital staff took me to dinner.

[1] Tracy Caswell, *Tea With Tracy: The Woman's Survival Guide to Bermuda* (Hamilton: Print Link, 1994/2003).

CHAPTER THREE

The Move

On Saturday, December 2nd, 1995, my wife and I and our two children flew to Bermuda. We arrived on a sunny, windy day, the thermometer hovering around 23 degrees Celsius (73° F). Dr. Trouts and his wife were waiting for us at the airport. They drove us to temporary accommodations at one of the private clubs where Dr. Trouts was a member. On the way there, two incidents suggested to me that I did not know my new associate very well. The first occurred when a black teenager on a motorbike tried to overtake us. Dr. Trouts pinned the boy against the sidewalk, nearly knocking him off his bike. I suggested he let the boy overtake him. Dr. Trouts then lectured me on Bermuda's driving rules. He informed me that in Bermuda one drives on the left side of the road and that it is illegal to overtake on the left, as the teenager had attempted to do. The boy gave up trying to overtake our car when he realized that Dr. Trouts was going to hurt him.

The second incident was Dr. Trouts' insistence that I replace his reflex hammer after my son had chewed on it. We had taken our son on vacation a few times before and he had never cried, but he seemed to sense something unusual about this trip. From the moment we reached Bermuda he cried non-stop, calling out for his grandparents. We found a reflex hammer in the back seat of Dr. Trouts' car and gave it to him. He chewed on the plastic end of the hammer and stopped crying. Dr. Trouts was upset about this, repeating over and over again that our son had chewed his reflex hammer. I thought he was joking, but realized he was not when he accepted a new hammer from me, worth three dollars. He not only accepted the new hammer, but kept the old one!

When we reached the Floral Beach Club, my family and I were assigned a two-bedroom cottage. The daily rate for select members of the club was $600 US, but we were billed only $100 because we were Dr. Trouts' guests and because the occupancy rate was low at that time of year.

On Monday morning I called a cab to take me to take me in to Hamilton. When the cab arrived I was waiting outside the cottage. I opened the door and sat in the front seat. The driver, a black man, said nothing, but stared at me as if I were a ghost. When he finally spoke he said he was there to pick up a Mr. Bah. I replied that I was Mr. Bah. He hesitated before heading towards town. He did not speak and I sensed that something was bothering him. Finally he asked if I was a guest at the Floral Beach Club and was staying in the cottage where he had picked me up. I responded in the affirmative. He told me that he was in his late sixties and had lived in Bermuda all his life and had driven a cab as long as he could remember and had never known a black man to stay in that cottage. This was my first insight into Bermudian society.

For the next three days I went in to town again, to open a bank account, take driving instruction and obtain a driver licence. On Thursday I was ready to buy a car, a small 4x4 similar to the one Dr. Trouts drove and had suggested I buy. In the documents he had faxed me in Montreal, he had written the following:

> "By way of providing you with costs of set up I [Dr. Trouts], will help you with moving costs, rent, car etc… in some organized fashion. These will be eventually deducted from your profits."

When it came time to pay for the car, Dr. Trouts presented me with a contract to sign. It stated that I was to reimburse him the money he gave me to purchase the car at ten percent per year. I asked him what the phrase "help in some organized fashion" meant in the document he had faxed me. He answered that when he left the United States he had managed to save only $30,000 and was not going to give me any of that money free. Instead of borrowing from Dr. Trouts, I paid all my expenses, including the $15,000 US it cost to move our furniture from Montreal.

On Thursday, December 7th, I was ready to start working at the hospital. Before doing so, Dr. Trouts and I met at the Boat Club, another private club he was a member of, to finalize our contract. In October 1994, Dr. Trouts had said that, because we were "friends," withholding anywhere between zero and twenty percent of my income after expenses would be acceptable to him. In June 1995, when he was eager for me to join him in Bermuda, he had suggested withholding only ten percent. Now he said that ten percent before expenses would be easier to calculate than ten percent after expenses. I said that ten percent before expenses was equivalent to twenty percent after expenses. I asked about his earlier promise and his comment that we were "friends." Dr. Trouts smiled and said I was negotiating at a disadvantage now that I had moved to Bermuda. I told him I could move back to Canada the next day, especially since our furniture had not yet arrived. I did not feel like arguing, however, so I agreed to give him ten percent of my earnings if I earned more than $300,000 US a year. Somehow, Dr. Trouts knew that I would be seeing more patients and making more money than he. He therefore asked that I agree to share with him any money I made above and beyond twenty percent of his income. I agreed on the condition that he be involved in the practice of medicine full time in any given year. Then he suggested that I be paid a monthly salary of $6,000 US and receive the rest of my money as an earned bonus at the end of every quarter. He said that this would be to my advantage since I would be paying income tax, the equivalent of nine percent, on my salary only, and that this was legal under Bermuda tax law. I agreed on the condition that a clause be included in the contract that I would receive the remainder of my money at the end of every quarter.

After more than three hours of discussion, with Dr. Trouts drinking beer and I eating peanuts, I thought we had an agreement. But apparently not, for Dr. Trouts suggested I give him twenty percent of my income if I earned $0.5 million US, thirty percent if I earned $0.6 million and so on up fifty percent if I earned $1 million a year. I said that the main reason I had moved to Bermuda was to spend more time with my family and would have gone to the United States if I wanted to make more money. He suggested we move to a more private corner of the club, then whispered, "You can easily make more than a million a year." I said, "I'm not interested in making a million a year. It is getting late and I want to return to my family." We agreed to the first part of our discussion, that I would give him ten percent of my income if I made more than $300,000 US. He said he would put our agreement in writing the next day, have his attorney review it on Monday, and give me a copy for review by an attorney of my choice the following week. He said we would have a signed contract within ten days, as originally promised.

The next day, Friday, December 8th, I started working at the two-hundred-bed King Edward VII Memorial Hospital, the only hospital in Bermuda. The work was pleasant and the patients respectful and appreciative. There is no workers' compensation or unemployment insurance on the Island. The most an unemployed person can expect to receive from the government is enough to barely cover their rent. Therefore, most patients return to work shortly after surgery, three times earlier than similar patients in Canada. In my Friday clinic I saw an average of twenty to thirty patients instead of the eighty or more I was accustomed to in Montreal. By noon I had already finished consulting on all the patients that were scheduled at the clinic.

I was on duty over the weekend and saw half a dozen patients instead of the thirty to forty I had been accustomed to. One drawback in Bermuda was that most of the patients I saw on the weekend had injuries sustained in traffic accidents related to alcohol and were brought to the emergency room late at night. Another drawback was that the operating room was not nearly as efficient as those I was used to in Montreal, because of a combination of many factors that I would slowly discover. For example, it took me more than four hours to operate on my first femur patient instead of the usual two. One of the problems was that the operating table dated back to the 1950s.

On December 14th-, I was asked to attend a meeting at the hospital. Present at the meeting were Dr. Jameson, the chief of staff, a black Bermudian in his sixties, Dr. Joneson, the chief of anaesthesia and surgery, a white English woman in her fifties, and the four orthopaedic surgeons working on the Island, Drs. Chalvin, Cooperson, Fascioni and Trouts. Dr. Jameson was the first to speak. He told those assembled that because of my arrival there would now be five orthopaedic surgeons working on the Island, which warranted the creation of an orthopaedics division. He said that Dr. Cooperson would head up this division since he was the most senior orthopaedic surgeon and asked if anyone objected to Dr. Cooperson's becoming chief of orthopaedics. For a while nobody said anything. Then Dr. Joneson spoke. She said that health care in Bermuda was very costly and suggested that in order to reduce costs all the orthopaedic surgeons would have to use the type of prosthesis that Drs. Cooperson and Fascioni were using. She said that Drs. Chalvin, Trouts and I would have to seek Dr. Cooperson's approval if we wanted to bring any implants into the hospital. Dr. Joneson and Jameson spoke for half an hour and presented us with more guidelines and rules, which all boiled down to the fact that Dr. Trouts and I would need the approval of Dr. Cooperson to do anything at the hospital.

Dr. Fascioni spoke next. He went on for five minutes, but said nothing new or constructive. Dr. Jameson then asked if anyone had anything to add. Dr. Chalvin, the doctor from India, stared at the floor and said nothing. Dr. Trouts had his arms folded and looked proud, a grin on his face and nodding in approval at everything that was said. His reaction surprised me because of what he had told me regarding his working relationship with Dr. Cooperson. (Dr. Trouts had told me he had been unable to work at the hospital his first three months on the Island because Dr. Cooperson had refused to give him clinic time. He said it had taken the intervention of a Canadian hospital administrator and a meeting with Dr. Cooperson and all other interested parties for Dr. Cooperson to agree to give him clinic time. Later I would learn that for some time Dr. Cooperson would still show up at Dr. Trouts' clinic and see his patients.)

I had attended many meetings, but never one so cold and autocratic. I had been in Bermuda only a week, but I knew that the talk of keeping health-care costs low was just empty words. Drs. Joneson, Cooperson, Fascioni and Jameson did not really care about health-care costs in Bermuda. They cared about their pockets and feared that American-style managed care would reach the Island. For example, in just one short week I had discovered that Drs. Cooperson and Fascioni were using very costly non-cemented prostheses for all the patients they operated on irrespective of the patient's age and condition and contrary to practices in the United States and Canada. Their choice of prosthesis resulted in many complications and repeat operations for the patient and unnecessary costs for the hospital.

I raised my hand and requested permission to speak. I suggested that we have regular scientific meetings to review the orthopaedic literature and discuss cases. I explained that this would help us determine what type of prosthesis or implants to use at the hospital. I also suggested that we have morbidity meetings, which were non-existent at the hospital, to discuss complicated cases. I would be glad to attend these meetings and present my cases, I said, if they were conducted in a spirit of comradeship with the intention of helping the patients and each other. Nobody said anything, but I felt that Drs. Cooperson and Fascioni were not interested in my "scientific meetings" or my "comradeship." They gave me the impression I was not welcome at the hospital. They were upset because Dr. Trouts had caught them off-guard by bringing me to Bermuda. Dr. Trouts had misled them by suggesting that I would be coming to the Island occasionally to replace him when he went on vacation while at the same time convincing the immigration ministry of the need for a permanent spine specialist in Bermuda.

I later asked Dr. Trouts why he had not spoken up at the meeting since he disagreed with everything that was being said. I would never have set foot in Bermuda, I said, if he had told me everything. He smiled and said, "I told you that the water looks beautiful and calm, but I'm sorry I didn't tell you that there were some sharks out there." I would soon discover that in Bermuda the dolphins were as harmful as the sharks.

The next evening Dr. Trouts phoned me. He had bought a two-bedroom cottage near the hospital for $535,000 US and was going to convert it into offices for our use. The renovations would be completed in six months. The reason he was calling, he said, was to inform me that I would have to pay him $3,400 US a month for the next six months to "retain" the building. I asked if I would then be an equal owner, since $3,400 represented half the mortgage payment. He said no. I asked why I would invest in something that would never belong to me. He said I had advised him to buy the building. (For two years Dr. Trouts had been negotiating with the owner, who had repeatedly refused his offer of $500,000. Upon my arrival, thirteen days earlier, Dr. Trouts had shown me the cottage and asked whether he should purchase it. I told him the $35,000 difference between the asking price and the bid was insignificant considering the total price.) I told him I would never have expressed an opinion about the price of the cottage had I known it would automatically oblige me to pay half the mortgage. I said it was ludicrous to expect me to pay half the mortgage on a building that does not belong to me. I would call the movers the next morning to cancel the arrival of our furniture, I said, and my family and I would move back to Canada as soon as I had sold my car and closed my bank account.

When I hung up the phone I told my wife about the conversation and suggested we move back to Canada. She could not have been happier. An hour later Dr. Trouts called back to say that he had consulted with his wife and to expect me to pay the mortgage on a building that did not belong to me was not such a bright idea. He apologized and admitted that he had thought only of himself. He begged me to stay, promising that, when we moved into the building in July 1996, my rent would be no higher than what I was currently paying. My wife and I discussed this second phone call and decided to stay.

The Floral Beach Club invited my family to a Christmas Eve gift-opening event, but we declined. The management placed a Christmas tree in our cottage and sent us a bottle of wine and a box of chocolates. At New Year's, Dr. Trouts and his wife joined my family and me for dinner at the club.

To find permanent accommodation I called Kate, the Canadian woman I had met on the flight to Toronto after my first trip to Bermuda. Kate had promised to help me find accommodation in the event that I moved to the Island. Her husband said she was not at home, but he would pass on the message. That evening Kate phoned and I reminded her of our meeting. I told her I had moved to Bermuda and was calling to ask for her help in locating a house. She said there were no rental houses on the market, but she would phone me if she happened to hear of any vacancies. I knew by the tone of her voice that she was not going to call me, and she never did. My wife and I contacted two real estate agents, who showed us the few rental houses available. In late December we settled on a three-bedroom house in Paget parish, not far from the hospital and downtown Hamilton, and on January 3rd, 1996, we moved in.

By early January I had enough surgical spine cases to start operating, but I lacked the implants (rods, plates and screws) and instrumentation (hardware) to perform the surgeries adequately. The implants that were used at the King Edward dated back to the 1970s and were no longer used in Canada. I took the issue to the head operating room nurse, Mrs. Santini, a black Bermudian. She said she had no objection to importing the implants since the hospital and the insurance companies had allocated money for this purpose, in order to decrease the number of Bermudians travelling abroad for surgery. She suggested I get in touch with Dr. Cooperson to discuss the type of implants I required. With regard to the surgical instruments, Mrs. Santini said there was no money allocated for this purpose. The best she could do was to purchase an instrument of my choice worth no more than $3,000 US. (A year earlier Dr. Trouts had told me that the hospital would buy whatever instruments I needed to operate on spine patients if I were to settle in Bermuda.) Mrs. Santini suggested I purchase whatever other instruments I required and submit the invoices to Mrs. Anderson, the executive director of the hospital.

On the morning of Wednesday, January 10th, at the end of the surgical meeting, I approached Dr. Cooperson, the newly designated chief of orthopaedic, to show him the literature on the spine implants I wished to bring in. Dr. Cooperson said he had no time to see me, as he was late for his office, then rushed off. I ran after him, handed him the documentation on the implants and asked him to read it at his leisure. Thirty minutes later I saw him in the surgical ward talking with Dr. Fascioni, in no rush at all. He never returned the documentation to me and never spoke to me about the implants I wished to purchase. I told Mrs. Santini of my brief encounter with Dr. Cooperson. She bypassed Dr. Cooperson and ordered the implants for me.

I performed surgery on the spine patients using the few instruments I had brought with me and the few old instruments the hospital possessed. After a few weeks I realized that these instruments were inadequate to the task and in the long run could create problems both for the patients and for me. I went ahead and purchased the instruments I needed, at a cost of $28,000 US. I took Mrs. Santini's advice and sent the invoice to Mrs. Anderson, along with a letter explaining why the additional instruments were necessary and requesting that the hospital help cover the cost. Mrs. Anderson did not answer my letter. Instead, Dr. Jameson wrote to say, "I commend you for the initiative of buying the instrumentation, but the hospital will not reimburse you nor give you any money."

Initially I performed an average of one spine operation per week. After a month I was operating on an average of two per week. Most of the patients I operated on had already had one or more back operations, either in Bermuda or abroad. I thought that after a while I would have fewer patients requiring surgery, but instead I had more and soon had a short waiting list. There were many patients requiring surgery considering Bermuda's small population. The older generation had worked hard throughout their lives and continued to do so into their late seventies, so that many elderly people had developed severe degenerative arthritis and other debilitating spinal pathologies. In addition, there has been inbreeding within the small local population for three hundred years, resulting in a prevalence of pathologies like diabetes, hypertension and arthritis. Furthermore, before my arrival many patients with spinal problems had chosen to endure their pain for years rather than submit to surgery at the King Edward.

After operating on a few patients, I noticed that my patients' pre- and post-surgical x-rays were missing. Initially I thought the radiology department was losing the x-rays, but then I realized that was not the case, for the radiology employees did their best to find the films, to no avail. Then, on March 20th, Dr. Tom, a senior gynaecologist, a black Bermudian, approached me to say that Drs. Cooperson and Fascioni had been complaining that I was operating on too many spine cases. This indicated to me that it was probably Drs. Cooperson and Fascioni who were taking my patients' x-rays. Dr. Trouts and I tried to obtain from Dr. Jameson the minutes of the meetings at which Drs. Cooperson and Fascioni had complained about me. Dr. Jameson told us that the minutes were unavailable to us. My patients' x-rays continued to disappear and all I could do was wait and see what motives Drs. Cooperson and Fascioni had.

After working in Bermuda for four months, I planned to travel to Mont-Tremblant, Quebec, for a trauma conference. Dr. Trouts informed me that he was tired and stressed and had already paid for a three-week trip to the United States to attend a magic convention during the same period. Before he left for his convention, he and I met to discuss money matters. I had billed an average of $31,000 per month since my arrival in December and was entitled to a bonus every quarter. I asked Dr. Trouts why he had not produced the contract he had promised when we met at the Boat Club in December 1995. He said the contract was ready, but he had been unable to pick it up because he had been away on vacation a few times since our meeting. As soon as he returned from the convention, he said, he would give me the contract as well as make the necessary calculation and pay me my quarterly bonus. I told him I wanted my salary increased to $8,000 because the $6,000 I was receiving barely covered my rent ($5,000) and because I had discovered that Dr. Trouts – who had no dependants – had been paying himself a monthly salary of $8,000, in addition to paying his wife a monthly salary.

Dr. Trouts said his attorney had already prepared the contract and the figures could not be changed. I said the figures could be changed because neither of us had signed the contract. He said I had agreed to $6,000. I said I had agreed to this figure only because he had advised me to and had told me it meant that I would pay less income tax. I asked him why he had proposed that I get $6,000 while he had been paying himself $8,000. He smiled and did not answer. He told me not to worry – we would sign the contract and I would get my money as soon he returned. Our meeting ended sooner than I wished because Dr. Trouts had a dental appointment. I asked him to give me the name of his dentist because I needed a routine dental examination and cleaning.

CHAPTER FOUR

Easter 1996

On March 28th, 1996, Dr. Trouts' dentist saw me and conducted routine physical and x- ray examinations of my mouth. He showed me the x-rays, which indicated that the root of one of my upper left molars and adjacent jawbone had been replaced by a hole. The dentist poked at the tooth and the hole with one of his instruments. He looked at the x-rays and poked at my mouth again. He took a book from a shelf in his office and scanned it unsuccessfully for images with which to compare the x-rays of my mouth. He told he did not know what I had and suggested I seek a second opinion in Montreal. I went home that evening feeling very ill. I thought that, like many people in Bermuda, I had the flu. For the next three days I managed to work despite feeling sick and having pain in the left upper molar that the dentist had poked.

On the afternoon of Thursday, April 4th, I drove my wife and children to the airport, as they were travelling to Montreal. On the way I developed a severe headache and by the time we reached the airport my vision was blurred and I could not see. I paid a taxi driver to drive me home in my car. When I arrived home I took two Tylenol tablets and went to bed. I slept only a few hours that night and woke up feeling no better. I had a problem on my hands for I was on duty (responsible for all orthopaedic traumas) for the four-day Easter holiday and I was barely able to get out of bed. Easter weekend marks the beginning of spring in Bermuda. It is when Bermudians fly their kites and tourists return to the Island. There could be a lot of motorbike accidents. Three orthopaedic surgeons, Drs. Chalvin, Fascioni and Trouts, were away. Dr. Cooperson and I were the only ones left. Dr. Cooperson had been practising in Bermuda for more than twenty-five years and had been on call only the first year. Apparently he had declined to go on call after that, leaving the general surgeon to deal with orthopaedic traumas while he concentrated on treating wealthy patients and those with insurance. He took calls only occasionally, when Dr. Fascioni was away. I paged Dr. Cooperson and left a message for him to call me back, hoping he would cover for me. When he failed to respond I realized that nothing short of a miracle or divine intervention would get me out of the situation I was in. I went down on my knees and asked God, if he existed, to help me. I made a promise that if God helped me I would forever listen to him and do his will.

The vast majority of orthopaedic traumas in Bermuda are due to motorbike accidents, so I specifically asked God to prevent any motorbike accidents that weekend. On Friday I sat all day anxiously listening for the ambulance's siren and waiting for my pager to ring. When I lay down inside the house I felt worse because the dampness in the house, which was made of limestone, penetrated my flesh and bones. Therefore, I sat outside most of the time and moved around like a lizard following the sun. I wore a heavy ski jacket both inside and outside the house.

A three-month-old Labrador had been left in my care. We had bought the dog when we arrived in Bermuda because we had been told that a dog was the best alarm system there. When I left him inside he barked constantly. When I left him outside he jumped over the fence we had installed around the property in order to visit the neighbours' dog and eat their plants. In spite of all the trouble he caused, however, the dog kept me company that day and made me laugh. I ordered a vegetarian pizza, but it was topped with pineapple and pickles and other incompatible garnishes. I was weak with hunger, but the sight of the pineapple mixed with pickles made me nauseous so I gave the pizza to the dog. He developed diarrhea the moment he ate it. Its behind would make a gushing sound and scare the dog whenever he had a stool. He would run away from his behind and I would laugh. These were my only moments of joy that day.

There were no motorbike accidents on the Island all day. My prayers had been answered. In the evening the emergency room physician called to say that he had a child with a broken wrist, sustained while rollerblading. The physician told me the boy's fracture was displaced and needed closed reduction and casting in the operating room. I said I would be at the hospital shortly, then called the operating room to schedule the patient for surgery. The staff there informed me that the operating room would be available in thirty minutes, as soon as the ongoing surgical case was finished. I dressed and sat in my car, but realized that I was so weak it was unsafe for me to drive, let alone operate. I went back to the house. I called the operating room and asked to speak to Dr. Berger, the general surgeon from Germany who had just finished operating. I explained my predicament to Dr. Berger and asked him to operate on the boy for me. Dr. Berger, with whom I had enjoyed a good working relationship, agreed to do so.

Dr. Berger's agreeing to operate on the boy came as a relief, but did not solve my biggest problem, which was that I was on duty for the next three days. I was beginning to think that maybe there was a God, because my prayer that there be no motorbike accidents on Friday had been answered. I felt that if there was a God he had not failed me because the young man had broken his wrist while rollerblading and not riding his motorbike. I realized that I was so concerned about motorbike accidents, the most common cause of trauma in Bermuda that I had forgotten about other road-related injuries. I needed to expand my horizon of prayer. So I went down on my knees again and asked God, if he existed, to prevent all road-related injuries over the next three days while I was on duty, or at least until I got well. To cover myself further I prayed that no one would fall in his or her house. To be on the safe side I also prayed for rain so that people would not venture outside their homes. When I rose from my knees I was sure I had covered every eventuality of an individual sustaining an orthopaedic-related trauma in Bermuda.

I went to bed early Friday night, but did not sleep well and woke up Saturday morning still feeling febrile and weak. I called the emergency room and discussed my symptoms with a physician there. He said that many people in Bermuda were sick with a virus. I told him that I had had a cold almost every year in Montreal, but had never felt this weak or missed work because of the flu. The physician said this flu was very virulent and untreatable and advised me to rest and take a lot of liquids. I felt relieved after speaking with him. I drank a lot of orange juice and lay in bed all day. It rained all day on Saturday and most of the day on Sunday. This meant that I had to stay inside the damp house, but I could not complain because I had prayed to God to send the rain. My only wish, besides the wish to get well, was to be taken to an arid place because of the penetrating dampness. For the first time in my life I felt my bones, which served to confirm to me that I was made not only of flesh.

All day Saturday I listened for ambulances going to the hospital. Late in the afternoon the emergency room physician called to advise me that an elderly woman had sustained a hip fracture requiring surgical treatment. I wondered how this had happened, as I thought my prayers had covered every eventuality of a person getting injured on the Island. I asked the physician how and where the woman had sustained the injury. He said she had fallen in a convalescent home. I could not argue that God had not answered my prayers, for I had asked that no one be hurt in their home or on the road and the woman had fallen not in her own home, but one where she was staying temporarily. The next time I prayed to God I would have to expand my horizon and cover the eventuality of an individual getting injured in a home other than their own. For now, though, I had to deal with this woman's injury, and I felt no better than I had the previous day. I asked the physician when the woman had had her last meal. He went to ask her and returned to say that she had had her last meal in the afternoon. I felt relieved because it was preferable to postpone the surgery until the next day and anaesthetize the patient when her stomach was empty. I asked the physician to admit the patient and inform her and her family that I would operate the following day. I called the operating room and scheduled the surgery for Sunday at noon.

At this stage I was beginning to get the idea that there was a divine being out there, because my prayers had twice been answered. For two days during a spring holiday no one in Bermuda had fallen in their home or sustained a motorbike-related injury. This time I really thought I had figured out how to pray. I dropped to my knees again and asked God to prevent all accidents in Bermuda, whether on the road, in a house or in any public place. I asked God that no individual be hurt within two hundred miles of the Island. I went to bed hoping I would feel better the next day and assured that God would answer my prayers as he had done on the two previous occasions. I got little sleep that night.

I woke up Sunday morning feeling febrile and as weak as ever. When it came time for me to operate on the woman with the broken hip, I did not have the strength to do so. I called the operating room and asked to speak to the anaesthetist on call. I spoke to Dr. Joneson and told her I was too ill to operate. I proposed that we postpone the surgery until the next day, when I hoped to be better, or until I reached Dr. Cooperson and asked him to operate for me. Dr. Joneson panicked. She asked if I knew whose mother we were dealing with. I said the emergency room physician had told me she was the mother of the tourism minister. Dr. Joneson asked if I knew that Mr. Dodge, the tourism minister, could be the next premier. I answered that, given my health, it was not in the patient's interest to have me operate on her. I said I would explain to the minister why I had to postpone his mother's surgery. I spoke to Mr. Dodge, a white Bermudian, and described the situation to him. He was very understanding. "By the tone of your voice," he said, "I can tell that you are sick and in need of a doctor yourself." I told the minister I would try to get Dr. Cooperson to operate on his mother as soon I reached him. I paged Dr. Cooperson again, but he did not reply.

It rained most of the day on Sunday as I had requested and I got no calls from the hospital. I went to bed that night relieved that God had answered my prayers a third time. Around midnight my pager vibrated. It was the emergency room physician calling to inform me that he had a woman with an open fracture of the leg (a fracture with the bone piercing the skin and muscles). My first thought was that this was impossible because God had answered my two previous prayers – why not this time? I asked how the woman had sustained the injury. The physician said the woman, a flight attendant for an American company, had sustained it when her plane hit turbulence en route to New York. "The plane was two hundred miles from Bermuda when it encountered the bad weather," he reported, but flew back to Bermuda because it was safer to return than to continue on to New York. I felt temporary relief when I realized that God had not failed me. I had specifically asked that no individual be hurt within a two-hundred-mile radius of Bermuda! Still, the injury required urgent treatment. I got up and tried to make my way to the hospital, but was drowsy from the medications I had been taking all day to relieve my flu-like symptoms. My only alternative was to call Dr. Berger, the physician who had operated on the young boy for me, and ask him to treat the flight attendant as well. I phoned Dr. Berger, but he was reluctant to become involved in the case, for two reasons. Before my arrival on the Island, Dr. Berger, a general surgeon with trauma training, had been treating orthopaedic-related injuries while on call. Dr. Cooperson had reprimanded him for this. The other reason for his reluctance to become involved was fear of being sued, since the flight attendant was an American. I begged Dr. Berger to treat her and he finally relented.

If in the past I was not sure if there was a God, now there was no doubt in my mind that there was a divine being. For three days God had answered my prayers. For three days he had saved me. He had seen to it that no individual suffered as of result of my illness. He had seen to it that I would not be sued and lose my hard-won licence. My short relationship with God made me realize many things. I had been too specific and restrictive in my prayers. I was sitting in the driver's seat, asking God to sit in the back seat and guide me. He could do much more for me if I did not limit him. It would be wise to let God sit in the driver's seat. I had a lot to learn about praying. I went down on my knees and simply asked God to help me with the whole situation and with my health problem. Then I went back to bed. I slept better than I had the previous three nights and the hospital did not call again.

On Monday morning I phoned the emergency room physician and described my symptoms. He said my weakness and fever were not related to the flu. In addition, he said, people with the flu usually improve with rest and I was not getting any better. He told me to take care of myself and suggested I call Dr. Cooperson at home and ask him to cover for me. I called Dr. Cooperson and left a message on his answering machine. Dr. Cooperson called me back a few hours later. I asked him to operate on the woman with the broken hip, the minister's mother, and promised to return the favour to Dr. Fascioni, his associate. He agreed to perform the surgery.

Now that the first part of my prayer had been taken care of, I turned my attention to my health. It occurred to me that if my symptoms were not caused by the flu, my upper left molar, which had eroded into the jawbone, was the culprit. I therefore phoned the dentist I had seen the previous week and asked if I could see him again. Being unable to drive, I took a cab to his office. I told the dentist what I had been through over the weekend and begged him to do something. He suggested removing the offending tooth and I consented. I felt relief the moment he anaesthetized my mouth, which strongly suggested to me that my symptoms were related to the tooth. He removed the tooth and showed to it to me. A granulomatous tissue, something that looks like a red mushroom, had destroyed and replaced the root. The fact that the root was destroyed explained why I did not experience severe pain in the tooth. The dentist asked me if the tooth should be sent for analysis. I replied that this was for him to decide. He took the tooth and threw it in the garbage. I went home and took two Advil tablets to relieve the surgical pain.

Overall I felt better after the tooth had been removed. In the evening, however, I felt worse than I had the previous four days. The symptoms worsened, my body shook, my teeth chattered and I was barely able to get out of bed. I called my wife in Montreal and asked her to come home.

Next, I tried to reach Dr. Trouts because I was scheduled to be on call the following Friday and did not want to run into the same problem. I telephoned his mother, who resided in Bermuda, and asked her where he could be reached. She gave me the number of a hotel in Maine. I called the hotel, but the clerk said that Dr. Trouts had checked out three days earlier. He told me that Dr. Trouts was part of a travelling magic convention that moved to a new hotel every second day. He said that Dr. Trouts could be anywhere in New England, but gave me the name of a hotel where he might be found. I called that hotel, but the clerk said the convention had moved yet again and gave me the number of a third hotel. I called this hotel and was referred to a further one. I do not remember how many hotels I rang. Finally, after three days of phoning, I reached Dr. Trouts at a hotel somewhere near Portland, Maine. I described the situation and suggested he cut his vacation short and return in order to cover for me. Dr. Trouts said he had already made reservations at various hotels and it would be difficult to cancel them. He also said he was very much enjoying the magic convention, not having attended such an event since moving back to Bermuda. He suggested I ask Drs. Fascioni or Chalvin, who were due back on the Island before he was, to cover for me on Friday. He said he would try to return a day earlier than scheduled.

The following day I called the dentist and asked if I should have been taking antibiotics as the tooth that he removed had looked infected. "Oh, yes, you should be on an antibiotic," he said, "but I thought you would prescribe it yourself." "I'm sick," I said, "I'm the patient and not the doctor in this situation." He suggested I write myself a prescription for penicillin.

My wife flew back the next day, leaving the children behind with her parents. As soon as she arrived I gave her the prescription and she picked up the antibiotic from a pharmacy. I began to feel better less than twenty-four hours after taking the medication. Tired of the whole ordeal, but no longer running a fever, I was able to see patients in the clinic and in the office on Wednesday and for the rest of the week. I asked Dr. Fascioni to cover for me on Friday, which he did (I would later repay him).

Dr. Trouts did return a day earlier than scheduled. Over the following months he would remind me frequently that he had ended his vacation a day early in order to cover for me. (When Dr. Trouts had asked me, in June 1995, to join him in Bermuda, I told him I had headaches that were probably related to my heavy workload. He said that the work pace on the Island was much slower than what I was used to in Montreal, but that he would gladly cover for me if I were to fall ill.)

The day after Dr. Trouts returned to Bermuda my wife and I left for Montreal.

CHAPTER FIVE

In Search of the Truth

After my illness of Easter weekend I could claim to have some kind of relationship with God. Previous to that weekend I had little or no relationship with God, although I had been searching for the "truth" for many years. I had been born in West Africa into a Muslim environment. I started learning the Koran, the holy book of Islam, when I was five years old. My uncle, who was my teacher, would transcribe verses from the Koran onto a wooden tablet for me to read. Early in the morning and in the evening the other students and I would read aloud from our wooden tablets under my uncle's supervision. The objective was to memorize the verses by the end of the week. Then we would erase the writing from the tablets and my uncle would write new verses on them. We spent hours erasing the writing, using water and leaves from a special tree. The children produced the ink my uncle used by fermenting the leaves of another tree, gathered from the forest on weekends. My uncle could have easily written the verses in a notebook, or we could have learned them directly from the Koran, but it was traditional to write the verses on tablets similar to those that God gave to Moses. In addition, the tedious act of erasing the tablets was intended to make us appreciate the learning process.

My uncle was very open-minded. Once, he allowed me to purchase, cook and eat pork. I ate the meat and gave it to the other children. My aunt, who was very religious, was so upset that she threw away all the cooking utensils that had been "tainted" by the pork. She reprimanded us children for eating the pork, but said nothing to my uncle, even though he had allowed me to cook it (I never once heard my uncle and aunt argue).

By the age of eleven I had memorized part of the Koran without having a clue what it was I had memorized, because the Koran is written in Arabic, which is not my native language. At age eleven I started learning Arabic in order to understand what I had been memorizing for six years. Like most of the other children, however, I soon gave up. Only one of us, as far as I know, continued studying both Arabic and the Koran past the age of twelve. After that I would use verses from the Koran that I had memorized in childhood only when I prayed during the month of Ramadan. During Ramadan, the ninth lunar month in the Muslim calendar, a Muslim is supposed to abstain from food and drink during daylight hours. I did not like fasting, as it made me dizzy and made it difficult for me to concentrate in school, but I fasted anyway, because my parents urged me to and because there was no food available during the day. After sunset we prayed and ate a light meal, at nine in the evening we ate a sustaining meal and before going to bed we ate again. My parents rose before sunrise to eat a fourth meal, but I was too sleepy to eat at that hour in the morning. Sometimes we ended up eating more in the month of Ramadan than at any other time of year.

I watched my parents and their peers pray five times a day, repeating the verses from the Koran they had memorized in childhood, but understanding little. I think that most prayed genuinely, some prayed because it was the thing to do and a minority prayed because they feared they would not be buried when they died. The religious leaders had decreed that any dead person who had not been seen praying while still alive would not be laid to rest.

I arrived in Canada as a teenager in order to join my father, who had left Guinea, our country of origin, a decade earlier for political reasons. The things that impressed me most about Canada were the size of the library in my school and the fact that I could borrow five books at a time. In the city where I grew up, a city of a hundred thousand people, there was not a single library. The only book I could afford to read was the school textbook, which we often had to leave at school. When I saw the library at my school in Canada I thought my classmates had read all the books in it and I had a lot of catching up to do. Before long, however, I was the only kid in my entire high school who read regularly. I was an avid reader. At first I read so slowly that it took me a month to read a three-hundred-page book, but soon I was able to read such a book in a week and within a few months I could read it in a day.

I developed a particular interest in science fiction and for the next three years read science fiction books at the rate of one a week. Then I started reading science fiction short stories because I could consume more stories in a given period. I watched the *Star Trek* television program and any science fiction movie that was shown in a theatre or on television. In college I became a founding member of a science fiction club. The president of the club, who was especially passionate about the subject, suggested we push our passion for science fiction "to the next frontier" by taking skydiving lessons. All the club members consented. However, everyone, but the president quit the course when they learned that a person in the group ahead of us had broken his ankle upon landing. I bailed out of the course because I thought I had pushed my interest in science fiction too far. It occurred to me that I should try to find the reason or reasons why I was on earth before jumping from the sky and killing myself in the process.

I thought that getting close to God would help me discover the meaning of life and why I was put on earth. I knew only one way to get close to God, and that was to pray as I had been taught to do as a child. A Muslim is required to pray five times a day. Praying includes genuflecting and prostrating oneself while facing in the direction of Mecca, the Muslim holy city. So I started bending, kneeling and reciting verses from the Koran as I had been taught to do. It soon became clear to me, however, that I was a total failure at this. My schoolwork and other matters crept into my mind every time I prayed. I thought this was because I was not familiar with Arabic, the language of the verses I recited when praying.

I reasoned that my distraction problems would be resolved if I learned Arabic so I could understand the meaning of the prayers, so I bought a book and began teaching myself Arabic. I gave up after a year. Then I reasoned that the fastest and most efficient way to know what I was saying when I prayed was to read translations of the Koran. I read French and English translations of the Koran as well as books about Islam. My concentration while praying did not improve, but a few things caught my attention during my reading of the Koran. I noticed that the names of Moses and Jesus were mentioned a hundred and seventy-five times and twenty-nine times, respectively, and yet I had only the vaguest clue who these men were and what they did. I also noticed that "the book" (the Bible) and "the people of the book" (Jews and Christians) came up frequently. For instance, the Koran states:

> **"If thou were in doubt as to what We have revealed unto thee, then ask those who have been reading the Book from before thee: The Truth hath indeed come to thee from the Lord: So be in no wide of those in doubt"** (Sura 10:94).

I was not at a doubting level, but I was completely ignorant when it came to Moses, Jesus and the Bible. Therefore, I followed the advice of the Koran and start talking to "the people of the book," in the hope of better understanding why I prayed and to whom. One of the first "people of the book" I spoke to was a Jewish classmate. I asked him questions about Moses and bombarded him with other questions related to his religion. He talked to me about Moses and recommended that I read up on the subject. I took his advice and learned a little about Moses. I found that I was more ignorant about the Bible than I had thought.

Next, I decided to ask a Christian, a member of the other "people of the book," about Jesus and the Bible.

I am not a historian, but I am aware of events in the history of humankind such as the colonization of Africa, slavery in America, and World War II and the holocaust. When I looked at these events and other atrocities committed by Christians against both non-Christians and Christians, the last thing I wanted to know about was Christianity. However, in the end I decided to set aside my distrust of Christians and to focus on Christianity as a theology and on Jesus Christ, the spiritual leader of the Christians.

Two young Jehovah's Witnesses were the first Christians I talked to about Christianity. They knocked on my door and spoke about the kingdom to come. I told them I had been raised in a Muslim environment, but was interested in learning about Christ and the Bible. They promised to bring me a Bible. The following Saturday the two young men brought me a Bible, the *New World Translation*. I told them I would read it and suggested they return in two weeks to discuss what I had read.

I started reading the Bible and had a problem with the second paragraph:

> **"Now the earth proved to be formless and waste and there was darkness upon the surface of [the] watery deep; and God's active force was mo-**

ving to and fro over the surface of the waters."[1]

The words "**active force**" caught my attention. They reminded me of science fiction. In science fiction movies such as *Star Wars* I had heard phrases like "the dark force." To say that God has an "**active force**," I believed, was to imply that he also has a passive force. I stopped reading the Bible and waited eagerly for my two visitors to come back so I could ask them why God had an active force and maybe a passive force.

Two weeks later the young men returned. They said that God's active force did not imply that God has a passive force. They would come back the next week, they said, to explain to me the meaning of God's active force.

The young men came back as promised. One of them opened his bag and pulled out a book different from the Bible they had given me. He flipped through the pages and read me the definition of active force. I reluctantly accepted his explanation and said I would try to read the Bible again. I tried again, but, as before, never made it past the second paragraph. I knew it was perhaps a little semantic, but I could not reconcile the fact that God had an active force and maybe a passive force. I had stopped reading science fiction years before and did not want to read anything remotely resembling it. I finally completely gave up trying to read the Bible my two visitors had given me, but I kept it anyway. It never occurred to me that there existed other versions of the Bible besides that one.

My encounters with the young Jehovah's Witnesses and my failure to read their Bible did not discourage me from trying to learn about Jesus and Christianity. One day I read a French book by Gérald Messadie titled *L'homme Qui Devint Dieu,*[2] which translates literally as The man who became God. Messadie tries to prove that all the miracles Jesus performed, including the healings, were not miracles at all, but a result of Jesus using His knowledge and wisdom. He suggests that Jesus did not die on the cross, but that Pontius Pilate, the Roman governor, Nicodemus and Joseph of Arimathaea, two rulers of the Jews, conspired to remove Him from the cross before He died. Messadie concludes by suggesting that Jesus was a good man Who had been turned into God. At first I was glad I had read this book, but slowly I realized that it had destroyed the notion I had of Jesus as a prophet and more than an ordinary wise man. But what upset me most about the book was that, despite his writings about Jesus, the author still professed to be a Catholic. I wondered how he could destroy the foundation of Christianity and at the same time profess to be a Catholic (which I believed to be Christian).

In his second book, *Les Sources,* Messadie apparently tries to substantiate the allegations made in his first. I went to a bookstore and looked at this book, but it did not interest me.

I did not give up reading about Jesus, His life and His speeches until I learned that He had said, "**I am the way, the truth, and the life and no man cometh unto the father, but by me.**" I thought that this statement was very categorical and denied access to God all those who did not believe in Jesus. I failed to understand how one person could claim to be the only way to God and heaven. In an era of rapprochement between the different religions, this was the most divisive statement I had ever read. I stopped reading about Jesus and Christianity.

Next I read the writings and biographies of Malcolm X, Abraham Lincoln, Karl Marx, Benjamin Disraeli and other well-known people in the hope of finding some enlightenment as to my purpose, and that of humankind, on earth. But nothing I read by and about these people helped in this regard. At one point I thought the communists might be right when they suggested that religion and God are the invention of the well to do to keep the less fortunate numb and accepting of their plight.

Next I read books by and about philosophers. I read Khalil Gibran extensively and proudly quoted Socrates in my conversations. But none of what the philosophers wrote helped me to discover why mankind was put on earth. In the case of some philosophers, in fact, the contradiction between their writings and the lives they led left me even more confused about the purpose of humankind on earth.

Next I read many self-help books. These helped to boost my ego, but did not help me in my quest to understand why I had been put on earth.

Then I read books about Africa and my origins, which made realize that I had no reason to envy others.

When I ran out of topics to read in my quest to understand why I had been put on earth, I read books about war in an effort to understand human behaviour. I read about most of the wars of the nineteenth and twentieth centuries. At one point in my reading, I thought that religion was responsible for most of the wars and that perhaps there would be no armed conflict in the world if religion did not exist. But later in my readings on war, I understood that violence is inherent to humankind and that religion is just one of the pretexts for it. Then I lost faith in man's ability to peacefully control his destiny and wished that there were a compassionate and loving being to control the destiny of humankind. After this, I did not read any books for a while.

When I picked up reading again, I chose more entertaining themes. For a few months I read playwrights. I spent some time reading Bernard Shaw, perhaps because of his satire and concern with social justice.

Then one day a friend lent me *The Rajneesh Bible,* by Bhagwan Shree Rajneesh. I started reading it in the afternoon and couldn't put it down until I finished all thousand pages late at night. Rajneesh was a philosopher, a guru in Eastern religions and a very smart man. In the book he expounds on life and God. He says, "God is the greatest fiction that man has created."[3] He is of the opinion that the universe is so vast that one little man on planet Earth could not influence events in the universe and get the attention of a busy God, if in fact there happened to be one. To illustrate his point, Rajneesh tells the story of an elephant crossing a bridge. The bridge gives way when a fly sits on the elephant's back halfway across the bridge. The fly thinks the bridge has collapsed because of its added weight on the elephant's back. Rajneesh says that, like the fly, human beings think they have influence in the vast universe. He believes that human beings invented a God and pray to him because we are not centred. He suggests that meditation is one way to achieve equilibrium on the path to enlightenment, and that dropping one's ego is one way to achieve enlightenment. Finally, I thought, I had found a way to understand the purpose of man on earth and had found everything I needed to know about humankind. I immediately tried to drop my ego, learn to meditate, find the god in me and reach enlightenment. I also read the second volume of *Rajneesh's Bible.* However, I found that it was just a repetition of the first volume.

The more I read Rajneesh, the more I became disenchanted with his theories about life and the god in me. In one book, he attacks a former follower of his, equating her with the devil. I wondered why he was suggesting there was a devil when in his previous book he had written that there was no God. I also learned that he had accumulated vast wealth and collected luxury cars. I wondered why he had accumulated so much wealth yet suggested that the way to enlightenment was to drop one's ego and not to rely so much on materials things.

If I had become disenchanted with Rajneesh, I had not given up on the idea of achieving enlightenment even though I had little clue of what it meant. Next I read about Buddhism and Nirvana, "the state of perfect blessedness achieved by the extinction of individual existence and by the absorption of the soul into the supreme spirit, or by the extinction of all desires and passions."[4] Buddhist philosophy suggests that an individual has to follow four paths or noble truths in order to attain Nirvana. These are:

1. Suffering is universal.

2. Suffering is caused by desire.

3. To eliminate suffering is to eliminate desire.

4. A path must be followed in order to achieve this.

The four paths are divided into eight steps: "(1) right belief, (2) right feelings, (3) right speech, (4) right conduct, (5) right livelihood, (6) right effort, (7) right memory, (8) right meditation (concentration)."[5]

After reading books on Buddhism, I immediately set out to follow the eight steps to be followed in order to achieve Nirvana. At the end of every day, I assigned myself one point for every step I felt I had successfully followed. I did not do well on my self-evaluation. After three months of trying to achieve perfection, I felt not a sparkle of light let alone enlightenment. I decided that maybe the best way to understand and attain enlightenment was to read about and try to emulate the spiritual leader of Buddhism. I learned that Buddha, a prince, had at the age of twenty-nine left his throne, his wife and his newborn son, just a few days old, to become a mendicant. He wandered around the country in search of truth. Apparently he attained Nirvana after a long period of intense meditation and fasting.[6] When I finished reading about Buddha I realized I could never achieve enlightenment his way because I love children. No matter how sad and tired I am, I smile and become energized when I see a child. I could not contemplate having children and leaving them behind to attain Nirvana. My feeling was confirmed when one day I saw a television documentary about religion in

India. A Sannyasin, a homeless disciple in search of enlightenment, cried the moment he spoke of his family and the son he had left behind. My heart would have been torn apart and I would have sobbed like Sannyasin every time I remembered the family and children I had left.

I wished to study Hinduism, but was reluctant to do so because I could not understand how a god, the Hindu god, could assign the majority of his followers to the lower end of the class system for socio-economic and racial reasons. However, at one point I put aside my prejudices and asked a colleague from India to tell me why the caste system existed in Hinduism. He told me that the Hindu gods had instituted the system to make society more efficient. Initially, people were assigned to a class according to their social aptitude. The caste system was intended to be accommodating and allow individuals to move from caste to caste based on merit. Over the years, however, the people in the higher castes made the system very rigid, jealously keeping the upper echelons for themselves and preventing individuals in the lower castes from moving up. My colleague's explanation satisfied me somewhat and for a while I was open to learning about Hinduism.

My interest in Hinduism dissipated again when, one day, a patient from India walked into my office. Around his neck he wore a pendant with a picture of an old man with a long white beard. I asked the patient whose picture he was wearing. He said it was his god. I asked him to tell me a little about his god. He said he did not want to talk to me about his god and added that there were thousands, perhaps a million, other gods like his. I asked him which god was the best among the thousands or perhaps a million, for if I was going to worship a god I wanted it to be the best one. I did not want to serve a god only to discover when I died that I had not served the best one and would have to be reincarnated as a miserable human being or, worse, as an animal or a plant to feed earthly predators. I wanted to serve a god who would assure me of an eternal life free of the constraints of this life and of the endless cycle of death and reincarnation dogma of Hinduism. The patient said he did not know who was the best god. He said he chose his god because it happened to be the god of his people. Then I made a quick calculation in my head and concluded that it would take me at least ten million years (10 years x 1 million gods = 10 million years) to find the most suitable god among the one million Hindu gods if I spent more than a decade searching for one and did not find him. I reached the conclusion that I did not have that much time to live and gave up trying to find a suitable Hindu god.

The closest I got to studying Hinduism was when I read New Age books. Every large North American city has at least one bookstore devoted entirely to New Age books, and Montreal is no exception. In addition, the religion sections of regular bookstores feature more books devoted to New Age than to the three major religions (Judaism, Christianity and Islam) combined. For more than a year I shopped for New Age books and music almost every second week. At one point I tried to stop buying New Age books because it was becoming costly and I was getting nowhere. However, I was unable to kick the habit. I kept on buying and reading New Age books in the hope that the next one I read would give me the answer to life and god and lead me down the path of enlightenment. When someone gave me a gift, it was usually a New Age book.

For two semesters I took evening classes on transcendental meditation. The instructor taught us how to focus and channel our energies from our rectum to our head. The other students said they succeeded in channelling their energies. I failed despite trying hard. We hummed and learned how to relax. We had Tarot, crystal ball and other New Age sessions. I learned to burn a candle while taking my bath. At the end of the course I did not feel enlightened. On the contrary, I felt darker inside because the classes were always held in the dark.

One day an acquaintance suggested I attend a conference given by a Maha something, a guru from the East. The acquaintance told me the guru was probably the only enlightened person alive. I went to the conference eager to meet an enlightened person and hoping to finally discover the se-cret to enlightenment. The conference was held in a hotel in a Montreal suburb. The parking lot of the hotel was full of cars bearing licence plates from Ontario and northern U.S. states. Most of the people who attended the conference had serious looks on their faces. Like me, they all seemed preoccupied and searching for something. The hall, which could hold a thousand people, was full. I expected the guru to be an old, white-haired man wearing a robe. Instead, he was in his early fifties, had dark hair, and wore a business suit and tie – and appeared well fed. He did not appear to be enlightened even though I still do not know what an enlightened person looks like. He spoke English very well. The guru told us repeatedly that two words, ego and greed, summarize all the problems of humankind. He gave us an example. He said that in the Middle Ages men aspired to having a castle and the best horse, and that today men aspire to having the biggest house and the most beautiful car. He said we labour hard to get all this and then die. He suggested everything would be fine if we were to stop this flow of desire. I later learned that the guru had come to Montreal in order to have maintenance work done on his private jet. For me it was all déjà vu. I had heard the same thing from Mr. Rajneesh. I dislike it when people say one thing and do the opposite. The participants at the conference did not pay a fee to attend, but we were all given a card with the address of the guru's centre in Montreal where we could buy books and other items and also sign up to become members. I never went to the centre.

At one point I thought that perhaps science could me help me understand about life and God. I read books about astronomy and astrophysics and watched television shows on these subjects. I learned that earth and eight other large bodies called planets currently known to humankind, some sixty satellites gravitating around the planets, and billions of comets (celestial objects with a luminous tail) and asteroids gravitate around the sun to form the solar system. I learned that a group of stars (suns) can form a pattern in the sky known as constellations, which are given names such as Ursa Minor (Little Bear), Ursa Major (Great Bear), Taurus (Bull) and Leo (Lion). I learned that from a million to as many as trillions of stars can be grouped together to form an entity known as a galaxy.[7]

I learned that our sun (a star) and more than a hundred billion other stars form the Milky Way Galaxy. I learned that the sun and the hundred billion or more stars that make up the Milky Way circle around the centre of the galaxy. I learned that the Milky Way has a diameter of about a hundred thousand light years. I learned that our solar system, moving at a speed of two hundred and twenty-five kilometres per second, takes two hundred million years to make a complete revolution around the centre of the Milky Way. I learned that there are probably more than a hundred billion galaxies in the universe. I learned that a group of galaxies ranging from ten (a cluster) to as many as a thousand (a supercluster) can form a group and travel in unison away from other galaxies and groups of galaxies. I learned that the galaxies in a cluster are held together by the gravity of the members of the cluster and possibly by dark matter. I learned that the dark matter makes up about ninety percent of all matter in the universe. I learned that the dark matter can also be found in the form of black holes (collapsed massive stars). I learned that the universe is expanding with the galaxies and clusters of galaxies, getting away further and further from each other and from the centre of the universe. I learned that even if one were able to travel at the speed of light (300,000 kilometres per second), it would take 4.3 light years to reach the nearest star, a hundred thousand years to cross the Milky Way, two million years to arrive at the next galaxy and twenty million years to reach the next cluster of galaxies.[8] At the end of my astronomy-reading spree, I realized that the universe is vast, complex and organized, that we know little about the universe and finally, that humankind is infinitesimally small in the infinite or perhaps finite universe. However, knowing a little about the universe did not enlighten me as to how humankind came to be and our purpose on earth.

One day I saw a documentary about Stephen Hawking, the English physicist. I watched him explain the origin of the universe. I liked the documentary and admired his determination to crawl up the stairs despite his physical limitations. I remained motionless for the entire presentation and followed it with all my senses. Finally, I thought that this time I had nailed it, I finally understood everything about creation and maybe the creator. In the documentary, Professor Hawking explained how the universe evolved from fifteen billion years ago to today. I thought I understood everything until he talked about the Big Bang, the explosion that is said to have occurred at the beginning of the universe. Professor Hawking said he did not know what happened a split second before the Big Bang, or "time zero." He did not know who initiated the implosion, which collapsed all the mass of the universe together, for the Big Bang to occur. He did not know if there was a creator of the collapsed mass and, if so, who it was. Professor Hawking said he did not know what came first, "the chicken or the egg," the creator, the implosion or something else. I became confused. I thought I had missed something he said because of my inattention for a split second.

I immediately went out and bought Professor Hawking's book.[9] I took time off work and went up to the Laurentien Mountains, north of Montreal, in the quietness of winter in the hope that I would understand it. For three days I tried in vain to read and understand the book. I could not understand how, by itself, an explosion of universal magnitude like the Big Bang could produce billions of complex organized galaxies, trillions of stars and millions of life forms on this planet. I was comforted when an English woman told me that many people in England had bought the book and not read it. She said people carried it with them into the Underground (the subway), opened it and then placed a gossip magazine in front of it. I lent the book to a friend, who never gave it back. This was one book I was not unhappy to never have returned to me.

I thought that maybe Albert Einstein, one of the world's greatest scientists, would help me to understand something about the universe. With my inability to read and understand Professor Hawking's scientific writings still fresh in my memory, I tried not to dwell too much on Einstein's scientific writings. Instead, I concentrated on his philosophical work and life.[10] Nothing I read about Einstein enlightened me as to how humankind came to be and why we are on earth.

At the end of my scientific readings about the universe, I thought that Professor Hawking and other scientists who profess that the universe started at a given point and time, is expanding or is expanding and contracting are probably right. However, I felt that most likely a very intelligent being initiated the creation and evolution of the universe, for the universe is too complex and organized to be just the result of a random explosion. I felt that a very intelligent being must have initiated and overseen the evolution of the universe, because we know that "motion cannot initiate itself, but must be motivated by something already in motion." I felt that an intelligent being must have created and supervised the evolution of the universe, for I have never seen an explosion create complex organized bodies revolving around themselves and other complex bodies. Chaos and rubble are all that explosions create. I also felt that an explosion of universal magnitude like the Big Bang could not, by itself, without any intelligent intervention, have created the complex organized universe and elaborate life forms on this planet. If this were the case, it would contradict the principle of ownership as we know it and I could walk into a car dealership, take any car I wanted and say the car was created by an explosion and chance. I could also move to any property and say the house came about by some kind of implosion or explosion. In the end I concluded that humankind will probably never know what happened at time zero and beyond unless the creator of the universe tells us, and even then we will probably never fully understand it.

At one point in my search for the purpose of humankind on earth, I read books on anthropology (the study of human culture). I learned a lot about the inhabitants of this planet and their culture. I noticed that all nations, even those that exist deep in the jungle, seek and worship some kind of divinity. I noticed that the more technologically advanced a society becomes, the less its citizens entertain the notion of a divinity and the more they spend on pets. However, reading anthropology did not help me to understand the meaning of life.

In college, the theory of evolution was part of my curriculum. Other than this, I never bothered to study the theory of natural selection, which states among other things that life forms on this planet evolved over millions of years through natural chance. I did not subscribe to the theory of natural chance because I felt there were many missing links. For example, it does not adequately explain the relationship between the monkey, Neanderthal man and contemporary man. My understanding of the theory of chance is that primitive species A (the monkey) gave rise to the ancestor of the chimpanzee, the ancestor of the gorilla and a less evolved species B (Australopithecus, or southern ape), the ancestor of humans. Apparently this latest species B gave rise to an intermediate evolved species C (Homo erectus, or upright man), which in turn gave rise to the more advanced species D (Homo sapiens and Neanderthal man).

Then, apparently, Homo sapiens finally gave rise to the most evolved species of all, contemporary man. I felt that if the theory of natural chance was correct, the most evolved species (contemporary man) and perhaps the more advanced species (Homo sapiens and Neanderthal man) would still be around and the lesser-evolved species gorilla and chimpanzee would have disappeared long ago. Today, we are still guessing as to what happened to Neanderthal man, and we know that if it were not for humankind destroying the monkey and his environment the apes would outlive us. Another reason I was not enthusiastic about the theory of evolution was as non-scientific as the theory of evolution itself. When I was young and living in Africa, the other children and I had a pet monkey named Booboo. We grew up with Booboo. We spent more time playing with Booboo than any evolutionist will ever spend with a monkey. Booboo knew many things and we taught him many other things, but it never once occurred to me that Booboo would have become like us even if we had spent a million years with him. At the end of my study of the theory of evolution I felt that it is probably correct to say that a species adapts to its environment, but that it is unrealistic to claim that the changes brought about by this adaptation cause the species to mutate into another species (from monkey to mankind).

After more than one decade of reading, bending, kneeling, humming, prostrating, candle burning, bead counting, listening to New Age music and doing many odd things, I had not found the reason for humankind's presence on earth. I had not found enlightenment or what will happen to me when I die. Someone once said, "A man without a cause is like a tree without roots." If I had failed in my search for the reason or reasons for humankind's presence on earth, I had not failed to find what I thought was a good cause. In my years of reading I had come across and read a book by John Robbins, *Diet for a New America: How Your Food Choices Affect Your Health, Happiness and the Future of Life on Earth.*[11] Robbins refers to the scientific literature to show that a vegetarian diet is beneficial to one's health. He also shows that society's craving for meat products is contributing to the destruction of the environment and mistreating animals in the process. To me the book made a lot of sense and being a vegetarian became my cause. In any event, it was a convenient cause for me, for I rarely ate meat.

As for my quest to discover why I was placed on earth, I decided to put this on the back burner. I decided that I was going to enjoy myself, lead a good suburban life, make some money, give a little to charity, be kind to most people and ignore those who are not kind. I decided that I was going to do all this in the hope that I would be allowed into heaven when I died and there happened to be a God and heaven. Meanwhile, I started reading financial books.

That was my plan until my wife and I had children. Suddenly I realized that I had to worry about and care for not only myself, but our children as well. I realized that I needed to give our children some spiritual guidance or some day strangers might do it for me and enrol them in a cult. I could tell our children to follow tradition and embrace Islam, my grandparents' religion, but I rather doubted they would follow my advice since I did not practise that religion myself. I could tell them I had explored many religions and had not found the truth and God, but I realized that this would have amounted to an invitation for them to search for God where I had failed. I decided to ask for my wife's input. My wife cared less about spirituality than I did. She remembered her fervent Catholic grandmother "dragging" her to church, which she hated with a passion. Her only desire was to have the children baptized to please her grandmother. I acquiesced to the wishes of my wife and her grandmother and had the children baptized. I did not know that infant baptism is not described anywhere in the Bible. Meanwhile, I hoped that some day our children would wisely choose their own spiritual path. It was a few months after this that my family and I moved to Bermuda.

[1] *New World Translation Of the Holy Scriptures* (Brooklyn, New York: Watchtower Bible And Tract Society, 1961).

[2] Gérald Messadie, *L'homme Qui Devint Dieu* (Paris: Éditions Robert Laffont, 1988).

[3] Bhagwan Shree Rajneesh, *The Rajneesh Bible* (Oregon, USA: Rajneesh Foundation International, 1985)

[4] Excerpted from *Compton Reference* (Carlsbad, CA: Compton News Media, 1995).

[5] George A. Mather and Larry A. Nichols, *Buddhism: Dictionary of Cults, Sects, and Religions and the Occult* (Grand Rapids, MI: Zondervan, 1993), p. 46.

[6] Sherab Chodzin Kohn, *The Awakened One: A Life of the Buddha* (Boston: Shambhala, 1994).

[7] Terence Dickinson, *Night Watch: A Practical Guide to Viewing the Universe* (Buffalo, New York: Firefly books, 1998).

[8] Terence Dickinson, *The Universe and Beyond* (Buffalo, New York: Firefly books, 2004).

[9] Stephen Hawking, *A Brief History of Time: From the Big Bang to Black Holes* (New York: Bantam, 1988).

[10] Albert Einstein, *Ideas and Opinions* (New York, New York: Bonanza Books, 1954)

[11] John Robbins, *Diet for a New America: How Your Food Choices Affect Your Health, Happiness and the Future of Life on Earth* (Tiburon, CA: H. J. Kramer, 1987).

CHAPTER SIX

To Mexico

Dr. Trouts returned to Bermuda on Monday, April 16th, 1996. My wife and I departed for Montreal the next day.

I was feeling better since I had started taking the antibiotics a week earlier, but nonetheless I saw a dentist in Montreal for a second opinion. The dentist was gentle and polite. She listened to my story, looked in my mouth and referred me to a periodontist, a gum specialist. The periodontist saw me the next day. He examined my mouth, poked my mouth and gums with a pointed instrument, and told me that my teeth were good and solidly anchored, but that I had a mild inflammation of the gums. He said that this type of pathology was common in certain parts of Africa and he had treated a few persons of African heritage with the problem. He recommended that I have my molars removed and replaced with titanium implants. I didn't know much about dentistry, but it seemed to me that the periodontist's recommendation did not make sense, especially since he had said my teeth were good. Therefore, I rejected his recommendation. That evening I started to feel unwell again. I thought I was tired and needed a vacation, so I booked a ten-day vacation in Mexico at an all-inclusive club.

Two days later my wife and I left the children with her parents and flew to Cancun. When we arrived at the club we asked for and were given a room far from the centre of activity so I could rest. But I was unable to rest because eighty young Americans and Canadians who met once a year were vacationing at the same time as we were. These young people would have dinner and watch a show until eleven p.m. Then they would go to their rooms to change before heading for the discotheque. Somewhere between three and five in the morning they would return to their room, making more noise than at eleven because by now they were intoxicated. At seven the whole group would go for breakfast, making more noise than in the wee hours because they had enjoyed their catch of the night. As soon as the young guests left for breakfast the cleaning staff would arrive, dragging the beds on the tile floors and calling out to each other across the hall.

I got little sleep because of all the noise. I thought I might sleep better at night if I exhausted myself during the day. For two days I ran more than an hour every morning, but had to give it up because of the heat and humidity. For the next two days I worked out in the weight room, which was air-conditioned. My second day in the weight room, an employee came running in to inquire if there was a doctor. When I said I was a doctor she asked me to follow her to the clinic, which was located nearby. In the clinic I found a club employee of Mexican origin lying on a stretcher, badly burned and in shock. Apparently he had tried to fill the gas tank of a boat while the engine was on. Eyewitnesses said the boat had caught fire and exploded like in the movies and the worker had been blown out of the boat.

Two women were standing beside the burned man. One said she was the club's nurse and the other introduced herself as a doctor. I asked the doctor to install a large intravenous line on her side of the patient and I would do the same on my side. She said, "I am an ophthalmologist [an eye doctor]; I will assist you." Therefore, I knew the patient was mine. We managed to revive and stabilize the patient and then waited for the ambulance.

Usually the club had a resident doctor on duty, but the nurse told me there would be no doctor for the next ten days. The following day when I went to the weight room to work out I was asked to go the clinic to attend to another patient. I had to repair a laceration that had been sustained by a guest. The following day I was again asked to attend to a patient. To thank me for my services, the manager gave me beads, which I used to purchase water at the bar. I didn't mind helping the nurse, but I was afraid I would be liable if I treated all these patients, some of whom were American, without malpractice insurance. To avoid being called to the clinic again, I decided to go snorkelling. I spent several hours every day in the water. I snorkelled to the point where my left ear got clogged with algae and I had to go the hospital in town to have it irrigated.

After a week of resting and snorkelling I still did not feel well. I slept little and had pain on the left side of my face. I tried to forget my problems by minding other people's business. Every evening the club nurse, a married couple from Montreal – also doctors – and my wife and I would sit and gossip. The nurse would tell us which employees used the most condoms, for these were distributed free to all employees. The woman doctor, who spent most of the day spying on people, told us who had sex with whom. Ironically, the most sexually active people were the American and Canadians girls who went to the best schools and seemed very proper when they arrived. One of these girls had said to her friends, "My daddy would never imagine what his little girl is doing here." Gossiping helped me forget my problems temporarily, but after a few days I still was not feeling well. I decided I needed to deal with my own problems and stopped sitting with my gossip group.

One evening I sat by myself and thought about the events surrounding my illness. I thought about my severe headaches and the ensuing hospitalization in Montreal in 1995, and I realized that I had seen a dentist a few days before falling ill. I thought about the events surrounding my flu-like symptoms in Bermuda and realized that they had started the night after my first visit to the dentist. Then I reviewed my current state and realized I had felt very good when I left Bermuda and begun to feel ill the evening after I saw the periodontist in Montreal. I reached the conclusion that I had a tooth-related problem, which flared up with every dental manipulation. I realized that I had been misled into thinking that the headaches I had in Montreal were work-related. I realized that I had hastily moved to Bermuda based on this assumption. I decided that I needed to take care of my teeth more than I needed rest, and that I stood a greater chance of finding a suitable dentist in Montreal than in Bermuda.

I also felt that the hospital in Bermuda, with Dr. Cooperson and his group, was not an ideal place for me to work. I reached the conclusion that I should move back to Montreal at once. All I would have to do was tell my wife that I had made an error in judgement in moving to Bermuda and apologize to her. In any event she would be delighted to hear of my decision. I rehearsed all the above in my mind and was going to break the news to my wife when God gave me a directive to go back to Bermuda, find a church in my neighbourhood and attend services there. I thought God had made a mistake, because even though I had searched for the truth for many years it had never occurred to me to change religions and go to church, even if this happened to be part of the truth. I wanted to question the directive, but I remembered that two weeks earlier I had promised God I would listen to him and do his will if he helped me with the difficult situation I was in. I had no choice, but to return to Bermuda.

My wife and I took an earlier flight than planned and flew to Montreal via New York. We spent one night in Montreal, then flew to Bermuda with the children.

CHAPTER SEVEN

"A Church in My Neighbourhood"

I returned home still thinking I had misunderstood the directive from God. I thought I was supposed to find a Muslim temple and not a church. So my first Friday back in Bermuda (Friday being the Muslim holy day), I went looking for the mosque. I noticed that it was not located in my neighbourhood as the directive had indicated, but on the other side of town. I didn't know the exact location of the mosque and got lost. When I finally found it, they had finished praying and there was nobody around. I went back to the office still thinking I had misunderstood the directive. In fact, I was still a little sceptical about the whole business of finding a church in my neighbourhood and decided I was going to do nothing more about it. I would wait, and if God really wanted me to attend a mosque, or a church for that matter, he would find a way to let me know.

The following Friday I finished seeing patients in the clinic early in the morning and sat down to talk with Florence, the clinic receptionist. For a while we talked about things completely unrelated to religion and God. Then suddenly, for no reason, she changed the subject and invited me to her church. I was surprised by her invitation and didn't know what to stay. I stuttered when I tried to speak. When finally I was able to speak, I began to tell her that I had been raised in a Muslim environment. Before I could complete my sentence, she interrupted and said, "Everybody is welcome in our church; we don't ask people who they are or where they come from." She told me her church was called Cobbs' Hill Methodist Church and gave me the address. I told Florence I would attend her church that weekend.

On Sunday I got up early, thinking that Florence's church was located at the other end of the Island. I dressed and asked my wife to come with me. I drove out of our property, took the main road, passed the first street, turned left on the second street, and immediately turned right to enter the lane where Florence's church was located. I couldn't believe the church was located in my neighbourhood just as God had instructed. It was the church closest to my home. I had walked past it on my way to Aikido lessons on numerous occasions and had never noticed it. The church has been built by slaves in the 1800s. The slaves, who had received permission from the master, had built it by the light of the moon at the end of their day of labour. The church could seat a hundred people and had about fifty members. It was one of the smallest churches in Bermuda. Florence introduced us to the members and they welcomed us. The church had a women's choir and a children's choir. The choirs sang so beautifully that my wife wept for joy. There were three preachers: Pastor E. Desilva (real name), who preached twice a month, and two schoolteachers, Mrs. Williams and Mrs. Smith, who each preached once a month.

After the service I immediately ran off to the hospital because I was on duty. When I arrived at the church the next Sunday the others politely told me I could not dash out immediately after the service the way I had the previous week. They said I had to stay after the service to greet people and chat with them. After that I made sure I stayed around at the end of the service to shake hands with some, receive hugs and kisses from others, and talk with many. I had never come across such a warm group of people, and I partially understood why God had directed me to that particular church.

Now that I had found a church, I wanted to buy an English Bible. It would have been easy to ask Florence what Bible they used in the church, but I wanted to shop for my own. I went to the Christian bookstore. I found the Bible section and discovered that there were many versions. I scanned them for one that suited me. The more I went through the Bibles the more confused I got. At first I thought the most expensive Bible would be the best and decided to make a selection based on that criterion. I picked a nice white leather-bound one and noticed that it was priced at a hundred dollars. I put it down as fast as I had picked it up. Next I thought I would choose a Bible on the basis of whether it was new or old, because I remembered trying in vain to read the *New World Translation* that the two young Jehovah's Witnesses had given me years earlier. I thought that maybe an older translation would not talk about "active force" as that one had. I looked on the shelves for a Bible bearing the title *Old World Translation*, but could not find one. I considered just asking Florence what Bible she and the church used, but was too eager to choose my own. I was not going to walk out of that bookstore without a Bible. So I went to the desk and asked the gentleman for advice. I told him I was looking for a good Bible, preferably an old one. He walked to the Bible section and without hesitation, picked up a Bible and said, "This is a good Bible – you can't go wrong." I glanced at the cover, which read, *Holy Bible: King James Version, Giant Print,* and looked at the gentleman with scepticism for he had not given me a Bible with the word "old" in the title. I asked him three times if he was sure he had given me a good Bible. My question did not annoy him and three times he responded that he had given me a good Bible. I paid the gentleman less than thirty dollars and left with my Bible.

I started reading my Bible that evening. I noticed that this Bible said "spirit of God" instead of "active force of God." Initially I used a dictionary to help me understand some of the words I was reading, but as the evening wore on I discovered, to my surprise, that I was reading fluently and understanding my Bible without the use of a dictionary.

The following Sunday I went to church proudly holding my Bible under my right arm just as I had first gone to school at the age of six proudly carrying my school bag. I was eager to know if the other members were using the same Bible. To my great joy I discovered that they were. Later I would learn that prior to my arrival there had been a debate because some members wanted to use the *New King James Bible* while others wanted to continue using the *King James Bible.* Apparently the most influential members of the church had won and the *New King James Bible* was ordered. However, the order was never received and the church had gone back to using the *King James Bible.* I didn't understand the controversy over Bible versions, but was happy that the church was using the same one that I had bought.

CHAPTER EIGHT

Looking for a Doctor

On my return to Bermuda I saw patients in the clinic and in the office. I operated on minor cases, but did not want to embark on long and arduous spine surgeries since I was still not feeling one hundred percent.

I went back to the dentist and told him I was having pain in my left cheek and thought it was related to my teeth. He said that the older generation of dentists to which his father belonged thought an infected tooth could produce systemic symptoms and make a person sick. He did not subscribe to that theory, he said, and had not read anything to that effect in his textbooks. I felt like saying that not so long ago doctors exsanguinated patients who presented with high blood pressure and put people to sleep using ether, that a hundred years from now people will say we were barbarians because of how we treated people, that something is not necessarily implausible or non-existent just because we have not seen it in our few textbooks. But I didn't say any of these things, because I was not in the mood to argue. I just wanted something to be done about my symptoms. I told him I didn't feel well and would rather be working than in his office complaining. He said, "You have to accept being sick like everybody else." I asked him to give me my x-rays and I left his office.

Next, I went to see an ear and nose specialist in order to rule out mandibular joint involvement. The specialist told me my temporo-mandibular joint was normal and there was nothing he could do for me.

Next, I went to see an internal medicine specialist. The internist told me my symptoms were related to my teeth and suggested I see a dentist. This was easier said than done. I wondered how I could find a dentist to help me since the best dentist on the Island (according to Dr. Trouts) had told me

I had to accept being sick like everybody else. At this stage I was desperate and did not know who to turn to.

Then I remembered a conversation I had had with Dr. Little, a young white Bermudian, when I first moved to the Island. The second time we talked, Dr. Little, who had trained in Montreal, said, "Bermuda is a rough place," and offered to help if need be. At the time I didn't know what she meant by this. Now I thought that maybe Dr. Little could help me. I called her, told her about my predicament and asked for her advice. She said she could not be my physician since we had a working relationship, but suggested I see her associate, Dr. Water.

On May 30th, I saw Dr. Water in the small office she shared with Dr. Little. She took the time to listen to my story and examine me. Then she told me I was sick, and not in the head. For once I could relate to my many patients who had been told by a doctor that they were sick in the head. (While it is true that no two individuals will react the same way to the same disease, and people may occasionally have a financial incentive not to return to work, I have never, in my fifteen years as a doctor, seen a patient who was sick in the head. On the other hand, I have seen many patients who were told by a physician or other health-care professional that they were sick in the head and who turned out to have a severe pathology such as a tumour. Thus I think that a health-care professional who tells a patient that he or she is sick in the head is either narrow-minded, arrogant, ignorant or all of the above.) Dr. Water ordered some tests and scheduled an appointment for me to see her the following week. She also suggested I see a dentist.

My pager vibrated as I was leaving Dr. Water's office. I used her phone to call the hospital and found that it was Dr. Cooperson who had paged me. He asked if he could see me. I told him I was in Dr. Water's office and would be there right away (Drs. Water and Little rented a former gardener's house that Dr. Cooperson had converted into an office.)

I crossed the parking lot and entered Dr. Cooperson's office. I sat in the waiting room with his patients until he was able to see me. He began by saying he knew I was sick and had learned that I had been sick in Montreal before coming to Bermuda. He said that as chief of orthopaedics he was entitled to know what was wrong with me. I said I had had headaches when I was Montreal and had informed Dr. Trouts of this before moving to

Bermuda. I explained that I now knew my headaches were related to a chronic dental problem, which I was trying to have taken care of. Dr. Cooperson was very cold and unsympathetic. He started questioning me about patients I had treated in Bermuda.

T.S., a young Portuguese-Bermudian boy, was the first patient Dr. Cooperson wished to discuss. I had been involved in the treatment of T.S. my first week on the Island. The boy presented with a "burst" fracture of the neck (shattered vertebrae fracture). Dr. Trouts, the treating physician, had asked for my opinion. I told Dr. Trouts and the boy's parents that he required surgery. The parents consented and I put in an urgent order for the necessary implants from Toronto. Meanwhile, Drs. Cooperson and Fascioni got involved in the boy's treatment. They suggested that my proposed surgical treatment was aggressive and sent the boy's x-rays to two of their friends, in Montreal and in Boston, for their opinion. Their overseas friends said the boy did not require surgery. Drs. Cooperson and Fascioni conveyed this opinion to the boy's parents. They became very confused by all the conflicting opinions and refused the surgery, yet they still wanted me, not Dr. Trouts, the treating physician, nor Drs. Cooperson or Fascioni, to treat their child.

The parents wanted me to fit T.S. with a neck brace and allow him to walk immediately, as per the recommendation of Drs. Cooperson and Fascioni. I could have told Dr. Trouts I did not want to be involved in the boy's treatment. But I did not. Instead, I chose to remain on the scene for the sake of the patient, who was too young to decide for himself. I explained to his parents that he had an unstable fracture that could collapse, causing compression of the spinal cord and nerves, if he was allowed to stand immediately. I recommended that the child remain in bed with traction to his neck for at least three weeks, to allow the fracture to heal, before he be allowed to walk. The parents consented to my compromise treatment.

Back in his office, Dr. Cooperson asked me why I had been so aggressive in my recommended treatment of the neck fracture. I noticed that on his shelf he had a book titled *Orthopaedic Knowledge Update 5: American Academy of Orthopaedic Surgeons*. I asked him to pick up the book and open the chapter on spine trauma. He did so. I asked him to read the section on "Fracture of the vertebral body with canal comprise"[1], which was what the boy had. He quietly read the section, blushed and put the book away. He realized that my proposed treatment was the right one. He tried to change the subject and discuss another of my patients. I said he might be interested to know what had happened to the boy. I told him that on March 23rd, 1996, four months after T.S. had sustained the trauma, his parents brought him to the emergency room because he was still having problems with his neck. I examined him at that time and found that the fracture had collapsed further and his neck was in kyphosis (abnormally bent forward). The parents told me they had recently taken him to Boston to seek an opinion on the treatment of the unhealed fracture and a surgeon there had recommended surgery from the back of the neck. The parents asked me to perform surgery from the back of the neck (my initial recommendation had been to perform surgery from the front of the neck as described in most spine books). I politely declined and strongly recommended that they take T.S. to Boston to have the surgery.

Dr. Cooperson began to question me about my treatment of some other patients, even after I had updated him on T.S. and had proved that it was he who had been wrong about the child's recommended treatment. I said I would not play his blame game. I told him about S.B., a young black Bermudian with severe low back pain who he had seen years earlier. I reminded him that he had told the girl that nothing was wrong with her back. According to the patient and her mother (see Letter 1 in the Appendix), Dr. Cooperson told the mother, "Nothing is wrong with her back and do not return to waste my time."

I told Dr. Cooperson that Dr. Bernis, a chiropractor who saw the girl some time after he did, discovered that she had a spondylolisthesis (slipped vertebrae). I had reviewed the x-rays and found that she had a spondylolisthesis, a pathology that we learn to recognize in medical school. Dr. Cooperson was not impressed by my pointing to his inability to make a simple diagnosis of a slipped vertebra. He wanted to discuss another patient who I had treated inadequately. I tried to reason with him and show him that I had treated this patient ingeniously. I told him the patient was doing well, even playing soccer, and his parents were very grateful for what I had done. Dr. Cooperson was not impressed by my arguments.

I realized that Dr. Cooperson's intentions were not to determine whether

I had treated my patients adequately, but to find patients he could accuse me of maltreating. I therefore put an end to the conversation by saying that I had completed my examinations successfully and was not going to put up with any more of his questions. Dr. Cooperson said he believed my judgement was inadequate and asked me to leave his office. On my way out he suggested I tell Dr. Trouts to stop taking vacations until I got well (since my arrival in Bermuda six months earlier, Dr. Trouts had taken three vacations).

That evening Dr. Trouts phoned to say he would be taking three weeks off to travel abroad. I would have to cover his practice and take his calls. I informed him of my meeting with Dr. Cooperson and said I did not want to have to see both his patients and my own, and respond to both his calls and my own, while I was not completely well and under the scrutiny of Dr. Cooperson. He advised me not to let Dr. Cooperson intimidate me. He said that when he moved to the Island Dr. Cooperson had also scrutinized his practice and accused him of treating his patients inadequately; at one point Dr. Cooperson had accused him of wrongly treating a patient with a wrist fracture and threatened to help the patient take legal action against him. I told Dr. Trouts I was not overly worried about Dr. Cooperson, but had a duty to my patients. He informed me that he was scheduled to sail to Russia with his family on a cruise ship and had spent $19,000 on the tickets. I suggested he find a locum to cover for him. He said that according to our contract it was my duty to cover for him while he was away. I reminded Dr. Trouts that he still had not produced a contract as promised and thus I was under no obligation. He offered all sorts of excuses as to why he had not produced a contract. A few days later Dr. Trouts said he had been unable to find anybody to replace him and pleaded with me to find somebody.

While Dr. Cooperson was harassing me and Dr. Trouts was pressuring me, many of my spine patients were urging me to operate on them in June so they would have the summer off. Some, like the girl whose slipped verte-bra Dr. Cooperson had been unable to diagnose, were even threatening to have their surgery abroad if I did not operate on them in June. The irony is that most of those who were threatening to have their surgery abroad had been suffering with back pain for years before my arrival. Now that I had determined the source of their problem and offered a potential solution, they could not wait any longer. I could have easily let the patients who were threatening to go abroad for their surgery make good on their threat, but this would have been to their detriment, because many of these spine patients were victims of failed surgery in Bermuda and abroad.

It suddenly occurred to me that it was not such a bad idea for Dr. Trouts to take his vacation in June. I would ask Dr. Morais, a friend and former professor, to help with my backlog of spine cases and serve as a locum for Dr. Trouts at the same time. Dr. Morais rarely took a vacation (less than two weeks a year), but I remembered that he occasionally took a week off during the summer. I phoned him in Montreal and asked if he could come to Bermuda for a week. He said his clinics and offices were booked for the next three months and he was scheduled to move house the week I needed him, but would nevertheless see what he could do.

Two days later, Dr. Morais phoned to say he was considering the offer, but would have to cancel and reschedule a clinic with eighty-seven patients and an office with thirty-seven patients, find surgeons to take over his two operating days and find somebody to supervise the movers. A few days later he phoned again. He had been able to reorganize his schedule and would come to Bermuda for seven days.

Now that Dr. Morais had agreed to come, I tried to deal with my health condition. One evening I was relaxing in the surgeons' lounge when a gentleman walked in and began to talk to me. The gentleman, a black Bermudian, introduced himself as Dr. D., a dental surgeon. I asked if I could show him some x-rays. I had been carrying in my briefcase the x-rays of my mouth taken in Montreal and recently taken in Bermuda in the hope of finding a suitable dentist. I showed the x-rays to Dr. D. without telling him the story behind them. He looked at the x-rays and said there was a lesion on a molar and the adjacent jawbone (the dentist who had ordered the x-rays had told me they were normal). He offered to examine my mouth and we went to a vacant operating room. I lay on the operating table and he examined my eyes, my neck, behind my ears and briefly, my mouth. He said I had a mild inflammation of the gum and probably an associated infection because he had found ganglions (lumps) behind my ears and in my neck.

Dr. D. suggested I take antibiotics. I told him I had recently taken penicillin and it had not helped. Dr. D. said that at this stage the infection was probably resistant to penicillin and prescribed tetracycline, another antibiotic. He asked me to see him in his office one week after I finished taking the antibiotics.

A few days later I went for my appointment with Dr. Water. She was not as warm and joyful as she had been in our first meeting. I told her I was feeling much better since taking the tetracycline that Dr. D. had prescribed. She said she could see that I was feeling better. I informed her of my meeting with Dr. Cooperson, which she seemed to be already aware of. She said, "Bermuda is a rough place." She told me that Dr. Cooperson had tried to intimidate Dr. Trouts when the latter had moved back to the Island, stopping only when he realized that he could not do much against Dr. Trouts, who was a Bermudian. Dr. Water said that Dr. Cooperson would do everything in his power to get at Dr. Trouts through me. She said I had to develop a thick skin. Then she said that she, being a white Bermudian, had a lot of difficulty when she moved back to the Island from the United States. She had trained in Connecticut at a school with an international reputation, worked in Connecticut as an internist for twenty years and was well respected by her peers. When she moved back to Bermuda, health-care professionals at the hospital questioned the treatments she prescribed for her patients and frequently put her down. Then, without telling me why, Dr. Water said she would be unable to see me any more and advised me to continue seeing Dr. D. I had a feeling that Dr. Cooperson, Dr. Water's landlord, had a lot to do with her decision not to see me any more. A few days later Dr. Water resigned from the hospital. She stopped practising medicine completely and went on to become a painter.

In June Dr. Morais came to Bermuda to cover for Dr. Trouts while the latter went to Russia. For a week he and I did marathon surgery and operated on the backlog of my spinal cases. Working with Dr. Morais was so refreshing and relaxing I was reminded of my training and working days in Montreal. I covered for Dr. Trouts the other two weeks of his vacation.

A few weeks after Dr. Trouts returned I decided to take some time off and go to Montreal to have my dental problems taken care of. I learned that dentistry is a complex field comprising many different specialists. I discovered that, as with the field of medicine, it is best to seek the opinions of different experts in the field. Finally, I learned that teeth, such seemingly non-vital organs, are very vital indeed. At the end of the treatments I was feeling much better, so I kicked myself in the behind and went back to Bermuda to work.

When we arrived home we found the sofas, beds and all the other furniture, kitchen counter and walls covered with mildew. My wife had cleaned all the furniture and walls with Clorox before we left, but this had not prevented mildew from forming. During our absence our neighbours had regularly opened the windows to allow the air to circulate in the house, but this had not prevented it either. My wife could not find an inch of surface in the house that was not covered with mildew to put down the sleeping children. She stood in the house and cried. I took the children outside while she washed the linen and prepared the beds. I was glad to see that the mildew had completely destroyed all my New Age, philosophy and similar books. I managed to salvage a few of my medical books.

[1] *Orthopaedic Knowledge Update 5:Home Study Syllabus* (Rosemont, Illinois: American Academy of Orthopaedic Surgeons, 1996).

CHAPTER NINE

The Inquiry

I started working as soon as I arrived back in Bermuda. I was enthusiastic and thought all my troubles were behind me until I received a letter from the chief of staff, Dr. Jameson. The letter, dated September 9th, 1996, stated:

> "As a result of inquiries made on the conduct of your practice, the Credentials Committee has reviewed and initiated inquiries into your Curriculum Vitae and four (4) specific cases under your care.

> In order to facilitate inquiries into your Curriculum Vitae, you are to Sign and authorize consent and release form [sic] of liability in order to obtain third party information on your professional career [sic]…

> The Credentials Committee has appointed a Committee of Drs. Cooperson, Chalvin, and Elliott, who have been requested to review the four (4) specific cases, to interview you in relation to the cases and submit a written report to the Credentials Committee."

The letter gave me some concern because I had given the Bermuda Hospitals Board details of my qualifications and had submitted references as a part of my application before moving to the Island. My greatest concern was the fact that Dr. Cooperson would be heading the committee charged with conducting the inquiry.

I asked Dr. Trouts for his advice. He suggested I seek legal counsel from the Williamson law firm, which handled all the legal affairs of the Medical Insurance Society. I had purchased malpractice insurance from the MIS.

I called the Williamson firm and secured an appointment with Mr. Romas, a senior partner. On September 16th, I met with Mr. Romas, a white Bermudian in his early fifties. He read Dr. Jameson's letter and listened to my story and to my concerns regarding the inquiry. Mr. Romas spoke in a vibrant voice. He brandished Dr. Jameson's letter and said, "This is a kangaroo court. They cannot do such a thing." He promised to reply to Dr. Jameson's letter within ten days.

On September 27th, Mr. Romas replied to Dr. Jameson's letter as follows:

> "Dr. Bah wishes to assist with your enquires and is confident that any concern that the Board may have as to his professional practice will be allayed.
>
> Before we are able to advance this matter, however, we will need to know the terms of the "enquires made on the conduct of Dr. Bah's] practice" which are referred to in your letter under reply [sic]. We will, also, need to know the identity of the parties making such enquires. It is clearly reasonable and just that if allegations are made regarding Dr. Bah's professional conduct he should be furnished with the particulars of such allegations and given a fair opportunity to respond to them.
>
> Dr. Bah also has concerns as to the composition of the Committee that has been appointed to review the four specific cases. He has reason to believe that this Committee as presently constituted will not be unbiased in its review.
>
> We would, also, [sic] be obliged if you could inform us of the statutory provision under which the Board is conducting this enquiry…
>
> As to Dr. Bah's Credentials and Curriculum Vitae please find enclosed a copy of the requested release to obtain third party information…we also enclose a list of persons that you may wish to contact who will speak to Dr. Bah's integrity and professionalism."

Dr. Jameson replied in a letter dated November 1st, 1996. He stated:

> "…There was one complaint by a patient and three by other members of the Department of Anaesthesia & Surgery…
>
> I anticipate that your client will be provided, in advance of any interview, the particulars of the complaint. I note your client's concern about the composition of the subcommittee and I should be grateful if you would share them with me right away. As indicated above, any staff member who initiated the complaint would be excluded from membership of the subcommittee….
>
> Under the circumstances, I have purposefully declined to reveal the identity of the persons initiating the inquiry as it would be imprudent to do so…"

While Dr. Jameson was reluctant to put in writing the identity of the persons initiating the inquiry, he was very forthcoming about giving me their names verbally. On November 6th, a few days after I had received his letter, Dr. Jameson approached me at the end of a scientific meeting and told me that it was Drs. Cooperson and Fascioni who had initiated the inquiry. I asked Dr. Jameson why he could not put what he had just told me in writing. He said he just could not and left.

A few days later, I phoned Mr. Romas to discuss Dr. Jameson's letter. His secretary informed me that Mr. Roma could no longer represent me because he was moving to another law firm. I suggested that Mr. Romas take my file with him. She said he could not do so since he would be in a conflict of interest. Another partner in the Williamson firm would be taking over my file, she said, and would be calling me shortly. I could not understand why Mr. Romas was suddenly in a conflict of interest for representing me. Later I would learn that he had moved to the firm that was handling the hospital's case against me.

Two weeks later, on November 15th, I met Mr. Kasson, my new attorney at the Williamson firm. Mr. Kasson, a Bermudian of Indian origin, was very soft-spoken and seemed to be timid. He asked me to explain in detail what had prompted Dr. Jameson to initiate an inquiry into my practice. After listening to my story, Mr. Kasson said he would write to the MIS and ask them to pay my legal fees. I had been paying Mr. Roma's fees out of my own pocket. Mr. Kasson said he would try to respond to Jameson's second letter within ten days.

A few days later Mr. Kasson called to say that the Medical Insurance Society had agreed to pay my legal fees and that he would respond to Dr. Jameson's letter at once. On November 27th, he wrote to Dr. Jameson, stating the following:

> 1. Without knowing in advance the identity of the complainants or persons initiating the enquiry it will be difficult for our client to satisfy himself that the members of the Committee are impartial.
>
> 2. Although you state that the sub-committee will not "assume any disciplinary role or function," if the sub-committee determines not to confirm [sic] our client in his appointment to the Medical Staff as a result of its conclusions, this will have a serious effect on our client's career by depriving him of the opportunity to continue in employment in Bermuda and also by

causing a blemish to appear on our client's credentials.

We, therefore, reiterate our request for full and complete disclosure of the identities of the complainants and the particulars of their complaint.

Dr. Jameson never replied to this letter.

CHAPTER TEN

The Case of Mr. D.

On Wednesday, October 23rd, 1996, I was scheduled to operate on Mr. D., a patient with a non-healed fracture of the tibia. Mr. D. had sustained the fracture to his leg in a traffic accident in 1983. He had been treated first by a general surgeon and then by Dr. Cooperson.

Seven months earlier, in March 1996, Mr. D. had consulted with me because he was still having pain in his leg. I had examined the leg and reviewed his x-rays and made the diagnosis of a non-union of the tibia (non-healed fracture). I advised Mr. D. to go back to Dr. Cooperson, his treating orthopaedic surgeon. I wrote a note to Dr. Cooperson suggesting that he use a combination of bone grafting (surgery to add bone at the fracture site) and electric stimulation to treat Mr. D.'s non-healed fracture.

Three months later Mr. D. came back to see me, still complaining of pain. He informed me that Dr. Cooperson had done the bone graft, but had not applied the electrical stimulation as I had recommended. I sent him back a second time, with a note advising Dr. Cooperson of another alternative treatment.

Three months later Mr. D. came back to me. He said that Dr. Cooperson had not followed my second recommended treatment to the letter and as a result the leg had not healed and he was still in pain. When I began to speak, the patient, who was very upset, interrupted and handed me a message from his supervisor. The message stated that Mr. D.'s supervisor was going to send him overseas to have surgery if I failed to treat him. When I finished reading the note, the patient said he would not be going back to Dr. Cooperson. I agreed to treat him and explained what type of surgery I would be performing.

At eight a.m. on the day I was scheduled to operate on Mr. D., Dr. Cooperson phoned Dr. Trouts and asked him why I was operating on this patient. Dr. Trouts replied that he did not know the patient and advised Dr. Cooperson to direct his queries to me.

At noon, as I was operating on Mr. D.'s leg, Dr. Cooperson walked into my operating room and began to question me. He asked what I was doing. I described the surgery I was performing and the reasoning behind it. I told him I was removing the nail from the patient's leg, over-reaming the tibia (increasing the size of the canal) to stimulate the blood flow, and inserting a larger nail. Dr. Cooper said, "You are destroying the blood flow to the patient's leg." I said that after a year there was no blood flow in the canal of the tibia, which was one of the reasons why the leg had not healed. Dr. Cooperson said once again that I was destroying the blood flow to the leg. I said that what I was doing would stimulate the blood flow and allow the leg to heal. I told him that this was the recommended treatment for this type of non-healed fracture and suggested he read up on the subject.

Dr. Cooperson approached the viewing box, looked at the patient's x-rays and said, "The patient's leg is healed." It was obvious, even to an untrained eye that the fracture had not healed. I asked Dr. Cooperson why the patient was still having pain if the fracture was healed. He hesitated, mumbled something and then said, "I know the patient; he is funny and unreliable." I continued with the operation. Dr. Cooperson fumed, paced up and down for a while, and then left.

Dr. Trouts, who was assisting and had witnessed the exchange, asked me how I had been able to keep my composure. I said I could have thrown the scalpel at Dr. Cooperson, but this would not have helped the patient.

After the operation I spoke to Mrs. Santini, the head operating room nurse, about Dr. Cooperson's odd behaviour. She said, "I saw him come in to the operating room and put on his greens, and I wondered what he was doing here since it was not his operating day." She suggested I write a letter of complaint to Dr. Jameson, the chief of staff, with a copy to Dr. Joneson, the chief of surgery. I did so that evening. In addition to describing Dr. Cooperson's unprofessional behaviour, I reminded Drs. Jameson and Joneson that at our meeting in December 1995, when I had first arrived, I suggested that scientific meetings be established in the orthopaedics division to discuss interesting cases. Had we had such meetings, I wrote, Dr. Cooperson would have known how to properly treat Mr. D. and the patient would not have consulted me on three occasions.

Mr. D. woke from the surgery free of the pain he had been suffering for thirteen years. Four months later his leg was healed and he went back to his job in the engineering department of the Bermuda government.

CHAPTER ELEVEN

Negotiating with Dr. Trouts

On October 17th, 1996, I decided it was time to talk to Dr. Trouts about our arrangements. I asked him about the contract he had been promising to produce since the previous December and about the quarterly bonus I was entitled to. As of September 1996, I had billed more than a $0.25 million and had received a monthly salary of only $6,000. Dr. Trouts said he could not produce the contract or issue a bonus until we decided how much rent I would pay, as my rent and other office expenses would have to be deducted. He suggested $3,200 a month for the rental of his two-bedroom cottage, plus $500 to cover property tax, fumigation and cleaning, electricity and water. Dr. Trouts was basically suggesting that I pay half the mortgage on his building. I said that this proposal was outrageous. I reminded him that we had been paying $800 a month each for the offices we occupied before moving to his cottage in July 1996. I also reminded him that in December 1995 he had assured me that my rent would not increase substantially and that I would not be paying half his mortgage. Dr. Trouts said he did not recall making any such promise and would use the cottage as his residence if I was not willing to work there. I said that would be fine with me; I would find office space in town. He said I could not do that since he held my work permit. I replied that this was a form of slavery. He gave me one week to determine what would be a reasonable rent for the cottage and to present him with an alternative proposal.

I asked several professional people such as doctors and accountants what kind of monthly rent they were paying. I found that the going rate for office space in Bermuda was $20 to $40 US per square foot, and calculated that Dr. Trouts was asking me to pay the equivalent of $104 US per square foot.

A month later, on November 16th, I wrote to Dr. Trouts summarizing my findings and making a counterproposal. I put this information in writing because I noticed that he had a tendency to deny yesterday the things he would say today. Dr. Trouts had once said he did not like to keep a paper trail of what he said. (In September 1996, I had organized a meeting with Dr. Trouts and the staff because he had yelled at the staff and made a secretary cry in the waiting room in front of the patients because the staff had used metal fasteners in the patients' files. Dr. Trouts told the secretary the metal fasteners could cut his "valuable hands," preventing him from earning a living. At the meeting I asked a secretary to type and keep the minutes of the meeting for reference so that the staff would know what was expected of them. Dr. Trouts told the staff that all copies of the minutes should be given to him or destroyed in front of him because he did not like to keep a paper trail of what he said and did.)

In my letter, I pointed out that Dr. Trouts had misled me by telling me that most physicians on the Island were paying a significantly higher rent than what he had suggested I pay him. I wrote that physicians were paying an average of $2,000 a month for office space larger that what he was making available to me. I proposed that I pay him $2,000 a month even though I used the office only one afternoon a week. I also wrote that, given the choice, I would rather fight Drs. Cooperson and Fascioni than argue with him because he was supposed to be on my side. I closed by suggesting it was time we had an agreement signed and sealed and put the discussion behind us.

Upon receiving my letter, Dr. Trouts said my proposal was very reasonable and he would put it in the contract.

Two days later Dr. Trouts confronted me in a fury because I had tried to destroy his reputation by telling other physicians that he wanted to charge me $3,700 for rent. He said he was not asking me to pay $3,700; this figure was merely a negotiation ploy. I assured him that my intention was not to destroy his reputation, but to find out what other professionals were paying. I said I was tired of negotiating and wanted him to give me my money. He said he would get back to me with what he thought was a reasonable rent for his cottage. I asked him about the figure of $2,000 that two days earlier he had found reasonable and was going to put in the contract. He said he had to think about it. I had a feeling he had to discuss it with his wife.

In November 1996, to my great satisfaction, the insurance companies took care of another aspect of my relationship with Dr. Trouts. They wrote to advise us that they would no longer pay us to assist each other. They complained that we were assisting each other too often. Dr. Trouts had assisted me on all the spine cases I operated on and I had assisted him on every single case he operated on. The insurance companies had a point: it was not necessary for me to assist Dr. Trouts on minor surgery such as the removal of wires or screws. But Dr. Trouts wanted me to assist him at all times. He would not operate unless I was in the operating room.

Dr. Trouts wrote the insurance companies asking them to reconsider. He referred them to the agreement between the Bermudian Medical Society and the insurance companies, which stipulated that doctors could assist each other when necessary and the insurance company would pay the assisting physician twenty-five percent of the surgical fee. They refused to reconsider. Dr. Trouts wrote a second letter pointing out the unfairness of the decision. He rightfully noted that they continued to pay Drs. Cooperson and Fascioni when they assisted each other on similar cases. Neither the companies nor the BMS responded to the letter. Dr. Trouts suggested that he and I keep assisting each other and bill the patients the amount that the insurance company refused to pay. I declined on the basis that I did not want to over bill my patients. The truth was that I preferred to have the resident doctors assist me. I could perform the average spine operation in less than two hours when assisted by a resident; it took me significantly longer to complete the same surgery when assisted by Dr. Trouts.

Three weeks after receiving my letter Dr. Trouts proposed I pay $3,000 a month for his office. I was furious. I felt he was taking advantage of me. I wrote him again, reminding him that in my survey I had found that physicians on the Island were paying an average of $2,000 for an average of four rooms available to them at all times, while Dr. Trouts made available to me only one room one afternoon a week; the rest of the time he, the physiotherapist and a pain specialist used the two rooms in the little cottage.

On January 10th, 1997, he sent me an unsigned letter. It stated:

"I have received your letter of December 27th 1996 and find it like your previous one antagonistic and disturbing... I will await a signed contract prior to any further discussion of other matters and must defer any disbur-

sements until that time. Attached is the version of the contract that we have
been working under from the beginning."

I mulled over my relationship with Dr. Trouts and concluded that I
had not been antagonistic towards him. If anyone had been unreasonable,
contradictory, misleading and antagonistic, it was he. I immediately paged
him, but he failed to respond. I phoned many times, but he refused to take
my calls. So I drove to his house and rang the bell. When he opened the
door I told him I wanted to talk. He came outside and we sat in my car
talking for two hours. At the end of our conversation, Dr. Trouts apologized for sending me the threatening letter. He promised to have a contract,
including a reasonable proposal regarding the rent, ready to be signed upon
my return from vacation, for I was scheduled to leave the next day. I asked
him why we couldn't come to an agreement about the rent right away. He
looked towards the house and said he had to think about it (he could never
make a decision without consulting his wife). He also said he would make
the necessary calculations and give me my money upon my return.

CHAPTER TWELVE

Interview with the Subcommittee

In November 1996, I partially understood why Dr. Jameson had told me earlier that it was Drs. Cooperson and Fascioni who had initiated the inquiry against me. Dr. Cooperson, who had been diagnosed with cancer, had had to travel abroad for treatment. Apparently his father had passed away in his late fifties from a similar illness. With Dr. Cooperson gone, the orthopaedics division became calm and functional. Dr. Fascioni, who was usually very outspoken, became withdrawn, probably because his father had recently passed away and also because he realized that should Dr. Cooperson not return, Dr. Trouts, the only other Bermudian in the orthopaedics division, would be its next chief. For once I felt welcome in the hospital. Dr. Joneson, nicknamed "The Dictator" and a staunch ally of Dr. Cooperson, approached me and took me on a tour of the new operating room, then under construction.

Even before I read the Bible, I never rejoiced at other people's misfortunes. Now that I was reading the Bible daily, I tried to apply what I read, which included being more compassionate towards others. The Bible teaches that one must:

> **"Love your enemies, bless them that curse you, do good to them that hate you, and pray for them which despitefully use you, and persecute you"** (Matthew 5:44; Luke 6:27; Acts 7:60; Romans 12:14; I Peter 3:9).

I did not think I could ever love Dr. Cooperson, but pray for him was something I was able to do. So I went down on my knees and prayed for Dr. Cooperson's health.

In February 1997, Dr. Cooperson returned to the hospital. I was happy to learn that he was well and knew that God had answered my prayers, or somebody else's. I was even happier when I met him in the operating room a week later and he initiated a conversation with me, something he had never done in the past. He was open about his illness and the treatment he had received. He said one realizes that life is precious and other things are superfluous only when one becomes sick. We spoke at length and I could not believe this was the same Dr. Cooperson who four months earlier was in my operating room arguing with me. When I told Dr. Trouts that I thought Dr. Cooperson's illness had changed him for good, he did not share my enthusiasm. "Evil now, evil forever," said Dr. Trouts. "We will have to wait and see."

It turned out that Dr. Trouts was right about Dr. Cooperson. On Wednesday, March 26th, Dr. Jameson wrote to advise me that I was "required" to attend an interview. The letter stated:

> "The Credentials Subcommittee of the Medical Staff Committee has required you to attend for interview the committee pursuant to Section 6 (2) of the Bermuda Hospitals Board (Medical Staff) Regulations 1996.
>
> The committee has advised me that the interview will focus on the management of the following patients:
>
> Mr. D.S. (Your involvement in the planning of the his operative procedure)
>
> Mr. G.C. (Choice of operative procedure)
>
> Mr. B.S. (Failure to provide medical report requested by the patient)
>
> Mr. E.G. (Choice of operative fixation…)
>
> Charts of the above patients are available for review at the Medical Secretary's office in the Clinical Records Department."

I had three working days to prepare for the interview. I called my attorney's office and asked to speak to Mr. Kasson. The secretary told me that Mr. Kasson was off the Island, but scheduled an appointment with another partner in the firm when I explained the urgency of the matter. I went to the medical records department as Dr. Jameson had suggested in his letter and asked the secretary to let me consult the charts of the four patients I was to be questioned about. She unlocked a filing cabinet and allowed me to consult the four charts under her supervision. I asked if I could make copies of the charts. She said that she had been instructed not to let me do so.

On Monday morning I went to the Williamson law offices to meet Mr.

Black, my new attorney. I gave Mr. Black a copy of Dr. Jameson's letter and discussed with him the four patients that I would be interrogated on.

On Tuesday, April 1st, Mr. Black, Dr. Trouts, who had been invited to attend the meeting as an observer, and I went to the hospital to meet with the Credentials Subcommittee of the Medical Staff Committee. I had spent the weekend preparing my defence and brought two large hockey bags full of books, a spinal model and x-rays concerning the four patients. I asked Dr. Trouts to carry one of the heavy bags for me. For the occasion Dr. Trouts, who was already heavy, wore an oversized beige pullover. He said this might intimidate the interviewers. Mr. Black, a white Bermudian, was by not small either. He was built like a slightly out-of-shape rugby player. We arrived early and sat in the boardroom waiting for the committee members, who arrived one by one. They included Dr. Jameson; Mrs. Anderson, a black Bermudian and Executive Director of the Board (who I had never seen smile); Dr. Joneson; Dr. Paytons, a white Bermudian and a close friend of Dr. Cooperson's; Dr. Ember, a black Bermudian gynaecologist; Dr. X., the dentist who had told me I had to accept being sick; and Dr. Jamieson, a white physician from Tasmania who had achieved Bermudian status through marriage. We were told that Dr. Cooperson had been invited to the meeting as an observer.

I could see by the composition of the committee that I was not in friendly territory. I felt that only two of the seven members, Dr. Ember and (perhaps) Dr. X., would be objective in their assessment of my treatment of the four patients. Before the meeting began, Dr. Jameson told Mr. Black that he would have to leave the room. This led to a long and heated argument. Mr. Black told Dr. Jameson that I would not attend the meeting if he were not allowed to do so. Mr. Black, Dr. Trouts and I walked out of the boardroom. For more than half an hour, Mr. Black tried to reach the hospital's attorney, but the latter never returned the numerous phone calls and pages. Mr. Black advised me not to attend the meeting, but said the decision was mine to make. He said that if I did attend, I should do so under protest. I decided to attend under protest, while Mr. Black waited outside. (I wondered if I was making the right decision. I would get the answer a few months later.)

Mr. S.D., a sixty-three-year-old black Bermudian with a prostate tumour, was the first patient I was questioned about. Dr. Cooperson had complained that I had delayed operating on Mr. S.D. for twenty-four hours and the committee wanted to know why I had done so. I had first seen Mr. S.D. on Tuesday, April 1st, 1996. The patient, who was known to have terminal cancer, had been admitted with back pain, weakness in the leg and inability to walk. I had ordered x-rays, which showed that a tumour was compressing his spinal cord. I explained to Mr. M.D.'s daughter the type of surgery her father required. The next evening the family met to discuss and approve the surgery. Unfortunately I became ill on Wednesday, the morning I was scheduled to operate (this was the day after I had seen Dr. X.). An anaesthetist suggested I transfer the patient to Dr. Cooperson, which I did. Dr. Cooperson operated on Mr. S.D., whose condition then deteriorated until he passed away three weeks later. Dr. Cooperson said the patient would not have died had I operated on Tuesday instead of Wednesday. In my defence, I read out literature showing that my delaying the surgery for twenty-four hours had no bearing on the prognosis. In addition, I could not operate without the family's consent, which was obtained only on Tuesday evening. I read out literature indicating that the surgery (laminectomy) performed by Dr. Cooperson was inappropriate for the pathology presented. I indicated to the committee that it would have been better if Dr. Cooperson had left the patient alone instead of performing the type of surgery he did. I also said that, despite his apparent concern for the patient's welfare, Dr. Cooperson saw him not once after the operation.

The second patient was Mr. B.S., a twenty-six-year-old black Bermudian with a fracture of the left forearm. He was the only patient who had complained about me. Dr. Jameson said my treatment of the fracture was "fine", but he and the committee wanted to know was why I had "failed to provide the medical report requested by the patient."

Mr. B.S.'s file contained summaries of all his office visits and phone conversations, which I had dictated and my secretary had transcribed. I read out these summaries, which indicated the date and time the patient had requested the medical report and the date and time it had been delivered to him. Mr. B.S. failed to mention in his complaint that he disagreed with the conclusion of the medical report I had produced. My report based on my findings and on the evaluation of the physiotherapist, showed that aside from a barely visible scar the patient had no sequalae and the surgery was a success. Mr. B.S. had asked me to change the medical report to indicate that he had some sequalae so that he would receive insurance benefits. I had refused to comply with this request, which may be why he complained that I had not produced the medical report.

Dr. Fascioni, who saw the patient after me, urged him to lodge a complaint against me. Mr. B.S.'s complaint stated:

> "Dr. Fascioni told me that the plate was stopping [sic] healing process and suggested removal of the plate so that the bone heal properly [sic]…he told me that if it was to break arm [sic] with the plate still inside of it without it being removed of course I would lose my arm."

I asked Dr. Jameson if this statement was true. Dr. Jameson said he had spoken to Dr. Fascioni, who denied having said what the patient contended. I then asked Dr. Jameson why; if he acknowledged that the patient had lied about the conversation, the complaint still stood. Dr. Jameson did not reply, but simply looked at the floor.

The next two patients I was questioned about were a young man and a boy who had sustained severe leg injuries, to the extent that both risked losing their legs. In the case of the man, two consulting physicians had recommended amputation. I rejected their recommendation and, by the grace of God, we were able to save the leg. The patient and his family were so happy that they invited me to the young man's wedding.

In the case of the boy, also by the grace of God I was able to save his leg and he ended up being able to play soccer without any handicap.

Dr. Cooperson complained that I had used unconventional methods to treat the two patients. I read out paragraphs from the books I had brought to show that the treatments I had administered were described in the medical literature and were not my invention. Dr. Joneson argued with me about the treatments, while the other members of the committee remained silent. I reminded Dr. Joneson that she was an anaesthetist and I a surgeon. I said that, with all due respect, I knew surgery better than she did and in any case there was no point arguing with the recent orthopaedic literature. I handed her the relevant books and suggested she read them. She pushed back the books and stopped arguing. That put an end to the interview.

Dr. Jameson told Dr. Trouts and me to leave the room. Dr. Trouts asked why he was asked to leave while Dr. Cooperson was allowed to stay for the deliberations. Dr. Jameson did not reply, but merely repeated that Dr. Trouts was to leave. Dr. Trouts protested, but left anyway, while Dr. Cooperson stayed behind.

Dr. Jameson never informed me of the outcome of the meeting. I would learn, however, that Dr. Ember and Dr. X. behaved as I had predicted. Apparently they strongly objected to Dr. Cooperson's complaining about me and investigating my work at the same time. They recommended that the committee have an independent surgeon from overseas conduct a review of the entire orthopaedics division, including Dr. Cooperson's work.

CHAPTER THIRTHEEN

The Contract

I returned to Bermuda in January 1997 to find that Dr. Trouts had not paid me as promised. On February 5th, I met with him and asked why. Initially he said he had not promised to pay me. Then he acknowledged that he had promised, but said he had changed his mind and would not pay me until I signed the contract. I reviewed the contract and found that he had omitted many items we had agreed to and had included many other items we had not even discussed. Of course, all the omissions and additions were to his advantage. For example, we had agreed that, by way of protecting Dr. Trouts and in the interests of income sharing, I would pay him fifty percent of any income I earned that exceeded his income by fifteen percent. This was conditional on his being engaged in the practice of medicine *full time*. In the modified contract he had changed the conditional clause to read as follows:

> "7.01 Additionally, by way of protection for the practice of the Company's employee, Dr. G. Trouts, Dr. Bah agrees that if the receipts exceed by 15% or more the receipts of Dr. Trouts in any calendar year Dr. Bah will pay 50% of the excess by way of an additional fee to the Company provided that Dr. Trouts practices medicine full time during the calendar year. For the purposes of this paragraph Dr. Trouts shall be deemed to have practiced medicine full time during a particular calendar year if he has worked at least *350 (three hundred and fifty) hours* during the said calendar year." [emphasis added]

This meant that I would be giving Dr. Trouts fifty percent of my income if he chose to work only one hour a day or two months a year.

After I reviewed the contract, Dr. Trouts and I met to discuss it. We talked for an hour and did not come to an agreement. He said we would have to end the meeting because he was hungry. I said I would resign the next day if there was no agreement.

The next day Dr. Trouts gave me the contract with the changes I had requested, but now it stated that I would pay him $2,200 a month in rent. I felt that this was too much for the little use I made of the clinic, but I was so tired of arguing with him that I was willing to compromise and settle for that amount.

I took the contract and went to seek professional advice before signing it. Mr. Clancy, the attorney I consulted, and I discussed the contract at length. He saw as unfair the clause stating that I would pay Dr. Trouts any money I owed him "within three days" whereas he would pay me any money he owed me at a "convenient time." Mr. Clancy suggested that a time frame for Dr. Trouts to pay me be included in the contract.

I took the contract back to Dr. Trouts and told him of the minor changes I wanted. He said he would give me the revised contract within a few days.

Three weeks later Dr. Trouts still had not given me the contract. On March 3rd, Mr. Clancy called Dr. Trouts' attorney in the hope of ending the stalemate. Dr. Trouts' attorney told Mr. Clancy he did not have a mandate from his client to talk to my attorney.

By this time Dr. Trouts and I rarely met. However, we bumped into each other on the morning of March 7th. I asked him about the long-overdue contract. "Don't worry," he said. "It's ready. I'll pick it up from my attorney shortly and give it to you."

When I went to the office that afternoon, Mr. Robbins, our English bookkeeper, was smoking outside the office, nervous and anxiously waiting for me. He pulled me into the examining room and said Dr. and Mrs. Trouts had asked him the day before to erase and reallocate figures in the ledgers that related to me. Mr. Robbins said he had suggested that Dr. and Mrs. Trouts make the changes themselves, but they told him it had to be in his handwriting. Mr. Robbins said the couple threatened to withhold his paycheque and dismiss him if he refused to comply.

On March 20th, Dr. Trouts gave me the revised contract to sign. Instead of making the minor changes I had suggested he had added new clauses, including the following:

> "7.05 If Dr. Bah is the sole occupant of the clinic supplied by Dr. Trouts then Dr. Bah shall pay 100% of the cost of rent, water, electricity, gas, telephone, laundry service to the clinic, medical supplies and drugs legally supplied to the clinic, carpet cleaning and fumigation of the clinic, salaries of the staff, accountant and any locum, and any other operations made for the operation of the clinic."

This meant that I would being paying the mortgage on Dr. Trouts' clinic plus the items listed above and the salaries of the staff, which technically included Mrs. Trouts when Dr. Trouts was absent from the clinic for any length of time (such as on vacation).

The thirteen-page contract was full of similar irritants, but the most distressing part was a clause stating that the contract was not between Dr. Trouts and me, as we had agreed, but between a company and me. The contract also stated that I would have to pay the directors of the company, Mrs. Trouts and Dr. Trouts' mother, seventy-five percent of my income should Dr. Trouts take a leave of absence. I asked him if this interpretation of the contract was accurate. He replied that it was, adding, "It's a take-it-or-leave-it situation."

Mr. Clancy advised me not to sign the contract. He suggested sending the police to the office to confiscate the ledgers that Dr. Trouts had ordered altered and taking him to court. I reminded Mr. Clancy that Dr. Trouts held my work permit and would revoke it the moment I sent in the police, and that if I did not have a permit I would have to leave Bermuda within days. He said I could sue Dr. Trouts from abroad and recuperate my money within six to nine months. I asked about my chances of recuperating my money, which I estimated at $0.2 million US, if I sued from abroad. Mr. Clancy said they were poor because I would be suing Dr. Trouts "at arm's length." I said I did not think it a good idea to send the police to Dr. Trouts' office and sue him from abroad. I was going to sign the contract, I stated, because under the circumstances a bad agreement was better than none. I said I did not care about the vast majority of the contract because I did not think it was possible for me to continue working with Dr. Trouts. What mattered most, I explained, was that the paragraph stating that Dr. Trouts owed me money was still included in the contract.

On March 27th, 1997, seventeen months after I had arrived on the

Island, Dr. Trouts and I signed the contract and I waited impatiently for him to make the calculations and give me my money.

CHAPTER FOURTEEN

"Jungle House"

Being in the midst of a fight with the hospital and negotiations with Dr. Trouts, I had neglected my wife's repeated crying over our children's health and our rental house. A month after arriving in Bermuda we had moved into a three-bedroom house in Paget, an upscale, mostly white, residential area. We had seen many houses, but chose this one because it was located far from the main street and had a yard for the children to play in. My wife and I met the owner, Mr. Connelly, a white Bermudian. He spent more time showing us the garden, which he was very fond of, than the house. He loved the garden so much he had named the house after it. After renting us the house, Mr. Connelly instructed us not to use the few nails or pieces of wood he had left in the garage because wood was very expensive in Bermuda. When I asked why he didn't take these with him, he replied that he had nowhere else to store them. On December 11th, 1995, we signed a three-year lease on the property. We were to pay $4,250 a month the first two years and $4,462.50 a month the third year, plus $1,600 US a year for property tax and water, in addition to paying for the electricity. Mr. Connelly wanted us to pay $250 a month for the gardener to cut the grass once a month. We found this fee exorbitant and suggested we find another gardener to cut the grass. He agreed, but advised me not to let any Portuguese gardener cut anything higher than ankle height.

The first thing we did was buy a ton of soil to fill the holes in the yard because we were afraid our children would fall into them. Before ordering the soil, we sought the advice of our neighbour, a retired white Bermudian who we had befriended. The landscaping company brought sand instead of soil, but fortunately the grass grew on the sand anyway. Later we would discover that our neighbour was reporting to Mr. Connelly everything we did around the property.

The second thing we did was try to make the landscaping safe. A hurricane in 1987 had uprooted many trees, which were still lying around the property. A huge tree, covered with bougainvillea and ferns, had been left lying in the narrow driveway. Once I backed my car into it and broke the rear lights. For years Mr. Connelly had instructed his gardener to only cut the grass and not trim the hedges, prune the trees or tend the flowers. The property was neglected and looked scary at night. It looked more like a jungle than a garden so I renamed it "Jungle House." When it came time to look for a gardener, although I had found Mr. Connelly's comment about Portuguese gardeners discriminatory, I decided to follow his advice because I did not know the Island.

I called six landscaping companies. Five of them were Portuguese owned and operated. The sixth was also Portuguese owned, but was managed by a man from the West Indies. This company's bid was $1,000 to do the initial work of pruning the trees and trimming the hedges and $100 a month to maintain the property.

Even though its bid was the highest, I hired the last company in order to comply with Mr. Connelly's wishes regarding Portuguese gardeners and because the West Indian manager, who, unlike the other bidders, spoke English, had told me he would be present to supervise the work. I took the day off when the landscaping was scheduled to be done. Instead of coming in the morning as scheduled, the workers arrived in the middle of the day, and they appeared without the West Indian manager, because, I was told, he was being married that day. I told the men, who spoke little English, that my wife and I were going to town for an hour and to wait for us before starting the work. One of them, who seemed to be the supervisor, nodded in approval and said, "Yes, no problem." The men sat dawn to have their lunch.

My wife dropped me at the hospital, for I had to see a few patients, while she went to see the real estate agent who was managing the property in order to reimburse Mr. Connelly the sum of $21. The phone company had mistakenly billed him for a long-distance call we had made during our first month in the house. Mr. Connelly, an investment banker based in

Hong Kong, had called us a few times early in the morning to tell us it was urgent we reimburse him the $21.

My wife and I arrived back at the house an hour later. The men must have been working for about thirty minutes at that point, but it was as though a hurricane more powerful than the one of 1987 had hit the property. The gardeners had used their machetes to cut every green thing that was standing or climbing. They had removed all the bougainvilleas, all the ferns and flowers climbing the wall, the house and the fence. My wife became hysterical. She yelled at and ran after the workers, who were still holding their machetes. I was shocked at what I saw around the property, but I could not, but laugh at the scene of my wife with her bare hands charging at five men holding machetes. I ran after her and calmed her down. Then I asked the gardeners what they were doing. The man who seemed to be the foreman said, "Prune tree, clean, prune tree, prune tree..." I said, "I told you to wait for us." He said again, "Prune tree, clean, prune tree." I realized then that he spoke no English at all. I told the men everything was fine and instructed them to leave. They left, but I could see by their demeanour that they felt they had done nothing wrong.

My wife and I went around the garden assessing the damage. We salvaged and replanted a few plants. The next day, before our neighbour had time to report the disaster to Mr. Connelly, we informed the real estate agent of our misadventure with the gardeners. Mr. Connelly sent his brother-in-law to inspect the property.

Within a few days Mr. Connelly sent us a long letter from Hong Kong with a list of things to be done around the property. Here is an excerpt:

> "Parking Area: Ground Cover – Juniper, Bougainvillea or Buddleia – in front of remaining pride of India trunk – 3 or 4 plants needed, Double Yellow Hibiscus – 2 plants needed, Silver and Buttonwood – 1 of each needed.
>
> Rockery (garden just right of entrance steps): Dwarf Sages – 2 plants needed, Cuphea.
>
> Under High Wall (where ferns were removed): Day lilies – 5 plants needed, Lilly grass.
>
> Bed under kitchen window (Plants were removed): Arthwian – 2 plants needed, Bromeliads – 2 plants needed.

General: Stone edges to be properly finished or replaced.

Top soil: Get good quality soil for beds and lawn. Very poor quality has been used…"

Bermuda is a very damp and humid environment and left alone most of the plants would have grown back within six months, but Mr. Connolly wanted everything on his list done right away. The real estate agent suggested I sue the landscaping company. I did not take her advice because I had enough problems with my associate and the hospital and because I felt it would not be a good idea to sue a minister of the government, because that was who owned the landscaping company. Instead I chose to settle with the company.

Our problems with Jungle House did not end there. After the fiasco with the garden, Mr. Connelly had his brother-in-law check up regularly. He also ordered the owner of the real estate agency to visit, who reported back to Mr. Connelly that the garden looked cleaner than it had when we moved in and the house was in good condition. We no longer felt comfortable living there. Slowly we realized that Jungle House was a source of headaches and an expensive undertaking, especially since Dr. Trouts still had not paid me. The logical thing was to move out, but the lease stipulated that we had to stay for three years unless we were leaving Bermuda or had some other pressing reason to move out. The pressing reason we had was that our children had been sick with respiratory infection, in the case of our son more than eleven times, since moving into Jungle House. My wife had pointed this out to me numerous times, but I had not heard because I was too busy dealing with the hospital and Dr. Trouts.

Our children had been sick because Jungle House, which was built of limestone, was unusually damp, especially in the winter months. The old wood-frame windows allowed wind, lizards and cockroaches to enter the house. I often teased my wife and referred to the lizards and cockroaches as her pets. The house, like all Bermudian houses, had a water tank built underneath the main floor to collect rainwater. The water tank contributed to the dampness inside the house. Apparently the way the house had been painted also contributed greatly to the dampness. We met Mr. Connelly's painter, who was kind enough to explain this to us. He said there is a particular sequence to painting houses in Bermuda in order to minimize the dampness. Apparently one paints the inside wall first (I think it is the inside wall) and allows the paint to dry before painting the outside wall. The painter said he did not follow this sequence in the case of our house because Mr. Connelly had instructed him to paint it quickly so he could rent it.

We tried to manage the dampness in the children's room by using a dehumidifier, which collected more than two gallons of water per night, and using heated blankets on their beds. However, these measures did not improve our children's health. Our son coughed constantly.

I asked Mr. Clancy, the attorney handling my case with Dr. Trouts, to advise us on how to break the lease on Jungle House. He suggested we obtain the children's medical files from the pediatrician and the pharmacy to prove that they were constantly sick. Mr. Clancy hired an engineer to inspect the house and produce a report. The engineer's report read partly as follows:

> "I confirm our todays visit to this property, which is occupied by Dr. & Mrs. Bah and their children...
>
> The dwelling is very damp even by Bermuda standards. Mrs. Bah showed us mildew on the interior walls, their new furniture, curtains, in closets and on the children's toys. I felt dampness on the room side of walls [sic] that had even been paneled or furred with plasterboard. There was a general damp and musty feeling in the house. The general use of furring indicates that this is not a new problem and I have been told that the previous owner disposed of this property because of this problem. Parts of the residence are quite old but the problem also occurs in a recent addition.
>
> Mrs. Bah is a good housekeeper and explained about her regular use of Clorox to wipe down surfaces to little avail.
>
> I suggest that contributing causes to the dampness are:
>
> 1. The position of the house being in a valley where a considerable depth of the soil would be expected. The soil would not permit sufficient drainage, as would a thinner layer overlaying the more porous Bermuda rock.
>
> 2. There is little sun shining on the property because of its orientation and the shielding effect of the surrounding trees and the position of the residence to the west. Foundation planting also obstructs the sun. All of which prohibit proper drying out of the residence...
>
> I suggest that this condition makes the residence uncomfortable, inconvenient as the housekeeping and unsuitable for children and adult occupation."

Mr. Clancy submitted the report and the children's medical files to Mr. Connelly's real estate agent. He wrote to Mr. Connelly telling him that my family and I wished to vacate Jungle House based on the children's medical condition and the engineer's report. In February 1997, Mr. Connelly replied, in a letter, that though he did not agree with the engineer's report he would allow us to break the lease and vacate the house subject to his finding a suitable tenant.

My wife did not leave it to Mr. Connelly to find a new tenant. She immediately placed an advertisement in the newspaper. She held a garage sale to sell many pieces of our furniture that had been damaged by the dampness. She enjoys buying, selling and talking to people. In one weekend she sold almost everything we had in the house. I asked her not to sell my clothes or the children and took the children to the park. During the garage sale, my wife found three serious prospective tenants and referred them to the real estate agent.

A clause in our lease stipulated that we had to paint the interior of the house before moving out. I asked Mr. Tony, a Christian acquaintance who worked as a technician at the hospital during the evening and as a painter during the day, if he was interested. Mr. Tony came to the house, made an assessment of the work to be done and agreed to do it. I asked him how much the job would cost. He said to trust him; he would give me a special price because he was aware of my problems with Jungle House and at the hospital. I told him I had not found many people in Bermuda I could trust and asked for an estimate. He smiled and said I could trust him. He refused to give me an estimate.

My wife suggested we hire another painter because Mr. Tony would not give us an estimate. I hired Mr. Tony anyway. He did a good job and charged us $282, whereas another painter had estimated $1,000. After dealing with Dr. Trouts and the others, I found it refreshing to work with somebody like Mr. Tony.

To find a new house to rent, we consulted the same real estate agent we had dealt with the first time. I had dealt with many real estate agents and had found this person, an English woman, to be very sincere. After a week of searching, she and my wife found a newly built two-bedroom split-level cottage with a one-bedroom apartment on the lower floor. Yellow Bird

Cottage, which was constructed of brick, was situated on one of the highest hills in Paget. The owner, Mrs. Richards, a young black Bermudian bank executive, was asking $2,500 a month for the two-bedroom unit. This seemed high so I suggested we look for something cheaper. My wife said this was the best she had found and she was exhausted from looking. Someone else might snap it up, she cautioned, if we didn't hurry and rent it. I knew she was right so we went ahead and rented it. (I am told that similar apartments currently rent for $3,500.)

We moved out of Jungle House on April 24th and paid for the full month. The new tenant my wife had referred to Mr. Connelly moved in on June 1st. Mr. Connelly increased the rent to $5,000 and demanded that we pay him $4,250 for the month of May. My attorney advised us not to comply with this request since we had made an effort to find a tenant willing to move in on May 1st. For reasons unknown to us, Mr. Connelly had asked the tenant not to move in until June 1st. His attorney phoned and threatened to take me to court if I did not pay the $4,250. I referred him to my attorney. A few days later he phoned again and suggested we settle out of court: I would pay his client $2,150 instead of the $4,250 he said I owed. I refused and again referred him to my attorney. I heard nothing more about Jungle House.

We moved into Yellow Bird Cottage on April 24th. Our neighbours, with the exception of an older couple from France, were not pleased about the construction of the building and our arrival in the neighbourhood. The problem was that for two hundred years the same white Bermudian family had owned the land on which the new building stood, as well as the surrounding property. Apparently the members of the family had agreed not to sell the land to a foreigner until an aunt, a woman in her eighties who occupied one of the houses on top of the hill, passed away. The brother of the elderly woman had broken the agreement and sold land to our landlord, a foreigner and to make matters worse, a black woman. All the neighbours had written the government-planning agency, which was responsible for supervising all construction on the Island, objecting to the construction of Yellow Bird Cottage.

The planning agency had approved the construction of Yellow Bird Cottage despite the many letters of protest it had received. Hence the entire neighbourhood with the exception of the couple from France anxiously waited to direct their anger at the tenants. Two days after we moved in, the husband of the elderly aunt delivered a nasty letter to our house. The man, who was in his late seventies, said he did not agree with his wife. In her letter, the aunt complained that our house was obstructing her view of the sea, which was two kilometres away. She also complained about the packing boxes that we had placed outside our house for garbage collection. I was upset by the long letter and wanted to respond, but my wife convinced me not to, so I planted a tree that, when grown, would completely block the woman's view of our house and the distant sea. The good thing about our new quarters was that our son's cough ceased completely three days after we moved in and except for the occasional flu that all children pick up from the nursery twice a year, our children did not get any sick more.

Yellow Bird Cottage was not completely free of problems, but they were mild compared to what we had endured at Jungle House. One the problems was that our landlady, who was like I somewhat naïve, had hired a Portuguese Bermudian contractor with a poor reputation to construct the building. The contractor had taken many short cuts. Cracks appeared in the walls of the building and in the water tank, which began to leak soon after we moved in. The stucco ceiling of the apartment underneath us collapsed and damaged the tenants' furniture. The tenants, an American couple, had to move out temporarily while the ceiling was being repaired. They sued the contractor for the damage to their furniture and the inconvenience to them. Our landlady also tried to sue the contractor.

CHAPTER FIFTEEN

The "Witch Hunt"

On Tuesday, April 22nd, 1997, Dr. Jameson, the chief of staff, phoned me and said he wanted to see me his office on Thursday. He said he had things to discuss with me. I did not know the purpose of the meeting, but I did learn that Dr. Spencer, an anaesthesiologist from Scotland, would also be attending the meeting and would be acting as chief of surgery in place of Dr. Joneson, who was away from the Island. I learned that Dr. Spencer was reluctant to attend the meeting because he did not want to take part in a "witch hunt." On Thursday afternoon I went to Dr. Jameson's office with a tape recorder hidden in my pocket. Here is the transcript of the conversation between Dr. Jameson, Dr. Spencer and me.

> **Dr. Jameson**: Mrs. Aguilera [not real name] case cause to look at the blood transfusion in cases of spinal perfusion done by yourself and look at the literature on the subject and this is what he came up with [sic]. Of twenty-one patients, fifteen lost more than 7 units of blood. This is taking from the note [sic]. We have done some work to find about spinal fusion blood loss, average 3–4 units, and we have some rough average [sic] and I have here some paper here to show that again average is about 700 cc. This one here is 800 cc something. This is a British paper the average loss is 870 cc. Now the question is either the operation you are doing is in fact not the same as the literature or perhaps you have some literature to show that certain operations you are doing the blood loss is of this magnitude. We need to have this matter clarified because if this blood loss is extra high. I think you have, we cannot justify doing these operations. *You got to retrain or whatever* [emphasis mine]. So maybe you can justify this situation with other literature that you have been able to look at. The information that is brought to my attention shows that this is excessive.

Dr. Bah: Do you want me to sit down and comment on it or do you want me to come back later?

Dr. Jameson: Well, you can comment it now if you wish.

Dr. Bah: We can sit down and comment on it now. Mrs. M.M. is not on the list. Dr. Morais and I operated on her.

Dr. Jameson: Who is Dr. Morais?

Dr. Bah: Dr. Morais is a spinal surgeon from Montreal who came to Bermuda to operate with me on some spinal cases. The only patients listed here whose blood loss seems similar to Ms Aguilera is Mrs. M.M., who also I think lost about 12 units of bloods. The day I operated on Mrs. Aguilera, I brought the X ray of Mrs. M.M. with me in the operating room. I told the anaesthetist that Mrs. Aguilera case is complex and similar to Mrs. M.M.

Dr. Spencer: Now maybe I am not a special surgeon, Dr. Jameson is not a spinal surgeon. What we are trying to find is if the surgery you are doing, the exposure or whatever, results in greater tissue damage likely to result in greater blood loss…

Dr. Bah: I think we are comparing apples with oranges…

Dr. Jameson: That is why we would like you to give us some information either through personal letter from Dr. Morais…

Dr. Spencer: Because the concern is that either these are excessive or that they reasonable for the surgery that is being done, and that if this is the case we need to change rather drastically the information given to the patient because 12 units is a complete exchange transfusion. This is greater than their circulated volume [sic]…

Dr. Bah: We are talking about different things because all the surgeries that were done in the Island before I arrived were done using Harrington rods…

Dr. Spencer: So you see we are already talking about different…

Dr. Jameson: Could you get some information to back this up, because the information that I have does not support the situation…

Dr. Bah: I would like to know what prompted this investigation. Since I got here in Bermuda, I have been under constant investigation of all sorts.

Dr. Jameson: I investigated because I said 12 units of blood loss are excessive.

Dr. Bah: The list indicates that before Mrs. Aguilera, Mrs. C.G., another patient, lost 13 units of blood and there was no investigation. Why an investigation in the case of Mrs. Aguilera?

Dr. Jameson: Because this woman nearly died.

Dr. Spence: There was a complaint by the family.

Dr. Jameson: The family said we are not... We have to go look and see what the situation has been. Than we looked at the literature to see what is this... So we have to... My job as Chief of Staff statutorily is to be responsible for supervising the clinical care of patients in the Hospital. That's what it says in the act and I am backed-up by my chief to do that. Anything that relates to patient care that is unsatisfactory I am to investigate, and there have been complaints about 8 of your patients and complaints I would not say, but there were information brought to me about a certain patient care, which prompted this investigation [sic].

Dr. Bah: I do not find this hospital has been fair toward me. Since I arrived here in Bermuda, I have been under constant investigation and you call these investigations objective. Let's face it Dr. Jameson. There has never been any objectivity in all these investigations. You started an investigation of my work last year and you were not going to tell me who the complainants were. However, when Dr. Cooperson got sick you came and told me that Drs. Cooperson and Fascioni were the complainants.

Dr. Jameson: I never told you.

Dr. Bah: At the end of a Wednesday meeting in October, you told me that Drs. Cooperson and Fascioni made the complaints against me.

Dr. Jameson: That's not true because the complainants were not all Cooperson and Fascioni, they were from a variety of sources.

Dr. Bah: If you are objective, why were you not willing to tell us who the complainants were?

Dr. Jameson: Because the issue is not to satisfy the complainants as I pointed to you before in a letter in writing and at a committee. The issue is to...

Dr. Bah: It does not work this way in the Royal College.

Dr. Jameson: This is not the Royal College. This is Bermuda.

Dr. Bah: But this hospital receives its accreditation from the Royal College [Royal College of Canada]

Dr. Jameson: This is not the Royal College. This is Bermuda.

Dr. Bah: You are running under the rules of democracy then.

Dr. Jameson: We are running under the rules of our statue and our by-laws.

Dr. Bah: Which are democratic?

Dr. Jameson: I do not know what you mean by that…

Dr. Bah: So far there has not been any objectivity in all of this. I wrote to you a letter complaining about Dr. Cooperson who walked into my operating room and disrupted my surgery. I wrote you a letter of complaint with a copy to Dr. Joneson. Dr. Joneson and you did not answer my letter…

Dr. Jameson: The aspect of this is patient care, what you complained about was not patient care. They are different things. What you are complaining about is the attitude of one doctor against the other.

Dr. Bah: The attitude of one doctor against another doctor is also included in the bylaws of the hospital and you are supposed to answer to that.

Dr. Spencer: Under Collegiality [the Bermuda Hospitals Board Act defines Non-Collegiality as follows: "Non-Collegiality, broadly speaking, is the failure to work well with others, and where uncooperative, uncivil, abusive, and disruptive conduct is judged to adversely affect patient care, it is ground for disciplinary action, I.E., suspension, revoking of privileges, declining to appoint or reappoint."]

Dr. Jameson: It is not too late. I can deal with that.

Dr. Bah: Why have you not dealt with it so far?

Dr. Jameson: Because Dr. Cooperson took ill and the matter was not dealt with.

Dr. Bah: But he is back since.

Dr. Jameson: He is back and I have not dealt with it.

Dr. Spencer: Can we take it that Dr. Jameson will investigate?

Dr. Jameson: I am supposed to, I will answer.

Dr. Bah: You are supposed to answer to this matter also. I do not want to be here any more… I am treating Bermudians and I think I am doing a very good job. God wants me to be here. I do not want to be here. If you people would have the professionalism and the courage to tell me that you do not want me to be here instead of playing this cat and mouse game I will leave the Island.

Dr. Jameson: I heard a lot of stuff and I am not going to…

Dr. Spencer: As I am saying [sic] one of the ideas we got are that all spinal fusions are the same, obviously, they are not.

Dr. Bah: I am just saying if I prove this then what is next again?

Dr. Jameson: There got to be an outside assessor of orthopaedic surgeons [sic].

Bah: Selected by you?

Dr. Jameson: Selected by me, yes…

Dr. Bah: You know that there is a God. There is a God. There is a God and he is the last judge.

Dr. Jameson: I am not confirming or denying anything like this. I think you should stick to what I brought you here for.

Dr. Bah: I will stick to it, but I just wanted to summarize what have been my ordeals since I arrived here in Bermuda.

Dr. Jameson: I heard this before, this is not the first time that you gone into a harangue like this… In fact you did it in front of the whole credential committee.

Dr. Bah: The objectivity?

Dr. Jameson: The complaints, you did it in front of the whole credential committee, you have probably forgotten. You did not think it was fair.

Dr. Bah: If I do not think it is fair, maybe because it is not fair.

Dr. Jameson: I will give you a copy of that. You can get it off your chest now. You feel better?

Dr. Bah: No, I do not feel much better. I always feel good anyway.

Dr. Jameson: I have got to do what I have to do to protect the patient.

Dr. Bah: Sure!

At the beginning of the interview Dr. Jameson said I had "to retrain or whatever." The irony was that Dr. Jameson was doing to me what the chief of staff and all the white physicians at the hospital had done to him when he was trying to set up his practice. Apparently when Dr. Jameson returned to Bermuda with his surgical training, they would not allow him to work at the only hospital on the Island. He had been allowed to practise as the first black surgeon in Bermuda only after the teaching hospital in Canada where he had trained had threatened to sever its ties with the hospital.

I was not proud of how I had conducted myself at the meeting. I had been too angry and at times incoherent. One of the reasons I was angry and frustrated was because I could not explain why the blood loss of my patient as indicated on the list was extremely high. However, to put things in perspective, I learned a lot from the meeting. I learned that eight other cases had been added to the initial four complaints that had been brought against me. I also learned that Dr. Jameson would select an orthopaedic surgeon from abroad to come to Bermuda to assess the work of all "orthopaedic surgeons." Of course Dr. Jameson would never keep his promise to deal with my complaint about Dr. Cooperson's barging into my operating room.

On Saturday, two days after the meeting, Dr. Jameson and I met at the hospital entrance. He put his hand on my back and said, "Don't worry, everything is going to be all right." He said I was too Latin and told me to learn to control my temper. I gently removed his hand, remembering a line from a mobster movie I had seen. It went something like this: "If your enemy places his hand on your back, it is because he is trying to find a soft spot to put the knife."

CHAPTER SIXTEEN

The Case of Mrs. Aguilera

Who was Mrs. Aguilera, what happened to her and what prompted Dr. Jameson to initiate an investigation into her case?

Mrs. Aguilera was a Portuguese Bermudian who I first saw in my office on February 20th, 1997. She was accompanied by her husband, her son, her daughter and her daughter-in-law. Aged seventy-eight at the time, she complained of severe pain in her back and legs. Her symptoms of five years' duration had worsened to the point where she could walk only with the assistance of a family member and a walker. She was taking three types of pain medication, which did not give her much relief. A month earlier she had been admitted to hospital for ten days because of severe pain. A test carried out while she was in hospital found that she had a scoliosis and marked spinal stenosis (narrowing of the spinal canal with compression of the spinal cord and nerves). Mr. Aguilera's children told me they had first taken their mother to see Dr. Cooperson, who concluded that she was too obese and said he would not "touch her with a ten-foot pole."

I explained to the family that Mrs. Aguilera could continue taking the pain medications or have back surgery. I spent an hour discussing with the patient and her family the type of surgery that might benefit her. I told them that the surgery would consist of a laminectomy decompression (relieving the pressure on the spinal cord by removing bone from the back) and spinal fusion (using rods, screws and bone graft to stabilize the spine). I explained that this type of surgery is very complex, but I had done it in the past without complications. I said that any problems I anticipated would be due to the fact that she was overweight, diabetic and hypertensive. I told them I would be happy to operate on Mrs. Aguilera if the anaesthetist saw no medical contraindication to anaesthetizing her and if she was medically well prepared for the surgery. I referred Mrs. Aguilera to the pre-admission clinic run by the anaesthetists and wrote a note to the anaesthetists descri-bing her condition and recommending that they see her weeks before the procedure in order to adequately prepare her. Before Mrs. Aguilera and her family left my office, I gave them a handwritten summary of our discussion. I suggested they think about what we had discussed and call me if they had any questions.

On March 26th, I went to the operating room to perform surgery on Mrs. Aguilera's back as had been discussed with her family. As a reference, I brought along the x-rays of Mr. M., a patient on whom I had done similar surgery a few weeks earlier. I showed Mrs. M.'s x-rays to Dr. Morrison, the English anaesthetist, described to him the surgery I planned to perform on Mrs. Aguilera and advised him to be prepared accordingly.

We began the surgery and everything went well until I started the la-minectomy decompression. At that stage the patient began to bleed. It is normal for the blood vessels in the back to bleed when laminectomy de-compression is being performed, but in this case the bleeding was excessive because the patient was overweight and had high blood pressure. Bleeding during this type of surgery can be minimized by lowering the blood pressure with medication or by applying cotton swabs and gel to the bleeding vessels. In Mrs. Aguilera's case, Dr. Morrison, the anaesthetist, would not lower the blood pressure. When I asked for cotton swabs and gel to minimize the bleeding, I was told that the hospital had run out of cotton swabs and gel and an order from abroad had not been made. I continued the operation regardless because I was midway through. I did what I could to minimize the bleeding. Halfway through the operation, I told Dr. Morrison, who was absorbed in reading a newspaper, of the progress I had made so far and what remained to be done. He listened to my briefing and then went back to reading his paper.

A few minutes later Dr. Morrison threw down the newspaper, rose from his chair in a state of panic and told me to stop the operation. The problem was that one of the anaesthetic machines had stopped beeping. The elec-trocardiogram reading had suddenly gone flat. There was no heart rhythm. The patient was basically dead. The solution was to turn the patient, with her wound open, onto her back and start cardiac massage and resuscitation. Before we did that, Dr. Morrison gave her intravenous fluid under pressure and within a few seconds her heart rhythm was back to normal. When the patient revived with the fluid, it became obvious what had been the problem: she had lost of lot of fluid – four litres of blood – which had been replaced by only 1.5 litres. I stopped the operation for ten minutes while Dr. Morrison replaced whatever blood had been lost. Mrs. Aguilera became stable again once the fluid had been replaced. I decided to end the operation. I closed the surgical wound and transferred the patient to the intensive care unit.

I was exhausted and felt very bad about what had happened to Mrs. Aguilera. This sort of thing had never occurred during my surgeries. After the operation I went to the office of Mrs. Santini, the head operating room nurse, and sat down, discouraged. I thought Mrs. Santini was going to reprimand me for what had happened. Instead she said, "It isn't the first time something like this has happened in the operating room, and nothing has been done about it."

Next I went to see Mrs. Aguilera's family, who were waiting for me in the hospital café. I did not have to explain to them what had happened. Someone had already told them in detail. (When I arrived in Bermuda I was told that when a person at one end of the Island sneezes, people at the other end feel it. Now I knew what the expression meant. News travels fast in Bermuda.) I expected Mrs. Aguilera's family to blame me for her misfortune, but before I had a chance to speak her son said, "We trusted you so much with the surgery that we forgot about the anaesthesia part." The family said they would have requested a different anaesthetist had they known that it was Dr. Morrison who was going to be on duty. They said that Dr. Morrison was involved in the case of the Fisher boy and similar cases. All I knew about the Fisher case was that a few weeks before my arrival a little boy had died at the hospital after undergoing a tonsillectomy.

Dr. Jameson, Dr. Joneson and Mrs. Santini met with Mrs. Aguilera's family members, who were very upset about her near-death experience in the operating room. According to the family, Dr. Jameson told them that "it was all Dr. Bah's fault" and suggested that another surgeon complete the surgery on Mrs. Aguilera. They rejected this proposal and said that "nobody, but Dr. Bah" would operate on her. They demanded to have an anaesthetist of their choice, other than Dr. Morrison, for the procedure. Dr. Jameson had no alternative, but to acquiesce because he feared they would take legal action against the hospital.

At the suggestion of Dr. Jameson, Dr. Morrison and I met with the family to try to defuse their anger. I attempted to give them some plausible explanation as to why Mrs. Aguilera had bled more than usual. I said that one of the reasons was that the prone position (flat on the stomach) in which we had to place her for the surgery might have caused compression of the vessels in her unusually protuberant stomach (this is a known fact in the spine literature and one explanation for excessive bleeding during spine surgery). Dr. Morrison said I was not telling the truth and began to argue with me. The family members looked at each other and at me in amazement – shocked that Dr. Morrison was contradicting me in front of them. I did not argue with Dr. Morrison, but suggested to the family that we end the meeting. They agreed and the meeting ended without further discussion.

On March 27th Dr. Joneson wrote the following note in Mrs. Aguilera's chart:

> "Next week if well [Mrs. Aguilera], re-operate to fuse T11 to S1. More aggressive per-operative management is needed. A line, Foley, IV lines, Blood and Inotropes [fluid replacement] all freely."

Dr. Joneson had in one short paragraph summarized everything that was required in terms of anaesthesia in a major surgical procedure such as that performed on Mrs. Aguilera. Before the surgery commences, the anaesthetist should install an "A line (arterial line)" in order to obtain constant and accurate monitoring of the pressure. In Mrs. Aguilera's case, an arterial line was not installed during the operation. Before a major surgical procedure such as this, the anaesthetist should install at least two intravenous lines in case the patient requires a lot of "inotropes (fluid replacement)." During Mrs. Aguilera's surgery only a small line had been installed. Dr. Joneson also wrote that "more aggressive pre-operative management" is needed in a major surgical case, which means that the anaesthetist should be on his or her feet, trying to keep the blood pressure low and stable in order to minimize bleeding.

Mrs. Aguilera remained in intensive care for three days before being transferred to the ward to await the second procedure. On the ward, I asked an internist to follow her for her diabetes and high blood pressure.

On April 2nd I operated on Mrs. Aguilera a second time. Dr. Harold was the anaesthetist chosen by the family. This time around, because proper anaesthesia was performed, the patient lost only 800 cc of blood, as opposed to 4,000 cc during the first operation. The second procedure, which consisted of rod insertion and bone graft to stabilize the patient's back, went well. Mrs. Aguilera once again stayed in intensive care for three days before being transferred to the ward.

On the ward, I opened the bottom part of Mrs. Aguilera's wound to prevent the formation of an infected hematoma (collection of blood) because she had bled profusely during the first operation. I prescribed Cloxacillin, an antibiotic, to prevent infection because she was diabetic and had had a hematoma. After Mrs. Aguilera had been on the ward for three days, the internist who I had asked to follow up the patient told me she would not be following her any more; she wrote in the chart that the patient was obese and should lose weight.

One week after I prescribed the antibiotic Mrs. Aguilera was doing well and the wound was slowly healing. When it came time for the antibiotic to be renewed, the nurses asked a resident to do so. Without telling me, the resident discontinued the Cloxacillin and prescribed Gentamycin, another antibiotic, which, if not monitored with frequent blood testing and dose adjustment if necessary, can cause kidney damage. This is exactly what happened in Mrs. Aguilera's case. She was transferred to intensive care and underwent dialysis for kidney failure caused by Gentamycin. Progressively, her kidneys regained their function, her wound healed and she was discharged home. I read the literature and spoke to one of my former professors about the case. Both the literature and my professor recommended a long-term antibiotic such as Cloxacillin, to eradicate any possible infection, and removal of the rod in the back once the fusion has healed. I again prescribed this antibiotic for Mrs. Aguilera. Without my consent, Dr. Paytons, the chief of medicine, discontinued it and openly criticized me in her chart for prescribing it.

A few months later Mrs. Aguilera was admitted to hospital with a fever. Her back was healed, but she had an infection in her bloodstream. I withdrew from the case because everything I tried to do for this patient was criticized. She was transferred abroad to have the rods removed.

Mrs. Aguilera's family told me she was doing relatively well and no longer had the leg pain. They said they intended to take legal action against Dr. Morrison, but would delay the process until my fight with the hospital was over, because, they reasoned, the hospital authorities might try to shift the blame for their mother's misfortune onto me if they sued Dr. Morrison. Mrs. Aguilera's son said, "We do not want to see your reputation tarnished."

The Aguileras were a genuine and loyal family. A few months later when a family member broke his leg in a motorbike accident, they asked the emergency room staff to call me to operate on him.

CHAPTER SEVENTEEN

Blood Loss and Operating Room Problems

After my meeting with Drs. Jameson and Spencer, I set out to determine why my patients' blood losses were higher than what was found in the literature for similar surgical procedures. First, I copied the medical records of the twenty-one patients on Dr. Jameson's list. When I sat down to compare the blood loss for each patient as indicated in the records and the blood loss for the same patient as indicated on the list, I found significant discrepancies. In some instances the blood loss as indicated by Dr. Jameson's list was five-hundred-percent higher than as indicated in the patient's chart. The list showed that the average blood loss was 3,228 cc, while the records showed that it was 1,750 cc, a difference of eighty-four percent. The average blood loss as indicated by the hospital records was consistent with the average blood loss for similar cases in the literature.

I took this information to Mr. Kasson, my attorney. I suggested we let the hospital fire me on the grounds of Dr. Jameson's erroneous figures and then take legal action against it. Mr. Kasson said we were under an obligation to inform Dr. Jameson that his figures were erroneous. I did not understand his reasoning, but nonetheless followed his advice.

I met with Dr. Spencer and showed him the enormous difference between Dr. Jameson's figures and the actual figures as recorded in the medical charts. I told him I found it unfair and malicious to produce an erroneous list in order to frame me. Dr. Spencer asked me if I thought life was fair. I answered that I guessed it was not. I asked him who had produced the list. He said it was probably Dr. Morrison, the anaesthetist who had been involved in Mrs. Aguilera's case. He added, "Sometimes the best defence is offence."

In a letter dated May 27th, 1997, Mr. Kasson wrote to Dr. Jameson expressing concern about the investigation into the blood loss of my patients and asking about the procedure to be followed. In a letter dated June 20th, Dr. Jameson stated:

> "Please also be advised that the Medical Staff Committee *is not* investigating any complaints for which disciplinary action may be invoked in accordance with Section 25 (e) of the 1993 Medical Staff Bylaws, and the Policy & Procedures of Appendix 19 related to Medical Staff discipline is not being applied to address any complaints against Dr. Bah."

Dr. Jameson did not bring up the issue of my patients' blood loss again, at least not for some time.

My experience with the Aguilera case and Dr. Jameson's erroneous figures made me reconsider how I did things in the operating room. Upon my arrival at the hospital I had tried to change the way things were in done during my procedures. After six months I gave up because I had not had any success. Now I had no choice, but to change things if I was to continue operating in that environment.

When I had discovered that the hospital did not have the instrumentation needed for spine surgery, I purchased my own instruments. I made it very simple for the staff by assigning the instruments to only two trays, one for all the instruments pertaining to neck surgery and one for all those pertaining to thoracic and low-back surgery. Even with this simple method, I found that instruments would be missing from the tray every time I operated. I therefore resorted to going to the operating room the evening before I was scheduled to operate in order to verify, in the presence of a nurse, that the instruments I needed were in the proper trays. Even then I would find, during surgery the next day, that many of the instruments I needed were missing from the tray. More often than not I would manage to operate without them because the search for the missing instruments would take forever.

The problem was compounded by the fact that the implants (screws, rods and plates) I needed for my spine operations required six trays. However, the implant salesman from Canada had devised a system to ensure that no implants would be missing during surgery. He sent us a list of all the implants contained in the trays. Each time we used an implant from a tray during an operation, the nurses were to cross it off the list; the list would then be faxed to Canada. When this procedure was followed, we usually received the missing implants from Canada within three days. More often than not, however, when an implant was taken from a tray during surgery the nurses would fail to cross it off the list or the list would not be sent to Canada, and in the middle of an operation I would discover that an implant was missing. I discussed this issue with the head operating room nurse. She put it down to the extremely high turnover of nurses in the operating room.

The high turnover of nurses was a particular inconvenience in the case of spine surgery. When I reviewed my patients' charts, I saw that in thirty consecutive back operations I had worked with twenty different nurses and never had the same nurse scrub with me twice in a row. As a result, in addition to performing the surgery I had to train the nurses every time I operated. At first I did not mind because I thought it would increase efficiency in the operating room, but eventually I all but gave up because I felt I was wasting my time; few nurses remembered what I had taught them, or even cared. At one point I made a list of everything I needed for a particular type of operation and gave it to the head nurse, who then made it available to all the nurses. However, this did not make the operating room more efficient when I performed my spine procedures.

I told the nurses that having to ask for each item I needed and then wait while they got it from another room was like going to a restaurant and asking for a fork, a knife, a spoon, a napkin and a glass of water and waiting while the waiter brought the items from the kitchen one by one. They were not impressed with my analogy. Fortunately for me, though, I realized early on that to get upset was detrimental to my health.

There were only two Bermudian nurses in the operating room. Until the early 1970s black Bermudians did not go into nursing because they were barred from working at the only hospital on the Island. The few Bermudians who trained as nurses remained abroad, practising in the United Kingdom, Canada or the United States. The nurses in the operating room were English, Scottish, Irish, Jamaican, Australian, Canadian or American – and many of these left almost as soon as they arrived because of the stressful environment. One day I witnessed exactly why the operating room was such a stressful place for nurses. I heard the surgeon who was operating in the room adjacent to mine – a white Bermudian in his early fifties – use the "f" word like a teenager. I wondered why this man, who was conducting a laparoscopy (a tube in the stomach), one of the simplest operations to perform, was swearing. Afterwards I approached him in the locker room and said, "Life is stressful!" He replied, "Oh yes, life is stressful," and began complaining that he had to pay $30,000 a year for his son to attend one of the best schools in the United Kingdom. At first I could not understand why a surgeon who was probably a millionaire was swearing at the nurses instead of being happy to have his son attend such a good school. With time, however, I came to understand why he had been swearing and why the operating room was such a stressful place. The problem was that the surgeons, who already made a lot of money, were stressed and stressed others because they wanted to make more, while the nurses were stressed because they wanted to make as much as those who were stressing them. The motto of the few nurses who remained in the operating room for any length of time became "We are here for the pay," to make a mockery of one of the hospital's mottos, "We are here for the patient." No doubt workplaces everywhere are stressful to a certain extent, but the operating room at the King Edward VII Memorial Hospital in Bermuda was particularly so. I once had a visit from a hospital administrator from Boston who was on the Island to recruit patients. We talked for a few minutes, then she sank into a chair, breathed a sigh of relief and said, "It's comforting to be in your office." She told me that she frequently visited hospitals in the United States, Canada and the Caribbean. Just before coming to my office she had been in the surgeons' lounge at the King Edward. "I wouldn't say this is the friendliest place I've visited so far," she said.

CHAPTER EIGHTEEN

The Solution to Operating Room Problems

When I started operating in Bermuda I noticed that my patients were bleeding significantly more than similar patients I had operated on in Montreal. The reason was that many of the anaesthetists I worked with in Bermuda did not lower the patient's blood pressure during surgery. I had politely asked them to do so. They told me that this would not reduce bleeding during surgery and asked me to bring literature to support my request. I brought literature showing that lowering the blood pressure serves to minimize bleeding and is common practice all over North America. Many of the anaesthetists brushed aside the literature, and my patients continued to bleed during surgery and to require transfusions. The haematologist at the hospital and I organized a system whereby my patients would give blood a few weeks prior to their surgery and then receive their own blood during their operation.

When I reviewed my patients' charts after the Aguilera case, I discovered what I had always suspected, that none of them required a transfusion when I operated with Dr. Mill, a young anaesthetist from the United Kingdom who had been hired by the other anaesthetists; when he was on duty the average blood loss of my patients was 567 cc. Dr. Mill rarely talked during surgery. The only thing he would say to me was, "How much longer?" He would be in the operating room during the entire procedure, monitoring the patients. On the other hand, a review of my patients' charts indicated that when I operated with Dr. Morrison, the anaesthetist who had been involved in Mrs. Aguilera's case, my patients' average blood loss was 3,500 cc and they all required multiple transfusions.

I therefore decided that only Dr. Mill and two other anaesthetists who were willing and able to lower patients' blood pressure during surgery would anaesthetize my patients. I developed the habit of writing on the patient's admission sheet the name of the anaesthetist I wanted for the surgery. I was aware that my plan would make me unpopular with the anaesthetists who carried the most weight in the hospital, but I preferred to have my patients alive and well than to be popular. My strategy worked until June 18th, 1997.

On June 18th, I was scheduled to operate on Mrs. Steele (not real name), a seventy-two-year-old with cancer that had spread to her back. The tumour in Mrs. Steele's back was pressing on her spinal cord and preventing her from walking. I discussed the possibility of surgery, which would consist of removing the tumour and stabilizing the back with instrumentation, with the patient and her family, and they decided to go ahead with it. I was very enthusiastic about operating on Mrs. Steele because I had operated on few similar cases in Montreal with a one-hundred-percent success rate. It is very gratifying to operate on individuals who are unable to walk and then see them walking after the surgery. For Mrs. Steele's operation, I asked Dr. Mill to serve as anaesthetist and an excellent Jamaican nurse who liked working on spine cases to scrub with me. I asked Dr. Winston, a Bermudian resident doctor and an excellent assistant, to assist with the surgery.

At the beginning of the operation Dr. Mill wrote the following in Mrs. Steele's chart:

> "Hypotensive technique employed to minimize the high anticipitated blood loss aiming for MAP [mean arterial pressure] 55–60."

We started the procedure around midday. Two hours later I had finished the most delicate part of the operation, removal of the cancerous tissue around the spine, and was starting the second part, stabilization of the spine. At this stage the patient had bled only 500 cc because Dr. Mill had kept her blood pressure very low. I was satisfied and relaxed until Dr. Mill informed me that he was leaving because he had been on duty the night before. He said that Dr. Joneson would replace him. I was not thrilled at all about this, because a review of my patients' charts had shown that they bled profusely and required transfusion when Dr. Joneson was involved. However, I had no choice but to continue. As soon as she walked into the operating room, Dr. Joneson discontinued all the intravenous medications Dr. Mill had been administering to lower the blood pressure. The patient began to bleed profusely. I used a second suction to aspirate the blood from the wound and tried other methods to stop the bleeding, but in vain. I could not perform the operation properly, for the bleeding was too profuse. I asked for Dr. Joneson, who had left the operating room, and was told that she was busy on the phone. She returned to the operating room only at the end of the operation.

I walked out of the operating room quiet and sad. I could not believe that Dr. Joneson had purposely raised the patient's blood pressure to make her bleed. I thought I was paranoid until Dr. Winston joined me in the surgeons' lounge and said, "Did you notice?" I said, "What?" He said, "She purposely raised the blood pressure to make the patient bleed." Although I was relieved to know that I was not paranoid, I was not fully convinced that Dr. Joneson, a professional, was capable of risking a patient's life in order to frame me.

The next day Drs. Browne and Butterman, two family physicians, phoned to inform me that Dr. Joneson had written something very compromising about me in Mrs. Steele's chart. She had written that the patient bled excessively because of the unnecessary surgery I had done. They advised me to be careful because Dr. Joneson was trying to frame me.

It was not until a year later that I became fully convinced Dr. Joneson had purposely raised Mrs. Steele's blood pressure in order to frame me. On November 23rd, 1998, I ran into Dr. Brock, an African-American vascular surgeon, and his wife and Dr. Sale, a Canadian cardiologist, in a restaurant. I had already had dinner so I joined them for dessert. Dr. Brock described in detail how on numerous occasions Drs. Morrison and Joneson had tried to manipulate the blood pressure of his patients in order to sabotage his operations. He described many arguments he had had with Drs. Joneson and Morrison in this regard.

After hearing Dr. Brock's accounts of his interactions with Dr. Joneson, I understood that Dr. Joneson had put Mrs. Steele's life in jeopardy in order to frame me. After this I believed more than ever the following passage from the Bible:

"And GOD saw that the wickedness of man *was* great in the earth,

and that every imagination of the thoughts of his heart *was* **only evil continually.**

And it repented the LORD that he had made man on the earth, and it grieved him at his heart" (Genesis 6:5,6; 8:21; Job 15:16).

Mrs. Steele's condition did not improve after the operation and she was never able to walk again. Her family remained kind to me and never blamed me for her condition. In fact, her daughter said, "We are Christian and understand that you did your best for our mother." I never told the family what had happened to Mrs. Steele during the surgery. After that operation, I vowed to never again let any person frame me and destroy my reputation.

Mr. Fred (not real name) was my next big spine operation. Mr. Fred, who was seventy-six years old, had had severe low-back and leg pain for seven years. He had undergone physical therapy, taken many medications and received six epidural injections, without any relief. I met with the family and explained to them that surgery might be a viable alternative. Mr. Fred and his family decided to go ahead with the surgery.

On the morning of August 18th, 1997, I began operating on Mr. Fred as planned. The operating room was noisy, which was usual. The patient was bleeding more than usual because the anaesthetist, who was engrossed in a conversation with the nurses, was not adequately monitoring his blood pressure. I asked the nurses and the anaesthetist to keep quiet. I reminded the anaesthetist that out of respect for him I never entered the theatre and talked while he was anaesthetizing a patient. Meanwhile I stopped the operation, sat on a stool and asked the anaesthetist to control the patient's blood pressure. I resumed the operation only when he had done so. Halfway through the operation I asked the scrub nurse to hand me a particular surgical instrument that I needed. The nurse looked in the tray and said she did not have it. The previous evening I had verified that the tray was complete and no instrument was missing. I asked the circulating nurse to look for the missing instrument. She left the operating room and came back a few minutes later without it. Normally I would have continued regardless because I was tired of always fighting to get what I wanted. But this time I stopped the operation, removed my surgical gown and went to the head nurse's office. I told the head nurse about the missing instrument and said

I would not leave her office to resume the operation until the nurses found it. The head nurse and a team of nurses went off in search of the missing instrument. Within a few minutes she came back with it. From that day on, not one of my surgical instruments ever went missing from the tray and the anaesthetists always monitored my patients' blood pressure. Word had spread that I would discontinue the surgery if the proper conditions were not in place.

Apart from the events described above, Mr. Fred's operation went well. The patient bled minimally and did not require a transfusion.

After Mr. Fred's operation, an Irish operating room nurse complained that I had raised my voice to her during the procedure. Dr. Joneson, who headed the ensuing investigation, asked me to give her my version of the incident and wrote down everything I said. After she finished questioning me, I reminded Dr. Joneson that she had not responded to the letter I had written her more than a year earlier regarding Dr. Cooperson's barging into my operating room and disturbing me while I was operating. Dr. Joneson made no comment.

I had the feeling that Dr. Joneson's investigation of the nurse's complaint against me would be carried further and that my version of incident would be dismissed. Therefore I asked the resident physician, an Englishwoman of Asian origin who had been assisting me on Mr. Fred's surgery, to write a letter describing the events surrounding the incident. The resident wrote:

> "To whom it may concern: This is to inform you that I, Dr Z. Shah A., surgical resident at the KEMH, was scrubbed with Dr. Bah as a first assistant in the surgery performed on Mr. Fred.
>
> During the procedure, Dr. Bah was very concerned about the distraction caused by the non relevant conversation [the nurses had been talking about what they had done on the week-end, and about their upcoming vacation] held in the theatre by the non scrubbed staff and expressed his concerns in a raised voice. However, they were not directed to any one person in particular. It was purely in the interest of the patient's welfare.
>
> As we all know the objective of this hospital is to be a "center of excellence" and "the patient is the reason why we are here" [two of the slogans posted around the hospital]. Therefore in my opinion the expression of his concerns was not unjustified."

Dr. Joneson's investigation continued until Mrs. Lightbourn, a black

Bermudian nurse administrator, put an end to it. Mrs. Lightbourn came out in my favour, especially after learning that the nurse had threatened me by saying, "Two strikes and you're out." Mrs. Lightbourn told the nurse that two strikes and she would be out.

Mr. Fred's recovery was not without incident. On the ward, Mr. Fred, who was unable to get out of bed by himself, was left lying in bed most of the day. He urinated in his diaper and wet the bottom part of his wound, which became infected. I ordered a urinary catheter in order to prevent the urine from contaminating the wound. The wound began to heal once it was free of contact with the urine, but Mr. Fred developed a urinary infection because of his permanent urinary catheter. I ordered that the catheter be removed, that the patient be seated in his chair for thirty minutes after each meal and that the nurses help the patient to walk. Often, the nurses sat Mr. Fred in a chair and left him there all day until he was exhausted and in pain. After two weeks on the ward, Mr. Fred, who had come to my office walking and well except for his back and leg pain, began to deteriorate due to the inadequate post-operative care.

I called Mr. Fred's children and told them that their father would die in hospital if they did not come to take care of him. They took turns coming to the hospital and caring for him around the clock. One week later Mr. Fred was continent, his wound healed and his urinary infection eradicated. He left the hospital free of leg and back pain and walking unassisted. He continued to do well after that.

One of the things I learned from Mr. Fred's post-operative care was that I should refrain from operating on elderly patients at the King Edward VII Memorial Hospital. The post-operative care of the younger patients on the ward was not much better.

CHAPTER NINETEEN

Problems on the Ward

There were two surgical wards, A and B. They were located on the same floor, separated by elevators. Two black Bermudian nurses ran Ward A. Mrs. McRae, an older white Bermudian, and her assistant, a Portuguese Bermudian, ran Ward B. The staff on Ward B were mostly made up of English nurses and a few Bermudian nurses. Many of my patients complained that they did not receive adequate post-operative care on Ward B. They complained that the nurses would not help them get out of bed following their surgeries. The few patients who were helped out of bed complained that they were left sitting in their chair all day. I first discussed my patients' complaints with Mrs. McRae, who brushed aside my concern and told me the patients were well taken care of. Next, I discussed their complaints with Mrs. McRae's assistant, who told me she would do something about the situation. However, the situation did not improve at all. I then advised my patients to bring their complaints to the attention of Mrs. Park, Director of Nursing and Patients Services. Mrs. Park brought the issue to Mrs. McRae, who once again could not be bothered by my patients' complaints. I then advised my patients to write a letter to the hospital ombudsman. All but one were afraid to do so.

Mr. D.M., a fifty-year-old Portuguese Bermudian, took courage and wrote to the ombudsman. Mr. D.M. had had a back operation with four screws and two rods inserted. The morning after his surgery he asked the nurse to help him get out of bed. According to the patient, the English nurse told him to get out of bed by himself because she was pregnant. He suggested she get another nurse to help him and she replied that she was the one assigned to his care. Mr. D.M. said he then asked the nurse to give him the pain medication he had been prescribed so he could try to get up by himself, but she refused and reminded him that he had had an alcohol problem in the past (Mr. D.M. had been an alcoholic, but had been cured years before after joining Alcoholics Anonymous). In his letter to the ombudsman, Mr. D.M. wrote:

> "To the attention of Mr. Savory, Manager of Quality Improvement and Patient Relations.
>
> My name is [D.M.]. I was recently a patient on Perry's ward [Ward B] while recovering from major back surgery. I found it necessary to inform you that I received no after care beyond changing of dressings, getting cleaned up and taken out of bed where I was sat in a chair and left there sitting [sic]. I had to teach myself to walk. I hope this letter will bring to your attention the need for further after care to ensure the safety of all of your patients."

In reply to Mr. M.D.'s letter, Mr. Savory, the ombudsman, a black Bermudian, wrote:

> A review of your medical record was carried out and both the doctors' and nurses' documentation clearly stated what care was provided and how your post operative recovery progressed. The nurses had written that at times you were very drowsy as a result of additional medication you required and that you were reluctant to either move in bed, sit up in a chair or walk.
>
> Your doctor ordered a back brace for you to wear and this was fitted by staff from the Orthopaedic Clinic two days after your surgery. There was no indication in your medical records that your doctor felt you required any other treatment/assistance related to aftercare than what was prescribed.
>
> As it is our commitment to continuously work towards improving patient care and service, I have shared your concerns with the staff on the ward.
>
> I am sorry you are unhappy with the care you received."

Since the hospital authorities refused to address Mr. D.M.'s complaints, I felt compelled to find a solution to my patients' lack of care. The problem with Ward B was that it was only the black and Portuguese patients who were not properly cared for there. My white Bermudian patients were treated like royalty on Ward B and never complained. I went to the admitting department, where it was decided which ward a patient would be assigned to. I did not want to start a discrimination process in choosing which ward my black, white, poor and wealthy patients were sent to, but the fact that my patients were not being properly cared for on Ward B increased their risk of complications such as infection, phlebitis and loosening of hardware, and possibly posed a risk to my reputation as well. I told the head of admitting, Mrs. Shirley, a black Bermudian, that some of my patients were having problems on Ward B. Mrs. Shirley did not let me expand. She told me that before she had become head, Mrs. McRae would come to the admitting department to select the white and wealthy patients she wished to have admitted to Ward B. Mrs. Shirley said she immediately put an end to this practice. She sent Mrs. McRae away and told her never to return. I told Mrs. Shirley I did not want to make it a rule, but I would prefer that my black and other non-wealthy patients be sent to Ward A. (I had noticed that the white doctors preferred to have their patients sent to Ward B, and the black assistant nurse on Ward A had confirmed this to me.) Mrs. Shirley said she would see what she could do.

The racial problems at the hospital were not a figment of my fertile imagination. A letter published in a local newspaper read as follows:

"First of all I am a dark skinned black Bermudian.

Everybody is making a big deal about racism. They say it is black against white and white against black. What about black against black and white against white? You have light-skinned blacks turning their noses down at dark skinned blacks. You have one white nationality hating another white. Take this for example: Monday July 19, I went to the hospital to have a mammogram. The Pink Lady that directs you on where to go was very helpful. She was white. The lady that took the form from me seemed like it would hurt her to smile and say good morning. She was light skinned. I got all the forms I needed and went to where I was directed to go. I walked up to the desk, smiled and said good morning. No answer, just a hand put out for the form. I didn't think anything of it because I don't let things like that bother me. What did bother me was that a minute later a white English woman came up to that very same window and got the biggest, brightest smile and the loudest Good Morning. Can someone please explain that to me? But then again maybe it needs no explanation! Light skinned receptionist – dark skinned patient versus light skinned Receptionist – white patient. People get with it; we are all in this together.

NOT A RACIST

Southampton"1

Fortunately for my patients, not all wards were like Ward B. Patients were treated well in the emergency room and on the pediatric ward because the head nurses there (both black and white) were not like Mrs. McRae. On one occasion Dr. Joneson went to the emergency room, something she rarely did, to fetch a prominent white patient and take him to the operating room. Mrs. Louise, the black assistant head nurse in emergency, said to her: "I never see you coming down here to fetch a black patient or a poor white one. You go back to the operating room now and wait until we finish preparing the patient and send him to you." Dr. Joneson, who was feared by everybody in the operating room, did not utter a word. She bowed her head, turned around and went back to the operating room as fast as she had come.

[1] "We're All in This Together," *The Royal Gazette,* July 19th, 1999, p. 4.

CHAPTER TWENTY

Dr. Trouts' Guidelines

On March 27th, 1997, Dr. Trouts and I signed our work contract. I waited for him to make the calculation and give me my money. Mr. Robbins, his bookkeeper, estimated that Dr. Trouts owed me $200,000 US. On April 8th, Dr. Trouts wrote me a cheque for $12,764.24 for all the work I had done in 1996. He gave me no paper indicating why he was paying me so little (he did likewise when paying his employees). Something was obviously wrong, for I had billed for $400,000 over the period. I tried to meet with Dr. Trouts, but was unable to corner him until May 29th. At first he said he owed me nothing, but I when I pressed him he admitted that he had based his calculation on the altered figures in the ledgers. I asked him why he had ordered the bookkeeper to alter the ledgers. He replied, "For negotiation purposes." I reminded him that we had finished negotiating and had signed a contract two months earlier. Dr. Trouts said he "might revisit the figures in the future." I asked how far into the future that would be. He did not answer.

I had been involved with Dr. Trouts in another venture, a physiotherapy clinic. The contract stated that he was to take sixty percent of the profit (the percentage that he said was required by law to be Bermudian-owned). Dr. C.R., an Irish sports medicine specialist whose work permit was held by Dr. Trouts, and I were each to take twenty percent. Six months after the clinic opened the first physiotherapist we had hired was so busy that we had to hire a second, who became an instant hit with the patients. I asked Dr. Trouts about my share of the profits. He said the clinic had not generated any profit and I would have to invest more money if I wanted to stay in the venture. It was obvious he was not telling the truth. The bookkeeper had shown me the income generated by the physiotherapist and I knew all the expenses entailed in running the clinic. I told Dr. Trouts I wanted out of the venture and asked him to return the money I had invested. Three days later he wrote me a cheque for the amount I had invested. As for the profit I was entitled to, it is probably lost forever in the Bermuda Triangle.

The third subject I brought up with Dr. Trouts in our meeting was the money he owed Dr. Morais. Dr. Morais, my friend and former professor from Montreal, had acted as a locum for Dr. Trouts while the latter was on vacation in Russia. (Dr. Morais and I also operated on several spine cases while he was in Bermuda.) The two had met at the Boat Club and come to an agreement on how much Dr. Trouts would pay Dr. Morais. According to this agreement, Dr. Trouts owed Dr. Morais nearly $40,000 US. When I asked him about this money, Dr. Trouts said that Dr. Morais had acted as a locum for him and that Dr. Morais' money belonged to him. I reminded Dr. Trouts that he and Dr. Morais had a verbal agreement and he had a moral duty to pay Dr. Morais. He was not impressed with my lecture on ethics.

Dr. Trouts was very proud during our meeting. I was dealing with a completely different Dr. Trouts from the shy and broken man who had called me in Montreal in October 1993 to ask for help with his exam. That Dr. Trouts, when begging me to move to Bermuda and work with him, had said, "The devil you know is better than the devil you don't." Now I realized that I did not know Dr. Trouts at all and that it was not good to know any devil.

I could not help, but ask Dr. Trouts if there was anything for me in all of this. Without hesitation, he said it was a privilege for me to be in Bermuda. What sort of privilege, I asked. He looked outside and said, "The sun and the beaches." I reminded him that before my arrival he performed one knee arthroscopy a month, whereas once I was there to assist him he was operating much more; he had benefited more from our association than I. As for the "sun and the beaches," I told him that my family and I used to travel to Mexico and other sunny destinations twice a year when I was living in Montreal, and my travel expenses were significantly less than the $200,000 he was withholding from me. Moreover, I said, I did not particularly care for the beach (the first year my family and I were in Bermuda we went to the beach every second day late in the afternoon, as it was too hot during the day; the second year we went only on weekends from June to October, as the water was too cold for swimming the rest of the year; the third year I went only once the whole summer).

On that note our meeting ended, and that was the last time we spoke. Whenever we met after that we would greet each other with a "Good morning" or "Good afternoon." Even Drs. Cooperson, Fascioni and I would greet each other this way. It is the custom in Bermuda. It was what I liked the most when I first visited. But after a few months on the Island I realized that people would greet you with one hand and stab you in the back with the other (guns are not allowed in Bermuda). As one of my Bermudian patients told me, people do not really mean it when they greet you and ask you about your welfare; they start talking about you and backstabbing you moments later. Now, I prefer to live in a large city where people do not generally greet each other, but where the odd greeting and smile I get are, I think, genuine.

One week after my last meeting with Dr. Trouts, he passed along several documents to me. These included a balance sheet and a letter for me to forward to Dr. Morais. The flow sheet indicated that Dr. Morais had billed $65,481.50 for the work he did while in Bermuda and that he owed Dr. Trouts $11,009.21. I was completely mystified as to how Dr. Morais could have paid all the expenses (including travel and malpractice insurance) related to his work in Bermuda and still owe Dr. Trouts money (I would reimburse Dr. Morais for his expenses).

Enclosed with the flow sheet was the following statement:

"I, Dr. G. Morais F.R.S.C.(C), do release Orthopaedics and Sports Medicine of Bermuda Ltd. [Dr. Trouts] and all of their employees and shareholders [Dr. Trouts' wife and his mother] from all indebtedness to me as a result of work performed by me in Bermuda during 1996. I further authorize any payments due to me for said work to be made to Dr. C. Bah F.R.S.C.(C)."

In order to be paid, Dr. Morais was to sign this statement and have it notarized. In reality, had he signed it he would have had to pay Dr. Trouts $11,009.21. When I gave him the various documents, Dr. Morais smiled and said, "The most important thing is that you get the money Dr. Trouts owes you."

The signed contract between Dr. Trouts and me stipulated that at the end of every year Dr. Trouts would make the necessary calculations, show me the final figures and pay me based on those figures. The contract also stated that:

"10.01 Either the Independent Practitioner [Dr. Bah] or the Company may within 30 days of each and every year during the term of this Agreement, engage an accountant acceptable to both the Independent Practitioner and the Company to perform a review of the books and records of the Company and the Independent Practitioner for the purposes of calculating the Receipts, draws against Receipts, Personal Expenses and Shared Expenses of the Independent Practitioner…"

Thus I wrote him indicating that I wished to avail myself of the right, as stipulated in the contract, to review all financial documents (billing, receipts, draws against receipts, personal expenses and shared expenses) in order to verify the accuracy and completeness of the financial records. I explained that I had retained the services of an accountant to review the books and records of the company and asked him to supply the financial documents to my accountant in order for her to conduct the review.

My accountant called Dr. Trouts on numerous occasions, and also wrote to him, concerning her review. Dr. Trouts ignored her requests. Instead, he sent me a letter stating that I had to pay him in order to access the financial documents.

On June 16th, 1997, I wrote Dr. Trouts pointing out that nowhere in our contract did it state that I had to pay him for access to financial records concerning me. I asked him again to supply the financial documents to my accountant.

On June 20th, he sent me a letter stating the following:

"Please return a signed copy by yourself and your agent [accountant] prior to commencing work.

Guidelines for Review of the Books of Orthopaedics and Sports Medicine of Bermuda Ltd:

1. All expenses of engaging a third party to review the records will be borne by the person making the request.

2. No record will leave the premises of the Company.

3. No photocopies will be made of the records of the Company…

5. Any third party will be supervised at all times.

6. Expenses incurred for supervision, time spent with auditors or their staff
or in preparation of additional reviews by the Company will be charged out
at a rate of the cost per hour of that employee during regular working hours
or time and one half for any after hours…"

I felt that Dr. Trouts' guidelines were a scheme devised to avoid giving
me my money. I found them unacceptable. I felt that I should not have to
pay an employee who I was already paying to supervise my accountant, a
professional.

I sought the advice of a new attorney, Mr. Traut. I had ceased doing
business with Mr. Clancy, who had been handling my case with Dr. Trouts,
partly because I thought his fees were too high, but mainly because of a
conversation I had overheard in his office. Mr. Clancy's assistant said that
the fee of $5,000 they were billing a client was very high for the work done
and that $3,000 might be more appropriate. Mr. Clancy responded that
the client did not know that and to leave it at $5,000. This upset me, espe-
cially since Mr. Clancy had told me he was a Christian and we had become
friends, with our children playing together. Later I would realize that no
Christian is perfect and that perhaps I had judged Mr. Clancy too harshly.
Later, after dealing with other attorneys, I would admit to Mr. Clancy that
his fees were not so high after all and that he was perhaps the most honest
attorney I had ever met.

Mr. Traut, a black Bermudian in his mid-thirties, dressed like a model
in *GQ* magazine. It took me less than five minutes to describe my situation
regarding Dr. Trouts. Mr. Traut was all pumped up and enthusiastic. He
said he understood the matter very well and would take the case. He said
he liked fighting and got up every morning ready to do so. I thought, well,
good for you, because I got up every morning hoping not to fight and not
to have complications with my surgeries. Mr. Traut advised me to send
another letter to Dr. Trouts requesting that he give the financial documents
to my accountant.

As suggested by Mr. Traut, I again wrote to Dr. Trouts asking him to
give the financial documents to my accountant. On July 9th, Dr. Trouts
responded by sending me three new guidelines:

"The undersigned hereby agrees as follows:

1. The confidential records shall be used solely for determining the amount

of monies Dr. Bah is entitled to…

2. The undersigned shall keep the confidential records strictly confidential and shall not disclose their contents to any person or entity.

3. The undersigned shall deliver to the Company upon demand all Confidential records, any copies of the same, together with all papers, documents, studies, reports, brochures, analyses, compilations, forecasts, studies or other documents prepared by the undersigned in connection with his/her examination of the Confidential records."

My interpretation of the new guidelines was that I could not "disclose" the records to any "person" (judge, arbitrator) or "entity" (court, arbitration tribunal) if the need arose. I found Dr. Trouts' new guidelines even more stringent than the previous ones.

My accountant said she had conducted many audits and had never encountered guidelines of this nature. Mr. Traut found the guidelines unacceptable and advised me to send another letter to Dr. Trouts requesting access to my financial records.

On August 19th, I wrote Dr. Trouts a fifth time asking him to give the financial records to my accountant. I enclosed a letter from my accountant, which was intended to allay any fears he might have about the handling of the financial records:

Dr. Trouts did not respond to my letter or that of my accountant. Instead he had the office computerized and he and his wife ordered the staff not to give me the computer passwords. At the end of every month the staff provided me with a printout of the financial records that Dr. Trouts and his wife did not want me to have.

CHAPTER TWENTY-ONE

The Scientific Meeting

In a letter dated June 18th, 1997, Dr. Cooperson advised me that a "scientific meeting" of the orthopaedic subdivision would be held on July 2nd. This meeting notice, unlike his previous ones, was well structured and included an agenda. Five items were to be discussed, the last being "emergency room coverage." I knew that the real purpose of the meeting to discuss the case of, Mr. B.J.

On Sunday, June 1st, 1997, an ambulance had brought Mr. B.J., a black Bermudian, to the emergency room. Mr. B.J., an indigene patient (many indigene patients are itinerant and do not have insurance coverage) was the victim of a hit-and-run accident. He presented with a fracture of the right leg. Mr. B.J. requested that Dr. Fascioni, who had treated him in the past for a fracture of the same leg, be paged to attend to him. The emergency room staff duly advised Dr. Fascioni, who responded that he was unavailable. The emergency room staff then called Dr. Trouts, who was on call. Dr. Trouts declined to attend to the patient and suggested he be kept in the emergency room until the next morning when I would be on call. The emergency room physician phoned me at eight a.m. when my shift began. I immediately went to the emergency room to attend to Mr. B.J.

The patient, who was under the effects of alcohol and probably upset that two physicians had declined to treat him, began to argue with me. He told me he wanted Dr. Fascioni to treat him. I waited in the emergency room while the nurses tried to convince the patient to let me treat his fracture. The patient refused, insisting that Dr. Fascioni be called. The nurses called Dr. Fascioni, who again refused.

I waited in the emergency room for a while, but left when the patient continued to insist that he wanted only Dr. Fascioni. On my way home I realized that I had not been patient with Mr. B.J. because I was upset at Drs. Fascioni and Trouts for refusing to treat him. I rarely argued with patients and realized that had I been more patient I could have easily convinced Mr. B.J., who felt rejected by the other surgeons, to let me treat him. When I got home I called the emergency room and asked the staff to tell the patient that I would operate on him if he was willing. The staff informed me that the patient was willing. I immediately called the operating room and scheduled the surgery for noon. A few moments later Dr. Joneson, of Dr. Cooperson's group, called and asked why I did not want to treat Mr. B.J. I told her that it was not I, but Dr. Fascioni who did not want to treat the patient and that I was on my way to the hospital to operate on him.

Mr. B.J.'s surgery went well. After the operation he was a gentleman. He was one of the most courteous patients I had ever treated. He even apologized for his behaviour in the emergency room.

On July 2nd, I went to Dr. Cooperson's so-called scientific meeting. The two other orthopaedics meetings held during my two years in Bermuda took place in the surgeons' lounge, the loudest and busiest place in the operating room. Each had lasted less than five minutes. This time, the meeting was held in the tiny, six-by-twelve-foot residents' sleeping room. Drs. Cooperson and Fascioni sat on the bed, while Drs. Chalvin, Trouts and I sat in chairs we had managed to cram into the room. The meeting began as the two previous ones had, with Dr. Cooperson telling us he had ordered some orthopaedics equipment that had not been received. As usual, the discussion about equipment lasted five minutes. Then he introduced the subject of Mr. B.J. I had brought a hidden tape recorder with me. Following is a transcript of the discussion about "emergency department coverage," which lasted more than thirty minutes:

> **Dr. Cooperson**: Emergency department coverage, just to remind you that if you call somebody in… There was an incident that was reported to me and that the orthopaedic surgeon who was on call was not willing to treat the patient. That is unsatisfactory. If you are on call, you have to take the patient. If for some reason…that's what the patient requested that's fine. But if it is not that [not] it is your responsibility to take care of the patient.

> **Dr. Fascioni**: Since you brought up the fact, I think I have to bring the

issue of [B.J.], a patient who fall in the category of *undesirable, a bump, a guy who none of us like to have,* who I have operated [sic] twice in the past for very complex fractures of the same femur requested me on the day that I was not on call. I refused to come in because I had other commitments. That led to you [Dr. Bah] on call, and that led to Barbara Joneson having to call you. There are two things that you should know: First of all, I had a long discussion with Barbara and some of the comments you made I think were close to libel. You cannot say that, you know what you said and I am happy not to say it here. The second thing, which is easy to say here, is that you consider your taking over the patient humanitarian [sic], which, is not [sic]. In a word, it is your duty to take the patient if he is unpleasant and abusive. It is your duty to take the patient. Third it is a hospital bylaw. I do not think it is new but it has been revised that for certain patients especially those patients who are as we know in orthopaedics, patients like [B.J.] who will continue to be self-destructive and continue to… When we talk about indigene patient care that category of patient you can be bored by, I remember as a resident we used to do it all the time [you find an excuse to not treat and to get rid of the patient], the first thing you did was to look for whether anybody had treated or another service had treated them then you were free… Thank God, they had them last year. That does not apply anymore. It is not right, Ok? That is the kind of patient who has no loyalty to the surgeon and the surgeon on call must take that patient. It is not out of [sic] humanitarian reasons, but your duty.

Dr. Cooperson: Yes.

Dr. Fascioni: Professional duty, and I feel strongly about that and I know the discussion you [Dr. Bah] had with Barbara and I was not very pleased, Ok?

Dr. Bah: I do not remember.

Dr. Fascioni: I remember clearly and she probably has it written down, because it was practically very libellous what you said.

Dr. Bah: Well if you want to take legal action me against me. That is fine with me. I do not remember saying anything against you that was libellous.

Dr. Fascioni: I do not want to pursue it, but the consensus should be clear that *patients like B.J. are a pain in the ass,* but you have to take him. They will never pay you, they…

Dr. Bah: To you he was a pain in the ass, but to me he was not a pain in the ass. They called you first because the patient requested you. Then they called [Dr. Trouts], who was on duty…

Dr. Fascioni: They did.

Dr Bah: I never worked in a private system before, but my understanding is that no physician is allowed to refuse to take care of a patient in an emergency situation.

Dr. Fascioni: If you are not on call.

Dr. Cooperson: I have no knowledge of this.

Dr. Fascioni: That is right.

Dr. Bah: What had happened in the past was that even though I was on call, you or Dr. Chalvin would come to the emergency room because the patient requested you. [Dr. Fascioni would roam the emergency room on the days when Dr. Trouts and I were on duty, in search of insured patients to operate on.]

Dr. Fascioni: And I do 90% of the time unless I had a glass of wine or another commitment. So, if I am not on call, I answer the doctor and say sorry I have another commitment.

Dr. Bah: Anyway, when they call me, I never ask whether the patient is indigenous.

Dr Fascioni: I know that.

Dr. Bah: I came and saw the patient.

Dr. Fascioni: You should not ask that.

Dr. Bah: I do not ask the patient…

Dr. Fascioni: I am not accusing you of asking that question.

Dr. Bah: But…

Dr. Fascioni: I am saying that you implied that the reason that I did not come in was for that reason. I said I did not want to bring it up in particular. The general concept is that if patient requests you and you are fit to come, you come.

Dr. Bah: Would you have come had the patient not been indigenous?

Dr. Fascioni: That never had any bearing on how I treat patients, no bearing.

Dr. Bah: I never inquired whether the patient was indigenous. [I believed that Drs. Fascioni and Trouts, who had been called first, had declined to operate on the patient because he was not insured.]

Dr. Fascioni: You should not... I was not available and he needed acute care. The patient needed to be treated.

Dr. Bah: The bottom line is that I treated the patient anyway.

Dr Fascioni: As you should have.

Dr. Bah: It is humanitarian.

Dr Fascioni: It is not humanitarian. It is your duty.

Dr. Cooperson: That had nothing to do with it. You are on call and it is your responsibility.

Dr. Fascioni: It is unpleasant you do have a patient who is aggressive or is abusive like [B.J.]. I have known [B.J.] for a quiet a few years, the guy is my patient in terms of his previous fracture, that moment I could not come in. When a patient requests me in the middle of the night or anytime I come in most of the time. That is a fact. If you wish to discuss it with Barbara [Dr. Joneson]. She feels very strong [sic] about it and I do not want to discuss it.

Dr. Bah: I have already discussed it with Barbara. I came and treated the patient anyway.

Dr. Fascioni: I made my point about a specific thing, it should be clear.

Dr. Cooperson: Ed Schulte [the chief of emergency] is not aware of this case, which is why it was brought up to me. Dr. Jameson [the chief of staff] is aware of this case and he agreed. It seems to me the obvious thing is that whether or not you are on call it is your responsibility as long as somebody else is not available to take care of the patient.

Dr. Trouts: There are couples of thing that come to mind [sic]. Patients' bill of right to be able to request their physician...is there not something listed about being able to pick your surgeon?

Dr. Fascioni: If they are not available, they are not available.

Dr. Trouts: That's fine, I see the point, but we have to be careful that we do not force a treatment on somebody that is totally refusing.

Dr. Cooperson: If they refuse that is fine. Let them sign a refusal.

Dr. Trouts: I just think that there should be some understanding...

Dr. Cooperson: If they refuse either you get them to sign...sometimes they will refuse to sign, in this case, get a witness like a nurse. If this has not happened to you, it will. It has happened to me a bunch of times over the years, usually a patient on the ward who is psychiatric or drunk or something, and if they will not sign it get the nurse to witness it in the notes.

Dr. Trouts: But we do acknowledge in the patients' bill of rights to choose...

Dr. Cooperson: Absolutely.

Dr. Trouts: ...their physicians...

Dr. Cooperson: Absolutely.

Dr. Fascioni: I know this was a particularly difficult situation. Dealing with a particular patient who is self-destructive, who continues to do irresponsible things and injure himself and need something done. *But he was an asshole with you.* It is a tough situation.

At the end of the meeting everybody was happy. Drs. Cooperson and Fascioni were happy because they had had their so-called scientific meeting and, in addition, Dr. Fascioni had been able to say to me what he wanted to say. Dr. Trouts was happy because he had got a word in. Dr. Chalvin was happy because he did not have to say anything. I was happy because I had not allowed Dr. Fascioni to defeat me.

With regard to the rights of Mr. B.J., the rules and regulations of the Bermuda Hospitals Board stated the following:

Responsibilities to the patient

An Ethical Physician:

5. Will recognize that a patient has the right to accept or reject any physician...

6. Shall, except in an emergency, have the right to refuse to accept a patient.

Thus Drs. Fascioni and Trouts did not have the right to refuse the patient, since he was an emergency case, and I could not impose medical treatment or myself on the patient.

CHAPTER TWENTY-TWO

Summer 1997

Dr. Cooperson's scientific meeting was not the last forum where Dr. Fascioni and I got involved in a discussion. When I began operating at the King Edward VII Memorial Hospital I had to purchase an operating frame, an indispensable tool for performing back surgery. I had asked the hospital to reimburse me for the cost of the frame and other instruments I had bought. It refused. During one of the rare orthopaedics meetings, I suggested to the other surgeons (Drs. Cooperson, Fascioni, Chalvin and Trouts) that they reimburse me a fraction of the $2,000 US I had spent on the frame, and then it would belong to everyone. They completely ignored my proposal. However, I noticed that all the surgeons were using my frame without asking my permission. Initially I ignored their behaviour and let them use the frame for the benefit of the patients, but when their harassment and arrogance toward me intensified I decided to hide it.

One morning a few weeks later, Dr. Fascioni called me from the operating room and angrily asked why I had removed the frame and where I was hiding it. I reminded him that the frame belonged to me and I had suggested in vain that he and the other surgeons reimburse me a fraction of its cost. Dr. Fascioni said he had used the frame all along thinking it belonged to the hospital. He asked me if he could borrow it because he and a visiting spine surgeon from Boston were about to operate on a patient. The irony was that for years Drs. Fascioni, Cooperson and the surgeon from Boston had been operating on back patients without the frame and now they could not do without it. I asked Mr. Tony, the technician and my honest house painter, who had stored the frame for me, to give it to Dr. Fascioni.

One might think that Dr. Fascioni would thank me for lending him the frame. He did not. For the next three months he raised the issue of the frame at every single surgical meeting (where all the surgeons and anaesthetists discussed matters related to the operating room). Dr. Fascioni said that no surgeon should use his or her personal instrument, in my case the frame, at the hospital. If it was faulty, he said, the frame could endanger the patient and render the hospital liable. Dr. Fascioni was not going to spend $400 of his own money to partially reimburse me, but he wanted me to donate the frame to an institution that had an annual budget of more than $100 million. I told the meeting that I had invited the hospital and the orthopaedic surgeons to buy the frame from me and had been refused. I then ignored Dr. Fascioni and let him argue with the other surgeons who were using their own personal instruments at the hospital. Dr. Cooperson did not say a word because he was using two personal arthroscopy instruments worth less than $2,000 that he declined to donate to the hospital and hid from the other surgeons. Dr. Fascioni discussed my frame at every ensuing surgical meeting, insisting that I donate it to the hospital, until one day Dr. Miles, an ear, nose and throat specialist, told him outright to get on with life.

Dr. Fascioni and the other orthopaedic surgeons continued using my frame without my permission and without ever thanking me. I could have removed the frame from the operating room, but I chose to leave it there for the sake of the patients.

In the summer of 1997, I decided to concentrate my energies on my work. I tried to ignore Dr. Trouts, who was not going to give me my money, and Drs. Cooperson and Fascioni, who were not going to get off my case. I worked hard, hoping that one day I would see the fruits of my labour.

When I had arrived on the Island Dr. Trouts told me that one could make as much money running offices as operating, and with less effort. He therefore spent more time running offices. To avoid crossing paths with him, I spent more time in the operating room and less time in the office. Another piece of advice Dr. Trouts had given me was to avoid operating on American tourists who had sustained motorbike injuries because I could become liable to lawsuits. "It is better to wrap them up and ship them off," he said. I rarely gave advice and I listened to it as often. So I did exactly the opposite of what Dr. Trouts had advised. In the summer of 1997, I operated on as many Bermudians and Americans who had fallen off their bikes as I could. I liked operating on Americans because many wrote to thank me and to tell me that their physicians thought I had done a good job. Their letters allowed me to stay in touch with the outside world and suggested to me that what I was doing in Bermuda was all right.

I worked hard, but enjoyed it because the workload was still significantly less than what I had been used to in Montreal. I could have easily billed more than $800,000 US a year if I had kept up that pace, unhindered by my adversaries and overburdened by Dr. Trouts. The harder I worked, the more I became known on the Island. The pastor of my church, Mr. De Silva, a taxi driver, once asked me if there were any other surgeons at the King Edward. He said that every patient he picked up from the hospital said Dr. Bah was his or her surgeon. Dr. Browne, a family physician and politician, said people talked about me at almost every meeting he attended. I had had more positive impact on the Island in the short time I had been there, said Dr. Browne, than the orthopaedic surgeons who had been around for ten years.

However, not everybody appreciated my hard work. Dr. Fascioni roamed the operating room to see what I was doing and I sensed he was not a happy camper. Before my arrival he and Dr. Cooperson were each operating on an average of six patients a day, whereas now they were operating on an average of three small cases such as hardware removal or bunion surgery.

The more I operated the more people came to me. Even patients who were initially seen by Drs. Fascioni and Cooperson wanted to be treated by me. In the summer of 1997, one such patient, a schoolteacher with low-back pain, presented in the emergency room. Dr. Fascioni examined her, made a diagnosis of herniated disc and admitted her for surgery. The nurses on the ward suggested that the patient ask me for a second opinion. She did so and I agreed with the diagnosis of herniated disc, but suggested that conservative treatment (physiotherapy and anti-inflammatory medication) be tried since the patient had had the pain for only three weeks.

The patient agreed with my recommendation and asked that I be her treating physician. In the past I had strongly discouraged patients who had been seen by other surgeons to transfer to me, but since the surgeons were behaving unprofessionally I neither encouraged nor discouraged the practice. I told the schoolteacher that I would be her physician as long as she first discussed the matter with Dr. Fascioni. The patient told Dr. Fascioni that she wanted me to be her treating physician.

Dr. Fascioni phoned and gave me a piece of his mind. He said he could not understand how an "aggressive surgeon with an aggressive training" could recommend conservative treatment (to say that a surgeon is aggressive can be intended as a compliment or as an insult; Dr. Fascioni meant it as an insult). I tried not to argue and told him that the scientific literature stated the following:

> "The indication for discectomy is persistent pain with progressive weakness
> for more than 3 months and not responding to conservative treatment."[1]

I reminded Dr. Fascioni that the schoolteacher had been suffering from back pain for only three weeks. Moreover, the pain had already lessened slightly since she had been admitted to hospital. I promised to send Dr. Fascioni the literature I had quoted from.

I continued to work, seeing and operating on more and more patients. I knew, however, that sooner or later Dr. Cooperson and his group would do something to stop me, because I was taking away a lot of their business.

[1] Stephen Esses, *Textbook of Spinal Disorders* (Philadelphia, Pennsylvania: J.B. Lippincott Company, 1995).

CHAPTER TWENY-THREE

End of the Agreement

By September 1997, my accountant and I had written more than seven letters to Dr. Trouts requesting that he give us the financial statements for the purpose of calculating how much money he owed me. Dr. Trouts responded to our initial letters by asking us to sign and return his guidelines. Towards the end, he did not even bother to acknowledge our letters. On September 4th, Mr. Traut, my attorney wrote to Dr. Trouts' attorney stating the following:

> "...despite our client's repeated request to review the books and records of the company for the period ending 1996, your Mr. Trouts has failed and/or refused to provide our client's accountant with this information... In this regard he has instructed us to formally write to you to request that the company records be provided to our client's accountant within ten days from the date of this letter, failing which our client will assume that the Agreement of the 1st December 1995 has been repudiated by the company and, therefore, our client will consider his options. We trust, however, that as a result of this letter you will honor the terms of the agreement so that this matter may be resolved as amicably and expeditiously as possible."

On September 11th, Dr. Trouts' attorney replied as follows:

> "... Our client takes the view that for any accountant to be acceptable for the purposes of that paragraph, they must be willing to sign the confidentiality agreement provided...
>
> (1) Return the confidentiality agreement signed by both Dr. Bah and Mrs. Wilson..."

One week later, on September 18th, Dr. Trouts sent me a letter stating the following:

"…The Company [Orthopaedic & Sports Medicine of Bermuda Ltd] hereby gives you notice in accordance with Paragraph 11.00 of the Agreement that it is exercising its right to terminate the Agreement in accordance with that section, as of December 30th 1997."

I was happy that Dr. Trouts had terminated our agreement, especially since, in addition to failing to give me my money, he had joined the ranks of Drs. Cooperson and Fascioni in trying to undermine my professional reputation. Up until September 1997, even though Dr. Trouts and I avoided each other, we still worked from the same office and covered for each other during vacations. But Dr. Trouts had got into the habit of writing very compromising things about me in the charts of patients he saw when I was away. At first the secretary transcribed everything he dictated, but later she advised me that Dr. Trouts was trying to undermine my reputation and censored his comments.

Dr. Trouts had dictated the following with regard to a patient he saw when I was on vacation:

" He had a fracture of his left distal tibia on July 1st, 1996, which was treated by Dr. Bah. He gets ongoing stiffness with inactivity…and he is unhappy with his inability to discuss this with Dr. Bah and is here to see me in this regard…His last films apparently showed union."

The patient's surgery was successful, his leg was healed and as indicated by Dr. Trouts, his only complaint was stiffness in his ankle with inactivity. All Dr. Trouts had to do was refer the patient for physiotherapy. Instead, he added that the patient was "unhappy with his inability to discuss this with Dr. Bah," which was completely untrue. ·

Since Dr. Trouts had terminated my contract, my alternatives were to leave Bermuda or find another physician to hold my work permit. I chose the latter option. Dr. Browne, a black Bermudian family physician, was the fist person I thought of in this regard. I knew him mainly from what I read in the local newspaper. I had noticed that Dr. Browne, who was a member of parliament for the opposition party, was very outspoken. He was so controversial and made headlines so often that the newspaper was boring when he was away from the Island. I had decided to ask Dr. Browne to hold my work permit mainly because of a conversation I had had with a journalist at the newspaper. A few weeks earlier I had met a man at Dorval Airport in Montreal. Seeing that I was carrying a duty-free shopping bag from Bermuda, he asked if I came from "The Rock." I knew that Gibraltar and Alcatraz were referred to as "The Rock," and since I was not coming from either of these places I told the gentleman I didn't know what he meant. He informed me that Bermuda was also referred to as "The Rock." Our conversation led to his telling me he was a Canadian working as a reporter in Bermuda. Then he asked me where I worked and I said at the hospital. He asked if I knew Dr. Browne and I replied not very well. Then the gentleman said that as a parliamentary reporter he liked covering Dr. Browne's speeches. He said, "Dr. Browne speaks his mind, and within half an hour," whereas other members of parliament "talk for hours without saying anything."

My wife and I met Dr. Browne in his office. I described my situation and asked if he would hold my work permit. He asked us if we were "fighters." My wife said yes. I said I did not like fighting and tried to avoid it at all costs, but would fight if I had to. He said he had asked us this because "Bermuda is a rough place." He said that Bermuda, which was once known as the Devil's Island, is now sometime referred to as "Island of the Devils." Dr. Browne said he would be glad to hold my work permit. He said he would not ask for any money in return, only that I work for his clinic and refer patients to his radiology service. He said my practice would be completely independent of his and I would not have to report to him.

I had no objection to working from Dr. Browne's clinic and referring patients to his radiology service since I would be able to see my patients back in the office soon after they had their x-rays, whereas when I worked from Dr. Trouts' office I had to wait a week to have access to patients' films taken at the hospital and very often my staff, who had to go to the hospital to search for the films, could not find my patients' x-rays taken the previous week. Dr. Browne took my wife and me on a tour of his clinic and showed me the office space that would be available for me to rent.

A few days later, Dr. Browne and I met again. He told me he was still willing to hold my work permit, but I should be aware of the fact that this could be an asset or a liability to me because of his current political involvement and previous dealings with the establishment and the hospital. Later I would learn what Dr. Browne meant by this. One summer while studying abroad, he had returned to Bermuda on vacation and participated in the desegregation and human rights marches taking place there. The establishment chased him off the Island. After completing his medical studies in the United States, Dr. Browne returned to Bermuda to work as a resident at the hospital. Apparently he called the hospital racist and the hospital authorities did not allow him to return and work on the Island. He had set up a practice in California and only recently been allowed to return. Upon his return, he had set up a medical practice and become involved in politics. He informed me that he and his running mate ran against the immigration minister. Dr. Browne said the minister could either grant me a work permit to avoid controversy or refuse to grant it because of my association with Dr. Browne. He suggested it might be wiser for me to find another physician to hold my work permit.

After I left Dr. Browne's office I called Dr. Miles, an ear, nose and throat surgeon, to seek his opinion as to which physician should hold my work permit. Dr. Miles could not hold it as he was not Bermudian, but his advice had been very valuable to me in the past. Before I told Dr. Miles about my meeting with Dr Browne, he said he had been thinking about me. Dr. Miles said he had had dinner with Dr. Lightbourn two days earlier and the latter had indicated a desire to hold my work permit. Dr. Miles suggested I call Dr. Lightbourn.

Dr. Lightbourn was an internal medicine specialist in his early sixties. Although he referred many patients to me and we greeted each other when we met, I did not know him well. He was a very quiet man whom I knew to be a Christian. I also knew that he had been chief of staff at the hospital for a few years and had had difficulty with the establishment because he was an outsider.

I met Dr. Lightbourn in his office. Dr. Lightbourn, who was a staff physician at the hospital and ran the indigenous clinic, said that the patients he referred to me were happy with the treatment they received and that he would like to see me remain on the Island and continue seeing his patients. Thus he would be glad to hold my work permit. Other than the fact that I would continue to see his patients, Dr. Lightbourn gave no indication that he had any incentive for holding my work permit. I would not have to work from his office and could run my practice independent of his. My meeting with Dr. Lightbourn lasted less than five minutes and ended with his saying he would write a letter to the immigration ministry at once indicating that he would hold my work permit.

CHAPTER TWENTY-FOUR

A Review of the Orthopaedic Division

On July 15th, 1997, Mrs. Anderson, the executive director of the hospital, sent me a letter stating that my hospital privileges had been extended to February 25th, 1998. I forwarded the letter to Mr. Kasson, my attorney, who became optimistic and thought my problems with the hospital were over. Mr. Kasson said he would write a letter to the Medical Insurance Society to settle the legal costs in connection with the case and close the file. I was less optimistic. I felt that the renewal of my privileges was only a reprieve in my ongoing fight with Dr. Cooperson and his gang. I was operating too much for the liking of Drs. Cooperson and Fascioni, and I knew that sooner or later they would come up with something to hinder my work. My pessimism proved justified when I received a letter from Dr. Jameson, dated September 2nd, advising me that:

> " Dr. C.E. Brookson [from Canada]… has been invited to conduct a review of the Orthopaedic Division of the Department of Surgery…
>
> The Chief of Staff respectfully requests that you attend an interview by Dr. Brookson on matters related to the practice of Orthopaedic Surgery at the King Edward Memorial Hospital. Dr. Brookson will be in Bermuda from September 28th for one week. It will be appreciated if you could be available for a 15 minute period during his visit…"

At 9:30 a.m., on September 30th, I was interviewed by Dr. Brookson. The interview, which was general and unfocused, lasted thirty minutes.

On November 19th, I picked up the Brookson report from my pigeonhole at the hospital. It was divided into three parts. The first part consisted of interviews, entirely about me, that Dr. Brookson was said to have had with doctors and nurses at the hospital. In the second part he reviewed the hospital charts of thirteen patients and discussed their treatment at length. Twelve of the patients were mine. Concerning the thirteenth, a patient of Dr. Chalvin, Dr. Brookson wrote: "Operative procedure was difficult to assess and specific comments cannot be made." He did not review any patients of Drs. Cooperson, Fascioni or Trouts, all of whom had been students of his.

The third part, titled "Recommendations," was devoted solely to me. Under the heading "Dr. Bah," Dr. Brookson wrote:

> " The postgraduate training outlined by Dr. Bah appears adequate and his selection of equipment is likewise appropriate…The main areas of concern relate to his clinical judgment…

> Dr. Bah should refrain from performing elective spinal surgical procedures as he is operating in an isolated environment… His reappointment to the Subdivision of Orthopaedic Surgery should be seriously questioned as he appears to have difficulty in handling trauma, no doubt partially due to his training in spine surgery as well as the type of his Orthopaedic practice prior to coming to Bermuda…"

After reading the Brookson report I realized that I had been completely misled by Drs. Jameson and Brookson. Dr. Jameson had misled me because, at our meeting of April 22nd, he had told me that somebody from outside would be coming to assess "the orthopaedic surgeons," and in his letter of September 2nd he had written that Dr. Brookson had been invited to "conduct a review of the Orthopaedic Division," whereas the review centred solely on me. Dr. Brookson had misled me because at the beginning of our interview he said he would be "looking at the orthopaedics division as a whole." He also discussed twelve of my patients in his report without seeking my opinion as to my treatment of them. Nine of the twelve had spine pathologies, yet Dr. Brookson had told me during the interview that he was not a "spine surgeon."

I hoped that Dr. Brookson would be impartial. However, because my previous dealings with the hospital had been anything but fair, I had brought a hidden tape recorder to the interview. The following is an excerpt from our conversation:

> "**Dr. Brookson**: I was asked to come here to look at the division as a whole and just make some observations and comments. I am trying to make my way through to see what is going on and what you and the group…and

how are things going. You trained in Montreal, did you?

Dr. Bah: Yes, I did.

Dr. Brookson: U of M?

Dr. Bah: Yes, Université de Montréal.

Dr. Brookson: How come you did end up? [sic] down here, just curious?

Dr. Bah: I knew Dr. Trouts, who did a three-months rotation with us at the U of M.

Dr. Brookson: Dr. L. [the program chief at the university where Drs. Trouts, Cooperson and Fascioni trained and where Dr. Brookson was a professor] used to send people rotating through the University of Montreal.

Dr. Bah: Yes.

Dr. Brookson: I am trying to figure out the connection. I talked to [Dr. Trouts] yesterday.

Dr. Bah: I had been practising in Montreal for a few years and Dr. Trouts and I had not kept in touch. I think the year was 1994 when Dr. Trouts came to Montreal and asked me to come and work with him in Bermuda. Initially, I thought that the idea was a funny one. I was not too keen about moving to Bermuda, a very small place. I was doing a lot of spinal cases in Montreal and was very happy. Finally after two years of giving it a thought, I decided to come to Bermuda and give it a try.

Dr. Brookson: Where were you working in Montreal?

Dr. Bah: I was working in C.S. in Laval.

Dr. Brookson: So how are you enjoying it down here? It is working out? It is a very small place.

Dr. Bah: Yes, it is a very small place but I like my patients, I like the work I do.

Dr. Brookson: You do primarily spine or do you do other things like trauma?

Dr. Bah: Primarily spine and trauma.

Dr. Brookson: Is there a lot of spine stuff here?

Dr. Bah: Yes, but not to the same extent as in Montreal, but enough.

Dr. Brookson: Do you like the work?

Dr. Bah: Yes.

Dr. Brookson: I am just tying to sort out all of this, because I cannot understand, as I was saying yesterday, people just seem to pop out here and there. There are three groups, Jos. [Dr. Fascioni's first name; Dr. Brookson called Drs. Fascioni and Trouts by their first names because he had been their professor] and Cooperson, you and [Dr. Trouts' first name], Chalvin who is sort of on his own. There does not seem much to be many interactions [sic] between the groups.

Dr Bah: That is true.

Dr. Brookson: Is there a reason? To me it seems to be a little bit counter-productive in a place this small.

Dr. Bah: Physicians here work in small groups or solo... It is not only related to the division of orthopaedics but most other practitioners on the Island work in small groups.

Dr. Brookson: I am sure it is the same... I find it very strange to look at from the outside. There is no control over who is appointed to the division of orthopaedics. It seems that you can bring people you want to, all you need is the approval of immigration, something like that. They [immigration] seem to have a lot of power. So how do you get along here? Do you do a lot of spine surgery? It is working out for you? Are you able to get the instruments? *I am not a spine surgeon.* I have done trauma fracture and tumour. [emphasis mine]

Dr. Bah: I bought many of the instruments I use, because the hospital had little instruments for spine surgery...

Dr. Brookson: Are they pretty good at getting stuff for you?

Dr. Bah: The head operating room nurse is very good at getting me the implants...

Dr. Brookson: It is a little hard for me to get a handle on what is... I do not do a lot of spine, I have done a number of instrumentations for tumour and trauma and so on. Are your results reasonable?

Dr. Bah: It is very reasonable, which is very encouraging, because in Bermuda there is no workmen's compensation and Bermudians are very hard working. When my patients come to see me with their pain, they have usually seen other physicians on the Island and been to the United States for a second opinion. So they are usually in a lot of pain when they come to see me, and most of them do well after the surgery. Almost all of my patients get back to work three to four months after their operation...

Dr. Brookson: Where would your referrals come from? I just moved to Prince Edward Island and most of my referrals come from the GP.

Dr Bah: Initially most of my referrals came from the GP and the sport medicine doctors, but after a while patients hear form other patients and they come to see me on their own…

Dr. Brookson: Now the other thing I found out was that they [Drs. Cooperson and Fascioni] bring in another spine surgeon, Dr. White?

Dr Bah: Yes, Dr. White.

Dr. Brookson: Bink White? Does he operate down here? Does he come in? I cannot figure out here. I have a population of sixty thousand, you add in a few tourists, maybe you have a population of seventy to eighty thousand, you have five orthopaedic guys and they bring in another to do spinal fusion. I find it remarkable!

Dr Bah: Most of the spine patients I operate on now are patients who used to travel abroad to have their surgery… I operated on patients who suffered for ten to fifteen years without having had surgery. Currently I am operating on sixty percent of the spinal cases on the Island, twenty percent of the spine patients still prefer to go abroad and Dr. Cooperson's group operate on the rest.

Dr. Brookson: I find it hard to understand that you have five surgeons each in their niche. Do you think that it is ever going to work? To me, that would be the ideal scenario.

Dr. Bah: I do not know. When I first came here, I suggested that we have a journal club and grand round meetings as long as these meetings were held for the purpose of interacting and learning from each other. I did not feel welcome and felt that the environment vas very hostile…

Dr. Brookson: Everybody has complications. The guy who says he does not have complications is either not doing surgery or not telling the truth. One of the things I notice here is nobody in surgery seems to address the problem that you raised, there does not seem to be any forum for morbidity rounds. It is just not there, not only in orthopaedics but everybody. I found that rather strange… Do you think you are here for life?

Dr. Bah: No, I hope not. I do not think so.

Dr. Brookson: If you want to change things, how would you change it? From what I see you have three groups at each other's throat, not terribly friendly.

Dr. Bah: Not terribly friendly.

Dr Brookson: When you did come came here, you said you felt unwelcome. Who?… Did they give you a hard time or what?

Dr Bah: They sent me a letter to sign and asked me to give them consent to interview me on four cases I had operated.

Dr. Brookson: Who was interviewing you?

Dr. Bah: Dr. Cooperson, Dr Chalvin and Dr E.T.

Dr. Brookson: Oh, I see.

Dr. Brookson: So are you comfortable working under these circumstances? I find it tough, I would not want to work here.

Dr. Bah: Yes, I find it hard. I find it very stressful and counterproductive. I like my patients and think I am doing a benefit to the patients who for the most part used to travel abroad. The only reason why the other group does not want me here is for economic reasons.

Dr. Brookson: There seems to be a lot of politics… So, these cases, what were they? Were they all spinal fusion?

Dr. Bah: No, they were not spine cases at all.

Dr Brookson: What were they? I do not want to hear the whole thing.

Dr. Bah: The second patient was involved in a road traffic accident. The third patient was a young man with a fracture of the forearm who they told me I did not produce the medical report on time…

Dr. Brookson: I guess we…I have to sort out what is going on. I think the biggest problem here is that everybody does not get along very well. There seems to be a lot of political intrigue. So you think a lot is driven by economical reasons?

Dr. Bah: Yes, it is driven by economical reasons…

Dr Brookson: I get the feeling that money is a big issue in this part of the world too. So how long do you think that you are staying?

Dr. Bah: I believe in God. I came here for a purpose that I do not know. I will leave when God wants me to leave. I won't be here.

Dr. Brookson: It is hard to know.

Dr. Bah: My wife does not like it here any more. Since I came here, I like Canada. I think it is a beautiful country.

Dr. Brookson: I think this [Bermuda] is a very hard place to work. Thank you for coming. I appreciate your time. I hope things work out for you.

CHAPTER TWENY-FIVE

Witnesses

Mr. Kasson, my attorney, thought the Brookson report portrayed me as unskilled and incompetent, and he could not imagine that the King Edward VII Memorial Hospital and an eminent professor like Dr. Brookson could be wrong. I went over the cases reviewed in the report one by one and tried to show him that Dr. Brookson was wrong. I showed him the transcript of our meeting to illustrate how Dr. Brookson had misled me about the purpose of his review. Mr. Kasson gave me the benefit of the doubt. He said we would have to secure the opinion of an orthopaedic specialist of "greater eminence" than Dr. Brookson on each of the cases in the report. He said he would ask the Medical Insurance Society (MIS) to assist me financially in bringing such an eminent doctor to Bermuda.

After I left Mr. Kasson's office, I called Dr. Esses, one of my former professors, who was then working at Baylor University in Houston, to ask him to review the cases. When I described my situation to Dr. Esses, he reacted angrily. He advised me to fight Dr. Cooperson and his group because they wanted me out for financial reasons. Dr. Esses agreed to conduct the review and sent the following letter to Mr. Kasson:

> "It has come to my attention that there is some concern with Dr Bah's competency concerning spinal surgery.
>
> I am very familiar with the quality of surgery carried out by Dr. Bah. I personally supervised Dr. Bah during his fellowship at the University of Toronto.
>
> To the best of my knowledge, there has never been any question about Dr. Bah's competency. It comes, therefore, as a surprise that it has been questioned.

I would be happy to review any cases in which there is some concern about quality issues. I thank you for your attention to this matter."

Mr. Kasson forwarded Dr. Esses' letter to the MIS and we waited to hear whether they would provide financial assistance.

In his report, Dr. Brookson had written: "Dr. Bah feels that he has been treated unfairly, and is considering leaving the Island." I never told Dr. Brookson that I was "considering leaving the Island." The facts are as follows. During our meeting Dr. Brookson said: "I got the feeling that money is a big issue in this part of the world too. So how long do you think that you are staying?" I replied: "I believe in God. I came here for a purpose that I do not know of. I will leave when God wants me to leave. I won't be here." Since he had lied about his conversation with me, I supposed that he also had lied about his conversations with the other professionals. Hence I set out to find someone who would confirm my suspicions and be willing to put it in writing. Dr. Schulte, a white American family physician and head of the hospital's emergency department, was the first professional I approached in this regard. In his report, Dr. Brookson wrote the following with respect to Dr. Schulte:

> "Dr Schmaltz: In general felt that Drs Bah and Trouts had far less skills than their colleagues in handling patients in the Emergency Department."

Dr. Schulte told me he had already dictated a letter refuting the above statement. The letter, dated November 21st, 1997, was addressed to Mrs. Anderson, executive director of the hospital, with copies to the chief of staff and the chief of surgery. It read as follows:

> "On November 18, 1997, I was afforded the first opportunity to review the confidential audit of the Division of Orthopaedic Surgery, which was conducted by Dr. E. Brookson in October of this year.
>
> I wish to express my concern that this report does not accurately reflect the statements, which I made at the time of that interview.
>
> In my discussion with Dr. Brookson, I stated that both Dr. Bah and Dr. Trouts responded to their trauma calls in a timely and appropriate fashion. I told Dr. Brookson that there was a perception that the level of Orthopaedic trauma care which was provided by Drs. Bah and Trouts was not as good as that which was provided by certain other members of the Division of Orthopaedic Surgery [Drs. Cooperson and Fascioni]. I stated that this perception was widely held by nurses and physicians in the

Emergency Department but I specifically qualified this statement by telling Dr. Brookson that I had never assisted or observed Dr. Bah or Dr. Trouts in the Operating Rooms of the King Edward VII Memorial Hospital and therefore did not feel qualified to pass judgment on their surgical skills... I therefore could not state with any degree of certainty whether the "perception" was a "reality."

I find it of interest that a twenty minute interview was condensed into the single statement which was attributed to me in this report and that the auditor did not even take the time to research the proper spelling of my name [misspelt as "Schmaltz"].

I would strongly suggest that if this institution undertakes any future external audits, all interviews should be tape-recorded. That would ensure that a permanent and accurate audio record exists for all statements, which are made."

Drs. Cooperson and Fascioni spread the perception of my lack of competency that Dr. Schulte spoke of in his letter. However, other professionals in the emergency department did not hold that perception. On November 3rd, 1997, Mrs. Richard, head nurse in the emergency department and the orthopaedic clinic and a Christian, gave me a letter of reference for immigration purposes. It read as follows:

"It is a pleasure to supply this reference for Dr. Bah.

I have known him professionally for almost two years through his work in this establishment. He has provided services in our Orthopaedic Clinics and to acute trauma victims in this Emergency unit. He also provides specialist Orthopaedic therapies and surgery to patients suffering with chronic back problems.

Dr Bah is friendly and professional in his approach to his patients, and is very conscientious in seeing that they receive the best possible care. He works well in situations of stress and still manages to keep his sense of humor. He is always immaculate in appearance, honest and reliable with a good sense of integrity.

He has a good relationship with the nursing staff and the doctors in our unit."

I had also asked Edna Simmons, a nurse manager at the hospital and a Christian, to provide me with a letter of reference. Mrs. Simmons wrote:

"I have known Dr. C. Bah and his family for approximately sixteen months. Although Dr. Bah is a member of the staff of the Bermuda Hospitals Board

(K.E.M.H.) as I am, I did not really get to know him well until he began to attend Cobb's Hill Methodist Church, where I am a member.

Within a short period after his first visit to our church, he became a regular attendee, and a very special part of our church family. His friendly and loving manner has earned him the love and respect of all. We are a small congregation, and it did not take us long to recognize his sincerity in his love for us and for Our Lord and Saviour Jesus Christ. On several occasions, he has been a witness as to what faith in the Lord can do.

He participates in the Church activities on a regular basis, and even when asked on short notice he has assumed responsibilities without hesitation.

Dr. Bah and I also have a professional association, Dr. Bah as an Orthopaedic Consultant and Surgeon at the King Edward VII Memorial Hospital, and I as…Health Services Coordinator for the Bermuda Hospitals Board Employee Health Services (with Dr. R. Lightbourn as Employee Health Services Physician). We have referred several employees to Dr. Bah for his expert evaluation of conditions, which have required an Orthopaedic opinion.

We have been satisfied with the advice, treatment and positive results, and have not received comments of dissatisfaction from those employees referred to him.

We have been particularly pleased with Dr. Bah's very timely written responses (and verbal, when necessary) as to the employee's treatment, progress and fitness for work.

I believe that Dr. Bah is a valuable asset to Bermuda in his professional capacity, and as a member of the community."

These two letters and the fact that Dr. Lightbourn, a staff physician, and Dr. Pearson, the police and prison doctor, referred most of their patients to me completely contradict Dr. Schulte's perception. Even though Dr. Schulte's letter was not very complimentary regarding my skills as a surgeon, it was the only testimony I had to refute the Brookson report. Thus I needed to find other professionals willing to invalidate the report.

Dr. Chalvin was the next professional I approached. Dr. Brookson had written the following with regard to Dr. Chalvin:

"Dr. Chalvin is well liked and respected by all, but has expressed concerns with regard to the clinical judgment of Dr. Bah."

I suspected that this statement was incorrect because even in the period

subsequent to the Brookson review Dr. Chalvin and I had a working relationship. Dr. Kingsley, a black Bermudian surgeon, and Dr. Jameson had
hired Dr. Chalvin in 1991. Apparently Drs. Cooperson and Fascioni had
complained bitterly about Dr. Chalvin and his work when he first arrived.
The complaining and harassment had stopped only when Dr. Kingsley, who
was a member of the establishment, told Drs. Cooperson and Fascioni that
Dr. Chalvin had more judgement and skills than the two of them combined. Up until my arrival Drs. Cooperson and Fascioni did not work with
Dr. Chalvin. They began to do so when I arrived on the scene and became
their number one enemy (Dr. Bernis, a chiropractor, and Dr. Reynolds,
a sports medicine specialist, were numbers two and three). For my first
six months on the Island, Dr. Chalvin and I did not have a working relationship. Then, on June 27th, 1996, I received three simultaneous pages,
one from the head radiology technician, a white Bermudian who had never
spoken to me before, one from the radiologist and one from Dr. Chalvin.
They all wanted me to see a patient of Dr. Chalvin's, a twenty-four-year-old
man with a neck fracture who had been involved in a motorcycle accident
two months before. Dr. Chalvin had followed the recommendation of Dr.
Bink White, a visiting surgeon from Boston, and treated the patient with a
halo vest. When the patient presented for follow-up at six weeks, the x-rays
showed that his head was dangling in front of his lower neck and body.
The two body parts were held together only by the spinal cord and some
ligaments. It was fortunate that the patient did not die or become paralyzed.
It took Dr. Morais, who was visiting at the time, and me more than four
hours of gruelling surgery to put the patient's neck and body together. It
was fortunate for me as well as for the patient that the surgery was a success,
for I would have been blamed for the patient's misfortune and Drs. Chalvin
and White would have been exonerated.

After that, Dr. Chalvin referred all of his complicated emergency spine
cases to me and kept the elective (non-urgent) spine cases for himself and
Dr. White. He came to the operating room on two occasions to observe me
operating (assisted by the residents) on patients with broken backs. Then he
decided that he would no longer refer such patients to me, but would operate on them himself (Dr. Chalvin was a very good trauma surgeon, but had
no training in spine surgery). On October 5th, 1997, he called and asked

my opinion about a patient with a broken neck on whom he was about to operate. I told him I was at church, but would go to the hospital as soon as the service was over. When I got there he had already installed a halo on the patient's head and positioned the patient on the operating table and was ready to operate. For the patient's sake, I offered to help with the surgery. Dr. Chalvin and I were scrubbing up when a nurse said the anaesthetist needed us in the operating room. We went in and found Dr. McLean, the anaesthetist, holding the patient's head in his hands. Dr. MacLean calmly told us we had to reposition the patient on the table. The problem was that the halo pin, which had not been properly positioned, had come out and the patient's head and broken neck had fallen out of the halo and off the operating table. I installed the halo properly and repositioned the patient. For obvious reasons, I also performed the surgery. Afterwards, Dr. Chalvin thanked me for performing the whole operation and suggested that he bill for it as the surgeon and I bill a quarter of the surgical fee as an assistant. I told him not to put my name in the chart, neither as a surgeon nor as an assistant, because I did not know if the patient would be able to move his limbs when he woke up. I preferred not to make any money and not be involved in a lawsuit. Fortunately the patient did not wake up paralyzed. I was certain that Dr. Chalvin would be grateful to me for this case and similar ones that I bailed him out of and would act as a witness for me concerning the Brookson report.

On Thursday, October 23rd, I called Dr. Chalvin and asked if he had read the Brookson report. He replied that he had read it and disagreed entirely with what it said about him. He told me he was about to write a note to me indicating that the report did not reflect his conversation with Dr. Brookson. I asked him to please have his secretary type the note he was about to write. He agreed to do so and said he would put the note in my hospital pigeonhole over the weekend.

On Monday, I called Dr. Chalvin because I had not found the note in my pigeonhole. He said he had changed his mind about writing it because he had to "please everybody." I did not insist because I knew Dr. Chalvin's situation and his objective in Bermuda. His situation was that Dr. Jameson had hired him and he could not do anything that might upset Dr. Jameson. His objective in Bermuda was to make enough money to return to India and build a hospital, and he would not do anything that might jeopardize this goal.

Mrs. Santini, the head operating room nurse, was the next person I spoke to, in the hope that she would act as a witness for me. In his report Dr. Brookson wrote the following with regard to the operating room nurses:

> "Operating Room Nurses: The ongoing conflict between surgeons produces a poor atmosphere in the operating room. ...Nurses verbalized a concern that Drs. Bah and Trouts had considerable difficulty in planning an organized approach to trauma cases and were not familiar with the equipment or the usage of same... The feeling was that Drs. Cooperson and Fascioni have good surgical skills, are competent, quite familiar with the available equipment and show good management skills in both elective and traumatic situations."

I could not understand how nurses, whose training differed from mine, could assess my judgement and skill as a surgeon. However, I had no choice, but to deal with these erroneous statements because Dr. Brookson had relied on them to reach a conclusion about my competence.

On October 24th, I met with Mrs. Santini in her office. She said she had been off the Island when Dr. Brookson visited, but before leaving had instructed her nurses not to make remarks or pass judgement beyond their competency level when they met with him. Mrs. Santini said she learned, upon her return, that Drs. Jameson and Cooperson had chosen three nurses who did not work with me to be interviewed by Dr. Brookson. Two of these, both English nurses, worked at the front desk in the operating room and never scrubbed with me. The third, a white American nurse, did not even work in the operating room, but nursed on the ward. Mrs. Santini said that Drs. Jameson and Cooperson had purposely excluded all the nurses who usually worked with me and that she had already lodged a protest with them about their selection of nurses to be interviewed by Dr. Brookson. She said she disagreed with the Brookson report concerning the statement attributed to her nurses. "You should sue them [Drs. Cooperson, Jameson and Brookson]," she advised. I replied that I might have to do that one day. I asked Mrs. Santini if she would be a witness for me in the event the case went to court. She stuttered and told me she would not know what to say in court and would stutter. I assured her it was unlikely the case would go to court. I showed her Dr. Schulte's letter and asked her to put in writing what she had just told me about her disagreement with the selection of operating room nurses to meet with Dr. Brookson. She shook her head and said, "No, no, no."

I wrote to Mrs. Santini begging her to provide me with a written testimonial. She never acknowledged my letter and rushed away whenever she saw me. Even when I phoned her on completely unrelated matters she failed to return my calls.

Next, I asked Mrs. Basely, the nurse supervisor of the orthopaedic clinic, to write a letter refuting statements attributed to her. In his report, Dr. Brookson wrote the following with regard to Mrs. Basely:

> "Concern was expressed that Dr. Bah not infrequently had a confrontational approach towards the Head Nurse with regards to patient management, frequently would not answer his pager and, at times appeared indifferent to postoperative complications, such as infections following spinal instrumentation."

I never would have asked Mrs. Basely, a white Bermudian, to write a letter on my behalf had she not approached me first. After all, she had a close relationship with Dr. Cooperson and none with me. One piece of advice Dr. Trouts had given me when I arrived in Bermuda concerned Mrs. Basely. He warned me to get along with her or she might make my life miserable. I was also told that she "kisses the ground that Dr. Cooperson walks on." I try to treat all people the same, whether they are old or young, rich or poor, celebrated or ordinary. In fact, I rarely ask people what they do for a living. I ask my patients what they do for a living only when I suspect that their pain is related to their work. My first meeting with Mrs. Basely was disastrous because I did not give her the special treatment she thought she deserved. She struck me as overly proud. She declared that she had been running the orthopaedic clinic for twenty-three years and had taught Dr. Cooperson how to do casts. Everything would be fine, she declared, if I listened to her. I replied that I had learned to do casts as an orthopaedic resident. Mrs. Basely did not like my response and our relations remained cool. Fortunately for me, and to the joy of the clinic staff, Mrs. Basely was away from work, for all sorts of reasons, eight months of the year. After a while she came to me as a patient and referred her family members to me, but even then I would not have asked her to write a letter on my behalf had she not spoken to me about the Brookson report and expressed her disagreement with it. Two days after reading the report she approached me and told me she was unhappy about the statement attributed to her, saying it did not come close to what she had discussed with Dr. Brookson during their meeting. She said she was upset with Drs. Cooperson and Fascioni for having brought in a friend to produce the report. Mrs. Basely informed me that Dr. Cooperson had picked up Dr. Brookson at the airport and served as his host. (I also learned that Dr. Fascioni had hosted a dinner for Dr. Brookson at his home.) A few days later, I would find a memo confirming what Mrs. Basely had told me. The memo, which Dr. Brookson had inadvertently left in the chart of one my patients, was from Dr. Cooperson and it instructed Dr. Brookson where and with whom he was to have lunch.

After our conversation I asked Mrs. Basely to write a letter to the effect that Dr. Brookson, in his report, had misrepresented her comments during their meeting. Like Mrs. Santini, Mrs. Basely subsequently avoided me the rare times she came to the clinic and went the other way when she saw me.

Since Dr. Chalvin, Mrs. Santini and Mrs. Basely were unwilling to act as witnesses on my behalf, Dr. Esses was my only hope.

CHAPTER TWENTY-SIX

A Sheep Among Wolves

One day in a private conversation a well-known judge on the Island said to me, "You are a threat to Dr. Cooperson and his group." You have taken away their patients and you have alienated Dr. Jameson, a powerful enemy." I told the judge that it was not my intention to alienate anybody when I arrived, but with time I realized that I could not work with Dr. Cooperson and his group because we stood for completely different things. The judge, who knew that I read the Bible, said, "I realize that, but surely you know this verse from the Bible: '**Behold, I send you forth as sheep in the midst of wolves: be ye therefore wise as serpents, and harmless as doves**' [Matthew 10:16]. You must remember this verse in your dealings with them."

On Wednesday, December 3rd, 1997, Dr. Jameson called and asked me to meet him in his office two days later. On Friday I went to his office, once again armed with my hidden tape recorder. This time I remembered the judge's advice and instead of arguing with Dr. Jameson I acted like a sheep among wolves and wise as serpents. Here is a transcript of our conversation:

Dr. Jameson: Thank you for coming…the Brookson report, which I gave you a copy…You are familiar with it?

Dr. Bah: Yes.

Dr. Jameson: The credentials committee had a first meeting on the subject and… I think this report is going to affect you in a serious way. I do not know what the outcome is going to be but it is up to the medical staff and the board. I am just saying that it is going to affect you. The recommendation that they want to introduce is to stop elective spinal surgery now. They are of the opinion that your appointment should not be renewed come February. So…what seems to be coming down the pipe when the medical staff and the board reach their conclusion…I think that very likely it will get tough. I just want you to be aware of it from my point if view. From your point of view, I think unfortunately it is not good to have a public show down, Bermuda being a very small, *Bermuda is a very small place for this to get out.* I do not know if you have a comment? [emphasis mine]

Dr. Bah: You are saying, "show down." I do not understand.

Dr. Jameson: What I am referring to is what is likely to happen. You are a Doctor and I am a Doctor, we are doctors and I think I should talk to you simply. *The point I [am] making is that you could adopt a legal point of view and try to fight the regulation, by law, by going to court, appeal to the governor, do all these thing[s] and be a public spectacle which is not going to enhance your reputation at the end.* …your reputation will linger with you wherever you go and this will always follow you in public. [emphasis mine]

Dr. Bah: This report will always follow me anyway. What you mean if I go?

Dr. Jameson: If you make a public objection to the rule it will become public, appeal to the governor and so on like the Coxall's affair.[1] It becomes public and goes on and on and on and on and on.

Dr. Bah: So you mean a detriment to my reputation?

Dr. Jameson: Coxall will always be asked, what problem did you have in Bermuda? Do you know what I mean? I am trying to be…fair to warn you about what is coming down. The medical staff will do the same thing as the credentials committee and the board will do the same. This report if it gets public it would not be good to your reputation no matter how you try to defend it. You might just say well, fine I will decide to leave. You never told me this, but along the way, there were statements made by others that you are going to leave Bermuda. I do not know if that is true, yes or not, is that true?

Dr. Bah: It is not true.

Dr Jameson: It is not true! It is not true! There has been talk about you saying that you! About your appointment, you have privileges up to February 1998 and the recommendation is that they are not to be renewed at all. In the meantime your elective spinal surgery should be stopped.

Dr Bah: From now?

Dr Jameson: From now.

Dr Bah: Dr. Brookson's recommendation was that elective spine surgery should not be done at the hospital anymore. Will that recommendation be applied to me only or to everybody?

Dr. Jameson: That is something that is still not clear. The medical staff committee have to make that clear when it meet.

Dr. Bah: My privileges are due to expire in February. Will I receive a letter notifying me of these changes?

Dr. Jameson: I cannot, I cannot at this point, I cannot say that until the board meet.

Dr. Bah: Will this recommendation be in effect when I come back to the Island in January 98?

Dr. Jameson: What I will do is to try to get the medical staff committee to meet next week and to ask for a special meeting of the board since none is scheduled until January 98. But because of the importance of this, they should have a special meeting.

Dr. Bah: I just want to know what is my privileges status from now until February 98.

Dr. Jameson: The recommendation is not final... It may be likely that the board could have a final say before January 98.

Dr. Bah: I am just asking because I want to know what to tell my patients. Suppose I see a patient that need surgery could I book him for elective spinal surgery in January 98?

Dr. Jameson: No I would not do that. No I would not. I would refrain from elective spinal surgery cases at least. That will not be safe for you to do...that should not be considered my advice. That is clear, you should refrain from performing elective spinal surgery. I think as a chief of staff and the chief of surgery can implant that prior to the board.

Dr. Bah: So what you are telling me is that from now on I should not be doing elective spinal surgery?

Dr. Jameson: Yes, that is to be confirmed by the board but I think I have the power to do that.

Dr. Bah: He [Dr. Brookson] in his report talk about trauma. Should I be operating on trauma patients?

Dr. Jameson: It says difficult handling trauma, it says should be seriously questioned. We had difficulty interpreting this. *This is not fair to a person, that leaves you very little to earn income. The best is not to renew your privileges at all...* [emphasis mine]

Dr. Bah: So, I should continue doing only trauma cases?

Dr. Jameson: Yes.

Dr. Bah: Like you said, "between Doctors" it is best not do like the "Coxall affair"?

Dr. Jameson: Yes, Yes.

Dr Bah: I am just saying you gave me an advice?

Dr. Jameson: I gave you an advice if you want to, because this thing would become public to some extent. Some patients are going to ask why are you doing this? They will ask questions, people talk. *Bermuda is very small, it is not going to be the same if you publicly object to it, it is impractical…UBP* [the ruling United Bermuda Party, of which Drs. Jameson and Cooperson were members; Dr. Jameson was hinting that, considering his UBP connections, I could not win a fight against the hospital] and so forth…. You will have patients that will say he treated me fine, he is an excellent doctor. Then others will say, he operated on me and I am still not all right. You are going to have as many patients for you as you have people who are against you. It is a no win situation.

Dr. Bah: I do not agree with the Brookson's report, however if I were to leave the Island this report would follow me wherever I go.

Dr. Jameson: It does say something in favor of you. It says the ability to work in this type of environment is certainly compromised. It does suggest along the way that in a different setup other than Bermuda where you have other spine surgeons around such that you are not required to do trauma you probably could do quite well.

Dr. Bah: …That put me in a very difficult position.

Dr. Jameson: *It does, but it would be worse if it were a big public fight. You can probably get around it in a quiet manner. But if it were a big public issue… it would be worse in my opinion.* [emphasis mine]

Dr. Bah: It is worse for my reputation… You would not have hired me if I was coming to work here and there was a report like this in Montreal?

Dr. Jameson: I do understand.

Dr. Bah: Would you have hired me?

Dr Jameson: I understand it is difficult but…

Dr. Bah: I am in a kind of no win situation.

Dr. Jameson: You are in a kind of no win situation, but I think it is not a favourable situation. I cannot turn this into a favourable situation, but all I am saying is that a judgment and a public fight will make it look worse.

Dr. Bah: I do not know Bermuda. You know Bermuda better than me.

Dr. Jameson: I called you here because I wanted to be fair to you. I do not want to go on and on and on thinking that everything is well. …Knowing that I felt that I should in confidence take you aside and say this is what is happening and you can accordingly. You want to fight. *You can go to your lawyer and say I want to fight with the entire barrel and mussel you can master. It is your right and privileges to fight, but in my view it will be unwise to do that but you do not have to accept my advice. I felt that I owe it to you to give you as much warning as possible what to do. Think it over. Say to yourself what I am going to do what I am going to do. Am I going to enter into war engagement or give up? If you know, it gives you advance warning and I felt, that's why I wanted to. Ok?* [emphasis mine]

Dr. Bah: I just feel it is a no win situation. I did not come here to fight. I came here to treat patients. I spend 12 years of my life in Universities to learn how to treat patients. I came to Bermuda and have this in my file.

Dr. Jameson: Yes, it seems a logical situation statement to me. But I felt as a Chief of Staff, I felt the right thing to do was to tell you in confidence what is transpired and so that you can make your decision. You have to ask yourself what to do to protect yourself from a bad situation getting worse. It is bad situation. The situation is bad. You have to say to yourself what can I do to make the best of bad situation? *I just think that with a bad situation like this, going to public will make it worse* [emphasis mine].

Dr. Bah: You know politics in Bermuda better than I do.

Dr. Jameson: When the board and the medical staff committee meet I will give you a call after the medical staff committee meeting.

Dr. Bah: I am leaving next week and going to Montreal on vacation. I am coming back on January 3, 1998.

Dr. Jameson: You could if you are going back to Montreal and have knowledge of this information in advance…? Is that exact? [Dr. Jameson was suggesting I find a position in Montreal and not return to Bermuda.]

Dr. Bah: Yes.

Dr. Jameson: Yes.

Dr Bah: Ok, thank you.

While Dr. Jameson was trying to persuade me to leave the Island, the other members of Dr. Cooperson's group were spreading a rumour that I was indeed leaving. Mrs. Basely, the nurse supervisor of the orthopaedic clinic, started calling my patients to reschedule them for Dr. Cooperson's clinic.

On December 12th, one of my patients called to ask if I was leaving. I asked where she had got such an idea. The patient said that Dr. Joneson, who had performed an epidural on her earlier that day, had told her. The patient, who was upset with Dr. Joneson, wrote the following letter to the Board:

> "On December 12, I was scheduled to have an epidural at the hospital with Dr. B. Joneson was the anaesthesiologist. I asked her what follows this procedure? I was in recovery during our conversation. At this point, she told me to forget about Dr. Bah and make an appointment to see either Dr. Fascioni or Dr. Cooperson and not to bother with Dr. Bah as he was leaving. Later the same day I spoke with Dr Bah and asked him to confirm what Dr. Joneson had told me. He assured me he was not leaving.
>
> I believe Dr. Joneson acted in a very unprofessional manner, as Dr. Bah was my choice of surgeon.
>
> In all my visits following the operation, Dr. Bah has been completely honest and professional as would be expected from a person of his qualifications, and if ever I needed a specialist again I would not hesitate to select Dr. Bah."

I wrote a letter to Dr. Joneson asking her to wait until the Board officially informed me of the decision to revoke my privileges before telling my patients that I was leaving. I put the letter in her hospital pigeonhole. Two days later I found a bottle of white powder in my pigeonhole. The label indicated that the powder was to be used to remove dark spots from the skin. Until then I had naively been under the impression that I was not wanted at the King Edward VII Memorial Hospital because my presence affected the earnings of the other surgeons and that the colour of my skin was not an issue. Now I realized that I had been wrong.

---

[1] Mr. Coxall was a British police officer who spent three years in Bermuda with a mandate to fight crime, reorganize the police force and find a suitable Bermudian to replace him. At the end of his mandate he was praised for his work only to be criticized later because the police had discovered that a government minister had some relations with drug dealers. One day the local newspaper reported that Mr. Coxall's contract might be extended, and the next day, after a meeting with the immigration minister, it reported that if Mr. Coxall did not leave the minister would have to resign. Mr. Coxall finally left the Island.

CHAPTER TWENY-SEVEN

At the Discretion of the Minister

According to Bermudian immigration law, I had to seek a formal release from Dr. Trouts before obtaining alternative employment with Dr. Lightbourn. Mr. Dunkin, my new attorney, who had taken over the case from his associate, Mr. Traut, wrote to Dr. Trouts asking for a formal release. When it became evident that Dr. Trouts was not going to respond, Mr. Dunkin wrote to the immigration minister outlining my relationship with Dr. Trouts and asking the minister to use his discretion in granting me a new work permit.

On December 15th, 1997, Dr. Trouts' attorney wrote to mine objecting to my seeking alternative employment in Bermuda. He threatened to take me to court in the event that I stayed in Bermuda. The letter stated:

> "The clause [the non-competition clause] is specifically limited to preventing actions which would be in direct competition with the company and Dr. Trouts and no move. Accordingly, the clause is specifically structured to provide reasonable protection to Dr Trouts…
>
> Lastly, we note that Dr. Bah has only been on the Island for a short period of time and a restriction preventing him from practicing in Bermuda would not prevent him from returning to his native Canada and stepping back into the practice which he left in order to do this short stint in Bermuda."

Towards the middle of December my family and I flew to Montreal for a much-needed vacation and I left Mr. Dunkin to deal with immigration and with Dr. Trouts and his attorney. We kept in touch by phone on the little progress he was making with immigration. I did not know if I would be allowed back in Bermuda to work, or if I would be permitted only to collect my belongings. On December 19th, Mr. Dunkin called the immigration minister because he had not made any progress with the immigration officers. Finally, on December 21st, the minister granted my family and me a landing permit. The permit allowed us to return to Bermuda to reside and allowed me to "seek employment in Bermuda…but not to work."

On January 3rd, we returned to Bermuda. Two days later an acquaintance called from Montreal to tell me that an ice storm had hit the city. He said I was lucky to be in Bermuda. I told him I preferred not to address his comments as to who was the luckier of the two of us.

I set up my practice with Dr. Browne, a family physician and politician. His clinic, which was available to me at all times, consisted of one office, three examining rooms and a reception area. (In Dr. Trouts' two-bedroom cottage, I had had the use of only one room, which served as both office and examining room.) Dr. Browne and I agreed that I would pay him $800 in rent (I had been paying Dr. Trouts $2,200 for the use of one room one afternoon a week). Three days after I moved into Dr. Browne's building, he asked me to sign a one-page contract spelling out the conditions and our working relationship. Everything in the contract was as he and I had discussed and agreed to.

I had no difficulty finding a secretary, as all the personnel working in Dr. Trouts' clinic were eager to leave and come to me. I chose one secretary, the only one with medical training.

By the second week of January I had finished setting up my office and was ready to work, but I could not do so since my application for a work permit was still under consideration by the immigration minister. Meanwhile I was allowed to see my post-operative patients only after I submitted a list of the patients to my attorney, who then forwarded it to the minister for approval. This process was repeated every week while I waited for my work permit. Even more planning was required for me to see those patients who were on the ward. On January 21st, my attorney sent the minister the following letter with regard to one of those patients:

> "We have been advised that in August of 1997 our client performed a cervical fusion for a fracture of the neck upon a patient by the name of Mr. T.Y. The patient was subsequently transferred to L. Rehabilitation Center in Toronto where he received physiotherapy. In early December, the patient was transferred back to the King Edward VII Memorial Hospital.
>
> Since 9th January 1998, both the Resident and the Chief of Surgery, Dr.

Berger, have…repeatedly requested that our client see Mr. T.Y. because he has not been seen by any other Doctor for follow-up treatment. Our client advised both of the above named doctors of his immigration status and suggested that Dr. Trouts conduct the follow-up treatment. Dr. Trouts has refused to see this patient.

Mr. T.Y. does not have a family physician. In the premises [sic], we request that Dr. Bah be permitted to perform follow-up examinations upon this patient."

The patient, Mr. T.Y., a man in his sixties, had fallen from a ladder at work and presented with a broken neck and complete paralysis. Dr. Chalvin had seen the patient first and referred him to me for surgery. I performed surgery on Mr. T.Y.'s neck, which improved his neurological function to the extent that he was able to eat by himself and move his legs. He was subsequently transferred to Toronto for rehabilitation. Upon his return to Bermuda, Mr. T.Y. was admitted to the hospital until his family found suitable accommodation for him. Dr. Chalvin would not see him for follow-up. Drs. Cooperson and Fascioni, who were eager to take over my practice, would not see him. Dr. Trouts, who left my name posted on his office building months after I had left in the hope of attracting my patients, refused to see him. Besides his paralysis, Mr. T.Y.'s other liability was that he had no insurance, which probably explained why these doctors refused to see him. He did not have medical insurance because his employer of seventeen years had deducted money from his paycheque in order to pay the insurance company, but had kept the money. Mr. T.Y. could do nothing about this. After much negotiation and many letters the immigration ministry finally allowed me to follow up on Mr. T.Y.

When the minister granted me permission to see my patients, one of the major insurance companies, Bermuda Front Street Insurance Company (BFSIC), refused to pay me for treating its clients. Mr. Dunkin had to write to the immigration ministry requesting that the minister notify the BFSIC that I had been granted permission to conduct post-operative examinations on my patients. In the end, Mr. Dunkin's acting on my behalf, to ensure that I would be able to see my patients, cost more than I made for doing so (he billed me $300 an hour). However, I never doubted that it was worth it.

On January 26th, Mr. Dunkin phoned me, as he had done almost every day for three weeks. I knew by the tone of his voice that something had happened. First he asked me if I was prepared to pay his legal fees upon receipt. I answered yes. Then he said he had "hit a dead end" as there had been a change of heart in the ministry with regard to my case – "some intervention by the hospital." He said he would fax me a memo illustrating what he meant by change of heart in the ministry. The memo summarized a conversation between Mr. Dunkin and Mr. Painter, the Acting Chief Immigration Officer:

> "Mr. Painter said the Minister couldn't make a decision on the transfer of Dr. Bah's work permit to Dr. Lightbourn until the issues surrounding Dr. Bah's privileges at the King Edward VII Memorial Hospital have been resolved...

> The Medical Society has indicated that on the 2nd February, Dr. Bah's privileges at the King Edward VII Memorial Hospital will not be renewed. If the privileges are not renewed Dr. Bah cannot be given permission to work in Bermuda.

> Mr. Painter indicated that Dr. Bah should concentrate on resolving the problem of his privileges at the hospital after which he would be in a better position to secure the transfer of his work permit."

Mr. Dunkin sent me an invoice for more than $6,000, which I paid upon receipt.

In my conversation with Dr. Jameson on December 5th, 1997, he had said, "Bermuda is very small, it is not going to be the same if you publicly object to it, it is impractical...UBP and so forth..." At the time I did not know what he meant by "Bermuda is very small... UBP." Now I knew exactly what he meant. He was threatening to use his political influence to fight me in the event I stayed in Bermuda. I was beginning to understand the relations between the people in power at the hospital and the political apparatus in Bermuda.

It was late in the afternoon when I finished speaking with Mr. Dunkin. I immediately went to see Dr. Browne. I didn't need to inform him of the minister's decision, as he was already aware of it. I told him that although I had answered "yes" when he asked me if I was a fighter, obviously I hadn't fully understood his warning when he said that Bermuda is known as the "Island of the Devils." I told Dr. Browne I was upset that the minister, Mr. Ernest, a black Bermudian, had reneged on his promise. (A few weeks earlier a nurse at the hospital had discreetly approached me and said that her husband, the immigration minister, had a message for me. She didn't know what the message was about, but repeated a conversation she and her husband had had about me. He asked if I was pleasant and she answered that I was. Then he said to tell me "not to worry, everything will be all right.") I asked Dr. Browne why the minister had changed his mind. In response he related an anecdote. He said his aunt, who was a member of the United Bermuda Party (UBP) and a government minister, would say to him, "You cannot rely on these people's words. You have to get something in writing from them." Dr. Browne said he would speak to the minister and the prime minister and ask them not to intervene in the dispute at the hospital. A few days later, he told me they had both agreed not to intervene, but the minister said he would grant me a work permit only when I had won back my hospital privileges.

CHAPTER TWENY-EIGHT

The Advocate!

When I met Dr. Jameson on December 5th, 1997, he told me I could no longer treat patients with spine problems and he would convene an urgent meeting of the Board to ensure that I would be barred from treating trauma patients as well.

On Friday, January 8th, 1998, Dr. Jameson called and advised me to pick up a letter from my hospital pigeonhole. The letter, dated January 7th, was from Mrs. Anderson, the executive director of the hospital. It stated:

> "On behalf of the Bermuda Hospital Board, I must advise you that your status as a member of the Active Staff of the King Edward VII Memorial Hospital, which expires on February 25th, will not be renewed.
>
> The Board has also accepted the recommendation...of immediate withdrawal of privileges for elective spinal surgeries and the treatment of new trauma cases, following the in-depth consideration of the [Brookson's] report...
>
> Should you need assistance in winding down your practice in the hospital, please do not hesitate to notify Dr. C. Jameson. On behalf of the Board, I extend best wishes to you for the future."

Dr. Jameson called later that afternoon to make sure I had received the letter. He asked me what my plans were and if I had thought further about our conversation in December when he had advised me to leave the Island. I told him I would discuss the contents of Mrs. Anderson's letter with my attorney. Dr. Jameson was not pleased with my answer.

I consulted with Mr. Kasson, the attorney handling the hospital case for me, who responded as follows to Mrs. Anderson's letter:

> "Please be advised that Dr. Bah does not accept that the criticism of his skill

and judgment as an Orthopaedic surgeon by Dr. Brookson was justified. In our client's opinion, Dr. Brookson was not qualified to express the opinions about our client that were expressed in the External Review…

Our client feels that an independent evaluation of his cases will completely acquit him of the charges made against him by those who have made complaints about him and show that the External Review of Dr. Brookson ought not to be relied upon as a basis to exclude Dr. Bah from membership of the active medical staff of the hospital.

We would be grateful, therefore, if the Board would indicate that it is prepared to defer judgment in this matter until such an independent review can be conducted…"

On January 26th Mrs. Anderson replied as follows:

We certainly do not accept the very serious allegations, which have been made about Dr. Brookson's competency and qualifications. You have in our opinion done so without stating why you or your client believes these allegations to be true and we call upon you to substantiate these claims. We are certain that Dr. Brookson will be most interested to learn of these allegations and expect that he too, will also call upon you and your client to defend these views…

If it is Dr. Bah's wish to bring to the Board's attention the opinion of another surgeon, that is a matter for you and him…we are not prepared to unduly delay the process, particularly when your client's appointment is due to expire on February 25th, 1998…"

The hospital's regulations state that when the privileges of a staff member are withdrawn,

"The President of the Active Medical Staff shall inform the aggrieved person that he may…appear in person before the Board to explain any matter which he considers relevant to the decisions in question. (2) On appearing before the Board the aggrieved person may instruct legal counsel, or may request the services of the President of the Active Medical Staff in presenting his case."

Neither Dr. Jameson nor Mrs. Anderson informed me of my rights, as they should have done. However, when it became obvious to them that I knew my rights and was going to fight the hospital, Dr. Jameson phoned me and suggested that I have the president of the active medical staff, rather than my attorney, represent me in front of the Board.

A few hours later Dr. V. Jamieson, president of the active medical staff, a white family physician with Bermudian status (married to a Bermudian), called to ask if I would like her to represent me in front of the Board. Since I did not know Dr. Jamieson at all, I declined her offer. Several months later an article on the front page of the newspaper gave me an indication of who Dr. Jamieson, my proposed advocate, was. The article, titled "Women Should Have to Have a Licence to Have a Child," read in part:

> "A former Police medical officer is calling for sex offenders to be castrated as a form of punishment...
>
> [Dr. Jamieson]...claimed that the drastic measures were needed to help solve the problem of children growing up in Bermuda without parenting...
>
> Referring to her experiences as a Police medical officer [Dr. Jamieson] said: "I was struck by the number of prisoners who had not had a significant father in their lives."
>
> Dr. Jamieson was speaking out after a Sandy's man received just 18 months imprisonment after pleading guilty to having unlawful carnal knowledge with a teenage girl.
>
> And statistics released by the Department of Health show that, in the 12 months until April 1998, 27 girls 16 and under become pregnant. In the past four years, more than 100 girls have become pregnant...
>
> [Dr. Jamieson] said... "My other unpopular suggestion is that women should have to have a licence to have a child. You have to have a licence to drive a car and own a dog...
>
> "This licensing procedure could only be instituted if women – or men – had to take some sort of antidote to enable contraception rather than taking a pill to not conceive.
>
> "You and your partner – it would not necessarily require a marriage but you would have to be in a serious relationship – would have to show that you satisfy certain prerequisites before you have a birth permit. Two require-ments for example would be that you are at least 21 and employed..."[1]

A few days after Mr. Kasson and I received Mrs. Anderson's first letter, we received another from her, requesting once again that we explain why we believed Dr. Brookson was not qualified to express an opinion about my competence. We ignored this request and concentrated our efforts on trying to secure her assurance that the hospital would cooperate with the expert we would bring in to review the Brookson report and would provide my patients' charts and x-rays. Mr. Kasson phoned Mrs. Anderson and wrote her several letters, but it was not until February 13th, 2000, eleven days before the deadline she had given us to present our case to the Board, that she assured us that the hospital would cooperate with our expert.

[1] Gareth Finighan, *The Royal Gazette,* Monday, June 7th, 1999, p. 1.

CHAPTER TWENY-NINE

The Review

On Friday, January 9th, 1998, Mr. Kasson faxed me a letter confirming that the Medical Insurance Company (MIS) was prepared to financially assist me in bringing Dr. Esses to Bermuda to evaluate the Brookson report.

I immediately called Dr. Esses in the hope that he would be able to come to Bermuda for the review. I reached him when he was in the middle of office hours so he transferred me to his secretary so that she could make the arrangements. The secretary consulted Dr. Esses' schedule and said he would not be free until late March. She promised to send me his hundred-page curriculum vitae and suggested I speak to Dr. Essex to confirm the date.

I immediately spoke with Mr. Kasson and gave him the date in March when Dr. Esses would be available. Mr. Kasson said that would be too late, as Mrs. Anderson would not extend the deadline of February 24th for us to present our case before the Board. Mr. Kasson suggested I call Dr. Esses again to see if he could possibly travel to Bermuda earlier.

That evening I phoned Dr. Esses at his residence and described the time constraints facing me. Dr. Esses understood, but said he could not cancel his many engagements. He suggested my attorney send him a copy of the Brookson report and copies of my patients' hospital records, office records and x-rays so that he could review them and produce a report. I gathered all the materials he requested and sent them off. My attorney said that even though Dr. Esses would be examining more materials than Dr. Brookson had in conducting his review, the hospital would dismiss his report on the grounds that he had not travelled to Bermuda to produce his report. He said we would have to find an eminent physician who was prepared to conduct the review in Bermuda. But how to find such an eminent person within 11 days?

A name that came to mind was that of Dr. Klein, a spine surgeon and assistant professor of surgery in New York. Dr. Klein and I had met in October 1997 at a spine conference and had exchanged phone numbers. I called Dr. Klein, who was in his late thirties, described my situation and asked if he could come to Bermuda and conduct the review. He said he would speak to his wife and consult his schedule.

The next day Dr. Klein called and said his family had planned a ski trip to Quebec the weekend of Valentine's Day, but he would try to reorganize his schedule. He would also have to cancel a day of consultations and a day of surgery and have a colleague cover for him for few days. Dr. Klein asked me if this was agreeable to me. This was more than agreeable to me.

The following day he phoned to say he had reorganized his schedule and everything was set for his family to travel to Bermuda on Saturday, February 14th. He would be available to do the review on either Monday the 16th or Tuesday the 17th and then fly back to New York on Wednesday the 18th because he was scheduled to operate on Thursday the 19th. I thanked him for his help. "I understand your position," he said, "and hope somebody will come to my defence if I happen to be in a similar situation." Not once during our conversation did Dr. Klein mention how much the trip was going to cost or how much I would have to pay him.

I told Mr. Kasson that Dr. Klein had agreed to travel to Bermuda and do the review for us. He immediately set out to make sure the hospital authorities would provide Dr. Klein with my patients' charts and x-rays. He then set out to get a temporary work permit for Dr. Klein, which he would need in order to conduct the review.

When all the paper work for immigration was complete, Dr. Klein phoned to say he was not sure he could travel to Bermuda because his wife was laid up with back pain. Two days later he called back to tell me his wife was well and walking and the whole family would be coming as planned. The next day he phoned to say he was once again not sure he would be able to come because his older son had had a febrile convulsion. By the grace of God, both his wife and his son recovered sufficiently for the whole family to make the trip on February 14th as planned.

On Sunday afternoon Dr. Klein and I met with Mr. Kasson in his office. A few days earlier I had couriered copies of my patients' files and the Brookson report to Dr. Klein. He had studied all the documents and was very familiar with them. Mr. Kasson found it hard to believe that a professor such as Dr. Brookson could be wrong and I right. Dr. Klein spoke for more than three hours. He went over my patients' files one by one, compared them with Dr. Brookson's review of the same files and showed that Dr. Brookson had been wrong in every case.

At the end of Dr. Klein's presentation Mr. Kasson remained silent and thoughtful. He walked us to the entrance of his office building, said goodbye and closed the door behind us. When Dr. Klein and I had reached the parking lot, he opened the door and called us back. He looked to his left and right and whispered, "I hope what we discussed here will remain confidential, as you might be aware that the Island has only one hospital and we mustn't do anything to damage its reputation." "Of course," said Dr. Klein, and we left.

Dr. Klein said he could not believe that the instruction to protect the hospital was coming from my attorney, the person who was supposed to defend me. I replied that I was aware of Mr. Kasson's partiality towards the hospital, but had no alternative but to work with him.

On Monday, February 16th, at 2:30 p.m. Dr. Klein was scheduled to be at the hospital to review my patients' records. At eight a.m. he was scheduled to meet with Mr. Dills, a member of the Board, in a downtown hotel. (When I realized that the hospital had involved the immigration minister in the dispute, I decided to use my own political connections. At eleven o'clock one evening earlier that week, I had visited Dr. Browne at his home to solicit his help. At midnight he called two members of the Board, both black Bermudians, and asked them to meet with Dr. Klein. The two men were friends of Dr. Browne, but did not associate with him officially. Mr. Toby, chairman of the Board, said his schedule would not allow him to meet with Dr. Klein, but Mr. Dills agreed to do so.)

At seven o'clock on Monday morning Dr. Klein called me from his hotel. Speaking in a faint voice, he said he would be unable to attend the meeting with Mr. Dills or conduct the review at the hospital later that day. He and all his family with the exception of his younger son had been sick throughout the night with abdominal pain, fever and vomiting. They were laid up in bed and so weak that the younger son had to bring them water. Dr. Klein said he was worried for his older son as he had had a febrile convulsion in New York a few days earlier. He told me they would have to fly back to New York the next day if his son did not get better. All I could do was wish them well.

I immediately called Mr. Kasson and Dr. Browne. I asked Dr. Browne to cancel Dr. Klein's meeting with Mr. Dills. Mr. Kasson notified Mrs. Anderson of Dr. Klein's health crisis and rescheduled his meeting at the hospital for the next day at 11:30 a.m.

Mr. Kasson phoned me on two occasions during the day to inquire about Dr. Klein and his family. I told him I had not called them, preferring to let them rest, and was praying that they would soon be better.

At eight that evening Dr. Klein phoned me. His voice was less faint. He said he and his wife were feeling slightly better, but his son was still running a fever. They were going to go out to eat and would stay in Bermuda if they continued to improve and their son's fever came down. At midnight he called again and reported that they had eaten and his son was as energetic as if he had never been sick. He would be able to go to the hospital the next morning and carry out the review. I cannot describe the relief and joy that I felt.

At eight o'clock on Tuesday morning Dr. Klein met with Mr. Dills in a downtown hotel. He went over the Brookson report and over my patients' charts to show Mr. Dills that Dr. Brookson's review had been poorly conducted. He said that the review was more a witch-hunt than a fair assessment of my work and that some doctors (Dr. Cooperson and his group) had used the hospital to further their cause, which was to get rid of me, and in so doing had jeopardized the hospital's reputation and rendered it liable.

At 9:30 a.m. Dr. Klein was at the hospital to review my patients' charts and x-rays. Dr. Jameson escorted him to the medical records and radiology departments. At the end of the review, Dr. Jameson, who was anxiously waiting for Dr. Klein, asked for his opinion on my treatment of my patients and on the Brookson report. Dr. Klein replied, "Dr. Bah treated his patients according to standard North American practice and everything seems to be all right." Apparently Dr. Jameson was not happy with this answer. He told

Dr. Klein that he was too young and inexperienced and that Dr. Brookson (who was in his sixties) had more experience. I had not known Dr. Klein long, but I knew him long enough to know that a comment like that would make him very angry. The man was indeed young, but very brilliant. Ever since kindergarten he had won prizes in every academic activity he pursued. He was a graduate of Harvard and Columbia universities and well known in the spine community. Yet he remained humble. He never brought up his academic achievements, preferring to talk about how proud he was of his father, a blue-collar worker. Dr. Klein told me he had been angered by Dr. Jameson's comment about his lack of experience, but had remained calm and said, "I might be young but let me show you something." He showed Dr. Jameson the MRI of one of my patients with a huge disc herniation that even Dr. Jameson, as a general surgeon, could recognize. He told Dr. Jameson that Dr. Brookson had written, with regard to this patient: "Pre-operative x-rays are normal… Reason for operative intervention must be seriously questioned." Dr. Brookson should have known, said Dr. Klein, that a herniated disc cannot be seen on an ordinary x-ray; it can be seen only on an MRI.

Dr. Klein said that Dr. Jameson admitted that Dr. Brookson had perhaps made an error in his evaluation of this particular case, but wanted to know if there were other instances where I had operated on patients unnecessarily. Dr. Klein replied that he had not found any. Later that evening Dr. Fascioni called Dr. Klein to discuss his findings.

I asked Mr. Kasson if my having dinner with Dr. Klein would constitute conflict of interest. "By all means do so," he replied. Dr. Klein had his mind made up, said Mr. Kasson, and nobody could influence his judgement. So that evening the Klein family and my family met in a downtown restaurant for dinner. Dr. Klein's wife was friendly throughout the evening. Despite their recent misfortune, I did not hear her complain once. Dr. Klein said the hospital authorities would likely reinstate my privileges after reading his report, in which case he advised me to return to work, forget the whole thing and not become involved in litigation. If they refused to reinstate my privileges, he advised, I should leave Bermuda because I would probably never get justice there. Dr. Klein commented that Dr. Cooperson and his group seemed to look down on Dr. Trouts and seemed to fear me. He was puzzled as to how an Island so beautiful could harbour so much hatred. At the end of our meal he asked me why Dr. Jameson seemed to hate black people considering that he was black himself. I related a story I had heard. Apparently Dr. Jameson, who had been a member of parliament under the UBP, had stood in parliament one day and said, "If I were black…" The story goes that another parliamentarian tried to point out his mistake, but Dr. Jameson ignored him and continued with his speech. This seemed to suggest that Dr. Jameson wished he were white.

The next day, Wednesday, Dr. Klein flew back to New York with his family. On Thursday he dictated his report and on Friday morning he couriered the audiotape to Mr. Kasson, who received it late Friday afternoon. On Saturday morning Mr. Kasson's secretary transcribed the tape. On Saturday afternoon Mr. Kasson corrected the document and faxed it to Dr. Klein, who made further corrections. On Sunday afternoon Dr. Klein signed the final draft of his report. On Monday morning Mr. Kasson sent copies of the report and all relevant documents to Mrs. Anderson, in time for our meeting with the Board scheduled for Tuesday, February 24th, 1998.

CHAPTER THIRTY

The Klein Report

Within a short period, Dr. Klein had produced a well-thought out, well-written and objective twelve-page document. It was divided into four sections. In the first section he wrote the following:

"I have had the opportunity to review the report, and specifically those sections pertaining to Dr. Bah, as prepared by Dr. C.E. Brookson... I will comment on the cases contained in Dr. Brookson's report. My comments are based on –

1. The material in his report

2. The Hospital records

3. Dr. Bah's office records

4. The discussion with Dr. Bah regarding his treatment

5. A review of the x-rays and advanced imaging studies available at the King Edward VII Memorial Hospital...

6. A review of the actual imaging studies from outside the Hospital, including MRI scans primarily from the United States.

All of this information is necessary in order to properly evaluate indications for surgery and to be as fair as possible to all parties concerned."

In the second section, "Method of Outside Case Review," Dr. Klein looked at the methodology used by Dr. Brookson to review my practice:

"In terms of the actual methodology of the case review, there are some very specific problems. It is not possible to evaluate these cases on the basis of the hospital records and hospital imaging studies alone. It is necessary to review the office notes of the surgeon in question, as well as the outside imaging studies... Lastly, it would be best to directly question the surgeon involved regarding the individual cases… In the particular review…office notes and outside imaging studies were not reviewed and the surgeon involved was not questioned. This would put any reviewer at a great disadvantage, especially one who did not specialize in spinal surgery. The conclusions reached and the opinions rendered regarding the individual cases were often specific and quite condemning…The conclusions reached are inappropriate. It is hard for me to imagine that anyone would find my opinion here as anything but fair and ethical. The importance of a fair and complete review can only be appreciated if one considers the situation of the surgeon being reviewed. Such a review not only affects the current practice of Dr. Bah but his entire future and career."

In the third section, "Case Review," Dr. Klein compared my treatment of specific patients and Dr. Brookson's comments on those same cases.

The first case Dr. Klein reviewed was that of a forty-year-old woman, a white Bermudian bank employee who had sustained a spinal injury during a fall. The patient was treated non-operatively with various modalities for eight months without any significant lessening of her pain. An MRI done abroad had shown a herniated disc at T9-T10 (thoracic 9 and 10). I operated on the patient at the level indicated by the MRI and she did well after the surgery. Dr. Brookson looked at the report of a CT scan done in Bermuda that suggested the patient had a herniated disc at T8-T9, and said I had operated on the patient at the wrong level. With respect to this case, Dr. Klein wrote the following:

> "The prior review reported a CT scan with posterior spurs at T8-9 and nothing further. An outside MRI performed shortly thereafter revealed the pathology to be at T9-10. The initial reviewer did not mention this… The level would be more accurately seen on an MRI… The previous review implies surgery at the wrong level. After a long period of conservative treatment, surgery is a viable alternative in this case. Complete data reveal the operative level to be correct."

(In January 1998 many of my patients were upset upon learning that the hospital had revoked my privileges and that therefore I could not see them. They were even more upset when they learned that I had lost my privileges because a "professor from outside" had written that the surgeries I performed on them were "aggressive and not indicated." Many patients wrote to the Board on my behalf. The letters from three of the seven patients discussed in the Brookson report are reproduced in the Appendix.

The letter written by the above patient is labelled Letter 2.)

The second case Dr. Klein reviewed was that of a sixty-year-old Christian woman who had had low-back surgery overseas a few months before I arrived in Bermuda. After the surgery, the patient's symptoms worsened to the point where she was barely able to walk and had lost control of her bladder. I operated on this patient with great difficulty because her previous surgery had been recent. The second procedure was a success; the patient was walking and no longer incontinent. Dr. Brookson had written that it was "inappropriate" for me to operate on this woman, whereas Dr. Klein wrote:

> "This is a case of a posterior decompression and instrumented fusion in a 60-year-old female who had undergone previous decompression without fusion in Boston... The problem was a Spondylolisthesis [slipped vertebrae] at L4-5 associated with Stenosis [compression of the spinal cord]. This would not be considered the standard of care for this type of problem. The Spondylolisthesis already implies some level of instability. Following decompression, this could only worsen. Quite predictably, it did... Dr. Bah intervened when she returned from Boston and subsequently developed increased pain in her legs as well as worsening difficulty with her bladder...
>
> The previous review described that the patient was heavy and exhibited a depressive reaction for which she was receiving drug therapy. The conclusion was that this would appear to show poor patient selection for this type of surgery. "This is inappropriate." I would argue that Dr. Bah did not select this patient for surgery but rather the patient selected Dr. Bah. The greatest surgical error (I feel) happened at the time of the first surgery, which was performed on the mainland. Salvaging this situation at this time is appropriate. Failure to do so would probably be inappropriate."[See letter 3 in the Appendix, for a testimonial by this patient.]

The third case was that of a thirty-three-year-old woman with a five-year history of low-back and leg pain. An MRI had shown a transitional (non-fused) vertebrae and a disc herniation. To operate on such a patient by removing only the affected disc and not addressing the secondary problem of transitional vertebrae is not recommended since it would make the condition worse. A surgeon in Bermuda had removed the disc without addressing the patient's secondary problem. The patient awoke from the surgery unable to get out of bed and required more pain medication than she had before the operation. The surgeon asked me to see her in consultation and the patient begged me to be her treating physician. I accepted the transfer because I did not want to penalize the patient, who was in agony and had no clue as to what was happening to her. I performed the repeat surgery, and, except for the fact that she developed phlebitis (a blood clot in the leg) from being in bed too long after the first operation, the patient was improved. She was treated for the phlebitis and did well. She invited me to her wedding. In his report, Dr. Brookson never mentioned that the first operation had been unnecessary. Instead, he criticized me for performing the second one and having the patient get out of bed. With regard to this patient, Dr. Klein wrote:

> "The patient underwent initial surgery by Dr. Trouts… Post-operatively the patient did not experience significant relief… In July 1997 a repeat lumbar decompression and fusion was performed at L4-S1 [by Dr. Bah]. She developed post-operative phlebitis, which was treated. According to office notes, she is now pain-free post-operatively and doing well.
>
> In the original review, the selection of this patient for surgical intervention was found very questionable given her previous medical history and the fact that she apparently did not respond to her previous intervention. This is a salvage procedure, if you will, and it is difficult to say that the patient was selected." [See Letter 4 in the Appendix, for a testimonial by this patient.]

All the other cases Dr. Klein discussed in his report were similar to the above three in that Dr. Brookson concluded that my surgical interventions were "inappropriate" whereas Dr. Klein concluded that they were "indicated" and "appropriate."

Although Dr. Esses had been unable to travel to Bermuda, he reviewed the documents that had been sent to him and produced a concise and accurate report, which concluded as follows:

> "It is my opinion that due process has not been given to Dr. Bah. It is specifically my opinion that it is inadequate to review hospital records alone in forming an opinion concerning the care rendered to a particular patient. It is my opinion that due process necessarily requires review of all information available concerning that patient. This would include office records and information from the treating physician or physicians. It is my opinion that it is wholly unacceptable to render an opinion without discussing the matter with the physician so that all relevant information can be reviewed.
>
> It is clear in the report prepared by Dr. Brookson that there are significant and destructive interpersonal conflicts within the Subdivision of

Orthopaedic…It is crucial, in my opinion, that all allegations be substantiated by fact."

In addition to the letters from my patients in Bermuda, in his submission to the Board Mr. Kasson included copies of letters from some of my overseas patients. These show that in a critical, but objective environment professionals could appreciate my work for what it was. These are available on the following Website: www. theonlywaytoeternallife.com, Letters 5 to 12.

CHAPTER THIRTY-ONE

Meeting with the Board

On Monday, February 23rd, 1998, Mr. Kasson and I met to discuss how we would present my case to the Board. Mr. Kasson had prepared a nineteen-page document outlining my dealings with the hospital. It showed that the hospital had treated me unfairly and disregarded the rules and regulations of the Board in its handling of the complaints against me. I asked Mr. Kasson if he was also going to present the reports by Drs. Klein and Esses and the letters from my patients. He said he was going to present his document only; the Board members could read the reports and letters at their convenience. I told him that the hospital authorities needed no reminding of the fact that they had not followed the rules and regulations in handling the complaints against me. I said the most important thing was to show them that my patients and two prominent doctors had completely discredited the Brookson report. Mr. Kasson was unmoved by my argument and said he was going to present only his document. That evening I called Dr. Klein in New York and asked him to try to convince Mr. Kasson to include the reports and letters. The next morning Dr. Klein called Mr. Kasson on my behalf.

On February 24th, at three p.m. Mr. Kasson and I met with the Board members in the boardroom of the King Edward VII Memorial Hospital. A black man sitting at the head of the table introduced himself as Mr. Toby, the chairman of the Board. Mrs. Anderson, the executive director of the hospital, and Dr. Jameson, the chief of staff, sat on his left. Mr. Barry, the hospital attorney and a minister in the government, sat on his right. I did not know the other five Board members sitting around the table. A black man whom I guessed to be Mr. Dills, the gentleman whom Dr. Klein had met, sat away from the table in the right-hand corner of the room. I sat at the opposite end of the table to Mr. Toby and Mr. Kasson sat on my right. Mr. Toby told the assembly that forty-five minutes had been allotted for the discussion of my case, but that people arriving late had already used up fifteen minutes and therefore Mr. Kasson and I had only thirty minutes; he asked us to proceed with our presentation at once.

Mr. Kasson read out the document he had prepared. He also brought up the matter of the patients' letters and the reports by Drs. Klein and Essex. He reminded the Board of the rules and regulations to be followed in appointing a physician to the medical staff and pointed out that these procedures had not been followed in my case. To prove his point Mr. Kasson read out the following from his document:

> "The presence of Dr. Cooperson at the meeting of the credentials committee on 1st April 1997 was in breach of the rules of natural justice in that Dr. Bah firmly and with good reason believes that Dr. Cooperson was one of the complainants and could not be expected to act impartially in the circumstances. In any event, the credentials committee has no power to delegate its function to an independent reviewer [Dr. Brookson] as was decided in the meeting...

> The Board (or the Chief of Staff acting on behalf of the Board) does not have any power to delegate its function of considering applications for appointment to the medical staff of the Hospital to an independent reviewer..."

Mr. Barry interrupted Mr. Kasson and said in an authoritative voice, "What do you mean by 'the Board does not have any power'? You know we have the power and we can do whatever we choose to do." Mr. Kasson bowed his head, curled his shoulders and looked at the floor. There was a long silence, with everybody looking at Mr. Kasson and waiting for an answer. Mr. Kasson did not respond to Mr. Barry's question, but resumed reading from his document in a shy tone of voice. Mr. Kasson read the following:

> "It is a breach of the established and documented procedure of the Hospital to adjudicate a complaint of unprofessional conduct against a doctor without following the procedures established by the "Regulations, Rules and Policies of the Bermuda Hospitals Board."

> It is our respectful submission that the Board's decision cannot stand. The

Brookson report is thoroughly wrong in relation to the skill and judgment of Dr. Bah both in substance and in the manner in which its conclusions were reached. The Board's decision was entirely based on the Brookson report. It cannot therefore stand. Dr. Bah's privileges must be restored immediately…and his triennial appointment granted."

Mr. Kasson's presentation lasted twenty minutes. He then asked the Board's permission for me to argue my case. The Board members looked at each other and at Mr. Toby. Mr. Toby told me I had less than ten minutes left to make my case.

I began by saying the purpose of my presentation was not to criticize anybody, but since my work had been put under scrutiny the only way I could defend myself was to compare my work with the work of other orthopaedic surgeons in Bermuda and with similar work published in the literature. I also explained that everything I said would be supported by facts and that the data I was about to present had been obtained from the operative registry of all orthopaedic surgeons in Bermuda in 1997. I had analyzed the data five times and asked my secretary to review it to make sure there were no mistakes.

I first discussed the allegations made by Drs. Cooperson, Fascioni and Joneson, which were included in the Brookson report, that I was subjecting my patients to "lengthy and complex" surgical procedures. I projected the following table representing the operative time for different procedures performed by the surgeons at the hospital in 1997 as obtained from the operating room registry:

Average operative time for different surgical procedures (minutes)

Surgeons	L4-S1 Fusion	Discectomy	Ankle (Bim)	Ulna	Quadriceps	Patella	Hip (DHS)	Tibia (ORIF)	Femur (Nail)
Bah	191	75	67	45	50	60	66	53	165
Chalvin		125	71	45	80	63	86	65	131
Cooperson	305	139	158				125		
Fascioni	335	150	73	105			110		220
Trout		122				70	88	106	243

The first column shows that it took me three hours to perform a spinal fusion while it took Drs. Marvin (a visiting surgeon from Boston), Cooperson and Fascioni five or more. The last column shows that Dr. Trouts spent an average of four hours and sometimes as long as seven to operate on a femur fracture. I told the Board that while faster does not necessarily mean better, the table shows that in all cases reviewed with the exception of reduction of femur fracture my operating times were shorter than those of the other surgeons for similar procedures (Dr. Chalvin took less time to treat femur fracture because he did not use a distal screw, as recommended in the literature, to secure the nail in the femur). In view of these facts, I said, the allegation that I was subjecting my patients to "lengthy" surgical procedures was false.

I then raised the issue of infections rates and operative complications. Dr. Brookson had written, "[T] here was a perception amongst the surgical/ nursing staff that Dr. Bah had an increased number of postoperative infections as compared to his colleagues." In his report Dr. Klein wrote that the only fair way to assess this situation is to obtain accurate data on infection rates for the different surgical procedures performed at the hospital and compare these with the rates for similar cases reported in the literature. I did exactly what Dr. Klein suggested and found that the infection rate for my complex spine cases was five percent compared to the four to eleven percent reported for similar cases in the spine literature. Every one of my five patients who had an infection weighed more than two hundred and twenty-five pounds, four were elderly, two were diabetic and one had a tumour – all factors that are known to increase the risk of post-operative infection.

Since the other orthopaedic surgeons at the hospital performed mostly joint surgery (hip and knee replacement), I analyzed the infection rate for this type of surgery. I showed the Board the infection rates of the other surgeons for total joint (hip and knee replacement) in 1997:

Surgeon	Chalvin	Cooperson	Fascioni	Trouts
Infection rate	0%	12%	18%	25%

The infection rate quoted in the literature for similar surgeries was one percent (I did not do any total joint replacements in 1997 as my practice consisted mainly of spine surgery and trauma). One could clearly see, I said, that the "perception" that I "had an increased number of postoperative infections" compared to my colleagues was unfounded, and that in fact the infection rates of my colleagues were higher than mine and significantly higher than reported in the literature for similar procedures.

The third issue I raised was that of complications. There was a "perception" that I had an increased number of postoperative complications as compared to my colleagues. Again, a review of complications for my spine surgeries revealed that this allegation was unfounded. On the other hand, I showed the Board alarming statistics when it came to the complications of the other surgeons (Drs. Fascioni and Cooperson). My review of the operating room registry in 1997 showed that the revision rate of total joint replacement at the hospital was forty percent – that is, one out of every two patients who had a prosthesis implanted at the hospital required repeat surgery within five years. The revision rate for total joint quoted in the literature was five percent at ten to fifteen years.

The next issue I discussed in front of the Board was that of blood loss. Dr. Brookson had written that my patients experienced "excessive" blood loss. Dr. Jameson had given Dr. Klein a fabricated blood loss list for my patients and asked him to investigate. With regard to this, Dr. Klein wrote the following in his report:

> "I was asked by Dr. Jameson to investigate the issue of surgical blood loss. He provided me with a printed sheet of names, surgeries and units of blood lost…there were large discrepancies between the blood loss listed by Dr. Jameson and that, which appears on the charts in the Anaesthesia Record. Specifically with reference to Mr. J.D., the printed list revealed a blood loss of approximately 4,000 cc. The Anaesthesia Record indicates a blood loss of 1,400 cc. In the case of Mr. B.W. the list from Dr. Jameson reveals a blood loss of approximately 3,500 cc. The Anaesthesia Record indicates a blood loss of 1,800 cc. I do not know how to resolve these discrepancies and hence I think it is best that the various parties involved sort this out."

I showed the Board the real blood losses for my patients as found in the chart, versus the inflated blood losses as found in Dr. Jameson's list. I asked the Board why Dr. Jameson was trying to frame me.

The last issue I raised was the number of spines cases I had been operating on. The "concern" was that I was operating on too many spines cases. When asked to address this issue Dr. Klein wrote the following:

> "Again, accurate data would need to be collected regarding this matter. It

must be kept in mind that there are a certain number of revision surgeries that are being performed, which will somewhat raise the number of total procedures being performed. It might be worthwhile to compare the overall number of surgeries to that number of spinal surgeries that was being performed prior to Dr. Bah being on the Island. This might be a useful comparison."

In order to make this comparison, I tried to obtain the operating room registry for 1995, the year of my arrival, but Mrs. Santini refused to make it available to me. Because I was unable to make an objective comparison and respond to the concern that I was conducting too many spine operations, I resorted to showing the Board why it *appeared* that I was operating on too many spines cases. I indicated that twenty percent of the patients I operated on had had previous back surgery, either in Bermuda or abroad, before my arrival and that these surgeries had failed. I indicated that my patients had been suffering with back pain an average of eight years and all had sought alternative treatment in Bermuda or abroad before I operated on them. One such patient had been suffering for twenty years. I said that in light of the data I had presented I did not think I was doing unnecessary surgery.

Mr. Toby interrupted me and said I had used up the time allocated to me. He asked my attorney and me to leave because there were other matters on the agenda. Mr. Kasson and I packed up our papers as quickly as we could and left the room.

Mr. Kasson and I went downstairs to the lobby. Mr. Kasson remained quiet and thoughtful. I sensed that he had been shaken by the whole affair. When he finally spoke, he said, "They call this a democracy." I felt we had made a good presentation. And I should not have been, but I was glad that Mr. Kasson was shaken, because in the past he did not believe me when I told him the hospital authorities were wrong and deceitful. Mr. Kasson and I stood in the lobby speechless until a hospital employee, a black Bermudian who knew me, asked why I was standing there and when would I be returning to work at the hospital. Before I could answer, she said, "You know, everybody likes you." Mr. Kasson said, "That is our main problem." After the woman left, I asked Mr. Kasson when we were going to leave. He said that in our rush to exit the boardroom he had forgotten his raincoat. I asked if he wanted me to go back with him. He replied, "No, thank you," and said he would go by himself. I left Mr. Kasson standing in the lobby and went home.

CHAPTER THIRTY-TWO

Awaiting the Board's Decision

On Wednesday evening, the day after our presentation to the Board, I called Dr. Klein to inquire about his family's welfare and to thank him for what he had done for me. Dr. Klein said he had called the hotel in Bermuda to get the results of the tests that had been conducted on its drinking water. His son was still having abdominal cramps and he wanted to know if he had contracted a bacterial infection, which would require treatment with antibiotics, or a viral infection. Dr. Klein said the hotel managers had put him on hold for a long while and then told him everything, but the truth. While in Bermuda Dr. Klein had told me he was not a litigious person. He said all he wanted was for the family to return to New York, for his son to get better and for them to forget the whole episode. But the attitude of the managers had really upset him. Dr. Klein treated his son with antibiotics without waiting for the test results from the hotel, and his son's condition improved. (Other American tourists who had stayed at the hotel the same weekend and had become sick were more upset and less conciliatory than Dr. Klein. They hired attorneys and contacted the American television networks. The local newspaper reported that the hotel management had known the water tank was in need of repair for some time. It also suggested that the hotel management and the medical officer knew that the water was the source of contamination and had misled the guests and hotel workers who had been sick by suggesting their illness was from a viral source. One of the results of the fiasco was that the international firm that was renting the property from a Bermudian company closed the hotel and left the Island.)

During our phone conversation, Dr. Klein said he had already heard about our presentation to the Board. Mr. Dills had called him to inform him about our presentation and its outcome: the Board was reluctant to restore my privileges and was considering conducting another review of my practice. Dr. Klein said Mr. Dills told him he was so appalled at the Board's decision that he was considering resigning. Dr. Klein said he told Mr. Dills not to resign since he was the only sensible member of the Board and his resignation would represent a loss to the cause of justice.

In his report, Dr. Klein had written, "This evening I was also contacted by telephone by Dr. Fascioni…" Dr. Fascioni had called Dr. Klein because he wanted to know what his findings were in relation to my practice. Dr. Klein said he told Dr. Fascioni the same thing he had told Dr. Jameson, that nothing in my practice fell outside the norm for North America. Dr. Fascioni asked him if he was sure. Dr. Klein answered that he was positive and told Dr. Fascioni, "You are barking up at the wrong tree; maybe you should look at the whole forest."

Dr. Klein's comment about looking "at the whole forest" did not fall on deaf ears. The first indication I got that Dr. Fascioni had been looking at the whole forest was when a hospital employee called to inform me that Drs. Fascioni and Jameson (Dr. Cooperson was on vacation) were sitting in the operating room lounge plotting against me. I thanked the employee for the information.

A few days later Mrs. Louise, a black Bermudian and assistant head nurse in the emergency room, called to tell me that Dr. Ilea, a resident doctor from the United Kingdom, was in the emergency room boasting that the hospital had paid him $500 to review my patients' charts for the purpose of finding complications. Mrs. Louise said she was disgusted by the whole affair. I told her I knew that Drs. Jameson and Fascioni were plotting against me, but could do little about it. She asked if she could phone my attorney and tell him about it. I gave her his number. A few minutes later Mrs. Louise called back to say she had phoned my attorney and he was unmoved. She said she was not impressed with my attorney and suggested I find another. I told her I had thought of changing attorneys, but this was easier said than done. She suggested I speak to Mr. Halls, a black Bermudian attorney who was not afraid of the establishment. I told Mrs. Louise she was not the first person to suggest Mr. Halls, but I had heard he was ill. The more people said I should speak to Mr. Halls, the more I wondered if there was only one honest and fearless attorney on the Island.

That same evening Dr. M., an emergency room physician, called to inform me of Dr. Ilea's task. Two days later Dr. Winston, a black Bermudian, told me that Dr. Jameson had first asked him to review my patients' charts with the objective of coming up with complications. He said that Dr. Jameson had hired Dr. Ilea to do the dirty work only when he and another black Bermudian resident had refused.

A few days later several of my patients told me that Dr. Fascioni had called them to ask if they would be willing to file a complaint against me. The irony was that Drs. Fascioni and Cooperson had seen the very patients that Dr. Fascioni called and had done nothing for them. One of these patients wrote a letter to the Board describing Dr. Fascioni's behaviour (see Website: www.theonlywaytoeternallife.com, Letter 13).

The Board's rules and regulations prohibit one physician from contacting the patients of another in order to impugn his/her reputation. They state that the second physician can file a complaint with the chief of staff if he/she believes the actions violate his/her rights. But I could not report Dr. Fascioni's behaviour to Dr. Jameson, for Drs. Jameson and Fascioni had together devised the plan to contact my patients. I thought I might obtain justice if I sought help outside of Bermuda. Drs Cooperson, Fascioni and Jameson had all trained in Canada and held certification from the Royal College of Physicians and Surgeons of Canada. The King Edward VII Memorial Hospital also receives certification from the Royal College. I therefore wrote a letter to the Royal College describing my situation and complaining in particular about Dr. Fascioni's contacting my patients.

On February 18th, 1998, the Executive Director of the Royal College replied as follows:

> "The Royal College encourages all of its Fellows to behave in a professional and considerate way with all colleagues. However, the College is in no position to comment on the circumstances, which you describe in your letter. I would suggest to you that these are matters, which can only be properly resolved by the individuals and authorities at the King Edward Memorial Hospital. I would suggest to you that you should pursue your inquiries both with the Chief of Staff and the Chief of Surgery at that institution."

In my first letter I had described in detail my situation and the involvement of the chief of staff and the chief of surgery in the plot to contact my patients. I had explained that I was bringing the matter to the attention of the Royal College because the chief of staff and the chief of surgery were not impartial in my case. So for the Executive Director to refer me back to the same parties was just a way of formally acknowledging my letter. I wrote a second letter, again describing my situation and again asking for assistance.

On April 29th the Interim Executive Director of the Royal College (the previous Executive Director had left) replied to my second letter:

> "The Royal College has endorsed the code of ethics of the Canadian Medical Association. I therefore enclose a copy for your perusal and information. I direct your attention to the section
>
> Responsibilities of the Profession:
>
> 35. Recognize that the self-regulation of the profession is a privilege and that each physician has a continuing responsibility to merit this privilege.
>
> 37. Avoid impugning the reputation of colleagues for personal motives; however report to the appropriate authority any unprofessional conduct by colleagues."[1]

Since I could not rely on the Royal College or the hospital authorities, I thought I might be able to stop the harassment by Dr. Cooperson and his gang if I went on the offensive. I told Mr. Kasson I wished to sue Drs. Fascioni and Cooperson for defamation on the grounds that the Brookson report stated, "Drs. Cooperson and Fascioni have refused to assist or consult with Dr. Trouts and/or Bah feeling that their surgical judgment and technique is so poor," and on the grounds that Dr. Fascioni was calling my patients with intent to impugn my reputation. Mr. Kasson said Drs. Fascioni and Cooperson were entitled to their opinion and I could not sue them even if I were to prove that the Brookson report had been widely circulated in the hospital. In that case, I said, I would sue Drs. Brookson and Jameson for misleading me as to Dr. Brookson's mandate. He said I could sue Dr. Brookson, but not Dr. Jameson. I asked why I was able to take legal action against Dr. Brookson, "the hit man," but not Dr. Jameson, "the head honcho" who had orchestrated the whole affair. Mr. Kasson could not give me a plausible explanation.

A few months later I would discover why Mr. Kasson was adamant I not take legal action against Dr. Jameson. One of my patients, Mrs. G.A.B., had asked me to be a witness before a government commission so she could receive compensation for back injuries inflicted by her boyfriend. While the patient, her attorney and I waited outside the hearing room, we heard the commissioners laughing heartily at the attorney and client who had just exited. When we entered the room, I saw Mr. Kasson, Dr. Jameson and the judge sitting together at the table enjoying themselves. Both Dr. Jameson and Mr. Kasson bowed their heads and avoided eye contact with me. This episode gave me some insight into Bermudian society and why Mr. Kasson had not let me sue Dr. Jameson. Another thing I discovered at the hearing was that my patient, a black Bermudian, had lied to me. She had once brought her eighteen-year-old son to my office and told me he had defended her against the physical assaults of her boyfriend. At the hearing, I learned that her son had testified against her on behalf of the former boyfriend in court and was now living with him.

---

[1] *Code of Ethics of the Canadian Medical Association* (Ottawa, Ontario: CMA, 1996).

CHAPTER THIRTY-THREE

The Board's Decision

After our meeting with the Board, a reliable source called me to confirm what Mr. Dills had told Dr. Klein, that the Board unofficially admitted that Dr. Brookson's review of my practice had failed. The source said the Board had allowed Dr. Jameson to commission another review of my work. Meanwhile the Board would not restore my privileges. I conveyed this information to Mr. Kasson. I explained to him that what the Board was about to do was unacceptable: it could not find me innocent and yet penalize me until the hospital authorities built up a better case against me. Moreover, I said, I considered another investigation of my work to be harassment. Mr. Kasson said the hospital had the right to conduct as many investigations of my work as it wished. In that case, I said, any review should be conducted in a fair and objective manner. We should be able to participate in the selection of the reviewer, to ensure that he or she would be impartial, and should be advised of the terms of reference. Ideally, I said, the reviewer should examine the same cases that had been the subject of the original complaint, the cases that Drs. Brookson and Klein had reviewed. Mr. Kasson said he would convey my concerns to the hospital's attorney.

Mr. Kasson spoke to Mr. Barry, the hospital attorney, and then summarized their conversation in a letter:

> "Dr. Bah is quite content that the Hospital engage another independent reviewer to review Dr. Bah's spine cases... In the meantime, the question of Dr. Bah's privileges would need to be addressed... It would be unreasonable and unfair in Dr. Bah's submission for him to suffer the consequences of the decision while the further review is conducted...
>
> Dr. Bah justifiably feels that he should enjoy all the benefits of the pre-

sumption of innocence. To do otherwise would be to sentence someone who is still awaiting trial…

We sincerely hope that the Board will see fit to restore to Dr. Bah the means to support himself and his family. This requires restoration of all of his privileges, albeit temporarily, until the new report is in…

We would be pleased to collaborate with you and the Board regarding the terms of reference of the new review, producing a short list of candidates for appointment to conduct the review and agreeing on the methodology."

I told Mr. Kasson that I disagreed with this letter, for several reasons. I was not "quite content" to have the hospital conduct another review of my work. I did not want to have my privileges restored "albeit temporarily." We had always sought to have my privileges fully restored and to have my appointment to the medical staff extended to three years. I reminded Mr. Kasson about the document he had submitted and read out to the Board, which stated:

"The Board's decision was entirely based on the Brookson report. It cannot therefore stand. Dr. Bah's privileges must be restored immediately…and his triennial appointment granted."

On March 4th, 1998, my reliable source informed me that the Board had commissioned another review of my practice and the hospital would not be restoring my privileges. I therefore asked Mr. Kasson to write a strongly worded letter to the Board, threatening legal action if my privileges were not restored. Mr. Kasson sent the following polite letter to Mr. Barry:

"As you know, our client was charged and found guilty by Dr. C.E. Brookson of a number of matters ranging from negligent treatment to unethical conduct… Not only did Dr. Klein express the view that Dr. Brookson was an inappropriate person to evaluate our client's skill and judgment but he also found that our client's treatment in all of the cases reviewed by Dr. Brookson to be entirely appropriate in the circumstances…

It is clear, in our respectful submission, that the justice of this case requires a full restoration of our client's privileges forthwith. Further delay increases progressively the injustice done to him.

We would be grateful if you would impress these matters upon the Board."

In a letter dated March 5th Mr. Barry responded as follows:

"We do not propose to address at this time the matters which you have raised, but will instead in accordance with your request draw them to the attention of the Board for consideration in their deliberations...

We shall inform you of the Board's decision as soon as we are instructed."

It was clear from the tone of Mr. Barry's letter that he was not impressed with Mr. Kasson's plea and that my privileges would not be restored.

My source informed me that the Board was scheduled to meet on the afternoon of Friday, March 6th, and would not be restoring my privileges. The plan was to conduct a review of my practice any time after three to six months, the purpose being to deprive me of the means to earn a living so I would have no choice but to leave the Island.

I believed that the threat of legal action would force the Board to restore my privileges. I knew, and the Board knew, that the Brookson report would not stand up in a court of law. Since Mr. Kasson would not issue such a threat, I had to find, within twenty-four hours, an attorney willing to write a strongly worded letter to the Board threatening legal action. I called Mr. Dunkin, the attorney handling my case against Dr. Trouts, and asked his secretary to schedule an appointment. She said Mr. Dunkin was in court and would not be available for two weeks. I called Dr. Miles, an ear, nose and throat specialist whom I knew to be a close friend of Mr. Dunkin, and asked him to speak to his friend and secure an immediate appointment.

Meanwhile, I called another attorney, Mr. Richardson, who had been highly recommended to me, in case Mr. Dunkin would not be available. Mr. Richardson said he would see me at 4:30 that afternoon.

Dr. Miles phoned me back an hour after I had spoken to him and said he had been able to secure an appointment with Mr. Dunkin for 2:30 p.m. I told Dr. Miles of my appointment with Mr. Richardson and he suggested I keep both appointments.

On Thursday, March 5th, Mr. Dunkin, a black Englishman, and I met in his office in downtown Hamilton. He seemed to be in a hurry and spoke very rapidly, in an English accent I barely understood. Meanwhile, he had difficulty understanding my accent, a mixture of French and African. He asked me to briefly describe my case. I started to speak, but stopped when I realized that Mr. Dunkin was deeply absorbed in reading the file. He scanned the documents for five minutes and said, "I understand everything...

Bermuda is an expensive place to live. The hospital is trying to stitch up your pocket." The hospital authorities did not want me to work while they conducted another review, he said. They knew that I could not survive without working and that I would end up leaving Bermuda before the planned review. I told Mr. Dunkin I agreed with his assessment of the situation and needed an attorney who would prevent the Board from carrying out its plan. He said he could not help, for two reasons. Mr. Kasson's last letter to Mr. Barry had weakened my position. Mr. Kasson should not have said, "Dr. Bah is quite content that the Hospital engage another independent reviewer to review Dr. Bah's spine case." Mr. Kasson and I should have been intransigent and demanded nothing short of our initial demand of full and immediate restoration of my privileges. Mr. Dunkin said the second reason he could not help was that he was scheduled to travel to London the next day. He said he could help if things were not resolved when he returned. I left Mr. Dunkin and walked to Mr. Richardson's office, located a block away.

Mr. Richardson, a black man from the West Indies with Bermudian status, was calm and in no hurry. He did not speak until I finished describing my case. Mr. Richardson said he would take the case. "If we see them [the establishment or white people] kicking on one of us [black people] and we do not help each other," he said, "next they are going to quick on us." I was glad that finally someone was willing to help. Mr. Richardson gave me a brief history of his dealings with the establishment to show that he was not afraid of them. He had sued the local newspaper for defamation. He told me that the establishment had threatened members of the jury and their families during the court proceedings (the case ended up in a hung jury). He said that initially members of the establishment were afraid to be seen with him and would invite him to lunch in St. George, on the outskirts of Hamilton, but now he represented many of those same people.

Mr. Richardson said he needed to know the composition of the Board before writing to it. I said I did not know all the Board members, but knew that Mr. Toby was the chairman. He explained that Mr. Toby did not hold the power, but was mere window dressing; the establishment had fronted the Board with a black person to appease the black majority, but behind the scenes control remained in the hands of the establishment. Mr.

Richardson said he knew Mr. Toby, a bank executive, very well. He picked up the phone and without consulting a directory, called Mr. Toby's office. He spoke to Mr. Toby for a few minutes, hung up and said, "It is exactly as I told you." The Board consisted of the wife of the finance minister, Mr. Barry, a government minister, the wives of two government backbenchers, and two white Bermudians with political connections to the ruling UBP. Mr. Richardson said he would write to the Board. I left his office not fully convinced he would do so before the Board's next scheduled meeting, the following day at four p.m.

At eight the next morning Mr. Dunkin phoned me. He said he had cleared his desk and was about to write the letter to the Board and would have it delivered to the hospital before his afternoon flight to London. I told him I would be delighted to have him write the letter, but Mr. Richardson had already agreed to do so. I said I would call Mr. Richardson immediately and get back to him. I phoned Mr. Richardson and told him Mr. Dunkin was about to write the letter to the Board and asked if he was going to write it or would prefer that Mr. Dunkin do so. Mr. Richardson said he would write the letter and would call Mr. Dunkin to tell him. I asked if he could let Mr. Dunkin review the letter. He responded positively.

After we spoke, Mr. Richardson called Mr. Kasson's office and reques-ted that my file be sent to him. A few minutes later, Mr. Kasson phoned me. Mr. Kasson, who was usually very calm, was angry. He said, "What is happening?" I told him I had asked another attorney to write a strongly worded letter to the Board since he had been unwilling to do so. Mr. Kasson then told me he had spoken to the Medical Insurance Society (MIS) and they were not going to pay my legal fees any more. He faxed me a copy of a letter he had written to Mr. Richardson stating that the MIS would be under no obligation in respect of any work carried out by Mr. Richardson on my behalf. At noon Mr. Richardson called me and said he had received Mr. Kasson's letter and it was no cause for concern. He said we should con-centrate our efforts on getting my privileges restored. He faxed me, for my approval, the letter he had written to the Board. In the two-page letter, Mr. Richardson summarized the events leading to the removal of my privileges and concluded as follows:

"...Clearly, Dr. Brookson's report, the basis for the removal of our client's privileges, has been discredited and therefore any accusations about our client's patient care have not been substantiated...

It is our position that in all the circumstances, our client's full privileges should be restored immediately and we would request that that course be taken since due process has not been given to Dr. Bah.

We can do nothing about your Board's wish to conduct another inquiry or review, which we hope will be impartial of the Orthopaedic Division of the Department of Surgery in which everyone agrees there are significant and destructive interpersonal conflicts as between the members of that Division, but we are instructed to inform you that if our client's full privileges are not restored within 10 days we shall be moving for a Judicial Review of the Bermuda Hospitals Board's exercise of its statutory functions in connection with this matter."

On Friday afternoon Mr. Richardson's letter was hand delivered to the hospital authorities. On Monday Mr. Barry replied as follows:

"We write to advise that the Bermuda Hospitals Board has decided to reinstate your client with full privileges, pending a further independent review of your client's case management.

Terms of reference for the review are currently being drafted and will be shared with your client in advance, as will a list of potential candidates."

The Board had not granted me my triennial appointment as they were supposed to and as we had sought. Under the circumstances, however, I was happy to be allowed to work.

CHAPTER THIRTY-FOUR

Working Again

The hospital had granted me full privileges, but this did not allow me to work in Bermuda. In order to work, I also had to secure a work permit from the immigration ministry.

I called Mr. Dunkin, the attorney who was handling my immigration case, to inform him of recent developments with the hospital. He said he was aware that the hospital had restored my privileges and had already called Mr. Ernest, the immigration minister – he had agreed as promised to grant me the work permit and I could start working at once.

I immediately opened my office and began to see patients. Even though I had verbal permission from the minister to start working, I wanted to have the papers confirming this so no one could accuse me of working illegally. Mr. Dunkin told me he had sent the necessary documents to the ministry and all I had to do was call and have the permit sent to me. I called the offices of the ministry and spoke to a clerk, who told me the permit had been issued and sent to Dr. Lightbourn, my work permit holder. I went to Dr. Lightbourn's office, but his staff said they had not received anything from the ministry concerning me. I called the ministry and spoke to the same clerk, who said that the permit may have been sent to Mr. Dunkin. I checked with Mr. Dunkin's staff, but they had not received it. I phoned the ministry again and was assured that the permit had been mailed to either my attorney or Dr. Lightbourn's office. The staff at the ministry suggested that the mail had been misplaced by a careless employee in my attorney's office. I spoke to Mr. Richardson, my other attorney, and asked if he had received it. After consulting with his staff, he told me it had not been sent to his office. He said he was on his way to lunch and would walk to the immigration building, which was situated adjacent to his office, and verify that the permit had been issued. On April 13th, more than a month after the staff at the ministry had told me that my work permit had been issued and mailed, Mr. Richardson called me and said it had never been issued. He said he had to stand in front of the secretary at the ministry and wait for her to fill in the fourteen words on the form to prepare my permit. I got my work permit, but Mr. Richardson's walk to the immigration ministry cost me $1,000.

I went to see Dr. Lightbourn and brought him his copy of the work permit. He suggested I get things straightened out with the tax commissioner, as my adversaries could try to discredit me if my taxes were not fully paid.

The next day I called the tax commissioner's office and spoke to a very nice woman who set up an appointment for me. Two days later I met with the tax commissioner, a Bermudian gentleman of Portuguese descent. He asked me how much I wanted to pay in taxes. For a Canadian who was used to paying more than fifty percent of his income in taxes, I could not believe that someone was asking me how much I wanted to pay. I felt like replying the least possible, but knew that this was not an appropriate response. I gave the gentleman the income statement my accountant had prepared and after some friendly negotiation he and I agreed on how much tax I would pay.

Then I turned my attention to my clinic at the hospital. I called the secretary there and asked her to schedule my patients. She said that Mrs. Basely, the nurse supervisor of the orthopaedics clinic, had called my patients and advised them to see Dr. Cooperson. I spoke to Mrs. Basely, who referred me to Dr. Jameson as chief of staff. After a few phone calls and negotiations, my clinic time at the hospital was reallocated to me and I was able to schedule and see patients at the clinic.

Once I started seeing patients, I needed operating time at the hospital. Because I had had such difficulty getting time in the orthopaedics clinic, I decided to ask Mr. Richardson to write Mrs. Anderson, the executive director of the hospital, regarding my operating time. Mrs. Anderson sent me a letter allocating operating time and suggesting I present my list of surgical cases to Mrs. Santini, the operating room head nurse. When I gave the list to Mr. Santini she was upset that I had brought up the issue of operating time with Mrs. Anderson instead of with her. She said she would have readily allocated me the operating time had I asked her. I did not remind Mrs. Santini that she had refused to write a letter on my behalf and had refused to allow me to consult the 1995 operating room registry. Even though I had obtained the operating time that I had requested, I was not eager to work in the operating room. I felt that it was not a conducive and safe environment for me to operate on my patients. I feared that one of the anaesthetists would frame me as Dr. Joneson had done in the case of Mrs. S.A.

After I finished dealing with the hospital, I wrote the MIS to ask them to reconsider their decision not to cover my legal expenses. I described the circumstances under which I had been forced to change attorneys. The MIS responded that it was not the "policy of the Society to meet legal expenses for attorneys, instructed by members, without the Society's permission." I wrote again, asking them to reconsider the decision and stating that I had not been aware of that policy. The MIS declined once again to help cover my legal expenses. I met with Mr. Richardson, paid part of his legal fee and informed him of the MIS's decision. He said: "Don't worry. A lot of people owe me a lot of money. You will pay me when you can."

I did not worry too much about my legal bills, because I was working five days a week and was fully booked. My secretary sent invoices for the work I did after January 1998, when I left Dr. Trouts' office, to the insurance companies and we waited for them to pay me. In April 1998, Mr. Robbins, Dr. Trouts' bookkeeper, called to inform me that some of the insurance companies had sent payment for work that I had done after January to Dr. Trouts' office. He said that Dr. Trouts and his wife had ordered him to deposit the cheques in their account even though they knew the cheques were not intended for them and did not belong to them. I immediately called the insurance companies to inform them of the mistake and to ask them to reissue new cheques to me and retrieve the money from Dr. Trouts. They told me that it was not their policy to issue a cheque twice and that it was up to me to get the money from Dr. Trouts. I reminded them that it was their mistake and not mine, for I had notified them that I was no longer working from Dr. Trouts' office. I also pointed out that every invoice I sent had my new address typed at the bottom. They admitted their mistake, but still said the onus was on me to get the money from Dr. Trouts. I wrote to the insurance companies a second time and to some even a third time before they stopped mailing my cheques to Dr. Trouts' office.

Many patients who I had treated while working with Dr. Trouts came to my office to pay me, saying they would rather pay me than Dr. Trouts, or mailed cheques to my new office. My secretary suggested we cash these cheques in retaliation for Dr. Trouts' taking money that did not belong to him. I told her that the Bible says, "**Be not overcome of evil, but overcome evil with good**" (Romans 12:21), and that Dr. Trouts and I had a contract and I was going to honour it. If it was God's will, I said, some day I would receive the money that Dr. Trouts owed me.

CHAPTER THIRTY-FIVE

The "Independent Review"

In April 1998, Dr. Paytons, a white Bermudian in his late fifties and an internal medicine specialist, replaced Dr. Jameson as chief of staff. This change did not improve my situation – quite the contrary; it made it worse, for many reasons. First, Dr. Paytons was a close friend of Dr. Cooperson's. Second, he worked from Dr. Cooperson's office. Third, he seemed more intelligent and cunning than all my previous adversaries. Dr. Cooperson was emotional. He blushed and easily showed his anger when he dealt with me. Dr. Fascioni was very visible, loud and vocal, which made him predictable. Dr. Jameson apparently had not been mean when young, but had become an apprentice pirate once he managed to join the establishment that had initially rejected him. He never looked me in the eye when we spoke, but would instead look at the floor. I could sense that he was not proud of what he was doing. Dr. Paytons, on the other hand, was no amateur. He was always calm and looked me in the eye when we spoke. He even wore a faint smile and at the end of the conversation would ask if there was anything he could do for me. Of course, his intentions were anything, but good. Unlike the others, Dr. Paytons did not waste time. He wanted to get rid of me as quickly and efficiently as possible.

My first meeting with Dr. Paytons took place on April 15th, 1998. After a Wednesday meeting, he followed me to the hospital parking lot and asked if he could speak with me briefly. He probably chose the parking lot as a meeting place because he was aware that I had taped my conversations with Drs. Brookson and Jameson. Dr. Paytons said that two professors from Canada, one of whom he knew very well and had known for a long time, would be coming to Bermuda in May to review my work. I suggested he put anything he had to tell me in a letter and send it to my attorney.

On May 1st, Dr. Paytons sent a letter to Mr. Richardson, my attorney, stating that two "independent reviewers," Dr. Sonby of Kingston, Canada, and Dr. Voraks of Vancouver, would be in Bermuda from May 14th to 19th to review my work. Enclosed with the letter was a two-page document listing the names of sixty-two of my patients. The letter stated that this document constituted the terms of reference of the review.

Mr. Richardson said he would call the hospital's attorney to lodge a complaint because the hospital had not kept its promise of "sharing in advance the list of potential candidates and the terms of reference of the review." I advised him not to call the hospital's attorney and scheduled an appointment with him to explain why. I called Mr. Dunkin, my other attorney, and sought his opinion on how to respond to Dr. Paytons' letter. He agreed that we should not contact the hospital's attorney or the hospital authorities.

A few days later I met with Mr. Richardson and explained to him that the hospital's intention was not to conduct a fair review of my practice, but to remove my privileges and get rid of me, and that his intervention would not prevent the hospital from conducting the review they way they intended to. I did not see the point of reminding the hospital that it had reneged on its promise to conduct a fair and impartial review. Mr. Richardson had been billing me an average of $5,000 a month. I said that his arguing unnecessarily with the hospital's attorney would cost me more money and in the end his legal fees might do me more harm than the hospital authorities intended to. I showed him an e-mail that proved beyond a shadow of a doubt that Dr. Cooperson was acquainted with Dr. Voraks, one of the so-called independent reviewers. I also showed him a document dated April 27th, 1998, prepared by the hospital for the independent reviewers, and listing my patients' so-called complications. When I reviewed it I found the data it contained to be false and contrary to what was indicated in my patients' charts. Mr. Richardson finally agreed not to call the hospital's attorney and to write a letter to Dr. Paytons informing him that I would not meet with the so-called independent reviewers.

When I arrived in Bermuda in 1995, Dr. Trouts warned me that Drs. Cooperson and Fascioni would find cases I had not treated to their liking and file a complaint against me. He advised me to collect cases from Drs.

Cooperson and Fascioni's practice and file a complaint against them if they complained about me. At first I resolved not to play Drs. Cooperson and Fascioni's game, but after a while I found that I had no choice, but to take Dr. Trouts' advice if I was to defend myself. Thus I had collected cases from their practice that I thought could be the subject of investigation if my work was put under scrutiny. Now that the hospital had commissioned another review of my work, I felt that the so-called independent reviewers should also review Dr. Cooperson and Fascioni's work, especially since Dr. Brookson's mandate to review the work of all the orthopaedic surgeons had not been fulfilled. I wrote to Dr. Paytons suggesting that while his independent reviewers were in Bermuda they could address some issues that were of concern to me.

I suggested to Dr. Paytons that the independent reviewers investigate the number of arthroscopies conducted at the hospital. Drs. Fascioni and Cooperson performed more than two hundred and fifty knee arthroscopies per year. The problem was not only the number of arthroscopies being performed, but also the number of patients who were undergoing three or four of these procedures. I gave the example of a twenty-year-old woman whom I had seen in my office. She had had three arthroscopies on her knee and was scheduled to have a fourth. When I examined her, I found her to have genu-recurvatum (hyper-laxity in the knees) and all she needed was physiotherapy and some type of shoe insert. Neither of these measures had been proposed. The history of this young woman was not an isolated one.

When I first moved to Bermuda, Dr. Browne had asked me to co-sign forms for his patients to have an MRI abroad. He said it was the policy of the insurance companies that a family physician could not order an MRI, and he therefore needed the signature of a specialist. He said that the local orthopaedic surgeons did not order MRIs and he believed this was because without such tests they could operate at random and nobody would question them. I agreed to co-sign Dr. Browne's forms so that his patients could have an MRI abroad, but did not comment on the possible intentions of the orthopaedic surgeons since I was a newcomer and could not corroborate his story. With time, however, I realized that Dr. Browne was right, for none of Drs. Cooperson and Fascioni's patients with multiple repeat arthroscopies had an MRI or other diagnostic tests prior to their surgeries.

The second issue I brought to the attention of Dr. Paytons and suggested the so-called independent reviewers investigate was the case of Mr. J.P., a thirty-eight-year-old who had been involved in a road accident. From the time he was admitted to the emergency department until he left the hospital, Mr. J.P.'s chart was full of notes indicating he had a neck fracture. One of the first doctors who saw Mr. J.P. wrote:

> "C-Spine: Local tenderness…denies sensation below neck…continues to have upper back…neck pain…is complaining of neck pain…reluctant to roll because of neck pain…neck soreness."

Despite all of Mr. J.P.'s problems, he was never fitted with a neck brace and never had a CT scan of his neck. Dr. Fascioni, the treating physician, wrote in his chart, "MRI is of choice," but the patient was never sent abroad for an MRI. Dr. Paytons, who was asked to see the patient, wrote: "Management to date seems optimal. He should make a gradual and probably full recovery." Mr. J.P. never recovered. He remained quadriplegic and barely able to use his hands to eat. His attorney asked me to review his client's file and produce a medical report. My review of the patient's chart and x-rays showed that Mr. J.P. had a fracture of the neck that would have been better elucidated by a CT scan or an MRI and that he would have fared better with some sort of treatment. I do not know what the patient's attorney did with my report, but I doubt he could have sued the doctors or the hospital.

The third issue I brought to Dr. Paytons' attention was the case of Mr. H.M. I had seen this man in my office in October 1997. The referral from his family physician read as follows:

> "Many thanks for seeing this dear 81 year old for a 2nd opinion. His back problems started 3 years ago after a fall, since which he has constant low back pain…patient has been under Dr. Cooperson for 3 years for his back…"

The patient came to my office accompanied by his wife and a nurse. The nurse wheeled Mr. H.M. into my office, but had to transfer him to the bed because of his severe back pain. Mr. H.M. had fallen down the stairs three years earlier and sustained a compression fracture of three lumbar vertebrae.

The patient said that at the time of his injury he received physiotherapy in Dr. Cooperson's physiotherapy clinic, but was never fitted with a corset or advised to stay in bed until his back healed. He had had severe back pain for the last three years and had recently begun to have pain and weakness in his legs, to the extent that he was unable to walk. The patient said that Dr. Cooperson had performed arthroscopy on his right knee and told him the weakness in his legs was due to arthritis in his knees. Mr. H.M. said Dr. Cooperson had scheduled him for total knee replacement. My evaluation revealed that the patient's fractured vertebrae had healed in such a crooked way that it was pressing on his spinal cord and causing weakness to his legs. It also showed that the patient did not have pain in his knees. The knee x-rays were completely normal. The patient did not have any arthritis in his knees. I advised the patient of these results and told him to walk as best he could with the aid of a walker. I explained that any surgery on his back would be very complicated because of the crooked way the fracture had healed. The patient looked like Quasimodo. Mr. H.M. and his wife happy to learn that he did not require any more knee surgery.

I brought a total of ten issues to the attention of Dr. Paytons for the "independent reviewers" to investigate.

On Wednesday, May 6th, Mr. Toby, the chairman of the Board, phoned my office and asked to speak with me. Because I was absent, he spoke with Dr. Browne and asked him to convey the following message to me: Although Mr. Toby had assisted me after my presentation to the Board, my case would not be helped by my refusal to meet with the "independent reviewers." If I did not participate in the review Mr. Toby would not help me any more. Dr. Browne told Mr. Toby I would take the case to court if my privileges were removed again. Mr. Toby told him to inform me that the hospital had never lost a case in court and my case would be no exception.

On Friday, May 15th, at four p.m. I went to my hospital pigeonhole to see if I had any correspondence from the hospital authorities, as I was curious to find out if they were going to proceed with the review without my collaboration. There was none. I went to my office to finish some work before going home. At five o'clock my wife phoned. Dr. Paytons had called my home and left an urgent message for me to pick up a letter in my hospital pigeonhole. At seven o'clock I went to the hospital and fetched the letter. The "independent review" was scheduled for the next two days, Saturday and Sunday. Dr. Paytons provided me with his pager number and suggested I call him if I changed my mind about attending the review. As for my letter of May 2nd suggesting that the "independent reviewers" investigate the issues I raised, Dr. Paytons wrote: "it is not appropriate to expand the terms of reference of the External Reviewers." Enclosed with his letter was a document listing the names of sixty-two of my patients, which, I was told, constituted the "official" terms of reference. It was the first time I was given any indication of what the complaints against me were with regard to each patient – and this only fourteen hours before the review was to take place. When I read the terms of reference, I discovered that the complications ascribed to each patient were false, fabricated and diametrically opposed to the facts. Dr. Ilea, the resident whom Dr. Jameson, the former chief of staff, had hired to review my patients' files and come up with complications, had prepared the working documents for the review.

The next time I heard from the hospital was June 10th, when Dr. Paytons wrote to advise me that:

> "The Bermuda Hospitals Board has now considered the written report submitted by the independent external reviewers [Drs. Sonby and Voraks]. By reason of the matters contained in the report, I regret to inform you that your application for re-appointment to the medical staff has been refused. You therefore no longer have privileges at the King Edward VII Memorial Hospital."

The report produced by the "independent external reviewers" was a new and improved version of the Brookson report. Its conclusions were identical to those reached in the Brookson report, essentially that "Dr Bah should not be allowed to continue the practice of spine surgery at the King Edward VII Memorial Hospital."

I was glad I had not cooperated with the so-called independent reviewers, for the document they produced was anything, but objective. For example, they had reviewed fifty of my trauma and general orthopaedics patients and found that only two patients, with hip fractures, had minor complications that had been successfully treated. (The listed complications rate for hip fracture was over fifty percent. In the six-month period preceding the review, Dr. Cooperson had two of his patients with hip fracture die of bleeding, one during and the other immediately after surgery.) In their report, the reviewers wrote:

"Dr. Bah appears to recommend surgery for patients with traumatic Orthopaedic injuries according to current practice… His decisions seem to be appropriate with reference to the indication for surgery."

Despite writing the above, and despite having found that I had a success rate of ninety-six percent (forty-eight out of fifty patients), the reviewers concluded that I should not be allowed to "practice general Orthopaedics and trauma surgery on the island of Bermuda."

In essence, the "independent external reviewers" had fulfilled their mandate, which was to cover up the fiasco of the Brookson review and prepare a more complex report, one less subject to scrutiny. In his letter of May 15th, Dr. Paytons had indicated that sixty-two of my patients would constitute the terms of reference. The reviewers had reviewed ninety-six of my patients. The task that lay ahead of me, defending myself against the findings of this new review, was onerous, but not impossible.

CHAPTER THIRTY-SIX

Pocket Stitching

On June 18th, 1998, Mr. Richardson, my attorney, wrote an eight-page letter to the Bermuda Hospitals Board strongly objecting to the revoking of my privileges. He summarized my dealings with the hospital as follows:

> "Our client's failure to meet with Drs. Sonby and Voraks stems from his view that the dice were loaded against him and in our opinion he had good reason.

> You will recall that following our letter dated 6th March last to the Bermuda Hospitals Board, Mr. J. Barry acting for the Hospitals Board wrote to us on 9th March last informing us that the Board had decided to reinstate Dr. Bah with full privileges in Orthopaedic Surgery effective immediately, pending a further independent review of our client's case management. Mr. Barry further stated that the terms of reference, when drafted, would be shared with our client in advance, as will a list, of potential candidates. We assume he was so instructed by his client, the Bermuda Hospitals Board… No list of potential candidates was ever shared with us and our client is very aggrieved by that fact. He had a legitimate expectation that he would have some input in the selection of reviewers especially since he contended that previous dealings between the Bermuda Hospitals Board and himself smacked of unfairness and bias.

> When this whole matter started, it seemed that there was an intention to investigate the Orthopaedic Division of the Department of Surgery. As it turned out the whole investigation gravitated to an examination of Dr. Bah's practice. With that in mind Dr. Bah, in his letter dated 2nd May last to Dr. Paytons in addition to stating that he would not be available to meet with the two reviewers, referred to certain very serious matters with which the Bermuda Hospitals Board must be concerned. As far as we are aware nothing has been done about any of these very serious matters which, if

known, might very well shake the public's confidence in the running of the Orthopaedic Division of the Department of Surgery at least…

In all the [In the] circumstances, we would demand that our client's privileges, which were restored on 9th March last and withdrawn on 10th June last, be again restored.

If you are unable to comply with our demand within 48 (forty-eight) hours we will have no alternative but to seek judicial review of the Bermuda Hospitals Board's exercise of its statutory functions in connection with this matter."

The hospital authorities replaced Mr. Barry, the attorney who had written that the hospital would share with us the list of potential candidates and the terms of reference. On June 30th, Mrs. Ball, the new hospital attorney, responded to Mr. Richardson's letter as follows:

"You have supplied one reason only to support Dr. Bah's view that "the dice were loaded against him," namely that no list of potential candidate[s] was ever shared with Dr. Bah, as indicated in Mr. Barry's letter of 9 March, 1998… In fact, no list of potential candidates was ever created, since the Board instead sought recommendations from respected overseas professional bodies and persons.

Finally, we would address your, and your client's repeated request that the entire Orthopaedic department be reviewed… The Board has already obtained a report of the Orthopaedic Department, the Brookson Report. The status of the Orthopaedic Department is not a matter for your client, but rather a matter for the Board.

In summary, the fact that your client chose not to participate in the independent external review does not give him the right to make allegations of lack of due process and/or bias."

I met separately with Mr. Dunkin and Mr. Richardson to discuss my alternatives in light of the hospital's refusal to restore my privileges. Both attorneys were of the opinion that we would have to opt for judicial review of the Board's decision. Mr. Dunkin said that if everything proceeded according to schedule the case should be heard within six months. He said that meanwhile the hospital would try to "stitch up" my pocket – do everything in its power to prevent me from earning an income and thus hinder my ability to fight it. Mr. Richardson said the matter should be heard within six weeks and I should be back at work in September. He told me he had defended a schoolteacher who had lost her job and she was back at work within six weeks. Mr. Richardson said he would work on the court documents over the summer and would consult with Mr. Dunkin.

Mr. Dunkin was right when he said the hospital would do everything possible to "stitch up" my pocket. The first thing it did was to prevent me from obtaining my patients' x-rays. Some of the patients I saw in consultation had been referred by their family physician to the hospital for x-rays. The staff at the hospital told my patients they could not get their x-rays before seeing me because it was the hospital's policy not give x-rays films to any of Dr. Bah's patients. Dr. Paytons had posted a memorandum to that effect in the radiology department. Dr. Browne, my landlord, was furious when he learned of this policy. He said I was letting the hospital "step on" me. He phoned Dr. Paytons and gave him a piece of his mind. The radiology staff gave my patients their x-rays after that, but would give me either an empty envelope or the x-rays of another patient. To resolve the problem, I asked Dr. Maud, Dr. Browne's associate, to requisition x-rays on my behalf and instructed my patients not to mention my name when they went to the radiology department.

Another thing the hospital did to "stitch up" my pocket was notify the insurance companies of my status at the hospital. Shortly thereafter, the Bermuda Front Street Insurance Company (BFSIC) wrote to inform me that its policy stated that "a specialist is a medical practitioner who is properly qualified and hold a consultant appointment at the King Edward VII Memorial Hospital." The letter advised me that the BFSIC no longer considered me a specialist because I did not have privileges at the hospital, and it would therefore reimburse me for only half of the fees I was entitled to for seeing its clients; in addition, I could not refer patients abroad for MRIs.

Dr. Browne was furious when he learned of the BFSIC policy. He said once again that I was letting people step on me. I told him I could not fight on all fronts and I had chosen to concentrate my efforts on battling the hospital. Dr. Browne said he would call the vice-president of the BFSIC and lodge a complaint with regard to the policy of considering me a non-specialist and paying only half of my professional fee.

Dr. Browne urged me to call the Chief Medical Officer and complain about the BFSIC's discriminatory policy. I was reluctant to do this since I knew it would change nothing, but I did so because I had promised Dr. Browne that I would. I spoke to the secretary of Dr. Caisson, the Chief Medical Officer, since he was away from his office. Dr. Caisson, a black Bermudian, did not return my call but had his secretary advise me that the BFSIC was entitled to apply its policy of not paying me as a specialist. Meanwhile I discovered that Dr. Caisson was one of the directors of the BFSIC. When I told Dr. Browne what the secretary had said and that Dr. Caisson was a BFSIC director, he shook his head and advised me to concentrate on my legal fight with the hospital.

A few other companies followed the example of the BFSIC and advised me that they would reimburse me for only half of my fee for seeing their clients. However, the insurance company covering government employees, Government Employee Health Insurance (GEHI) and the largest insurance company in Bermuda, Somers Isles Insurance (SII), allowed me to treat their patients unhindered. I do not know why these two companies behaved differently from the others. In the end, more patients came to see me for consultations, which compensated for the income I lost by receiving only half of the fees I was entitled to.

When it became evident to the hospital authorities that their first two strategies had not worked – I was not about to leave the Island and would continue to fight them – they came up with another plan to limit my ability to earn an income. This plan was to publicize the fact that I had lost my privileges at the hospital. On August 18th a journalist from the local newspaper phoned me at home and said he wanted to talk to me about the matter. He said he had secured my attorney's permission to interview me and I could speak freely. This came as a surprise to me since my attorney and I had agreed that we did not want to have the case publicized. I told the journalist I would speak with my attorney and get back to him. The next day I called Mr. Richardson to verify that he had authorized the journalist to call me and had said I could speak freely. Mr. Richardson denied having given the journalist permission to call me.

On August 19th, the front page of the newspaper proclaimed "Banned Surgeon in Legal Fight."[1] The article stated that I had lost my right to admit patients to the hospital and to operate on them because "two doctors [Sonby and Voraks] claimed he was not properly qualified to perform spinal surgery at the hospital."

My accountant told me that my dispute with the hospital was also the subject of a radio talk show and that many of my patients called and spoke in my defence. My neighbour told me the story made the evening news on television. I tried to stay out of the limelight and concentrate on my work. Patients came to see me in greater numbers despite the hospital having publicized the fact that I had lost my privileges.

[1] Neil Roberts, *The Royal Gazette,* August 19th, 1998, p. 1.

CHAPTER THIRTY-SEVEN

Moving

My wife and children had spent the summer of 1998 in Montreal while I was busy with my legal fight in Bermuda. While there, my wife met Dr. T., the chief of orthopaedics and my former colleague, who invited her and the children to his home. Dr. T. asked my wife about me and my work. She could not hide the fact that she was unhappy in Bermuda. Dr. T. wrote me a four-page letter apologizing for our earlier misunderstanding and urging me to return to Montreal and work with him. He asked the other orthopaedic surgeons and nurses in the clinic, operating room and ward to also write urging me to return. I was touched to receive all their letters, but could not return to Montreal just yet.

In June 1998, Mr. Richardson had told me I should have my privileges restored by the end of the summer. In September it became obvious to me that Mr. Richardson had sweet-talked me and I was nowhere near having them restored. Nevertheless I decided to stay in Bermuda and continue my fight, at least for the time being. On the other hand, my wife decided that she had had enough of Bermuda and was going to move back to Montreal with the children. Before settling there, she returned to Bermuda to help me vacate the two-bedroom apartment. At the beginning of September I called our landlady, Mrs. Richards, and informed her of our desire to vacate at the end of the month. To my surprise she agreed to let us leave without setting any conditions. She even agreed to give us back the $2,500 deposit we had made upon signing the lease. After my unpleasant dealings at the hospital and with Dr. Trouts, it was refreshing to deal with somebody like Mrs. Richards. My wife arrived in mid-September and within one week had sold all our furniture. She even found suitable tenants for the apartment.

Before leaving Bermuda, my wife urged me to retrieve my surgical instruments from the hospital. I called the operating room and asked Mrs. Santini to prepare them for my wife to pick up. Mrs. Santini told me she would do so and said, "How about the operating frame?" (Which the other orthopaedic surgeons did not wish to buy, but were using anyway). "What about it?" I said. Mrs. Santini asked if I would donate the frame to the hospital. I told her I would be willing to exchange my frame for two spinal instruments belonging to the hospital, to which she agreed. When my wife arrived to pick up my instruments, Mrs. Santini gave her only one belonging to the hospital instead of the two we had agreed upon. My wife told her to return the frame if she was not prepared to give me two instruments in exchange for it. Mrs. Santini refused. My wife was furious when she arrived home and urged me to go to the hospital myself. When I verified the instruments Mrs. Santini had given my wife, I found that twenty-five were missing.

The following day, I went to the hospital and told Mrs. Santini she had neglected to include twenty-five of my instruments. She said she had given my wife all the instruments belonging to me. I produced a photograph of all my instruments displayed in an operating tray. I had taken it to illustrate to the nurses how I wished to have the instruments displayed during surgery. When Mrs. Santini saw the photograph she had no choice, but to acknowledge that she had not given me all of my instruments. She took the photograph and went to the storage room. She came back a few minutes later carrying some old, malfunctioning instruments and said these were my missing ones. I pointed out that these were not my instruments, but the hospital's and that mine were probably in a tray waiting to be used by the other orthopaedic surgeons. Mrs. Santini began to argue with me again. She said the instruments in the trays were hospital property and those in her hand were mine. I produced an invoice indicating that I had purchased all of my instruments from the same company and pointed out that the engraving on those she held did not correspond to the name of the company on the invoice. A black Bermudian recovery room nurse who had been witnessing our argument whispered audibly, "If they don't want him to operate here, why don't they give him back his instruments?" Mrs. Santini then acknowledged that the other surgeons were using my instruments. She said she would instruct the only nurse who was familiar with my instruments to find them and suggested I return in a few days. I told her I wished to take back my operating frame since she had not given me in exchange the two instruments as agreed. She gave me an additional one and I left the frame at the hospital. My wife departed for Montreal without my instruments.

The following weekend, I went back to the hospital and met with the nurse who Mrs. Santini had assigned to find my instruments. For two hours she and I opened all the orthopaedic trays and found my instruments prepared and waiting to be used by the other surgeons.

A few days later, I had an opportunity to have my instruments shipped to Canada. Mr. Pronovost, a pharmaceutical representative from Canada, was in Bermuda to retrieve the implants I had been inserting in patients, as the other surgeons had decided not to use them. Mr. Pronovost encountered problems similar to those I had experienced. It took a nurse and him three full days to gather all of his implants. By the time they finished he was scheduled to depart for Canada and was unable to take the seven trays of implants with him. Mr. Pronovost offered to ship my instruments with his implants. He wrapped and packed all the implants and instruments together, ready for shipping. By then it was late Friday afternoon and the courier companies were closed, so he asked Mrs. Santini to have the packages picked up on Monday. Mrs. Santini referred him to a gentleman in the shipping department of the hospital. Mr. Pronovost took the packages to the gentleman, who assured him he would call the courier company on Monday morning.

Two months later, Mr. Pronovost phoned me. He was worried because he still had not received his implants and my instruments. He had called Bermuda and spoken to Mrs. Santini and the gentleman in the shipping department, both of whom assured him the packages had left Bermuda months earlier. He had called the courier company, who had no record of the shipment. He sought my advice as to how he could recuperate my instruments and his implants worth more than $100,000. I told him not to despair – one day they would turn up. I advised him to keep calling Bermuda daily. Mr. Pronovost was not amused by my optimism. He said he was losing money every day because surgeons in Canada were waiting for his implant trays. On January 29th, 1999, four months after he had left his trays in the hospital's shipping department, Mr. Pronovost called to inform me that his office in Toronto had received some of the trays. He said that, contrary to what he had been told, the trays had never left the hospital. They had been left sitting all that time in the shipping department exactly where he had left them. Apparently the gentleman had gone on vacation and assigned another man the task of calling the courier company. A few days later, Mr. Pronovost phoned me to say he had received all of his missing trays.

Under normal circumstances it is very difficult to find suitable rental accommodations in Bermuda. Since I had only one month to find a place, this task was particularly onerous. However, I had learned that the best way to find accommodations was to let all one's acquaintances know that one is looking, and this is exactly what I did. When my neighbours, the Remonds, a couple from France whom I had befriended, learned that I was seeking accommodations they invited me to stay in their home. They were both retired, but Mrs. Remond, a workaholic, was running a bed and breakfast in their five-bedroom house.

The Remond house was full of guests most of the time, but Mrs. Remond offered me one of their bedrooms. Tourists paid a daily rate of $100, which is low by Bermuda standards, but the couple, who were aware of my fight with the hospital, said I could pay them whatever I could afford.

I accepted their offer and moved in. The Remonds and I had dinner together every evening. They waited for me even when I had to work late at the office. After dinner we would sit in the living room for tea and Mrs. Remond would enlighten me about Bermuda history and teach me some French wisdom. The Remonds had been living in Bermuda for more than four decades, and Mrs. Remond, who had a phenomenal memory, would tell me everything that went on there in the last forty years and had been published in the local newspaper. One of the French sayings she taught me was "Qui dit bon, dit bête," which translates as "a person who is too nice may be stupid." Fortunately, the saying did not apply to the Remonds for though they were extremely nice to me. I became part of the family. Even Romeo, their cat, adopted me, though not before first staring at me when I sat in his favourite chair.

CHAPTER THIRTY-EIGHT

Learning from the Bible

In April 1996, while on vacation in Mexico, I realized that I had moved hastily from Montreal to Bermuda and had not necessarily made the right decision. I thought of moving back to Montreal, but had returned to Bermuda because I believed God had indicated that I was to do so. I stayed there because I felt indebted to God for getting me out of trouble when I was ill and on duty at Easter 1996. I also found a church in my neighbourhood to attend.

Some of my acquaintances who knew I was going to church would ask which one I was attending. When I would answer Cobb's Hill Methodist Church they would say that was a small church and invite me to theirs, which was bigger and had a larger choir. I would say I had nothing against big churches and large choirs, but I liked my small church. I liked it because God had found it for me. I liked it because all the parishioners knew each other by name and we were like family. I also liked it because the preaching was intellectual and educational as opposed to yelling and screaming. I loved the singing by the small choir that was joyful and uplifting. I often clapped and sang with more enthusiasm than all the other parishioners. My fellow usher, for I had become an usher, standing across from me would look at me and smile. My children would say, "Please, Daddy, don't sing." My children's pleas did not prevent me from joining the male choir. After a while I even felt that I had a beautiful singing voice and the other choir members were polite enough not to tell me otherwise. In addition to joining the choir and regularly attending the services, I attended the men's fellowship once a week. There we prayed for each other, encouraged one another and learned about the Bible. Hearing the pastor, who was a taxi driver, and the other men talk about their problems reminded me that I was not the only one in the world who had problems. I also liked my small church because when we met for fellowship we greeted each other with a warm, genuine and caring attitude, ate a lot, teased each other, and talked about everything and nothing, but not about one another. I liked my church because nobody was looked up to or down upon because of the amount of money they gave to the church. In the two years that I attended the church, nobody asked me about my religious background or tried to push any religious ideas on me.

I attended the church freely, and neither the pastor nor the other members meddled in my personal or spiritual life. As long as I was married rather than living common law and not involved in any of the other activities that the Bible prohibited, I was accepted. Florence, the woman who had first invited me to the church, had been right when she told me that in her church they did not judge others, but let everyone make up their own minds about Jesus after hearing the sermon. I believed they acted that way not because they did not care about my soul, but because they were discreet and respectful of others.

In fact, every sermon I heard preached in the church was about salvation (deliverance from sin and from the sentence prescribed for sinning by accepting Jesus Christ as the Saviour). At the end of every sermon the preacher invited people to the altar, but did not embarrass anyone who had not accepted Jesus as the Saviour by asking us to raise our hands so he could pray for us. In the two years I attended the church I saw many people go to the altar to accept Jesus as their Saviour. Some were extremely joyful and some cried. I could not understand their emotional outburst. I liked Jesus all right, but I had a lot of conflicting ideas about who He really was. Growing up in a Muslin environment, I had learned that Jesus was a prophet like any other prophet who existed before him (*Sura 2:136; 3:84; 4:171*). I had also learned from the Koran that it was not proper to say that God had a son (*Sura 2:116; 4:171; 5:75; 6:101; 9:30; 10:68; 17:111; 18:4; 19:35, 88, 91; 23:91; 25:2; 39:4; 72:3*) and that it was heresy to equate God with man (*Sura 5:19,75; 9:31*). Although I had not been a very religious child, the teachings about Jesus I had learned in my childhood had impregnated my brain and conflicted with what I was hearing in my church in Bermuda. I was repeatedly hearing that Jesus was the Son of God. So I set out to read my Bible again, with the purpose of trying to understand who and what Jesus was. In the Bible, I discovered that Jesus was referred to as the Son of God on more than a hundred occasions (*Matthew 3:17; 4:3,6; 8:29; 11:27; 14:33, 16:16,27; 17:5; 26:63; 27:40,43,54; 28:19; Mark 1:1,11; 3:11; 5:7; 9:7; 13:32; 14:61; 15:39; Luke 1:32,35; 4:3,9,41; 8:28; 9:35; 10:22; 22:70; John 1:18, 34, 49; 3:16, 17,18,35, 36; 5:19, 20, 21, 22, 23, 25, 26; 6:40,69; 9:35; 10:36; 11:4, 27; 14:13; 17:1; 19:7; 20:31; Acts 3:13, 26; 8:37; 9:20; 13:33; Romans 1:3, 4, 9; 5:10; 8:3, 29, 32, I Corinthians 1:9; 15:28; II Corinthians 1:19; Galatians 1:16; 2:20; 4:4, 6; Ephesians 4:13; Colossians 1: 13; I Thessalonians 1:10; Hebrews 1:2, 5, 8; 3:6; 4:14; 5:5, 8; 6:6; 7: 3; 10:29; 11:17; II Peter 1:17; I John 1:3, 7; 2:22, 23, 24; 3:8, 23; 4:9, 14, 15; 5:5, 10, 12, 13, 20; II John 1:3,9; Revelation 2:18*). At the end of my many readings of the Bible, I was even more confused about who Jesus was. What I was about to learn at Bible study would confuse me even more about who Jesus was.

One Sunday, Rudy, a church member, invited me to attend a Bible study session. He introduced me to a young man who had recently joined our church and told me he was the Bible study leader. I was sceptical because the young man looked like a boy. I accepted Rudy's invitation anyway because Rudy, who was usually very quiet, was also very humble and knowledgeable about the Bible and because I was eager to learn more about the Bible in the hope of reconciling the two divergent views I held of Jesus.

The following Tuesday, Rudy and his wife, Kathy, picked me up at my home and we drove to the other end of the Island. The session, which was scheduled for eight p.m., started half an hour late because people arrived late and then chatted with each other. Finally, at around half past eight, twelve of us were sitting around the large dining table. When a new person joined the group, it was customary for the other members to introduce themselves and briefly explain how they had come to join the group.

Lloyd, the host, was the first to speak. He said that a few years earlier his eight-year-old daughter had indicated to her Sunday school teacher, Kelly, her wish to see her dad saved. He told us that his daughter and Kelly prayed for this. Lloyd said that God arranged it in such a way that he and Kelly started meeting at his home once a week so that Kelly could answer his questions about the Bible, and slowly the meetings turned into Bible study sessions, with more people attending. When it came my turn I spoke briefly about how I had come to attend Cobb's Hill Methodist Church and said that Rudy had invited me to attend the Bible study session. Kelly spoke last. He told us he had loved what he called "the word of God, the Bible" since his youth. Kelly said the purpose of the sessions was to learn about "the word of God, the King James Bible"; whatever we would discuss should centre on "the word of God, the Bible" and the Bible would be the final authority, not him. We prayed and then began. Kelly told me that it was customary for the newest member to ask the first question. I politely declined and said I would rather have another member ask the first question. When the session started I realized I had underestimated Kelly because of his apparent youth, for his knowledge of the Bible was impressive. Later I would observe that he always came with a prepared topic, but rarely presented it, instead answering the questions of the members. When someone asked a question, Kelly would, without hesitation, flip through the Bible and use the five fingers of his left hand as bookmarks. He would then refer to the passages he had bookmarked in answering our questions. He always brought a Concordance and a dictionary with him, but I saw him use the dictionary only twice. He never became irritated when one of us interrupted him. In any case the discussion was always civil. When we got carried away, Kelly would listen patiently and after a while, smile, politely bring the meeting to order and remind us that the discussion had to centre around the "the word of God, the Bible." The session finished around ten o'clock with a prayer, but the discussion would continue until eleven and then we would finally all leave.

The second week I was eager to avail myself of the privilege of asking the first question, as a new member. For the next few months I asked the first or second question at every session. Although my questions were elementary, neither Kelly nor the other members of the group became irritated or impatient with me. At the end of the evening Kelly and his wife, Stacey, would drive me home, and sometimes Rudy and Kathy as well, for we all lived in the same neighbourhood. On the way home I would ask more questions. We never got home before midnight because of my questions.

After six months of regular attendance, I told Kelly I understood everything about the Bible and would ask no more questions. Two weeks later I was asking Kelly and the others more questions about the Bible. I loved

Bible study so much that when I travelled away from Bermuda I left on Wednesday and returned on Monday in order not to miss a session, as Tuesday was Bible study night. The people were very considerate and respectful. Like the members of the church I attended, they spoke about Jesus and salvation, answered my questions and let me make up my own mind.

None of the members queried me about my religious background or my personal life. At the end of each session we would stand, hold hands and pray for one another. They prayed for me, and some even fasted for me, when they read in the newspaper of my problems at the hospital.

I became confused about who Jesus was until one day Kelly read the following passages from the Bible: "**In the beginning was the Word, and the Word was with God, and the Word was God**" (*John 1:1*); "**And the Word was made flesh, and dwelt among us, (and we beheld his glory, the glory as of the only begotten of the Father), full of grace and truth**" (*John 1:14*). Kelly said these verses proved that Jesus [**the Word**] was God and showed us other verses in the Bible that, he said, supported them (*Psalms 110:1; Isaiah 7:14, 9:6; Micah 5:2; Matthew 1:23; 22:43, 44; 28:17, 18; Mark 2:5–7; Luke 7:48; John 10: 30, 38; 14: 8–11; 20:28; Acts 7:59; 17:31; Philippians 2:6–8; Colossians 1:13–16*). I had come to the sessions not only to learn about the Bible, but also to reconcile the two conflicting views I held of Jesus: that He was only a prophet, as I had been taught as a Muslim, and that He was the Son of God, as I was learning in church. Now, Kelly and his group were telling me that Jesus was not only the Son of God, but also God. Had I not been around Kelly and his group long enough to know that they were not fanatical, I would have walked out never to return. Instead, I stayed and asked Kelly to explain to me how Jesus, a person, could be the Son of God and at the same time God. Kelly said I had to understand that God does not think the way human beings do, and the notion that Jesus can be the Son of God and at the same time God can be difficult for us to appreciate. To illustrate, he referred to three verses from the Bible:

> "**For my thoughts [are] not your thoughts, neither [are] your ways my ways, saith the LORD. For [as] the heavens are higher than the earth, so are my ways higher than your ways, and my thoughts than your thoughts**" (Isaiah 55:8,9).

> "**But the natural man receiveth not the things of the Spirit of God: for they are foolishness unto him: neither can he know** *them*, **because they**

are spiritually discerned" (I Corinthians 2:14).

"And without controversy great is the mystery of godliness: God was manifest in the flesh, justified in the Spirit, seen of angels, preached unto the Gentiles, believed on in the world, received up into glory" (I Timothy 3:16).

I never claimed to think like God, but my human mind needed a simple explanation, an analogy, something – anything – to help me understand the idea that Jesus is the Son of God and also God. Kelly gave me the following illustration. He said that water is the most important element in the world. Water from the rivers, lakes and oceans evaporates into vapour or steam. The steam condenses into clouds. Then the water droplets in the clouds fall back into the ground, rivers, lakes and oceans. He said that water, steam and cloud seem to be distinct and separate entities, but they are not. They are a continuum. He said it is the same for God the Father, God the Son and God the Holy Ghost.

He said, furthermore, that we know that water is made up of three molecules, two hydrogen and one oxygen. Kelly said that instead of thinking of God the Father, God the Son (Jesus) and God the Holy Ghost as 1 + 1 + 1 = 3 gods, we should think of them as 1 x 1 x 1 = 1 God. He asked if I understood. I said I understood his analogies. After that, I came to the conclusion that I could spend a lifetime trying to resolve the divergent views of Jesus as illustrated in the Bible versus the Koran and not succeed. I decided that I should try to assure myself of eternal life, enlightenment, salvation or a place in heaven instead of trying to figure out who and what Jesus was.

When it came to the topic of salvation, I found that the way to achieve eternal life as described in the Bible is completely different from the ways I had been taught as a child and as written in the Koran. The Koran teaches that there is no "**intercessor**" or "**protector**" between man and God, that every soul will have to deliver itself by it owns acts (*Sura 2:120; 4:123; 6:14,51,70; 116; 10:3; 13:37; 17:97; 18:17,26; 29:22; 30:13; 33:17, 65; 40:18; 42:8, 9, 44; 48:22; 86:4*). The Koran teaches that a soul has to fulfil two sets of conditions in order to attain salvation. The first is to believe in God, the Messenger Muhammad and the apostles, fear God and repent (*Sura 2:25, 62,277; 3:57,89, 114; 4:17,37, 57, 122, 152, 146,162, 173, 175; 5:10, 37; 7:42, 43; 10:9; 11:22–23; 12: 57; 14:23; 18:30, 107;*

19:60,96; 22:14, 23; 28: 80; 29:7, 9, 58; 30:37; 31:8; 32:19; 34:4; 41:8; 42:23, 26 47:2, 12; 48:5; 57:19; 66:8; 85:25, 11; 95:6). The second is that one has to "**fulfil if thy hope to be admitted to heaven is to be righteous and do good deeds**" (*Sura: 3:15, 133, 198; 13: 35,45; 16:30,31; 18:107; 22:14, 23, 56; 25:15; 26:90; 29:9; 30:15; 31:8; 32:19; 40:8, 40; 42:22,23; 43:72; 46:14; 47:12,15; 50:31; 51:15; 52:17; 54:54; 65:11; 68:34; 77:41; 85:11).*

The Koran teaches that a righteous person is a believer who will fulfil the five pillars or demands that are placed on him or her. The five pillars are:

1. Daily recitation of the Koran (*Sura: 17:45,106; 18:27; 29:45; 33:34; 73:4*).

2. Performing the five prescribed daily prayers (*Sura: 2:277; 4:77, 103; 5:13, 58; 6:72; 8:3; 9:5,11,18,71; 10:87; 11:114; 13:22; 14:31; 17:78; 21:73; 27:3; 30: 31; 107:5*)

3. The giving of alms (*Sura 9:58; 60,103*)

4. Fasting during the month of Ramadhan (*Sura: 2:183–185, 187; 4:92; 58:4*)

5. HAJJ or pilgrimage to Mecca (*Sura: 2:196–197; 22:1,7,30*)

The Bible's teachings on how to attain salvation are different from those of the Koran. The Bible teaches that God promised Abraham that he would bless him and multiply and bless his descendants (*Genesis 12:2; 17:5; 18:18; 22:12–17; 26:3–4*). God also promised Abraham that in his descendants would all the nations of the earth be blessed because Abraham believed God (*Genesis 12:3; 18:18; 22:18; 26:3–4*). Then, the Bible teaches that God gave the commandments and the law to Moses, a descendant of Abraham, to teach the nation of Israel how to love God, love their neighbour and live a holy life (*Exodus 20:1–17*). The Bible teaches that God did set up a system of offerings as a way for people to seek temporary forgiveness for their sins (*Lev: 1:1–17:16*). The law and the sacrifices were not designed to give people everlasting forgiveness and salvation. The Bible shows that people offered sacrifices year after year to obtain temporary forgiveness.

The Bible describes numerous instances in which God saved His people from their enemies and their troubles, but also that salvation was temporary and not soul-saving and eternal (*Exodus 3:8; Numbers 10:9; Deuteronomy*

33:29; Judges 3:9; 4:14; 7:7; 8:7; 10:11; 11:30,32; 13:15; I Samuel 7:14; 12:10; 17:37; 23:14; II Samuel 3:18; 19:9; 22:4; Nehemiah 9:27).

The Bible teaches that about 1,260 years after Abraham and about 740 B.C., the prophet Isaiah spoke of the promised eternal salvation (*Isaiah 25:8–9*), saying that salvation was near (*Isaiah 46:13; 51:5; 56:1*). Speaking in the future tense, Isaiah said, "**Israel shall be saved in the Lord with an everlasting salvation...**" (*Isaiah 25:9; 26:1; 30:15; 45:2,17; 51:8; 62:1; 62:11; 64:5*). Isaiah said that when eternal salvation would come to Israel it would also be for all the nations, as per the promise God made to Abraham ("**Look unto me, and be ye saved, all the ends of the earth: for I [am] God, and [there is] none else**") (*Isaiah 45:22, 49:6–8; 53:11*). Then, Isaiah portrayed the messiah as the Christ, the anointed one of God, who would bring eternal salvation to Israel and the rest of the world (*Isaiah 9:6–7*). He prophesized that the messiah would be a descendant of David (*Isaiah 11:1–5*), that a virgin would give birth to a son, who would be the messiah, (*Isaiah 7:14*). Isaiah also prophesized that the people would reject the messiah (*Isaiah 53:3*) and the messiah would be judged and condemned to die for the sins of many (*Isaiah 53:5–12*).

Then, a few years after Isaiah, about 627 B.C., Jeremiah, another prophet, reminded the people that eternal salvation had not yet come (*Jeremiah 8:20*). Jeremiah prayed for eternal salvation (*Jeremiah 17:14*) and speaking in the future tense, also prophesized that the messiah, the Christ, who would bring salvation to Israel and to the rest of the world, would be of the lineage of David (*Jeremiah 23:4–6; 33:15–16*).

Around 480 B.C., Zechariah, another prophet, said the messiah, who would bring salvation to Israel and to the world, would enter Jerusalem upon an ass and "**...he shall speak peace unto the heathen: and his dominion [shall be] from sea [even] to sea, and from the river [even] to the ends of the earth**" (*Zechariah 9:9,10*).

Then, 15 months B.C., Zacharias, the father of John the Baptist, became dumb and speechless when he learned of the imminent birth of his son. Zacharias, who regained his speech after the birth of John the Baptist, prophesized of the coming of the messiah and foretold that John was the forerunner of the long-expected messiah (*Luke 1:68–69*).

The Bible teaches that all of the above prophesies suggest Jesus as the messiah, the Christ, and that the prophesies were fulfilled with the birth of Jesus. It teaches that God revealed Jesus as the messiah, the Christ, the anointed one of God, first to Simeon, a devout man, and Anna, a prophetess (*Luke 2:25–38*). It is written that Simeon thanked God and spoke these words when he took the eight-day-old baby Jesus in his arms "…**mine eyes have seen salvation, Which thou has prepared before the face of all people; A light to lighten the Gentiles, and the glory of thy people Israel**" (*Luke 2:30–32*).

When John the Baptist started his ministry, the Bible teaches, he said he was not the messiah, but the one whom the prophet Isaiah spoke of, saying God would send a prophet to prepare the coming of the messiah (*Isaiah 40:3; Matthew 3:3; Mark 1:7–8; Luke 3:15–17; John 1:23–27*). John the Baptist told his disciples that Jesus was the messiah, the Son of God (*John 1:29–34*). The Bible shows that Jesus' first recorded word was when he told his mother, "**How is that ye sought me? Wist ye not that I must be about my Father's** [God] **business?**" (*Luke 2:49*). It shows that at the start of his ministry on earth Jesus preached and said he was the messiah spoken of by Isaiah and the prophets (*Luke 4:18–21; Isaiah 61:1–2*).

Unlike the Koran, the Bible teaches that there is a mediator between God and man and that Jesus is the "**mediator**," the "**advocate**" (*John 5:22,27; 6:35; 17:2; Romans 8:34; Galatians 3:14,24; I Timothy 2:2–6; Hebrews 2:8; 7:25; 9:15; 12:24; I John 2:1*). The Bible teaches that every soul needs to go through Jesus, "**the mediator**," "the **advocate**," in order to attain salvation (*John 5:22*), that salvation cannot be attained by obeying the laws God gave to Moses nor by doing good works (*Romans 3:20,27,28; 4:2,3,6,15,16; 9:11, 32; Galatians 2:16, 21; 3:11, 5:4; Ephesians 2:8–10; II Timothy 1:9; Titus 2:14; 3:5*). It teaches that God has looked at humankind and found that none is just, none of us do good and the righteousness of all humankind is a dirty piece of dusting cloth (*I King 8:46; 2 Chronicles 6:36; Psalms 14:1,3; 53:1,3; Proverbs 20:9; Ecclesiastics 7:20; Jeremiah 4:22; Micah 7:2; Luke 18:19; Romans 3:10–12, 23; I John 1:8*) (*Isaiah 48:1; 64:6,7*), and that God has found that every human being is at best hypocritical and vain (*Job 7:16; 8:9; 11:11; 27:8; Psalms 4:2; 10:7; 12:2; 39:5,6,11; 41:6; 49:10; 62:9; 89:47; 94:1; 144:4; Ecclesiastics 1:2, 14; 2:1,11,12; 6:12; 12:8; Isaiah 9:17; 41:29; 59:4; Acts 4:25; Romans 1:21; 8:20; I Corinthians 3:20*).

After painting such a dismal picture of mankind's character, the Bible teaches that humanity is deprived of the glory of God and thus deserves to perish (*Romans 3:23*) (*Isaiah 60:12; Jonah 3:9; Matthew 5:29–30; 11:22,24; Luke 10:12–15; 13:3,5; Romans 1:18–21; 2:12*). It teaches that God is merciful and desires that none should perish, but that all should be saved. This gives every human being the opportunity to have eternal life (*Isaiah 45:22; John 3:15, 16; Luke 13:3, 5; I Corinthians 10:33; 2 Peter 3:9*). The Bible teaches that God freely gives every individual the faith he or she needs to be saved and that it is not something one has to work for, but is a gift (*Galatians 3:22; Ephesians 2:5,8,9; II Timothy 1:9; Titus 3:5*). All an individual needs to do to be saved, to receive salvation – eternal life – is to accept the gift from God, the faith that allows one to believe the following:

1. Everyone has sinned (*Romans 3:23; 5:12; 1 John 1:10*).

2. The penalty of sin is death (*Romans 5:12,21; 6:23; 8:2; Ephesians 2:5; James 1:15; 1 John 5:17*).

3. Jesus Christ died for the propitiation (covering, reparation) of all the sins of humankind (*Isaiah 53:4,5; Romans 3:25; 4:25; 5:6,8,9; 8:3; I Corinthians 15:3; I Thessalonians 1:10; Hebrews 1:3; 2:17; I Peter 2:24; I John 1:7; 2:2; 4:10*).

4. Repenting (being sorry and turning away from one's sins), confessing with one's mouth and believing in one's heart that God has raised Jesus from dead will lead to one's salvation (deliverance) (*Matthew 3:2; 4:17; 10:32; Mark 1:15; Luke 12:8; Acts 2:38; 3:19; 8:22,35–38; 15:11; 16:31; 17:30; Romans 4:24; 10:8–10,13*).

The Bible teaches that God will justify ("without blame before God, God will declare him or her righteous") every individual who believes that Jesus paid with His life for the redemption (deliverance) of his or her sins (*Matthew 20:28; Acts 13:39; Romans 3:24,28; 4:25; 5:1,9,16,18; I Corinthians 1:30; 6:20; Galatians 2:16,17; 3:11,24; 4:4,5; Ephesians 1:7; Colossians 1:14; Titus 2:14; Hebrews 5:3; 7:27; 9:12; 9:15; I John 1:7; Revelations 5:9*) and that God will sanctify (purify) every individual who believes that Jesus died for his or her sins and he or she will be at peace with God (*John 14:27; 16:33; 20:21; Acts 10:36; 26:18; Romans 2:10; 5:1; 15:33; 15:16; I Corinthians 1:2,3,30; 6:11; 7:15; 14:33; II Corinthians 13:11; Galatians 1:3; 6:16; Ephesians 2:14–17; 6:23; Philippians 1:2; 4:7,9; Colossians 1:2; 20; 3:15; I Thessalonians 1:1; 5:23; II Thessalonians 1:2; 2:13; 3:16; II Timothy 2:22;*

Hebrews 2:11; 10:10,14; I Peter 1:2; 5:14; II Peter 1:2; 3:14; II John 1:3; Jude 1:1).

I was as confused as ever about how to attain salvation when I finished reading the Koran and the Bible and comparing notes on how these two books suggest the way to salvation. My confusion was compounded by the fact that the Koran teaches that Jesus did not die on the cross – it was only made to appear as if He had been crucified (*Sura 4:157*) – whereas the Bible teaches that the death and resurrection of Jesus is the centre of the Christian faith (*Matthew 16:21; 17:9,23; 20:19; 26:32; 27:63; 28:6; Mark 8:31; 9:9; 10:34; 14:28; 16:6,9,14; Luke 7:22; 9:22; 18:33; 24:6,7, 34,46; John 2:22; 11:24–25; 20:9; 21:14; Acts 2:23–24, 31, 32; 3:15, 26; 4:2,10,33; 5:30; 10:40; 13:30, 33,34,37; 17:3,18,31; Romans 4:24,25; 6:4,5,9; 7:4; 8:11,34; 10:9; 14:9; 15:12; I Corinthians 6:14; 15:4, 14–17; II Corinthians 4:14; 5:15; Galatians 1:1; Ephesians 1:20; 2:6; Colossians 2:12; 3:1; I Thessalonians 1:10; 4:14; II Timothy 2:8; I Peter 1:3,21; 3:21).* The Bible teaches that the death and resurrection of Jesus is so important that the faith of all would be in vain and indeed all of humanity would still be in sin had Jesus not died on the cross (*I Corinthians 15:14–17*).

My dilemma of which path to follow in order to be saved and assu-red of a place in heaven remained unresolved until I attended a lecture given by a physician. One day an American patient of mine, a preacher's wife, invited me to a talk at her church given by an American orthopae-dic surgeon, a missionary working in Bangladesh. The woman, Mrs. Sandy Payne, was so sweet and caring that I decided to go. The lecturer, Dr. Viggo Olsen, had been medically treating Muslim Bangladeshi men and women and converting them to Christianity. He gave a slide presentation on the work he and his wife were doing. Dr. Olsen said he won Bangladeshis over to Christianity not by dwelling on the doctrinal differences between Islam and Christianity, but by exploiting what the two religions had in common. I thought that maybe I would find the path to salvation if I followed Dr. Olsen's advice and exploited what Christianity and Islam had in common instead of trying to resolve their doctrinal differences. So I set out to find a middle path to salvation.

When I looked at what the two religions had in common, I found the following.

Both teach that there is only one God (Bible: *Genesis 21:33; 24:3; Exodus 6:3; Deuteronomy 4:35,39; 10:14,17; 33:27; Joshua 2:11; 22:22; II Samuel 7:22,28; 22:32; I Kings 8:23,60; 18:39; I Chronicles 17:20; II Chronicles 2:5; 6:14; 20:6; Psalms 136:2; Proverbs 26:10; Isaiah 9:6; 40:28; 42:5; 43:10–12; 44:6,8; 45:5,14,21,22; 46:9; 54:5; Jeremiah 10:10; Daniel 2:47; 3:26; 11:36; Jonah 1:9; Mark 5:7; 12:29,32; Luke 8:28; Acts 17:24; I Corinthians 8:4,6; Galatians 3:20; Ephesians 4:6; I Timothy 1:17; Hebrews 3:4; 10:31; James 2:19; Jude 1:4,25; Revelations 4:8;7 19:6,15; 17; 21:22*); (Koran: *Sura 2:133,163,255; 3:2,6,18,62; 4:87, 171; 5:76; 6:19, 102,107; 7:59,65,73,140,158; 9:31,129; 10:90; 11:14,50,61; 14:52; 16:2,22,51; 18:110; 20:8,14,98; 21:25, 87,108; 22:34; 23:32,91,116; 27:26,61,62,63,64; 28:70,71,72,88; 35:3; 37:1,35; 38:65; 40:3,62,65,84; 41:6; 43:84; 44:8; 47:19; 59:22,23; 64:13; 73:9*).

Both teach that the God of Abraham is the one and only God (Bible: *Genesis 26:24; 28:13; 31:42,53; 32:9; Exodus 2:24; 3:6,15; 4:5; Deuteronomy 6:10; 9:5; 29:13; 30:20; I Kings 18:36; I Chronicles 29:18; II Chronicles 30:6; Psalms 47:9; Matthew 22:32; Mark 12:26; Luke 20:37; Acts 3:13,25; 7:2,17,32; Romans 4:3; Galatians 3:6,8,18; Hebrews 6:13; James 2:23*) (Koran: Sura *2:124,130,133,136,258,260; Sura 3:33,84,95; Sura 4:125; 6:83,161; 12:38; 16:120,123; 19:47; 21:66; 29:16*).

Both teach that humankind fell from the grace of God and death and sin entered the world as a result of Adam and Eve's disobedience (Bible: *Genesis 3:1–24; Romans 5:14; I Corinthians 15:22*); (Koran: Sura *2:35–36; 7:19–35; 20:120–123*).

Both teach that humankind must fear, love, serve and worship God (Bible: *Exodus 3:12; 4:23; Leviticus 25:17; Deuteronomy 6:5 … Revelation 7:15; 14:7; 22:9*); (Koran: Sura *2:63,138,165,189,194; Sura 3:30…51:56; 98:5*).

Both condemn the worship of idols and images (Bible: *Exodus 23:24; 34:13; Leviticus 19:4; 26:1,30; Numbers 33:52; Deuteronomy 7:5,25; 12:2; I Kings 14:9; II Kings 21:11; 23:24; II Chronicles 24:18; 31:1; 33:22; 34:7; Psalms 78:58; 97:7; 106:36; 115:4; 135:15; Isaiah 2:8,18,20; 31:7; 41:29; 42:8,17; 45:16; Jeremiah 8:19; Ezekiel 6:4,5,6,13; 14: 3,4,5,6; 16:17,36; 18:5,6,12,15; 20:7,8,16,18,24,31,39; 22:3,4,7; 23: 30,37,39,49; 30:13; 37:23; 44:10; 44:12; Hosea 8:4; 11:2; 13:2; 14:8; Micah 1:7; 5:13; Habakkuk 2:18; Zechariah 13:2; Acts 15:20,29; 21:25; I Corinthians*

8:1,4,7,10; 10:19,28; 12:2; II Corinthians 6:16; I Thessalonians 1:9; I John 5:21; Revelations 2:14,20; 9:20); (Koran: Sura 6:74; 14:30,35; 22:30; 26:71; 29:17,25).

Both the Koran and the Bible (Old Testament) teach that humankind is to obey the Law God gave to Moses (Bible: Exodus 19:1–23; 34:1–34; Leviticus 1:1–27:34; Numbers 15:1–41; 18:1–19; 28:1–30 Deuteronomy 4:1–30); (Koran: Sura 2:53,93; 3:3,48,50,84,93; 6:154; 17:2; 19:51; 23:49; 32:23; 40:53; 46:12,30; 87:19). The Bible deals in depth with the reasons why God gave the law and commandments to Moses and why a person should obey the law.

The Bible teaches that when God created humankind He gave us a soul, a Godly one, a conscience to discern right from wrong, make choices and know the consequences of our choices (Genesis 1:26,27; 2:7,15,17; 3:2,3). God taught humankind that the price of sin and disobedience is death (Genesis 2:17; 3:3). From the beginning, humankind (Adam and Eve) disobeyed God, went against his nature (created in the image of God) and against his conscience, and sinned against God (Genesis 3:1–7). In spite of this, God continued to teach humankind to discern right from wrong (Genesis 4:7). Humankind ignored God's teachings and sinned to the point where we ceased to discern right from wrong (Genesis 4:8, 9, 23, 24; 6:1–13). Then God gave Moses, a descendant of Abraham, and the nation of Israel, His Law and charged them to observe His Law (Exodus 19:1–23:26) in order for them to be "a holy people," "a kingdom of priests," an example and a blessing to the rest of the world (Exodus 19:5–7; Deuteronomy 4:20; 7:6; 14:2; 26:18,19; 32:9; Psalms 25:10; 103:17,18; 135:4; Isaiah 41:8; 43:1 Jeremiah 10:16; Malachi 3:17; Titus 2:14).

God taught that the punishment for breaking the commandments and the Law was death because God, who is holy, hates sin (Exodus 21:12–17,29; 22:19; 31:14,15; 35:2; Leviticus 19:20; 20:2,9–16,27; 24:16,17,21; Numbers 3:10,38; 15:35; 18:7; 35:16–18, 21,30,31; Deuteronomy 13:5,9; 21:22). Knowing that "the imagination of man's heart is evil from his youth" (Genesis 8:21) and that people would continue to sin, God devised a system of sacrifices and offerings to allow people to atone for their sins and to be forgiven by God (Leviticus 1:1–17:16). Under this system, the sinner had to offer a cherished non-blemished (without imperfection) animal from his herd, put his hand upon the head of the animal, identify with the animal and symbolically transfer his sins to the animal, which represented moral perfection (absence of sin). The non-blemished animal symbolically took the place of the sinner (*Exodus 30:10; Leviticus 16:6-11, 21,22,29,30,34; 23:27,28; Numbers 29:7–11*). In voluntarily making this sacrifice, the sinner was expected to genuinely repentant.

The Bible teaches that the Law and commandments and system of sacrifices and offerings were intended to show people that they were sinners and were accountable for their sins (*Romans 4:15; 5:13; 7:5–14*). It teaches that the daily ministering by the priest and the yearly offerings and the animal sacrifices prescribed under the Law and commandments did not save any souls (*Job 15:15; 25:4,5; Psalms 143:2; Romans 3:20,28; Hebrews 9:9–14; 10:4,11; James 2:20–26*). One of the purposes of the offerings and sacrifices was atonement (purging, covering) for one's sins, so that one was temporarily acceptable to God (*Leviticus 1:1– 7:38*). The sacrifices and offerings under the Law and commandments could not render a soul permanently perfect (justification, eternal forgiveness of sins by God, sanctification), or they would not have continued year after year (*Hebrew 10:1–4*).

The Bible teaches that before the Law, humankind lived in darkness and committed sin in the dark, pleading ignorance. When God passed down the Law, it became daylight for mankind. The Law revealed to mankind his sins and removed all excuses of ignorance (*Romans 5:20; Galatians 3:19*). Thus instead of saving humankind from his sins, the Law made him aware of and responsible for them. Instead of becoming a light to humankind the Law became a burden to him. Instead of freeing mankind, the Law accused him, found him guilty and condemned him (*Romans 3:19, 20; 4:15; 5:13; 20; 7:9; 1 Corinthians 15:56*). Instead of becoming a blessing to humankind the Law became a curse (*Nehemiah 10:29; Daniel 9:11; Galatians 3:10, 13*). The Bible teaches that with time humankind was supposed to realize the hopelessness of his situation, being accursed by God, for he could not obey all the commandments of the Law all the time, which is what the Law dictates (*Deuteronomy 27:26; Matthew 5:19; Galatians 3:10; James 2:10*). With time, humankind was supposed to realize that the burden of the Law was too much to bear and he was being crushed under his sins, and that he could attain salvation only through faith and the grace of God (*Habakkuk 2:4;*

Romans 1:17; 3:28; Galatians 2:16; 3:11; Ephesians 2:8–9; Hebrews 10:38).
Humankind was supposed to pray for, wait for and hope for the grace that
God had prepared for him since the beginning of creation, once he realized
he could not attain salvation by the deeds of the Law (*Genesis 3:15; Psalms
40:7–9; Acts 26:6,7; Luke 24:27, 44; John 5:39; Acts 10:43; Romans 8:24;
16:25,26; I Corinthians 15:3,4; Ephesians 3:9–11; I Timothy 1:1; Titus 1:2;
2:13; Hebrews 7:19; 9:26; 10:7–9; I Peter 1:3,10,11,20; Revelations 19:10*).
Jesus was the blessed and only hope, which God had promised humankind
since the founding of the world (*Isaiah 53:5–12; Daniel 9:24; John 1:29,
36; Acts 2:38–39; 3:20; Romans 5:1–2; 8:3,11; 10:4; I Corinthians 5:7; II
Corinthians 3:6; 5:1; Ephesians 2:13,14; Colossians 1:20; Hebrews 2:14; 6:18;
10:19–22; 12:2; I Peter 1:18–21*). Jesus, who knew no sin, took upon himself all the sins of humankind (*Isaiah 53:3–12; John 1:29; Acts 7:60; Romans
5:18–21; II Corinthians 5:21; Hebrews 4:15; 7:26; 9:28; I Peter 2:22–24; I
John 3:5*). Jesus, who was sinless symbolically and physically, took the place
of the unblemished animal offered under the Law of Moses and paid for the
sins of all humankind (*Isaiah 53:1–11; Hosea 14:2; Matthew 1:21; 20:28;
John 1:29; Acts 13:39; I Corinthians 15:3; II Corinthians 5:21; Galatians 1:4;
3:13; I Timothy 2:6; Titus 2:14; Hebrews 1:3; 2:17; 4:15; 7:26,27; 9:14,28; I
Peter 1:19; 2:22,24; 3:18; II Peter 3:14; I John 1:7; Revelation 1:5*). Whereas
the blood of the non-blemished animal offered under the Law of Moses
covered the sins of the sinner only temporarily, and the process had to be
repeated year after year, the blood of Jesus Christ, who was eternal, paid for
the sins of all humankind once and for all (*Psalms 103:12; Isaiah 43:25;
44:22 Micah 7:19; Hebrews 9:13, 14; 10:1–18*). A person who believes in
the sacrifice and resurrection of Jesus Christ and puts his or her trust in
Jesus is reconciled with God and is no longer under the bondage of sins and
condemned by the Law (*Psalms 130:7,8; Micah 7:19; Matthew 1:21; John
1:17; 8:36; Romans 3:19,20; 4:16; 5:10,20,21; 6:12,15; 7:4–11; 8:2; 11:6;
14,20; 7:4,6; II Corinthians 3:6–9; 5:18–21; Galatians 3:23–25; 4:4,5,21;
5:18; Ephesians 2:13–16; Colossians 1:20,21; Titus 2:14; Hebrews 2:17; 8:10*).
Believers should not say they can now sin because they are no longer under
the dominion of the Law; on the contrary, they should exhort themselves
to respect the Law because they are under Christ, under grace (*Romans 3:5–
8,31; 5:20,21; 6:1–23; Galatians 5:13; I Peter 2:16; II Peter 2:18,19; Jude*

1:4). The believer should fight sin and aim to become Christ-like, a loving person (*Romans 6:13–23; 12:1–21; Ephesians 4:22–32; Colossians 3:1–17*). Believers should do this out of gratitude for knowing that God had sent Jesus, His son, to die for them and that their sins have been forgiven (*John 1:16; Romans 5:15; II Corinthians 4:15; Ephesians 1:7; 2:7; Philippians 2:12; II Thessalonians 2:16; Hebrews 2:9; 12: 1,28*). Believers will be tempted by sin even though they have the Spirit of God in them.

The Bible suggests ways for the believer to fight the temptation to sin (*I John 1:8–10*).

First, it exhorts believers to be aware that that they have an adversary, the Devil, "the tempter," who is busy plotting their downfall (*Job 1:7; II Corinthians 7:5; 11:3; 12:7; I Thessalonians 3:5; James 4:7; I Peter 5;8*).

Second, it teaches that believers have to understand that they have inherited from Adam and Eve an evil and sinful nature with a strong inclination to yield to temptation (*Genesis 3:3–7; I Chronicles 21:1; John 8:44; Romans 6:12; 7:14–25; 8:4–6; I Corinthians 15:43,44; Galatians 5:16–19; James 4:1–7; I John 2:16*).

Third, it teaches that believers have to understand that on their own they are unable to fight the temptation to sin (*Psalms 142:7; Romans 6:19; 7:23; 8:13; I Timothy 6:9,10; I Peter 2:11*). Thus, the Bible exhorts the believer to flee sin. It teaches believers to avoid being in a place or position where they can fall to temptation (*I Corinthians 6:18; 10:14; I Timothy 6:11; II Timothy 2:22*), (*II Samuel 11:2; Isaiah 28:7; 56:10–12; Hosea 4:11; Matthew 13:22; Mark 4:19; Luke 8:14; 10:41; 21:8,34; Romans 12:2; I Corinthians 5:11; 6:10; Hebrews 12:15; James 4:4*).

Fourth, it teaches that Jesus, who was righteous and won over temptation, is able to help every believer to resist temptation and sin (*Matthew 4:1–11; Mark 1:13; Luke 4:2–13; John 16:33; I Corinthians 15:57; Hebrews 2:15; 4:15; I John 2:13; 5:4,5*). Believers have to draw close to Jesus, submit to God and be in constant communion with God, for Jesus to help them resist and escape temptation (*Psalms 39:12; 119:19, 54; Matthew 26:41; Mark 14:38; Luke 21:36; I Corinthians 10:13; Hebrews 7:19; James 4:7,8*).

This has been a brief summary of how, according to the Bible, God expects humankind to deal with the Law He gave to Moses.

The Koran was written six centuries after the last chapter of the Bible was written, and it agrees with the Bible on many doctrines. The last significant point I found common to the two books is that every person, without exception, will one day die and stand in judgement before God (*Bible: Deuteronomy 10:17; 16:19; 18:18,19; II Chronicles 19:7; Job 34:19; Psalms 9:19; Proverbs 24:23,24; Matthew 7:21–27; 10:15; Luke 8:17; John 5:22; 12:48; Acts 10:42; Romans 2:11,12; Revelations 11:18; 19:2; 20:11– 15*); (*Koran: 2:85,113,275; 3:55,77,161,180,194; 4:87,109,136,141; 5:15,39,67; 6:12,51; 7:32,167,172; 10:60,93; 11:60,98,99; 15:35; 17:13,58,62,97; 18:21,36,105; 19:37,95; 20:74,100,124; 21:47; 23:16; 25:11,69; 26:82; 27:65; 28:41,42,61,71,72; 29:13,25; 34:23; 35:14; 36:32; 37:20,26; 38:78; 39:24,31,47,60,67; 40:46; 41:40,47,50; 42:45; 43:85; 45:17,26,27; 46:5,6; 51:12; 53:57; 54:1,46; 55:46; 58:7,18; 60:3; 64:7; 68:39; 69:18; 70:26; 72:7; 74:46; 79:14; 82:15,17,18; 83:11; 85:2*).

The Bible teaches that God, Who is just, will judge all humankind equally, irrespective of nationality, gender, age, social status or religion (*Deuteronomy 10:17; 16:19; II Chronicles 19:7 Job 34:19; Proverbs 24:23,24 Matthew 22:16; Luke 20:21; Acts 10:34; Galatians 2:6 6:7,8; Ephesians 6:9; Colossians 3:25; I Peter 1:17*). When God created humankind, He put in the heart and mind of humankind a conscience, which allowed humankind to differentiate between right and wrong, to know that killing, stealing, lying and coveting are wrong. God will judge all humankind who lived from creation to the time of Moses according to the work of Law (actions), written in the heart and conscience of humankind ("**For as many as have sinned without law shall also perish without law**" [*Romans 2:12–15*]). God will judge all those who had been under the Law of Moses (the Jews) by the Law God gave to Moses ("**and as many as have sinned in the law shall be judged by the law**" [*Romans 2:12*]). God promised the house of Israel that some day He would make a new perpetual covenant with them, not like the old covenant He made with them in the time of Moses (*Jeremiah 3:5; 30:3; 31:31; 32:40; 33:14–16; 50:4,5; Ezekiel 37:26; Amos 9:13*). He promised that some day He would write in the hearts and minds of all humankind, Jews and non-Jews, a new covenant, the Law of grace (*Isaiah 11:10; 42:1,6; 49:6; Matthew 12: 18–20; 26:28; Mark 14:24; Luke 22:20; I Corinthians 11:25; II Corinthians 3:6; Hebrews 8:6–13; 9:15; 10:16,17; 12:24; 13:20*). Under the new covenant, the Law of grace, God would be merciful to humankind, forgiving their iniquities and remembering their sins no more (*Isaiah 53:11; Jeremiah 31:34; Ezekiel 11:19; 36:25–27*). The promise of the new covenant was fulfilled with the death and resurrection of Jesus (*Hebrews 10:1–18; 12:24; I John 2:1,2*). All those who have the opportunity to hear the Gospel of Jesus and believe will have everlasting life; they will not be condemned by God, but will pass from death unto eternal life (*John 3:18; 5:24; 6:40,47; 17:3*). They will dwell with God in a new heaven, new earth and new holy city called Jerusalem (*Psalms 48:1–3; 87:3; John 14:2; Galatians 4:26,27; Hebrews 11:10; 12:22; Revelation 3:12; 21:2,10–27*). The walls of the city are made of jasper and the streets of pure gold. The city has no need of the sun or of the moon, but is lit by the glory of God and Christ. A pure river of the water of life flows through the city. The tree of life, which bares twelve types of fruit, lines either side of the river (*Revelation 21:2*). The people will have a glorified body, like Christ (*Exodus 34:29,30; Matthew 17:2; 28:3; Acts 26:13–15; Romans 8:29,30; I Corinthians 15:42–54; II Corinthians 3:18; Ephesians 1:5,11; Philippians 3:21; I John 3:2; Revelation 1:13–16; 10:1*). There will be no more pain, sorrow, crying and death (*Isaiah 25:8; Hosea 13:14; I Corinthians 15:56,53–57; Hebrews 2:14,15; Revelation 19:20, 20:14; 21:4*).

The people will not marry nor be given in marriage, but will be as angels of God (*Psalms 103:20 Zechariah 3:7; Matthew 13:43; 18:10; 22:30; Mark 12:24,25; Luke 20:34–36; John 5:28,29; I Corinthians 7:29–31; I John 3:1,2; Revelation 5:9–11; 19:10*). On the other hand, "**the fearful, and unbelieving** [those who rejected the Gospel of Christ]**, and the abominable, and murderers, and whoremongers, and sorcerers, and idolaters, and all liars, shall have their part in the lake which burneth with fire and brimstone: which is the second death**" (*Proverbs 19:9; Matthew 25:41; Mark 9:43–48; 16:16; John 3:18,19,36 14:6; Acts 4:12; Hebrews 2:3 12:25; I John 5:11,12; Luke 12:5; Revelation 19:20; 20:14,15; 21:8*).

The Koran, like the Bible, teaches that every soul will taste death and be judged by God. It teaches that those who believed in the Koran and the signs given to the prophets (Abraham, Moses, Jesus, Muhammad), "**those who believed and those who suffered exile and fought (and strove and struggled) in the path of Allah**," "**those…who fought hard (in His Cause) and remained steadfast**," "**those who have left their homes, or been driven**

out therefrom, or suffered harm…, or fought or been slain," those who
"fight in His Cause and slay and are slain," "the righteous," "those who
repent, believe and work righteousness," "those who feared their Lord,"
"those who spent (freely) and fought, before the Victory," will receive
recompense, which is to be admitted into the garden of eternal life (*Sura:
2:82, 218; 3:15, 142, 195; 7:42; 8:72; 9:111; 10:26; 11:23; 13:35; 19:60;
25:10,15; 26:90; 39:73,74; 40:40; 46:14,16; 47:15; 50:31; 57:10; 76:5*).
In heaven the believers will dwell in beautiful, lofty mansions with gardens
that have rivers of incorruptible water, milk, wine and pure honey flowing
underneath. The gardens will be "**in nearness to their Lord with rivers
flowing beneath, therein is their eternal home, with Companions pure
(and holy); and the good of pleasure of Allah**." The believers will rest on
reclining raised thrones and will feel neither the sun's excessive heat nor the
moon's excessive cold. They will wear garments made of silk and bracelets of
silver and gold. They will drink wine that is pure and holy and eat fruits of
every kind. "**And round about them will (serve) youths of perpetual (fres-
hness)**" (*Sura 2:25; 3:15,136,195; 4:13,57,122; 7:43; 9:72,89,100; 10:9;
13:3,35; 14:23; 16:31; 20:76; 22:14,23; 25:10; 29:58; 39:20; 47:12,15;
48:5,17; 54:54; 57:12; 58:22; 61:12; 65:11; 66:8; 76:5–21; 98:8*). On the
other hand, "**those who reject Faith**," "**the unbelievers**," "**those who seek
gain in Evil, and are girt by their sins**," "**those who devour usury**," "**they
do blaspheme who say: 'Allah is Christ the son of Mary'…Whoever
joins other gods with Allah**," "**the hypocrites**," "**the sinful**," "**the unjust**,"
"**the wicked**" and "**the wrongdoers**," will receive a severe penalty, which is
an eternal blazing fire (*Sura: 2:39,81,174,217,257,275; 3:10,116,131,151
,181,183; 4:10,14,55,56; 5:67,75; 7:36; 8:14; 9:63,68 10:27; 11:106,113;
13:5,35; 18:29, 53; 21:39; 22:4,51,72; 25:11; 29:25; 32:20; 33:64; 35:36;
38:27; 40:6,43; 46:20,34; 48:13; 57:15; 58:17; 59:3; 64:10; 67:11; 71:25;
74:31; 76:4; 82:14; 83:16; 85:10*).

The first thing that occurred to me after I finished comparing the Bible
and the Koran was that I would have gone to hell had I died at that instant
or earlier. According to the Koran, if I had died, God would have judged my
performance in obeying the Law God gave to Moses. In theory, God gave
the Law to Moses for the children of Israel, but in reality I became subject
to the Law when my ancestors adopted Islam, for the Koran teaches that the

Law of Moses is "**a light and guidance**" to all Muslims (*Sura 3:3, 84; 5:47; 6:91,154; 11:17; 23: 49; 28:43; 46:12,30*). I felt I had broken every one of the Ten Commandments in the Law of Moses. In order to convince myself of this, I went through the exercise of seeing how miserably I had failed in keeping each of the commandments. The first four commandments in the Law of Moses, which characterize humankind's relation with God, are as follows:

> "**1. I am the LORD thy God…Thou shalt have no other gods before me.**
>
> **2. Thou shalt not make unto thee any graven image, or any likeness of any thing that is in heaven above, or that is in the earth beneath, or that is in the water under the earth: Thou shalt not bow down thyself to them, nor serve them: for I the LORD thy God am a jealous God, visiting the iniquity of the fathers upon the children unto the third and fourth generation of them that hate me; And shewing mercy unto thousands of them that love me, and keep my commandments.**
>
> **3. Thou shalt not take the name of the LORD thy God in vain; for the LORD will not hold him guiltless that taketh his name in vain.**
>
> **4. Remember the Sabbath day, to keep it holy. Six days shalt thou labour, and do all thy work: But the seventh day is the Sabbath of the LORD thy God: in it thou shalt not do any work, thou, nor thy son, nor thy daughter, thy manservant, nor thy maidservant, nor thy cattle, nor thy stranger that is within thy gates: For in six days the LORD made heaven and earth, the sea, and all that in them is, and rested the seventh day: wherefore the LORD blessed the Sabbath day, and hallowed it**" (*Exodus 20:1–11*).

The Bible teaches that we break the first commandment when we honour, love and serve objects (money, pleasure, the world), the fruits of our imagination (fame) or persons more than God (*Joshua 24:15; I Kings 18:21; Matthew 6:24; Luke 16:13; Romans 6:16–22; Galatians 1:10; I Timothy 6:9,10,17; II Timothy, 4:10*). We break the second commandment when we make and worship any carving, figure, image or portrait of anything in heaven (sun, moon, angels), on earth (people, animals) or in the sea (fish). We should not even make representations of God Himself to worship. We break the third commandment when we carelessly mention the name of God, Christ, when we use the name of God other than for the purpose of earnestly giving glory or praying to God (*Isaiah 1:11,13; Matthew 15:7–9; James 5:12*).

The Bible teaches that God set aside the seventh day of the week as a day of commemoration for the creation of the world and humankind. We are to set aside the seventh day as a holy day to honour God and should do no cerebral or manual work for pleasure or profit on that day. We break the fourth commandment when we do any work except works of mercy and of absolute necessity on the seventh day (*Numbers 15:32–36; Matthew 12:1–12; Mark 2:23–28; Luke 6:1–5; John 5:8–12; 7:23; 9:14*). The only time I conformed to the fourth commandment was when I was ill or went on vacation and forgot my books. It was obvious I had broken the first four commandments countless times in my life. Next, I looked at how well I had fared with the fifth commandment:

"**5. Honour thy father and thy mother…**" (*Exodus 20:12*)

My parents would tell you that I have not always obeyed this command-ment and only God and them can forgive me. The next five commandments tell us how to treat our fellow human beings:

"**6. Thou shalt not kill.**

7. Thou shalt not commit adultery.

8. Thou shalt not steal.

9. Thou shalt not bear false witness against thy neighbour.

10. Thou shalt not covet thy neighbour's house, thou shalt not covet thy neighbour's wife, nor his manservant, nor his maidservant, nor his ox, nor his ass, nor any thing that is thy neighbour's." (Exodus 20:13–17)

I acknowledged that I had broken the last five commandments more often than the first five. Yes, I had probably even killed, because somebody once hypothesized that every medical student inadvertently kills at least one patient. Even though the death may have been accidental or not entirely my fault, under the Law of Moses a sin that occurs due to ignorance is still a sin (*Genesis 20:9; Leviticus 4:2,27; 5:15,17; Numbers 15:22–29; Deuteronomy 19:4; I Samuel 14:27; Psalms 19:12; I Timothy 1:13; Hebrews 5:2 9:7; James 3:10*). Even if I had not physically killed a person, I had broken the spirit of the Law, according to the Bible, if I had been angry with a person without cause, which I had on numerous occasions (*Genesis 27:41; Leviticus 19:16–18; Psalms 7:4; 25:3; 35:19; 69:4; 109:3; Proverbs 26:24–26; Lamentations 3:52; Matthew 5:21,22; John 15:25; I John 2:9,11; 3:12–15*). I had also committed adultery, according to the Bible, by lusting after a woman, thus breaking the spirit of the Law (*Genesis 34:2; 39:7–23; II Samuel 11:2–4; Job 31:1,9; Proverbs 6:24–29; Matthew 5:28; James 1:14,15; II Peter 2:14; I John 2:16*).

Finally, I had broken the tenth commandment when I desired more than I needed and more than God had given me (*Genesis 3:6; 14:23; 34:23, Joshua; 7:21; I Samuel 15:19; II Samuel 11:2–4; Psalms 10:3; 119:36; Proverbs 4:23 6:24,25; Ecclesiastes 4:8; 5:10,11; Isaiah 33:15; 57:17; Jeremiah 5:8; 22:17; Ezekiel 33:31; Amos 2:6,7; Micah 2:2; Habakkuk 2:9; Luke 12:15; 16:14; Acts 5:4; 20:33; Romans 7:7; I Corinthians 6:10; Philippians 3:19; Colossians 3:5; I Timothy 6:6–10; Hebrews 13:5*). How often had I broken this last commandment by coveting the latest car or the latest gadget? And if the Ten Commandments were not enough, some Jewish scholars count a total of six hundred and thirteen commandments in the Old Testament.

When I finished looking at how I had fared in obeying the commandments, I saw guilty stamped on my forehead, written all over my body like a prisoner wearing his black-and-white-striped uniform. I could only plead guilty on all counts. Instead of spending time figuring out how to atone for my past sins, for it was impossible to do so, I thanked God that I had not died earlier and began to think of what I should or should not do from then on to assure myself of eternal life. For a fraction of second I thought I would try to obey the commandments from then on, but I realized that this too was impossible. How could I not covet? How could I love God, all the time, more than anybody or anything, with all my heart, soul and mind, which the Bible says is the greatest commandment? (*Deuteronomy 6:5; 10:12 30:6; Matthew 22:37; Mark 12:29,30,33; Luke 10:27*). How could I love my neighbour as I love myself, which the Bible says is the second-greatest commandment? (*Leviticus 19:18; Matthew 19:19; 22:39; Mark 12:31; Luke 10:27–37; Romans 13:9,10; 15:2; Galatians 5:14; 6:10; James 2:8*). When I remembered that the Bible teaches that if a person breaks one commandment he is guilty and accursed as if he had broken all of them, I realized it was impossible to conform to the Law God gave to Moses (*Deuteronomy*

27:26; Matthew 5:18,19; Galatians 3:10; James 2:10). I finally came to the conclusion that though the Law may be perfect, it was made for an imperfect soul like me and I could never achieve righteousness.

Then, to my great joy, it occurred to me that if I believed what I read in the Bible, which I did, I was not under the Law of Moses any more. It occurred to me that if I were to die, God would not judge me according to the Law of Moses, but according to grace, for the Bible teaches that the covenant God made with Moses could not exist side by side with the new covenant that God, through Jesus Christ, promised to the children of Israel and the rest of the world (Deuteronomy 30:6; Psalms 51:10, Jeremiah 32:39; Ezekiel 11:19,20; 36:26; John 3:3–5; II Corinthians 3:18; 5:17; Galatians 6:15; Ephesians 2:10; Revelations 21:5) (Matthew 9:16,17; Mark 2:21,22; Luke 5:36–39). For a new covenant to take effect, the old covenant has to be abrogated and vanish (Hebrews 8:10–13).

The Bible teaches that when Jesus came into this world and died, He paid for the sins of all humankind, Jews and Gentiles alike (Isaiah 53:1–12; Daniel 9:24; Zechariah 13:7; Matthew 20:28; 24:14; 28:18,19; Mark 13:10; 16:15; Luke 24:47; John 3:16,17; Acts 2:38,39,41; 8:12–16,36–38; 9:18 10:47,48; 13:47; 16:15–33; 19:3–5; Romans 1:8; 3:24–26; 4:25; 5:6–10,15–21; 10:18 15:19; I Corinthians 15:3; II Corinthians 5:19–21; Ephesians 5:2; Colossians 1:6,23; 2:13; 3:13; Hebrews 9:12–15; 10:10,14; I Peter 3:18; I John 4:9,10; Revelation 14:6). When Jesus was resurrected, all humankind, without exception, came under the law of the Spirit of life in Christ (John 1:17; Romans 4:16; 6:14; 7:4–6; Galatians 2:21; 5:4,18). Thus, according to the Bible, every individual who hears the Gospel of Jesus Christ has only two options from which to choose. He or she can either believeth in the Gospel of Jesus, the gospel of grace, and be saved, or reject it and be condemned (Mark 16:16; John 3:16–18,36; 4:24; 6:40,47; 8:51; 11:26; 12:44; 20:31; Romans 10:11–13; I Peter 1:21; I John 5:1,11–13).

So, at the end of this long process of comparing the Bible and the Koran, I realized that all I had to do was accept or reject the notion that Jesus came into this world to die for my sins and was resurrected so that I could live. My mind understood the rationale and simplicity of salvation as taught by the Bible, but my heart refused to accept it. My heart wanted to accept part of Jesus and retain part of what I had been taught in my childhood. My mind reminded my heart that Jesus had said, "**No man can serve two masters: for either he will hate the one, and love the other; or else he will hold to the one, and despise the other. Ye cannot serve God and mammon**" (*Matthew 6:24; Luke 16:13*). My mind also reminded my heart that Jesus said, "**Jesus saith unto him, I am the way, the truth, and the life: no man cometh unto the Father, but by me**" (*John 14:6; Isaiah 35:8,9; Matthew 11:27; Acts 4:12; Romans 5:2; Ephesians 2:18; Hebrews 7:25; 9:8; 10:19–22; I Peter 1:21; Revelation 7:9–17; 13:7,8; 20:15*) and "**I am the good shepherd and know my [sheep], and am known of mine; Verily, verily, I say unto you, He that entereth not by the door into the sheepfold, but climbeth up some other way, the same is a thief and a robber**" (*John 10:14,1*). My heart obstinately refused to accept Jesus as Saviour, probably because of the many things I had seen and been taught in my childhood. In my childhood I learned that one can change many things (one's country, one's partner, etc.), but not religion, perhaps because in so doing one is telling one's entire family that they are on the wrong path.

My heart refused to yield to my mind and I remained in limbo. However, I continued to attend church and Bible study sessions and I continued to read the Bible.

CHAPTER THIRTY-NINE

"The Way, the Truth and the Life"

"O give thanks unto the LORD, for [he is] good: for his mercy [endureth] for ever.

Let the redeemed of the LORD say [so], whom he hath redeemed from the hand of the enemy" (Psalms 107:1–2).

I continued to attend Bible study and church because I feared God and somehow knew that some day God would show me the truth if I continued to be patient. One Tuesday in September 1998, I attended the Kelly Bible study session as usual. The discussion started when one member asked a question about sin and Jesus. I began to follow the discussion and then my mind wandered and I reminisced about what I had learned about sin, salvation and Jesus. I realized that God had given to Moses and the nation of Israel his law for them to be "**a holy people**" and an example to the rest of us. I realized that the people had sinned against God no sooner than God had given them the Law and taught them the punishment for breaking the commandments and the Law (Exodus 32:1–6). I realized that out of love God had spared the life of the people and forgiven them for their iniquity (Exodus 32:7–14). I realized that with time the people had not only made sin an acceptable way of life, but had also made the sacrifices and offerings by which they were to repent and by which God was to forgive them into meaningless rituals (*Isaiah 1:23; 9:13–17; Jeremiah 3:5; 5:26–28; 7:8–12; 8:12; 10:15; Ezekiel 2:6; 22:2–12, 25–31; Hosea 4:5,6; Amos 5:12; Micah 3:11; 7:1–6; Zechariah 7:10–12), (II Chronicles 36:14–16; Proverbs 1:24–33; Isaiah 1:4,5; 5:4–6, 24; 9:13–17; 50:2; 65:12; 66:4; Jeremiah 2:27,30; 3:6–11; 5:3; 6:28–30 ; 7:13, 26–28; 8:5; 11:10; 13:10; 17:23; 19:5; 25:3–7*

;Ezekiel 3:7; 16:59; 22:24; Hosea 7:1,9–16; Amos 4:6–12; Zephaniah 3:2,7; Zechariah 7:7,11–13). I realized that the destruction of the nation of Israel and the rest of humankind who were involved in greater sins would have been the natural thing to do since God no longer wished to accept the lives of animals offered in sacrifice as a substitute for the lives of sinners (*Leviticus 17:7; 18:6–23; 20:2–27; II Kings 21:6–11; II Chronicles 33:2–7; Jeremiah 8:13; 10:2–5; 14:12; Ezekiel 5:7–17; Amos 5:26,27; Zephaniah 1:4–5).*

Then I understood that God, who was not only a just God, but also a gracious, long-suffering, merciful and above all, loving God, had offered the life of His Son, Jesus, as a sacrifice to save all humankind (*Exodus 34:6; Numbers 14:18; Deuteronomy 4:31; II Chronicles 30:9; Nehemiah 9:17,31; Psalms 86:15; 103:8; 112:4; 116:5; 117:2; 119:76; 145:8; Jeremiah 3:12; Joel 3:12; Jonah 4:2; II Corinthians 13:11; Ephesians 2:4; I Peter 2:3; 3:20; II Peter 3:9,15; I John 4:7,8,16).* My heart yielded to my mind and I understood that if I were to admit that I was a sinner, feel sorry for having sinned, earnestly repent and believe that Jesus died for my sins, then God would forgive me (*Matthew 10:32; Mark 16:16; Luke 24:47; John 3:16,36; Acts 2:38; 3:19; 5:31; 8:12; 16:31; Romans 4:24,25; 10:9; I Peter 3:21; I John 4:2,3; Revelation 3:5).*

Then it occurred to me that Jesus Christ had walked every day of His life on this earth knowing that He was ordained to die for all humankind and their sins (*Isaiah 41:4; Matthew 11:27; 12:40; 20:19; Mark 8:31; 10:34; Luke 1:68–70; 18:33; 24:5–7; John 2:4; 7:6,8,30; 8:20; 10:15,18; 13:7; 17:24, 25; Acts 15:18; Romans 16:25; Ephesians 1:4; 3:11; Titus 1:2; I Peter 1:5; 1:20; Revelation 1:17,18; 2:8; 13:8).* I understood that Jesus Christ was innocent and tears started flowing from my eyes like a fountain. I wished I could stop crying, but I could not. Brother Kelly and the brothers and sisters at the meeting stopped talking for a while. They looked at me to see if I was all right, left me alone and went back to talking, which was the best thing to do. The tears flowed down my cheeks, but a sense of joy overwhelmed me when I realized I finally understood the meaning of life, Jesus and salvation. I felt an inner peace and joy as never before. By the grace of God, today I still feel that inner peace and assurance, not arrogance. Of course, stressful situations still affect me to some extent, because of my weak flesh and because I am slowly learning to be patient and have faith in God. When the tears finally ceased because there were no more, I thought of my family members who were not on the right way, the way of Jesus Christ.

The next day, instead of appreciating the fact that I had found the truth, I wondered why it had taken me so long to find God, especially in light of the Bible's stating that God is busy seeking all humankind and wishes that all be saved (*Exodus 34:6; Psalms 147:11; Jeremiah 3:17; 31:20; Lamentations 3:33; Ezekiel 18:23,32; 33:11; Hosea 11:8; Micah 7:18; Matthew 5:45; Luke 1:71; 5:32; 15:7; Romans 5:8; 8:28–30; 11:14,26,29; I Corinthians 9:19–22; 10:33; Ephesians 1:4; I Thessalonians 4:7; I Timothy 1:15; 2:3,4; 4:10; II Timothy 1:9; Titus 3:5; Hebrews 3:1; I Peter 1:15; II Peter 3:9; Revelation 2:21*). The Bible teaches that although God wishes that all be saved, He will not force any individual to accept the gift of faith that leads to salvation; every individual has to accept God's gift of his or her own free will (*Romans 3:24; I Corinthians 2:12; Revelation 21:6; 22:17*). I may never understand all the reasons why I accepted the gift of God when I did, but the Bible offers some explanations.

The Bible teaches that for an individual to find God, he or she has to seek God diligently with all his or her heart, soul and mind (*Deuteronomy 4:29; 6:5; 10:12; 13:3; 26:16; 30:2,6,10; I Chronicles 22:19; II Chronicles 12:14; 15:12; 30:19; 34:31; Ezra 7:10; Psalms 22:26; 84:2; 119:145; Jeremiah 3:10; Joel 2:12; Matthew 22:37; Mark 12:29,30,33; Luke 10:27; Romans 8:7; Hebrews 10:16*). After reading the above verses from the Bible I realized that I had not found God all those years because I had not sought God the way the Bible teaches. My search for God had been only intellectual. I had read dozens of books, but my heart was not open to God. Reading the books had served only one purpose. It had allowed me to stay away from many religious organizations that could have exploited me, for I never got deeply involved in any religious organization that I could not read about and understand.

If my heart had not been open to finding God all these years, I wondered, what changes in my life had made my heart receptive to God? I could find the answer to this question in the Bible. On numerous occasions the people of Israel forgot God and relied on their riches when God subdued their enemies and made the people prosperous. The people went so far as to worship other gods when they were at peace. On the other hand, God's chosen people humbled themselves and cried out to God for help when they were destitute and oppressed. Because He is long-suffering, merciful and loving, God forgave and came to the rescue of his chosen people every time they humbled themselves and sought God with their hearts (*Exodus 32:1–34:35; Judges 1:1–21:25; Books of Samuel, Kings, Isaiah, Jeremiah, Lamentations, Ezekiel, Micah*).

My relationship with God had been similar to that between God and His chosen people as described in the Bible. When I lived in Canada, I complained about everything and nothing even though I was healthy, wealthy, and surrounded by family and friends. I was so comfortable that my search for God had been only from the mind. Some drastic events had to take place in my life for me to open my heart to God. The first was when I, a tireless person, became sick and weak and lost of control of my life. The second was when people took my money, my security and my god. The third was when I ended up in Bermuda, an environment in which, for a while, I had no friends, woke up every morning to face people who sought my downfall, did not have the luxury of giving up, and did not even have a few seconds' respite from my enemies. In that environment God became my refuge, my saviour, and I slowly opened my heart to Him. The event that made my heart truly receptive to God occurred in August 1998, a few weeks before I was saved. When I arrived in Bermuda I treated many patients who had been suffering with low-back pain for years. When the hospital Board removed my privileges, many of those patients wrote letters to the Board on my behalf. In the letters, they described their suffering and many wrote that God had sent me to the Island in answer to their prayers. After reading those letters I was under the illusion that I had moved to Bermuda to bring help to patients; thus my patients became one of the reasons I fought to remain there.

In August 1998, one such patient, a black Bermudian woman in her sixties on whom I had operated two years earlier, came to see me for follow-up. She had suffered from back pain for twelve years and had seen many physicians, including all the orthopaedics surgeons on the Island. Dr. Cooperson had given her his usual line that she was too fat and he would not touch her with a ten-foot pole. The woman did well after surgery and wrote to the Board on my behalf (see Website: wwwtheonlywaytoeternallife.com, Letter

14). She had also initiated a petition demanding that my privileges be restored. After the surgery I received a Christmas card from her every year. She lost weight because she was able to walk and do things she had been unable to before the surgery. She lost so much weight that she could feel one of the screws I had inserted in her back. The protruding screw bothered her when she lay on the side where it had been inserted. I suggested we operate again, to remove the screw, in September 1998, for Mr. Richardson, my attorney, had said I would have my privileges restored by September. The woman agreed to have the surgery. Meanwhile, I gave her some medication to alleviate her discomfort. At the end of the visit she asked me to write a medical report because she wanted to take legal action against Dr. Cooperson for all the suffering he had caused her and for telling her she was fat and inoperable. I told the patient it would be very difficult for her to win a lawsuit against Dr. Cooperson on the grounds that he had refused to operate. Before she left my office, the woman hugged me and kissed me on the cheek, as she had done on every previous visit. She said she would continue to pray for me, as this woman was a Christian.

Three days later I entered my office to find my secretary in tears. She informed me that the patient who had been hugging and kissing me and saying she would pray for me had just been by to pick up her x-rays on her way to see Dr. Cooperson. My secretary said, "These people have no loyalty." My patient had told her the once-a-day tablets I had prescribed had relieved the discomfort she had been experiencing, but she would not wait until September to have the surgery. This event made me realize that I had not moved to Bermuda to help others. While I may have helped some patients, I now understood that I had moved to Bermuda to be afflicted and humbled by God.

I thought, why humble me, since I was already humble (but proud)? Then I realized that God regards as arrogance what humankind considers pride, and God hates pride (*I Samuel 2:3; Job 40:12; Psalms 10:4; 18:27; 73:6–8; 101:5; 131:1; Proverbs 6:16–19; 15:25; 30:13; Isaiah 2:11; 3:9,16; I Peter 5:5*). God needed to humble me because the humble seek God. God hears the cry of the humble. God offers grace and salvation to the humble and lifts them up so they can dwell with Him (*II Chronicles 32:26; 33:12,19; 34:27; Job 22:29; 29:12; Psalms 9:12,18; 10:12,17; 22:26; 34:2;*

69:32; 72:12–14; Proverbs 15:33; 18:12; Isaiah 57:15; Matthew 18:4; 23:12; James 4:6; I Peter 5:5,6).

A few months later my patient returned, as friendly as ever. She informed me that Dr. Marvin, a visiting surgeon from Boston, and Dr. Cooperson had removed the screw in her back, but she was still experiencing some pain. She was upset with Dr. Cooperson. In addition to billing her insurance company $4,000 US he had billed her $4,000 for the thirty minutes it took to remove the screw from her back. (I would have billed the insurance company $600, which was the fee agreed to by the Association of Insurance Companies and the Bermuda Physicians' Association for this type of surgery.) Her insurance company paid Dr. Cooperson the $4,000. He told the patient this had served to pay Dr. Marvin, while the $4,000 he had billed her was his fee for assisting. The patient complained to the insurance company, but they said they could do nothing. She had tried to speak to Dr. Cooperson, but his secretary told her he would not see her or speak to her until she settled her bill. She then consulted an attorney, who told her she would have to pay the $4,000 because she had already paid $50 on account, thus indicating that she agreed to pay the full amount. She had come to me because of residual back pain. I treated her residual pain and she left, once again promising to pray for me. A few days later, the woman called to tell me she was free of pain, and some weeks later I received her usual Christmas card.

Now that I could claim to be a believer, a worshipper and a servant of Jesus Christ, I wanted to understand the attitude of some Christians that had long puzzled me. On a few occasions Christian friends and acquaintances had told me they hated Jews. I suspected that these negative feelings towards people of Jewish descent were based strictly on religious beliefs (not that I advocated hating others on any grounds). I could not understand the attitude of people who on the one hand professed to love Jesus Christ, a Jew, and on the other hand professed to hate Jews. Nevertheless, I did not engage in any discussions on the subject because I had little knowledge of the Bible. Now that I was somewhat acquainted with the Bible, I eagerly waited for a Christian to express negativity towards Jewish people so I could get at the reasons behind it. Such an opportunity came up a few months after I was saved. One day when I had a friend in my car, I stopped at a pedestrian crosswalk to allow a Hasidic Jew with forelocks to cross the road. My passenger groaned and gave the pedestrian a dirty look. Then she said, "They killed Jesus." I said, "I thought Jesus died for the sins of all mankind and all humankind killed Jesus" (*Isaiah 53:1–12; John 1:29; Romans 3:25,26; 4:25; 5:6–9; 8:3; I Corinthians 15:3; Galatians 3:13; I Thessalonians 1:10; Hebrews 1:3; 2:17; 9:28; I Peter 2:24; 3:18; I John 1:7; 2:2; 4:10*). I could see that my passenger did not like my response because she looked at me with the same disdain she had used for the pedestrian.

I asked my passenger if she hated people of Roman descent. She looked at me as if pondering what I might say next, but did not answer. I said that Pontius Pilate, a Roman governor, sentenced Jesus Christ and Roman soldiers executed Jesus. She replied, "Pilate did not want to crucify Jesus; the Jews forced him to do it." I said that nobody forced Pilate to do anything, that Pilate himself told Jesus Christ, "**Knowest thou not that I have power to crucify thee, and have power to release thee**?" (*John 19:10*). I asked my passenger if she would appreciate having a judge put her on trial twice, as Pilate had in Jesus' case, declare three times that she was innocent, say that he washed his hands of her innocent blood and give the order to kill her (*Matthew 27:11–24; Mark 15:1–15; Luke 23:1–7, 11–25; John 18:29–19:16*). She would probably call the judge a coward, a hypocrite and all sorts of injurious names, I said. If he wished to, Pilate could have saved Jesus, as Lysias, the Roman chief, had saved Paul from the hands of the same people who killed Jesus (*Acts 21:30–34; 23:23–33*). My passenger did not respond, but was not about to give up. She declared that the Jewish people said, "**His** [Jesus] **blood be on us and on our children**" (*Matthew 27:25*). "So let it be," she said. There were times, I told her, when I wished I had said differently half the things I have spoken and had not uttered the other half at all. As for my thoughts, I wished that ninety-nine-point-nine percent of them had never crossed my mind. I said that if God were to hold us accountable for all of our thoughts, words and deeds none of us would make it past the age of five.

I asked her if she remembered the first thing Jesus said on the cross. She said she did not. I said it was "**Father, forgive them; for they know not what they do**" (*Luke 23:34*). I said the Bible teaches that God hears the prayers of the righteous and answers them (*Psalms 10:17; 34:15–17; 66:18,19;*

145:18,19; Proverbs 15:8,29; Matthew 7:7; 21:21,22; Mark 11:24; Luke 11:9; John 9:31; 14:14; 15:7; Acts 10:31; James 5:16; I John 3:22; 5:14). If Jesus, the Son of God, asked God's forgiveness for those who were responsible for his death, I said, surely God forgave them. Indeed the Bible teaches that God heard Jesus Christ, and for His sake forgave those who killed Him and all humankind, without exception (*Ephesians 4:32; Colossians 3:13*). I sensed that my passenger was searching for another argument to justify her negative feelings towards people of the Jewish faith. Before she had a chance to speak, I said the Bible teaches that God forgives those who forgive others, and in refusing to forgive others we are denying that we are sinners and that God forgives us (*Proverbs 21:13; Matthew 6:12,14,15; 7:2; 18:21–35; Mark 11:25,26; Ephesians 4:32; Colossians 3:13*). I was right in thinking that my passenger had not yet run out of arguments, for she said, "But they do not accept Jesus Christ." I said there are a lot of people in this world who do not accept Jesus Christ for who He is, **"the messiah"** (*Isaiah 11:2; 61:1; Jeremiah 23:5,6; Daniel 9:25,26; Luke 4:18–21; John 1:41; 4:25,26*), **"the only begotten Son of God"** (*John 1:14,18; 3:16,18*), **"God manifest in flesh"** (*Micah 5:2; John 1:14; 9:35–38; I Timothy 3:16) and "God"* (*Isaiah 9:6; Matthew 1:23; John 1:1,2,14; 10:30; 17:11; 20:28; Acts 7:59; Philippians 2:6; Colossians 1:15–17*).

I said the Bible does not advocate hating or persecuting those who have not put their trust in Jesus Christ, but it urges believers to bear witness to the unsaved and pray for both the saved and the unsaved (*Matthew 5:44; 10:27; 18:15–17; 28:19; Mark 3:14; 16:15; Luke 6:28; 9:2; 23:34; 24:47; Acts 2:47; 7:60; 10:42; 26:22; Romans 10:1; 10:14,15; I Corinthians 9:19–22; 10:33; II Corinthians 5:20; Ephesians 6:18; I Thessalonians 5:17; I Timothy 2:8; II Timothy 4:2; James 5:16*). I reminded my passenger that she belonged to a Christian denomination that does not believe that Jesus is God, and I did not hate her for that (although I doubt she could be called Christian if she did not believe that Jesus is God).

After that my passenger did not speak. I was tempted to remind her that the Bible teaches that a loving, joyful, peaceful, long-suffering, gentle, humble and faithful spirit is holy and of God and that an angry, envious and hateful spirit is not of God (*John 3:6; Romans 7:5,18–25; 8:3,5,9,13; I Corinthians 3:3; 6:8–11; Galatians 5:13,19–23; 6:8; Ephesians 5:5,9; I*

Timothy 3:3; 6:11; Titus 3:3; James 3:16,17; I John 3:10). But I did not, because the Bible exhorts worshippers not to engage in argument for the sake of arguing, but rather to fear God, be patient and be ready to teach the truth (*II Corinthians 10:1; Galatians 5:22; Philippians 2:3; Colossians 4:6; I Thessalonians 5:13,14; I Timothy 2:7; 3:2,3; II Timothy 2:24; Titus 1:9; 3:2; James 3:17; I Peter 3:8,15*). I was also tempted to remind my passenger that the Bible teaches,

> **"And if some of the branches** [unbelieving Jews] **be broken off, and thou** [believing Gentile]**, being a wild olive tree** [unbelieving world]**, wert graffed in among them** [believing Jews]**, and with them partakest of the root** [Abraham] **and fatness of the olive tree [Jesus Christ];**
>
> **Boast not against the branches. But if thou boast, thou bearest not the root, but the root thee.**
>
> **Thou wilt say then, The branches were broken off, that I might be graffed in.**
>
> **Well; because of unbelief they were broken off, and thou standest by faith. Be not highminded, but fear. For if God spared not the natural branches, [take heed] lest he also spare not thee"** (Romans 11:17–21).

I was not sure I had convinced her that she was not justified in hating people of the Jewish faith and others who have not accepted Jesus Christ as their Saviour.

Now that I had found and fulfilled what I thought to be my main purpose in Bermuda, I was eager to leave. Although I dislike giving up almost as much as I dislike fighting, my family missed me and I missed them. Instead of jumping on the first plane, however, I decided to pray to God for guidance. I concluded that a United Bermuda Party (UBP) victory in the upcoming election, which was very likely, would be an indication that God wanted me to leave, whereas a Progressive Labour Party (PLP) victory would be an indication that God wanted me to stay and fight, at least for a while.

CHAPTER FOURTY

November 9th

I knew little about the history and politics of Bermuda when I moved there, and I never expected politics to affect my medical practice or my life to the extent that it did. Dr. Trouts had told me the little I knew about Bermuda. When he had first asked me to join him there, I told him I did not like the vestiges of slavery I saw in the southern United States and in the one Caribbean island I had visited. Dr. Trouts said that slavery and the large plantations had never existed in Bermuda they way they had in the Caribbean, since Bermuda did not have a lot of land to cultivate. In the early part of its colonization, he explained, Bermuda was involved in shipbuilding for the British Empire, and the Bermudian ships were the fastest in the Empire because they were made of light Bermudian shedder wood. Dr. Trouts said that the black people, who came from the West Indies, were employed in the shipbuilding industry and were not slaves. He proudly told me that his white Bermudian ancestors were pirates. They would cunningly use lighthouses to trick the French and Spanish sailors into becoming shipwrecked off the coast of Bermuda. They pirated the ships, giving ten percent of the bounty to the British Empire and keeping the remainder. Dr. Trouts smiled and said his ancestors were supposed to give fifty percent to the Empire and keep fifty percent for themselves.

I soon realized that Dr. Trouts had not related to me the less colourful side of Bermuda's history and socio-politics. When I started reading about its history and politics I learned that a Spaniard, Juan de Bermudez, first discovered the Islands of Bermuda in about 1505, but apparently returned to Spain without ever be able to land because of high winds. After this the many sailors who saw the Islands but could not dock their ships because of the storms and rocks named it "The Bermudas." Other sailors named them the "Isles of Devils," either because of the unusual sounds they heard coming from the Islands or because of the many shipwrecks on the reefs. Then in 1609 a party of English colonists bound for Virginia under Admiral George Somers was shipwrecked on the Islands. Sir George and his party survived and established the first colony in Bermuda. In 1612 a second group of English colonists arrived on the Islands, then also known as Somers Islands. In 1684 the Island that was included in the third charter of the Virginia Company became a self-governing British colony and that is what it is today. Shortly after their arrival the white settlers imported black slaves from the West Indies as well as North American Indians, and later they brought in Portuguese labourers from Madeira and the Azores. At the conclusion of the American Civil War some white Americans from the confederate camp moved to Bermuda. During the Boer War (1899–1902), the British government sent Boer prisoners to the Island.[1]

Shortly after I arrived in Bermuda I met Mr. Ira Philip, a journalist and former senator, who gave me a copy of a book he had written.[2] Philip's book helped me to understand the Island's politics. It tells the story of two twentieth-century political figures in Bermuda, Charles Vinton Monk and Dr. Edgar Fitzgerald Gordon.

Charles Vinton Monk, an American-born clergyman and journalist, was posted to Bermuda as pastor of the African Methodist Episcopal Church. Shortly after arriving he joined the editorial board of one of the Island's largest black newspapers and began writing about the plight of the majority black population and poor whites who were oppressed by the few white landowners, lawyers and businessmen. Naturally, the "tyrannical oligarchy," as Pastor Monk labelled the oppressors, did not like his writings.[3] Pastor Monk's troubles with the oligarchy came to a head when he described as "appalling" the conditions of the Jamaican workers who had been brought in to work on the Islands. He was charged with criminal libel. Pastor Monk brought from Jamaica one of the best lawyers in the West Indies to argue his case because he could not find a lawyer in Bermuda willing to defend him. The West Indian lawyer died mysteriously in Bermuda and it was widely speculated that he had been poisoned. Pastor Monk went to court and defended himself. The trial lasted three months and he was found guilty of publishing falsehoods. He was sentenced to six months in prison but served only four. After his release, he returned to Philadelphia where he resumed preaching. Pastor Monk never returned to Bermuda and his story was never told until Mr. Philip published his book.

Dr. Gordon, a Trinidadian-born medical doctor trained at the University of Edinburgh in Scotland, arrived in Bermuda in 1924. He established his own private practice because the only hospital on the Island was restricted to white doctors and nurses. Dr. Gordon, who like Pastor Monk had a social conscience and hated injustice, started clashing with the oligarchy as soon as he arrived. He referred to the few white landowners, lawyers and businessmen who had ruled the Islands for three hundred years as "The Forty Thieves." His first battle against the oligarchy was on behalf of the black nurses who were barred from working at the hospital. Dr. Gordon later became a founder and leader of the labour movement in Bermuda. He realized that he could better serve the cause of social justice and achieves greater influence if he became involved in politics. At the time, there were no political parties and universal suffrage had not yet come about. In *Freedom Fighters,* Mr. Philip describes the outdated electoral system that still prevailed in Bermuda in the 1940s when Dr. Gordon ran for parliament:

> "The limited franchise which dated back to the feudal system was at the bottom of all problems. It restricted the vote to persons owing land assessed at a value of sixty pounds. Black persons' land was deliberately undervalued by the predominantly white assessors. While the number of coloured voters exceeded white voters by 134, plural voting whereby one individual could vote in each parish in which he owned land, the white vote exceeded the coloured cumulatively by 232. Only seven percent of the population had the right to vote." [4]

Dr. Gordon discovered that, in addition to this favouring of the few white landowners, lawyers and businessmen, a black candidate could run successfully in a predominantly black parish only with the consent of the oligarchy.

When Dr. Gordon ran for election against the designated black candidate, he discovered that the electoral list included duplicate names, the names of dead people and the names of people who did not own land in the parish. He ran for parliament twice and lost twice. The oligarchy used many other undemocratic ploys. He complained to the governor about these, to no avail.

Despite all odds, however, on two other occasions Dr. Gordon outma-noeuvred "The Forty Thieves" and got elected to parliament. On the second occasion, the black man who had seconded his nomination was fired by his white boss. Another tactic used to discourage a voter who challenged the status quo was to cancel his mortgage.

In his years of political life Dr. Gordon fought for social justice and for universal suffrage and against discrimination and segregation. However, he was frustrated by the lack of loyalty and solidarity of the people he tried to help. Former patients of his told me that Dr. Gordon would often say, "Your people will sell their own down the river." Dr. Gordon passed away in 1955. At the time of his death only nine of thirty-six members of parliament were black, black nurses could not work at the only hospital on the Islands, and all institutions in Bermuda were segregated.

Social change began in 1959, two years after the unrest in Montgomery, Alabama (1955–56), over segregated bus seating. In June 1959, black Bermudians boycotted all the movie theatres on the Island to protest the se-gregated seating arrangements. The theatre owners gave in after fifteen days. The major hotels and many restaurants followed suit and dropped their segregation policies. While allowing token desegregation, the oligarchy be-came very ingenious in holding onto political and economical power. While the white South Africans were establishing a system of apartheid, alienating the rest of the world, the Bermudian oligarchy slowly gave in to some of the economical aspirations of its majority black population. The oligarchy maintained a system of segregation and fear among the masses with no name attached to that system. The rest of the world never saw Bermuda as an apartheid state even though its political and economic structure was not unlike that of apartheid South Africa. In 1963 black Bermudians formed a political party, the Progressive Labour Party (PLP). In 1964 the oligarchy at-tracted two black parliamentarians to its ranks and formed a political party, the United Bermuda Party. In 1967 the PLP of Bahamas, the counterpart of the PLP of Bermuda, defeated the ruling oligarchy in that country. The oligarchy in Bermuda, unwilling to relinquish its political power, attracted more black Bermudians to its ranks. These black people were often used as window dressing, to appease the black population, but behind the scenes political control remained in the hands of the oligarchy. Mr. Philip refers to this scheme as a "façade of democracy." He concludes his book as follows:

> "Bermuda facing the onrush of the 21st Century in 1986 remained a British colony controlled by the descendants of the oligarchy... Dr. Gordon set in train the forces that broke the back of the organized viciousness that characterized the early and mid-century oligarchs. However thirty years after his death many of the attitudes remained, safeguarded by a façade of democracy given legitimacy by such statues as the Bermuda Constitution Act 1968...

> The Archibald commission found not only institutionalized racism rampant in Bermuda in 1985, but a climate of fear pervading all segments of society, which militated against the development of a strong democratic system. The Commission added: -

> "Institutional racism occurs throughout Bermuda Society – in government, business, banks, churches, schools, unions, political parties, clubs and courts – and generally seems to be committed in the name of preserving business traditions and maintaining standards...it is a serious problem.

> Dealing with the question of "ingrained fear of speaking out" in Bermuda, the commission stated that fear, among a sizeable number of the population seemed to be enforced on the basis of economic sanctions which were significant instruments in controlling the behaviour of both Bermudians and non Bermudian alike. Persons regarded as independent thinkers, or ones who spoke out on issues that were unpopular or had the potential of disturbing the statue quo, or who took unpopular stands, found certain areas of employment closed to them, or were threatened with either withdrawal or the non-granting of a mortgage... Control of the media, banks and parliament has been essential for the oligarchy to ensure smooth dominance."[5]

My family and I arrived in Bermuda in 1995, seven years after Mr. Philip's book was published, and the political and social climate was exactly as he describes.

My wife and son were the first to become aware of the no-name brand of segregation that existed in Bermuda. My wife did not want to put our three-year-old son in a nursery, but did want him to interact with children his age. She therefore asked our Portuguese neighbours if he could play with their son, who was also three. The mother and grandmother refused and never again greeted her. My wife then took our son to a park in the hope of finding other children there for him to play with. On weekdays only white children and their nannies or parents could be found in the park, for black parents were usually working and their children in school or a nursery. My wife said the white nannies and parents would leave the playground as soon as she arrived. At first I did not believe my wife, because even though I had come across individuals who were prejudiced I had never lived in a society where discrimination was institutionalized. I suggested to her that it was coincidental that the nannies and parents left when she and my son arrived.

My wife eventually decided to put our son in a nursery, since she could not find any children for him to play with. She visited a nursery that our landlord, the white Bermudian banker, had recommended, but saw only white children there, although only forty percent of the Bermudian population was white. The head of the nursery told her that they were booked and would not have an opening for several years. Finally, my wife found a nursery owned by a black Bermudian. Our son attended this nursery and within two months was speaking English (we spoke French to him at home). The first thing he said to us in English was that he liked the black children and the white children, but not the white adults. We asked him why he did not like the white adults, wondering if a teacher or one of the children had taught him to say such a thing. He would not answer and was too young to give us an explanation.

After my son's comment, I started to think that maybe what my wife had been telling me about Bermudian society was true. Then one day an English nurse bluntly told me that she did not let her children watch Bermudian television because she did not want them to pick up the local accent. And almost every day my wife came home from her shopping with a story about her negative interactions with white people around the Island. One day she exited a store to find that a woman had hit her parked car. When the woman discovered that the car belonged to my wife she began screaming and accusing my wife of hitting her car. Fortunately the Portuguese Bermudian cashiers in the store had witnessed the whole incident. Again, I did not believe my wife's story until one day I witnessed firsthand the arrogance of the oligarchy, which in 1996 was made up of not only white Bermudians, but also white expatriates. Even some white Canadians, who are usually politically correct, became part of the oligarchy when they moved to Bermuda. One day I saw a white Canadian doctor stop his car in the middle of the main street in downtown Hamilton to talk on his cellular phone. This is like stopping one's car in the middle of Fifth Avenue in New York. He could have pulled over to the side, as there was room to park. Apparently his wife, who was sitting in the passenger seat, did not suggest this either. Traffic was backed up for at least two blocks waiting for him to finish his conversation.

One of my patients summarized the type of institutional racism that was prevalent in Bermuda. This patient, a black Bermudian who had been secretary to a white government minister for eight years, said that for eight years the minister would pass in front of her desk, which was located at the entrance to his office, without greeting her or even looking at her. He would speak to the white office manager when he needed the secretary to prepare his speeches or do other tasks. She would occasionally draft laws for him to present in parliament. She said these laws were for show and to appease the black people, because the oligarchy and their friends were above the law and the courts. The country was not governed from parliament, she said, but from private clubs.

Another of my patients, a young black Bermudian pastor, expanded on how the oligarchy – less than seven percent of the population – had controlled the population for more than three hundred years. "They even control our spiritual life and how we worship God," by deciding who can preach on the Island.

On Tuesday, October 20th, 1998, the prime minister called a general election for November 9th. The political situation at the outset of the election campaign was as follows. Universal suffrage had been in place since 1968. Sixty percent of the sixty thousand eligible voters were black. The remaining forty percent (white) included Bermudians of Portuguese descent. The United Bermuda Party (UBP), which had been in power for thirty years, held twenty-two seats and had been led since March 1997 by Pamela Gordon, the daughter of Dr. Gordon – the same Dr. Gordon who had dedicated his life to fighting the oligarchy, from among whom the UBP was drawn. The opposition PLP held eighteen seats and was led by Jennifer Smith, a former journalist.[6]

The economic situation at the outset of the election campaign was that the tourism industry, which employed a third of the population, had been in decline since the late 1980s. A number of hotels were closed over the winter and a few were set to close permanently. During the election campaign the PLP blamed the UBP for letting the tourist industry slowly die and promised to restore it within a hundred days if elected. The UBP reminded voters that Bermuda had prospered under its leadership and that it was the party best suited to lead Bermuda into the twenty-first century with its "global economy and age of technology." In the past the oligarchy had suggested that foreigners and foreign capital would leave Bermuda if the PLP were to gain power. In 1998, the vast majority of the population were no longer impressed with this scare tactic. In addition, the tactic of withdrawal or non-granting of mortgages to scare the majority black population was no longer very effective.

The PLP took out a newspaper advertisement pointing out that positive events like the fall of the Berlin Wall (1989) and the United Nations passage of a resolution condemning apartheid in South Africa (1976) had occurred on November 9th. A reader responded in a letter to the editor that it was also on November 9th that

> "Napoleon became dictator in France, Mussolini formed the National Fascist party, the German National Socialists formed the SS, the Nazis led to the infamous programme against the Jews known as Kristallnacht, and Farrakhan's new friend Saddam Hussein declared a "holy" war on Iran in which millions died."[7]

I had never lived in apartheid South Africa or behind the Iron Curtain, but the fear I saw in the faces of Bermudians when I tried to discuss politics with them was something I had read about in *Nineteen Eighty-Four* by George Orwell.

I tried to discuss politics and the election with my some of my patients when I finished dealing with their medical problems, because I hate social injustice of any sort and because politics was taboo in Bermuda. When I brought up the subject of the election, they would look right and left and behind them to see if anybody was watching or listening. Of course nobody was watching or listening, as the door to my office was closed, but they had developed this mechanical habit of looking around them whenever anybody spoke about politics. Most would tell me that they would pray about it. I would answer that although God wants us to pray there are times when He wants us to act. I was not interested in knowing how my patients were going to vote, but I wanted them to vote with their conscience and without fear.

I was in Montreal visiting my family the day of the election, and all I could do was hope and pray that black Bermudians would have the courage that South Africans had shown and would say no to being oppressed on the basis of their skin colour. The evening of the election I had dinner with two visitors from Bermuda, a black woman married to a European. I asked them who they thought would win the election. Even though we were thousands of miles from Bermuda, they mechanically looked around the room to see if anybody was listening and nervously told me they knew nothing about politics. I begged them to call their family in Bermuda to find out who had won. Later in the evening they phoned me from their hotel. They were happy, excited and no longer nervous. They told me the PLP had won, with twenty-six seats in parliament; the UPB had retained only fourteen of the twenty-two seats they held before the election.

At this stage I had been in Bermuda for two years. I had seen the people smile, but it was not genuine – I could sense their uneasiness and nervousness. Many tourists would remark on how sunny it was in Bermuda. I would answer, without elaborating, that Bermuda was not sunny. They would look me at with amazement and puzzlement. When I returned to Bermuda a few days after the election, I noticed that the atmosphere at the airport was suddenly relaxed. People's faces shone. For the first time I saw the natural smile of black Bermudians. For the first time I saw Bermuda as sunny. I was not in South Africa when apartheid ended and did not see the joy of the South Africans. But I was in Bermuda when the end of oppression started and I am glad to have witnessed it. Some white Bermudians stated quietly that black Bermudians might have the political power, but white Bermudians still had the economic power.

The weekend I returned to Bermuda the two black Bermudians who had been elected in the parish where my small church was located attended my church – which suggests that even politicians know where to find God. Unfortunately, they would never return.

In October 1998, I had decided that a UBP victory would be an indication that God wanted me to leave Bermuda, for I could not fight a political machine and the hospital at the same time, and that a PLP victory would be an indication that God wanted me to stay and continue my fight against the hospital, in the hope that there would be no political interference in my case.

[1] *MSN Encarta,* Online Encyclopaedia (Microsoft, 2001).
[2] Ira Philip, *Freedom Fighters: From Monk to Mazumbo* (London: Akira Press, 1987).
[3] Ibid., p. 21.
[4] Ibid., p. 185. '
[5] Ibid., p. 244.
[6] Meredith Ebbin, "Gordon sets tone for election battle," *Bermuda Sun,* October 21, 1998, p. 1.
[7] Kathy Gibbons, "Nov. 9 Has Also Been a Day for Tyranny," *Bermuda Sun,* November 6th, 1998

CHAPTER FORTY-ONE

Applying for a Judicial Review

In June 1998, Mr. Richardson, my attorney, told me I would likely have my privileges restored by September. He would prepare my affidavit and application for judicial review, ready to be signed and submitted to court within six weeks. In August, I called his office to inquire if the documents were ready. His secretary said he was working on them. Finally, on August 19th, I was able to sign all the documents supporting the application for judicial review, and on August 31st, Mr. Richardson submitted them to court. He told me that in all his years practising law on the Island, first as a lawyer, then as a judge and then as a lawyer again, he never experienced such difficulty submitting a case to court. He said the white judge had tried to hinder him from submitting the documents, but fortunately for us this judge was due to retire in just a few weeks.

The arguments brought forth in the ten-page affidavit – objections that had already been raised by Mr. Kasson, my former attorney – were that the King Edward Memorial Hospital had been biased in dealing with my case and had used unfair methods to review my practice. Mr. Richardson and I were also counting on an e-mail I had obtained. Dated April 15th, 1997, it was to Dr. Cooperson from "HDMMD@...COM," who we believed to be Dr. M. D, one of the so-called independent reviewers regarding my patients' allegedly high levels of blood loss. The author of the e-mail is responding to an inquiry by Dr. Cooperson and concludes as follows: "Hope this helps. If I can help further let me know. My best to your family." We believed it would be a blow to the hospital's claim of an "independent review" if the e-mail was from Dr. D.

In August, Mr. Richardson gave me the task of investigating whether the e-mail was from Dr. D, and I had to do so before his next appearance in court, scheduled for September 10th. I travelled to Montreal the first week of September and phoned many private detectives. Most told me they did not conduct e-mail searches. Finally, however, I found a detective who agreed to do the search. I drove to his office, which was located in the northeast part of the city. The old red brick house looked like something out of a Sherlock Holmes movie. A huge white husky guarded it. I rang the bell and the detective opened the door. He appeared to be in his mid-thirties. He was slim and stood about five foot five. He led me to a room at the back of the house. The room was full of books and papers; some on shelves, some on a desk, the rest lying on the floor. The gentleman had a coat and a hat like Sherlock Holmes hanging on a hanger. He asked me to tell him the story behind the e-mail. He said he did not want to be involved in anything illegal.

After I finished telling my story he said he would take the case. A month earlier, he said, he had helped a client locate the owner of a Website that had sold the client a fake painting only to shut down the Website a few days later. For the next half hour the detective talked about himself. He then assured me he would find out who sent the e-mail, but might not be able to do so by September 10th because he was scheduled to go fishing.

In order not to put all my eggs in one basket, I called a friend in New York and asked him to find out Dr. D' e-mail address. A few days later, the friend called and gave me an address other than "HDMMD@...COM." However, I reasoned that Dr. D might have a second e-mail address.

By September 9th, the detective had not provided me with the information I needed. I called and informed Mr. Richardson's associate of this, as Mr. Richardson was away from the Island. The associate said he would be replacing Mr. Richardson in court; he said that the court appearance was merely a formality and the case would be postponed because the hospital's attorney was also away.

On September 15th, the detective told me he had found Dr. D' e-mail address and produced the same address my friend in New York had given me. I told him that this was helpful, but I had hired him to find out who owned the address "HDMMD@...COM." He said he had given the task to one of his informants and it would take a few more days, at which time he would immediately fax me the information. The detective never called me back. I phoned him several times, but he did not return my calls.

When I realized that the detective would not be calling me back, I set out on my own to find out who owned the e-mail address "HDMMD@… COM." After less than two hours searching on the Web, I was able to determine that it was Dr. Marvin, a surgeon from Boston who frequently travelled to Bermuda to operate with Dr. Cooperson. I had been led to believe that the e-mail was from Dr. D because he had the same initial as Dr. Marvin. Needless to say, I was greatly disappointed to learn that I could not prove a connection between Drs. Cooperson and D. However, I got over my disappointment within a few hours because I reasoned that we still had sufficient evidence to prove bias on the part of the hospital. I only hoped that my attorney had not built his case solely on the e-mail evidence and that he would put this mistake behind him.

I phoned Mr. Richardson and informed him of my discovery. I could feel the disappointment in his voice when I broke the news. On October 26th, we met in his office. He was less jovial than usual. He began by showing me a crystal-framed clock that was sitting on his desk. The edge of the frame was broken and he said this was because the cleaning lady had dropped the clock on his desk instead of depositing it gently. When he finished talking about his clock and the cleaning lady he pulled a number of documents out of my file and said these were the affidavits of the doctors from the other party. He started reading them one by one, line by line, page by page. He read Dr. D' first. In his seven-page affidavit, Dr. D said he did not know Dr. Cooperson prior to the review. He also wrote that the e-mail letter we suspected had originated from him was not his.

Next, he read Dr. Fascioni's affidavit, which was vintage Dr. Fascioni. Dr. Fascioni admitted that it was Dr. Cooperson and he who were the instigators of the complaints against me, which started the chain of investigations of my practice, something that Dr. Jameson had officially denied in the past. Dr. Fascioni said he was justified in complaining about me because I was inept.

Mr. Richardson then read Dr. Cooperson's affidavit. Dr. Cooperson admitted to having made the complaint against me in June 1996, but did not explain why. He did not deny attending my interview with the Credentials

Committee in April 1997 and influencing its decision to investigate my practice further. He admitted that it was he who had recommended that Dr. Brookson, his friend and former professor, conduct the review of my practice, and that in September 1997 he had assisted Dr. Brookston in that review. When the Bermuda Hospitals Board restored my privileges in April 1998, following the Brookson review, it had not intended to conduct any further review of my practice, but Dr. Cooperson pressured it into doing so. In his affidavit, Dr. Cooperson exhibited a letter dated March 13th, 1998, from Dr. Cooperson to Mr. Toby, chairman of the Board, confirming this:

> "I had confirmation this afternoon from the Executive Director's office that what has been merely rumor for the past week is in fact true in that the Bermuda Hospitals Board has seen fit to reinstate the surgical privileges of Dr. C. Bah.

> In my position as Chairman of the Sub-division of Orthopaedic Surgery, I feel it is my duty to inform you that I disagree with the decision for a number of reasons, not the least of which is the fact that Dr. E. Brookson, the former Orthopaedic Surgeon in Chief of 1000 bed Teaching Hospital, Royal College of Canada Examiner in Orthopaedics for many years and a highly respected member of the profession, did not feel that Dr. Bah's professional actives met the standards required to be on the Orthopaedic Staff at KEMH. In addition, the decision has put any medical staff required to work with Dr. Bah in a very difficult position. I feel the position of the anesthetic staff, in particular, is untenable.

> The decision was made by the Bermuda Hospitals Board and the ultimate responsibility for this action rests solely with them.

> The early resolution of this dilemma is essential and to this end I would be most happy to discuss it with you and co-operate in any way with the hospital administration."

In his affidavit, Dr. Cooperson admitted that in April 1998 Dr. Paytons had asked him to cooperate with Drs. Sonby and D, the so-called independent reviewers, in the third review of my practice, and he had done so; he had participated in the preparation of the (erroneous) terms of reference. In his affidavit he admitted that he had filed complaints against me in December 1995 when I arrived on the Island, June 1996 and March 1998, and had been the witness, prosecutor and designated judge against me in September 1996, April 1997, September 1997, April 1998 and May

1998. Oddly, nobody among the hospital authorities saw anything unusual or unfair about this.

Mr. Richardson read Dr. Sonby's fifteen-page affidavit last. Drs. Klein and Esses, in their reports, had indicated that it is inadequate and inadvisable to review the practice of a surgeon without seeing the surgeon's office notes and the imaging results with regard to a given patient. All the patients I operated on had had MRI examinations. Copies of these and the results were available in my office. Any person who has recently undergone spine surgery in North America will attest that their surgeon did not rely on ordinary x-rays when deciding whether or not to perform surgery, but based the decision on the results of an MRI. In his affidavit, Dr. Sonby wrote that the x-rays and hospital records of my patients were "comprehensive and provided more than enough information" for Dr. D and him to assess my practice and my judgement. Drs. Klein and Esses also suggested that in order to conduct a fair review of an individual surgeon, the reviewer must speak with the surgeon personally. In his affidavit, Dr. Sonby stated that he and Dr. D had sufficient "experience...competence, and ability" to assess my practice and reach a conclusion without reviewing the office notes or MRIs of my patients or meeting with me. My clinical judgement and skills were so lacking, he stated, that their meeting with me would not have served to change their conclusions.

It took Mr. Richardson two hours, at a rate of $500 an hour, to read the four affidavits. When he finished, he brandished them and said, "This cost a lot of money." He suggested I speak to Dr. Klein and solicit his help. He said that Dr. Sonby's affidavit was basically an attack on the reports of Drs. Klein and Esses. I told Mr. Richardson I did not want to call Dr. Klein because he did not have good memories of his visit to Bermuda and would not be eager to return. In addition, I remembered the advice Dr. Klein had given me before he left. He said the Brookson report was a fiasco and if I were to sue the hospital I would win, but he advised against this course. In light of his findings, Dr. Klein said, the hospital should restore my privileges and leave me alone.

Dr. Klein advised me to leave Bermuda if the hospital failed to restore my privileges or decided to conduct another review of my practice, because in such an environment I would never get justice. I felt I could not ignore

Dr. Klein's advice and call on him to bail me out whenever I was in trouble. Thus I told Mr. Richardson that instead of phoning Dr. Klein I would produce my own affidavits and find other means of defending myself.

CHAPTER FORTY-TWO

Help?

As soon as I left Mr. Richardson's office I started working on my affidavit in response to those of the other four doctors. However, I knew that no matter how thorough, accurate and truthful, my affidavit would not by itself stand a chance in a court of law against the testimony of the four doctors. I had to find some other means of neutralizing their opinions.

Then I remembered that someone had recently offered to help. In September 1998, while in Montreal, I had dinner with Mr. Pronovost, a pharmaceutical representative. He told me he had spoken with Dr. M. Domain, one of my former professors, who seemed to be aware of my misadventures in Bermuda. Mr. Pronovost said Dr. Domain had suggested I call him. Dr. Domain had been my supervisor during a six-month pediatric surgery rotation. He and I got along well, but I think he liked me most for the fact that I never bothered him at home when we were on duty together during those six months. He trusted me and I operated on his patients by myself. Dr. Domain had invited me to his cottage in Quebec's Eastern Townships on a few occasions during and after my training, but I had never been able to make it. Now he was chief of staff at a children's hospital affiliated with the other medical school in Montreal. Dr. Brookson had been a professor at that university until retiring a few months earlier so it was likely that Dr. Domain knew him well. Since he was involved in Canadian medical politics, Dr. Domain was probably also well acquainted with Dr. Sonby, one of the so-called independent reviewers. In September 1998, I had decided not to take Dr. Domain up on his offer of assistance, especially in light of his political connections. However, I phoned to thank him.

When, in November 1998, I was faced with having to defend myself against the four doctors, I reasoned that I had nothing to lose by soliciting the help of Dr. Domain. Mr. Richardson agreed. In order to minimize my legal expenses, I composed the letter to Dr. Domain and had Mr. Richardson correct it. The three-page letter summarized the events leading to the two reviews of my practice and withdrawal of my privileges and then asked for his assistance, as follows:

> "Dr. Bah has informed us that we may take the liberty of seeking your assistance in dealing with these matters and it is in this connection that we now write to you…
>
> We are of the view that because of professional jealousy certain members of the Orthopaedic Division of the Hospital engineered a decision by that Board to conduct an external review of Dr. Bah's practice with regard to his patient care…
>
> We feel that there is the likelihood that Dr. Cooperson, or Dr. Fascioni who were the original complainants against Dr. Bah, and Dr. Paytons know Dr. Sonby, Dr. D. We understand that the Orthopaedic community, and especially the teaching community in Canada, is very small and the likelihood of these gentlemen knowing one another is very great…
>
> We would be grateful for your opinion as to the approved method of selecting a candidate for peer review particularly in the context of this case, when the complainants and members of the same Orthopaedic Division and are in direct competition with the surgeon complained against in a private practice setting…
>
> May we thank you in advance for the offer to assist our client and ask that you submit your written views or comments as soon as possible…"

I made copies of all the relevant documents and took the copies to Montreal to meet Dr. Domain at his clinic. Dr. Domain, who at the time was recuperating from surgery, greeted my wife and me and asked about my well being. He briefly went through the documents and then said, "Nobody gets along with him [Dr. Brookson] anyway," and offered to help. When my wife and I left the clinic she said, "I don't trust that man." I said neither did I.

A week later, Mr. Richardson received a reply to his letter to Dr. Domain. When I went to his office to discuss it, he said, "You know, my staff is worried about your legal bill." I had not paid all of the legal fee, for two reasons. First, Mr. Richardson had told me in June 1998, when the

Medical Insurance Society indicated that it would not pay my legal fees, not to worry about costs. The priority, he said, was to get me back to work, which should be by September. Second, I realized that he was billing me more than his other clients because I was a doctor and therefore, presumably, could afford to pay higher fees. Mr. Richardson's attitude and tone suggested that something was wrong with Dr. Domain's reply. He did not read out the letter to me as he had the affidavits of the four other doctors, but instead handed it to me. It read:

> "The peer reviewers are well-known and respected orthopaedic surgeons. Dr. Brookson... has ample credentials, integrity and objectivity to analyze medical practices...
>
> From what I understand as an outsider, I feel that the methodology resembles what is usually done, when an evaluation is needed... It may be that the Bermuda surgeons knew Dr. Brookson reasonably well, but that would not influence his professional judgment..."

My misadventure with Dr. Domain was costly in terms of legal fees and travel expenses, but it taught me two lessons that I will remember forever: every opportunity that comes my way is not necessarily good for me, and my adversaries have friends in many places.

Before I left Mr. Richardson's office he reminded me once again about my legal bill.

I was determined not to let Dr. Domain's letter get me down. I would not give up. I continued working on my affidavit as soon as I left Mr. Richardson's office. Within two weeks I produced an affidavit of some thirty pages and a hundred pages of exhibits. While preparing it I realized that Drs. Sonby and D had included in their reports all the patients Dr. Morais and I had operated on. Dr. Morais, another former professor, had come to Bermuda in June 1996 to help with my backlog of spine cases. He had seen pre-operatively all the patients we operated on and in each case agreed with my diagnosis and indications for surgery. The so-called independent reviewers had concluded that those operations were not "justified" and that the surgeries we performed were too "aggressive." I called Dr. Morais and asked if he would be willing to prepare an affidavit to the effect that the operations we performed together were medically indicated and that the complications the two reviewers had ascribed to the patients concerned were a fraud. He agreed to do so.

I met with Mr. Richardson to give him my affidavit and to discuss the idea of Dr. Morais' helping us. At the commencement of the meeting I handed him an envelope containing a cheque for $5,000 in partial payment of my legal bill. I hoped this would revive his interest in the case. When Mr. Richardson took the envelope, which he may have thought contained payment in full, he smiled and said, "You know, these people [the hospital authorities] are afraid of me. You'll see what we're going to do to them." Mr. Richardson read my affidavit and said it was too long and contained far too many medical terms; he suggested I make some corrections. He agreed with the notion of having Dr. Morais produce an affidavit and said that both Dr. Morais' affidavit and mine should be ready to submit to the court before the end of the year.

I faxed Dr. Morais several documents and over the next few days he and I discussed the drafting of his affidavit. Then I flew to Montreal to meet with him and help finalize his affidavit.

On December 23rd, I met with Mr. Richardson and gave him Dr. Morais' affidavit and my revised one. He said he would work on both over Christmas and submit them to the court the first week of January. At that point I had paid Mr. Richardson $14,000 of the $24,000 I owed him and hoped he would proceed with the case.

CHAPTER FORTY-THREE

Fear

"And I say unto you my friends, Be not afraid of them that kill the body, and after that have no more that they can do. But I will forewarn you whom ye shall fear: Fear him, which after he hath killed hath power to cast into hell; yea, I say unto you, Fear him" (Luke 12:4,5).

For God hath not given us the spirit of fear; but of power, and of love, and of a sound mind" (II Timothy 1:7).

On January 12th, I phoned Mr. Richardson to see if he had finished working on the affidavits. He said he was still working on them and repeated his now famous line that his office was worried about the money I owed him.

Two weeks later, on January 25th, I phoned Mr. Richardson again. He said he had been very busy because his law firm was merging with another law firm. I realized that he had misled me when he said he was working on the affidavits. However, I was not going to give up; I would find a way to advance my case, with or without Mr. Richardson. I spoke to a friend about my case and the fact that Mr. Richardson had not finalized the affidavits I had given him a month earlier. The friend suggested that his wife, a lawyer, finalize them. I asked Mr. Richardson if he would mind submitting the affidavits to the court if another lawyer were to finalize them. He said he would not mind and I could drop by his office to pick up my file.

On March 5th, I went to Mr. Richardson's office to pick up my file. I sat and listened to him for some time. He began by saying he found the practice of law very easy while his associates became nervous when they had to go to court. He pointed to a large file lying on his office floor and told me he helped a lot of people. He said the file belonged to a gentleman who was in deep trouble and I would read about it in the newspaper in a few days. The file belonged to a policeman accused of sexually harassing a female colleague. A friend who was a police officer had already told me about the case. Then Mr. Richardson said I had a very good case and could win big. He said the hospital would have no choice, but to compensate me for the loss of income that I incurred if were to win. I asked Mr. Richardson how much more in legal expenses I could expect to pay before we reached that stage. He smiled and said that once the affidavits were prepared it would take three weeks of court hearings. I made a quick calculation in my head and concluded that at the end of three weeks of court hearings I could end up paying him $75,000 in legal fees. I smiled and told him I would think about it. Mr. Richardson said he was doing me a favour by letting me take my file while I still owed him money. He knew of no other lawyer who would do that, he said. He was probably right in that regard. Before I left, Mr. Richardson said I had done well in Bermuda (he had once been my patient) and no doubt would have continued doing well had I been left alone. He said, "You do not give up easily and I commend you for that."

As I left Mr. Richardson's office, I remembered what he had told me the first time we met: "If we see them [white people] kick one of us [black people] we should help the one being kicked; otherwise next they are going to kick the one who ran." Now that Mr. Richardson had saved me temporarily from being kicked, it was time to take my money, my shirt and my pants and leave for the others to kick. A few weeks later, I paid Mr. Richardson the full $10,000 I owed him. I asked his office to pay me the $600 they owed me for producing two medical reports for one of their clients. The junior partner refused, stating that it was up to the patient to pay for such medical reports. This was not true, as it is up to the party who requests the medical report to pay for it; all other law firms that I did business with paid me for such services.

I was confident that Dr. Morais' and my affidavits would prove that the review conducted by the so-called independent reviewers was a fabrication. But I also thought that the testimony of other professionals to this effect would give more leverage to my case. In their review of my work, Drs. Sonby and D had written the following:

"Dr. Ilea, a resident, has created a spreadsheet with brief clinical summaries listing Dr. Bah's surgical patients. This was reviewed to ensure complete-ness of our external review… Dr. W.R. Crook produced a review of the operative blood loss and complications associated with some of Dr. Bah's surgically treated patients. This review was provided to us…we were greatly helped by the meticulous review of operative blood loss and complications performed by Dr. W.R. Crook, and dated 15 May 1998. Our own review of the hospital clinical records confirmed the accuracy of the summary pro-vided by Dr. Crook."

Dr. Jameson, the former chief of staff of the hospital, had sought to hire Dr. Will Smith, a black Bermudian resident physician, to review the hos-pital records of my patients, with the mandate of coming up with compli-cations. When Dr. Smith declined, Dr. Jameson hired Dr. Ilea, an English resident physician, to do the dirty work. A few days prior to the review by Drs. Sonby and D, I found the document prepared by Drs. Ilea and Crook in the medical records. It was titled "Blood Loss list…Dr. Crook's chart review" and at the bottom was the initials JMSP, for Dr. Paytons, the new chief of staff. The document was completely erroneous. They had fabricated the evidence against me. Drs. Sonby and D found this erroneous document prepared by Drs. Ilea, Crook and Cooperson (in his affidavit Dr. Cooperson admitted to also working on the document) and approved by Dr. Paytons to be "accurate." They not only found it "greatly helpful", but also used the erroneous data in their review.

I thought my case would have more leverage if five physicians in Bermuda were to review my patients' hospital records, compare them with the data in the document prepared by the three doctors, and reach the inevi-table conclusion that these data were entirely erroneous. Dr. Burke, a black Bermudian family doctor, was the first physician I called in this regard. Dr. Burke, a man in his early fifties, had trained in the United States and worked there for many years because the oligarchy would not permit him to set up practice in Bermuda. Like Dr. Browne, he had only recently been allowed to practise in Bermuda. He had referred patients to me on a regular basis ever since my arrival on the Island. In private, he had often expressed support for me in my fight against the hospital. I explained why I was calling and asked for his help. Dr. Burke said he did not foresee any problem with helping me. I then faxed him the blood loss list of my patients prepared by Drs. Ilea, Crook and Cooperson, as well as a letter explaining exactly what

I needed him to do – which was to compare the blood loss of my patients as indicated in the hospital charts and compare it with the blood loss of the same patients as listed in the document prepared by the three doctors.

The next day Dr. Burke sent me a fax indicating that, on second thought, he could not conduct the review because it would represent conflict of interest. He informed me that the newly elected PLP government had just appointed him to the Board. He suggested I get in touch with Dr. Brock, an American-African vascular surgeon working in Bermuda. Two days later he faxed me a list of nine other physicians, all but one of whom were black.

When I looked at the names of the physicians on Dr. Burke's list, I had a feeling that none of them would support me. A meeting had been held every Wednesday, attended by all of the physicians at the hospital. The seating at the meeting was structured and segregated. The chief of staff, Dr. Jameson and later Dr. Paytons, sat in the front row on the right side of the room. Dr. Bazaar, an African family physician married to a Bermudian, sat next to the chief of staff, likes a water boy (Dr. Bazaar was one of the physicians on Dr. Burke's list). The other chairs next to the chief of staff remained empty. Dr. Crook sat by himself in the second row behind the chief of staff. Most of the female physicians sat in the third row behind Dr. Crook. Most of the black doctors and a few white ones sat in the fourth and fifth rows, while most of the white doctors, including Drs. Fascioni and Cooperson, sat on the left side of the room. I stood in the back near the food, to eat, observe and quietly exit and go to the operating room.

One particular meeting exposed the character of the doctors to me and made me see that none of the physicians on Dr. Burke's list would help. At that meeting a consultant from a well-known international consulting firm was the guest speaker. He presented his findings on the state of the health care in Bermuda, which were as follows: that health care in Bermuda was very expensive, that there was no leadership at the hospital, and that the general population believed the doctors took them for granted and were more interested in making money than in the welfare of their patients.

As usual, Dr. Fascioni was the first to speak after the presentation. He attributed all the negative findings of the consulting firm to the patients, who he said were spoiled and always wanted go abroad for an MRI. Then he lashed out at chiropractors. Dr. Fascioni had an aversion to chiropractors and anyone else who directly or indirectly competed with him. The other doctors followed suit and blamed the patients for the state of health care in Bermuda. The blaming of the general population went on for half an hour. No physicians commented on the finding that there was no leadership at the hospital. I stood in the back and bit my tongue because of the comment the judge had made, that I was a "sheep among wolves." Finally, however, I could restrain myself no longer. I raised my hand and requested permission to speak. I said the population had spoken and told us what they thought of us doctors. I said there were a lot of intelligent people in the general population and maybe we should consider their opinions. I saw two physicians nod in approval. I said we should investigate why the general population preferred to see chiropractors and other non-medical professionals over us. When I finished talking all eyes were on me and I felt daggers being shot at me. The whole assembly remained silent and the meeting ended. After the meeting all the physicians, including the black ones, walked by me as though I had a contagious disease. Dr. Wan, an oriental family physician from the West Indies, was the only one who dared speak to me. He approached me and whispered, "You are right," and hurried off.

Dr. Wan was not on Dr. Burke's list, but I knew he would not help me. When my privileges were withdrawn, Dr. Wan, who had been a constant source of patient referrals, had expressed his support for me. However, a few weeks later his wife phoned my secretary and asked her to go and work for Dr. Wan. My secretary, who was very loyal, declined the offer.

Dr. Miles, an ear, nose and throat specialist from the West Indies who had trained in Europe, was the second physician I asked to do a comparative review of my patients' hospital records and the list compiled by Drs. Ilea, Crook and Cooperson. Dr. Miles had moved to Bermuda two years earlier. He told me that four Bermudian physicians had hired him on the condition that he pay them forty percent of his income, but that once he arrived he realized he had to pay them more than sixty percent. The deal between Dr. Miles and the physicians fell through after a legal battle, but he had been able to remain on the Island because he had married a local judge.

Because of his connections and his intuition, Dr. Miles was more familiar with Bermuda's wheeling and dealing than anybody I knew and his advice had been very valuable to me. He now strongly advised me to drop everything and leave Bermuda because the establishment would waste my time and in the end, sweep everything under the rug. I asked him if the court would not be independent of the political apparatus now that the PLP was in power. He again said it would be better if I returned to Canada. I thought Dr. Miles must be right since he had privileged information. I asked him if I should also abandon my attempt to recuperate my money from Dr. Trouts. He said I should abandon everything, leave and forget the place. I said I would consider his advice, but for now I would like him to conduct the review for me. He agreed to do so and I faxed him the relevant documents.

Two weeks later, I met Dr. Miles at a meeting in the hospital, the purpose of which was to form a new association of doctors. Dr. Burke and many black doctors felt that the old association served only the interests of a small circle of white doctors. This sort of meeting would have been unthinkable a few months earlier when the UBP had been in power. After the meeting Dr. Miles said he did not have time to talk to me and hurried away. On April 8th, a month after he had agreed to conduct the review, I called and asked him if he had completed his report. He said he was busy and would call me back. He never did.

I then asked Dr. Boys, an African eye specialist married to a Bermudian, to conduct the review. Dr. Boys, a Christian, had once invited me to his church. He and his pastor, who were both aware of my situation, told me they often prayed for me. I thought that since Dr. Boys was sufficiently concerned to pray for me, surely he would be willing to offer his practical support. I called and asked if he could help. I also faxed him a letter and several documents detailing what I wanted from him.

Two weeks later, on February 19th, I phoned Dr. Boys and asked him if he had been able to do the review. He whispered and acted as if the phone was tapped. I asked him to speak louder as I could not hear him. He whispered a little louder, explaining that he had experienced difficulty-getting hold of my patients' charts due to some kind of conspiracy at the hospital, but that he would continue to try. I knew that Dr. Boys was not telling the truth about being unable to obtain my patients' charts. On March 8th, I called him for the third time and asked if he had been able to obtain the charts and conduct the review. He said he had not done the review because

I had told him I had also asked Dr. Miles to do it.

I next approached Dr. Warren, a black Bermudian internist. I would never have asked Dr. Warren to do the review had I not run into him one day in February 1999 as I was leaving my attorney's office. At that time he inquired about my legal battle against the hospital. I said things were progressing slowly. Dr. Warren said he could not understand why Dr. Trouts, who had depended on me to operate on his patients, was not supporting me in this fight. It was in light of this comment that I approached him to conduct the review, and he agreed to do so. On April 8th, a month after I had spoken to him, I called and asked if he had been able to do the review. He said he had not because he had been on vacation, and added that he would be unable to do it within the next month because he was too busy. I never called Dr. Warren again. On June 16th, I bumped into him in town. He said he had been unable to do the review and asked how things were. I told him everything was fine and we parted on that note.

After that I solicited the help of Dr. MacLean, a Canadian anaesthetist. Dr. MacLean had moved to Bermuda a year earlier and had had his share of problems with the anaesthetists at the hospital. Upon his arrival he joined the group of English anaesthetists and received a token monthly salary. He found that in addition to being paid a meagre salary he was working significantly more and billing more than the anaesthetists he was working for. He tried to improve his financial and work situation by asking to renegotiate his salary, with no success, so he left the group to work on his own. The group lobbied the surgeons to not work with him. The majority of the surgeons, including Drs. Cooperson and Fascioni, succumbed to the pressure and decided to stop working with Dr. MacLean. In addition to preventing him from making a living, the group tried to undermine Dr. MacLean's reputation. They did to him exactly what Drs. Cooperson and Fascioni did to me. They complained that he was not anaesthetizing patients according to North American standards and was putting their lives in jeopardy. Dr. MacLean had been practising anaesthesia in Canada for some fifteen years, with no complaints. He decided to fight back. He hired an attorney and won the first round. His task of defending himself against the hospital and the group was easier than mine by virtue of the fact that he was married to a Bermudian and thus had Bermudian status.

I called Dr. MacLean, described my situation and asked him to conduct a review. He said he would be more than happy to do so. He suggested I contact the Medical Insurance Society to see if they would agree to pay my legal fees if I worked with Mr. Diels, the attorney who had successfully defended him.

A few days later, Dr. MacLean did as he had promised. He compared the blood loss of my patients as indicated in the records with that listed in the documents prepared by Drs. Ilea, Crook and Cooperson and quoted by the so-called independent reviewers of my practice (see Website: www.theonlywaytoeternallife.com, Letter 46). He summarized his findings as follows:

> "The Blood loss set out in the "Blood loss List" [Dr. Crooks' Chart Review] does not correspond with the intra-operative blood loss recorded in the charts. It is consistently higher than the actual blood loss record at the time of operation, in some cases 300–400% of the actual blood loss."

Next, I approached Dr. Brock, an African-American vascular surgeon. Dr. Brock had moved to Bermuda two years earlier. His situation was better than mine because he had been a classmate and long-time friend of Dr. Browne, transport minister in the new government, and had many other friends in the new government. Also, he was the only vascular surgeon on the Island and therefore not in direct competition with anyone. Still, the other doctors had made life difficult for Dr. Brock when he first moved to Bermuda. They had tried to undermine his reputation by criticizing his practice. Dr. Brock, who was in his early fifties, said he had seen "the whole movie." He had grown up in the United States during the civil rights movement and had worked in the jungles of Los Angeles. Not one to mince his words, he had told Dr. Cooperson and his group at a meeting, "You f… with me, I will f… with you."

I asked Dr. Brock if he could do the review for me. He said he would if he was able to secure the charts of my patients. Two weeks later, he called and said he had done the review. I asked him about his findings. Dr. Brock said, "They framed you, man. They really f….. you." I told him I knew I had been framed, but would appreciate it if he used less harsh words in his report. Dr. Brock summarized his findings as follow:

> "The purpose of this communication is to describe my findings of a chart

review done on behalf of Dr. Bah. Of the eight charts I reviewed, no blood loss was recorded on two charts... In the remaining six charts reviewed there were major discrepancies in the recorded blood loss as indicated in the chart and that which was recorded on the "Blood Loss list" referred to as "Dr. Crooks' Chart review.

The discrepancies were so large that one would be hard put to say they were the result of error..."

When Dr. Brock gave me his report, he said the new PLP government would not rock the boat because "everybody has a finger in the pie." He advised me to negotiate with the new Board to restore my privileges and take legal action against Drs. Cooperson, Fascioni and the others who had framed me.

In the end, the only two doctors who agreed to conduct a review for me were a Canadian and an American. I wondered if Dr. Burke would have done so had he not been a member of the new Board. A few months later, I got my answer. In July 1999, the new government struck a race relations committee at the hospital. The organizer of a meeting of that committee told me what transpired there. Dr. Paytons was the first to speak. His said that professionals needed to be admitted at the hospital on the basis of merit and he deserved to be chief of staff. Dr. Miles also spoke. The meeting's organizer could feel Dr. Miles wanted to say something about racism at the hospital, but skirted around the subject because of fear. Of the thirty doctors who attended the meeting (Dr. Brock was away from the Island), only Dr. Little, a young white woman, had the courage to acknowledge the existence of racism at the hospital. That evening Dr. Burke phoned the meeting's organizer and said he wished to speak to her privately about racism at the hospital. She said the same fear found among black doctors in Bermuda was prevalent among black accountants and other black professionals.

CHAPTER FORTY-FOUR

The Promise

In November 1998, immediately after the election, many of my patients told me I would have my privileges restored because of the change of government. I wasn't so sure. Dr. Browne approached me and said I could have them restored if I wanted. I was not confident that Dr. Browne would carry through on his promise. Moreover, I felt I could reintegrate my work at the hospital unhindered and without my adversaries crying favouritism or political intervention if the court were to exonerate me of the charges. So I told Dr. Browne to wait a while and see what the court would decide.

In February 1999, after I realized that Mr. Richardson, my attorney, had practically abandoned me, I thought I would follow Dr. Brock's advice and negotiate with the hospital authorities to have my privileges restored. It was in this regard that I met Dr. Burke, the new member of the Board. In a January 1999 fax, Dr. Burke had said he could not carry out a comparative review for me because it would represent conflict of interest: "I really wish I could do this. You may not know, but I am now on the Board. Therefore I may be able to assist by another venue." I met Dr. Burke in his downtown office and I told him that Drs. Brock and MacLean had done comparative reviews and found that the hospital had framed me. If a court of law were to objectively review all the evidence in my case, I said, it would find that the hospital had wrongfully acted in removing my privileges and would have no choice, but to restore my privileges and compensate me for the loss of income and other damages. I suggested to Dr. Burke that the new Board consider all the evidence in the matter and restore my privileges, explaining that I would drop all legal action against the hospital if the Board were to do so, but would reserve my right to take legal action against the doctors who had initiated the complaints against me and commissioned the reviews. Dr. Burke was very understanding. He said he would talk to Mr. Dills, the new chairman of the Board, and get back to me. Mr. Dills was the only member of the old Board to survive the reshuffling. This was the same Mr. Dills who had met with Dr. Klein during his visit to Bermuda and had called him in New York to say he was considering resigning over the handling of my case.

On the evening of March 4th, Dr. Burke phoned me at home. He said he had taken the liberty of speaking with Mr. Richardson, who told him I had a very good case, but not the financial means to fight the hospital, especially if the case were to drag on. Dr. Burke stated again that he would discuss my case with Mr. Dills and get back to me.

A week later, on March 12th, I came across Mr. Dills in downtown Hamilton. He said that Dr. Burke had spoken to him about my case. "Some members of the old Board [Dr. Jameson and Mrs. Anderson]," he said, "had tried to convince the Board that patients would die if your privileges were restored. It was a scare tactic, and I never believed it." Mr. Dills said he would see what the new Board could do for me.

Late that afternoon Dr. Browne asked me to meet him in his office. He was always in a rush and preoccupied when we talked. He told me he had just spoken with Dr. Burke and Mr. Dills and it was "definite" that my privileges would be restored. He advised me to take legal action against the doctors who had framed me. I thanked him for his intervention and said I would look into taking legal action against them.

While waiting for written confirmation that my privileges had been restored, I reapplied for a work permit. I hoped that this time around, with the election of the new government, there would be no political intervention to obstruct the process of renewing my work permit. Dr. Lightbourn, my sponsor, wrote to the immigration ministry on my behalf. I filled in the application form and personally took it, along with Dr. Lightbourn's letter, to the immigration ministry. The clerk there was very nice. She said, "Everything is fine, Dr. Bah. You will get your work permit within two weeks." By this time many people in Bermuda who I had never met before knew my name, either because I had treated one of their relatives or because I had made the headlines.

Three weeks later, I went to the immigration office to get my permit. The front-desk clerk called her supervisor, who then appeared with my file. The supervisor was very polite. She looked at my file, smiled and said my work permit had been issued and sent to Dr. Lightbourn's office. I walked to Dr. Lightbourn's office, which was not far from the immigration office, but his secretary assured me that she had not received any papers from immigration concerning me. I walked back to the immigration office and was told this time around that the permit had been sent to Mr. Dunkin, my other attorney. I walked to Mr. Dunkin's office and his staff told me they had not received anything from immigration concerning me. I went back to immigration a third time and told the clerk that neither Mr. Dunkin nor Dr. Lightbourn had received my permit. The clerk and the supervisor checked once more and reassured me that it had been issued and sent to Mr. Dunkin's office. They suggested that Mr. Dunkin's staff had lost it because they had recently moved offices. I was not about to argue with the immigration staff. I went back to my office and recounted the afternoon's events to Dr. Browne. He immediately picked up the phone and called a senior civil servant in immigration, who then asked me to bring two passport photographs to her the next day. Two days later the civil servant called to inform me that she has just finished working on my work permit and I could pick it up. I immediately went to her offices and fetched it.

Towards the end of March Dr. Browne called me into his office and asked if I was going to stay in Bermuda. I was surprised by this question as three weeks earlier he had assured me that my privileges would be restored. He said he was thinking of bringing in a general surgeon from California and wondered if I would mind sharing my office with him. I said I didn't mind. The next day I went back and asked Dr. Browne what had happened to his assurance that my privileges would be restored. He said it had been impossible for him to keep this promise because Mrs. Anderson, the executive director of the hospital, had objected. He said his government could not terminate Mrs. Anderson, but in any event her contract was due to expire in June 1999.

CHAPTER FORTY-FIVE

The Tenth Attorney

On March 5th, 1999, I took my file from Mr. Richardson's office because a friend's wife, an attorney, was to review my affidavit and that of Dr. Morais. Once I had the file in hand, I called my friend, who told me his wife was laid up with the flu, like many people on the Island, and would not be able to work on it for at least two weeks.

I had not completely abandoned my legal fight even though Dr. Burke, Dr. Browne and Mr. Dills had promised I would have my privileges restored. I followed up on Dr. MacLean's suggestion that I ask the Medical Insurance Society (MIS) to cover my legal fees if I transferred my file to Mr. Diels, the attorney who had successfully represented him in his case against the hospital and the anaesthetist group. On March 8th, the MIS informed me they had asked Mr. Diels to provide a preliminary opinion on the merits of my case and indicated they would consider paying if he believed the case had merit.

On March 9th, I met with Mr. Diels in his downtown Hamilton office. Mr. Diels, a white Bermudian, tried to go through my file, but gave up after a while for he said the file was too disorganized. He said he would have his secretary put some order into it and asked me to return in a few days.

Three days later, after he had had time to look at the file, I met with Mr. Diels again. He said that the twenty-eight-day deadline for filing our affidavits was long past and we would have to explain to the court why we had not submitted them in December 1998. He said that I had a good case and he would write to the MIS with his opinion on its merits.

On March 26th, the MIS indicated that they would cover Mr. Diels' fee for advising and updating them on the merits of my case, but that I would have to continue paying for court proceedings. They suggested that they might cover my legal fees in the future if my application for judicial review was successful.

My alternatives were to continue the fight in the hope that the MIS would pick up the tab for the judicial review should I be successful, or to drop everything. Mr. Diels advised me to carry on. Having just defended Dr. MacLean, he knew the rules and regulations of the hospital better than my previous attorney and even better than the hospital's own attorneys. He went over them and showed me that in almost every instance the hospital had broken its own rules in conducting the reviews of my practice and removing my privileges.

I explained to Mr. Diels that I was hesitant to continue because Mr. Richardson had told me the same thing, only to bill me for $28,000 and drop the case midway through. Mr. Diels said that Mr. Richardson had over billed me and that his fee would be $7,000, which would include preparation of the documents and the two-day court appearance. I would have to pay him half that amount immediately, because his law firm was very small, and the balance the day before the hearing. He assured me there would be no additional charges. I agreed to Mr. Diels' proposal and wrote him a cheque for $3,500. He informed me that he was scheduled to travel to Australia in two days, but would take my file with him and work on it during the trip. As soon as I got back to my office I wrote to Mr. Diels outlining our agreement with respect to the fee we had agreed upon and his taking over my case and arguing it in court.

On April 7th, Mr. Richardson phoned to advise me that the hospital's attorneys were going to ask the court to dismiss the case unless we submitted the affidavits within seven days. I phoned Mr. Diels and asked him if he had worked on them. He said that so far he had not found the time and suggested I meet with him the following day. The next day he introduced me to Mr. Song, his junior partner, and said that Mr. Song would work on the affidavits. Mr. Song would be my tenth attorney in Bermuda. He briefly read the affidavits and said we would have to meet on a few occasions over the next two weeks to correct them. He suggested we request a two-week extension. Mr. Song said I had to first work on the affidavits by myself and instructed me on the corrections I needed to make.

For the next four days, I stayed up until two a.m. correcting the affidavits. Over the succeeding seven days Mr. Song and I met for a few hours each day to put the final touches on them. Midway through he asked me to pay his fee for this work. He explained that the $7,000 fee that Mr. Diels and I had agreed upon would cover Mr. Diels' court appearance, but not Mr. Song's work on the affidavits. Mr. Song said that I owed him for more than thirty hours of work and would have to pay him for those hours even if I decided not to proceed with the case. I therefore paid and we continued to work on the affidavits, with Mr. Song constantly reminding me that I would have to pay his fee in full once we finished. He was billing me $325 an hour. On April 26th, we finished working on the affidavits. I paid Mrs. Diels' law firm $15,000 to cover Mr. Song's work. This was in addition to the $7,000 I would have to pay for Mr. Diels to argue the case in court.

On Tuesday, April 27th, Mr. Diels reviewed the affidavits and the final drafts were ready to be signed. On Wednesday Dr. Morais' affidavit was couriered to him. On Thursday he received it, signed it, had it notarized and sent it back. On Friday, we received Dr. Morais' affidavit and submitted the two documents to court just under the deadline.

Dr. Morais' hundred-page affidavit was divided into five sections. In the first section he indicated that he felt compelled to analyse the Sonby/D review because it included thirteen of the sixteen patients he and I had operated on together. He indicated that he personally consulted pre-operatively with all sixteen patients.

In the second section he pointed out the many errors in the review. In the case of one of the patients, Drs. Sonby and D wrote that the blood loss was 3500 cc. In his affidavit Dr. Morais wrote:

> "The reviewers suggest that the blood loss was 3500cc, the Operative record which was available to the Reviewers exhibited hereto and marked "GM4" indicates a blood loss of 1200cc. Even given the vast array of data the reviewers misused the information."

In another case the reviewers wrote that the patient had a complication caused by a "Failed pedicle screw salvaged with a hook." They suggested that Dr. Morais and I encountered problems during the operation and had to replace a screw with a hook. The fact is that the patient never had such a complication and the reviewers were simply unable to differentiate between a screw and a hook on the x-rays. They were like hardware store employees who are unable to differentiate between a screw and a bolt. Dr. Morais provided a photograph of the patient's x-rays:

"A copy of the patient's x ray taken one week after the surgery which is exhibited hereto and marked "GM9" and a copy of an x-ray taken twenty months after the surgery and exhibited hereto and marked "GM10" do show that the patient had six pedicle screws. There was not and there is no evidence of a "hook" as applied in this case as suggested by the reviewers. I have reviewed these x-rays with other surgeons in my service and they also did not find any evidence of a hook or complications as suggested by the Reviewers... This case further illustrates the "independent review" contains many errors. Even when the relevant information was available and seen by the reviewers the reviewers still entered and misquoted information. The reviewers purposefully misused the information that was in the hospital records to reach their conclusion."

This patient, a retired nurse, wrote to the Board (which was exhibited in court and is available on the Website: www.theonlywaytoeternallife.com as Letter 17) indicating that she never had any complications as suggested by the reviewers and was very pleased with her surgery.

Dr. Morais provided many other examples of the reviewers purposely misinterpreting the x-rays and ascribing complications where none existed.

In the third section he showed that in all the cases he had participated in the patient had had an MRI. The reviewers did not see the MRI report or the scan itself, yet speculated on the validity of our decision to operate.

In the fourth section Dr. Morais compared our treatment with the treatment of similar patients in the North American spine literature. His conclusion was that ninety-seven percent of spine surgeons in North America would have treated their patients similarly.

He concluded his affidavit as follows:

"Drs. Sonby, D. Voraks, and myself can display our curriculum vitae, exalt ourselves and used frightening medical terms like "excessive surgery" but if we do not listen to the treating physician Dr. Bah and to his patients we end up sounding like idiots. Our concerns and the concern of the Supreme Court should be the patient's welfare. It must be kept in mind the reported success rate of spinal surgeries varies between 30% to 90%... It must be mentioned that 90% of Dr. Bah's spinal patients have written letters to the Board in support of him..."

(Some of the letters that were submitted to the court are available on the Website: www.theonlywaytoeternallife.com, Letters 14 to 45).

Dr. Morais pointed out numerous errors and contradictions in the review, and in my own thirty-page affidavit I highlighted many more. In the case of the following patient, Dr. Sonby's review stated that surgery was not justified:

> "It is our opinion that these patients should never have been subjected to the extensive back surgery which they have undergone. Indeed, there was one patient in particular who stands out in my mind whose age, weight, hypertension, diabetes when taken with her "bearable back pain" noted on her chart by the resident, rendered her among the most poor surgical candidates."

In my affidavit I exhibited a copy of the resident physician's note referred to by Dr. Sonby. It was in a typed discharge summary found on the first page of the patient's chart:

"PRESENTING COMPLAINT: *Severe low back pain*

HISTORY OF PRESENTING COMPLAINT: Patient with *severe low back pain* radiating to the left buttock and also with numbness in the same area. She received therapeutic epidural on 6.1.97 with no apparent relief..."

The resident also stated that the patient was barely able to walk and was unable to sleep despite taking many medications. It was clear from the note that the patient was in "severe pain" rather than the "bearable pain" suggested by the reviewers.

CHAPTER FOURTY-SIX

Another Promise

After Mr. Song and I finished working on the affidavits, I needed to get away from Bermuda for at least a few days. Before leaving I set out to deal with another matter I had left unresolved. Since December 1998, Dr. Paytons, the chief of staff, had been calling many of my patients and instructing them to go to Dr. Cooperson's office and be seen by Dr. White, a neurosurgeon from Boston.

Five of my patients advised me that Dr. Paytons had called them. One of the five said she refused to see Dr. White. Two patients said they saw him, but left after they realized what the purpose of the visit was. They said that Dr. Fascioni was present and the purpose was to recruit patients who were unhappy with the surgery I had performed.

The third patient who kept the appointment was told by Drs. White and Fascioni that she was having residual back pain because of the rods I had inserted in her back. They offered to remove the rods. I advised the patient, whose bone graft had not yet healed because she smoked, against the surgery. I explained that the rods were acting as a stabilizer in her back until her bone graft healed completely and she would have more pain without the rods. Drs. White and Fascioni removed the rods and, as I had predicted, she was in worse pain after the surgery. Drs. Cooperson and Fascioni told the patient that it was my fault she was in more pain.

The fifth patient phoned by Dr. Paytons was on my waiting list to have a plate removed from her neck. Drs. White and Fascioni would remove the plate as I would have done. The patient would later try to sue me, which confirmed what the other patients had told me – that Dr. Paytons' purpose in calling them was to recruit patients who might take legal action against me. Thus I felt compelled to write Dr. Paytons and point out that his behaviour was unethical and violated the rules and regulations of the hospital, and that the patients concerned had been suffering from low-back pain for many years before I operated on them.

I also pointed out to Dr. Paytons that he and Drs. Cooperson and Fascioni had previously seen many if not all of the patients I operated on and had done nothing for them. As an example, I enclosed a copy of a letter to the Board written by a patient on my behalf (see Website: www.theonlywaytoeternallife.com Letter 18); it stated that Drs. Paytons, Cooperson and Jameson had seen her in consultation and Dr. Cooperson had told her she "should not be having pain because there was nothing there!" I asked Dr. Paytons why he was suddenly concerned about the welfare of my patients when he had declined to treat them or to follow up on them. I suggested he stop calling my patients. I also included letters from four of my patients indicating that they did not appreciate being called by Dr. Paytons.

Before mailing the letter I asked a friend, Mrs. Austin, a Christian, to correct it for me. Mrs. Austin, who was Dr. Browne's office manager, asked if she could show it to Dr. Browne. Three days later she returned the corrected letter to me and said that Dr. Browne had been furious when he learned that Dr. Paytons had been calling my patients. She told me that Dr. Browne had spoken to the health minister and I would have my privileges restored.

Dr. Browne and I met in his office later that afternoon. He confirmed what Mrs. Austin had told me. He said he had spoken to the health minister and this time it was "definite" my privileges would be restored. He asked if I was going to take legal action against Drs. Cooperson, Fascioni and Jameson. I replied that I would have to think about it. I explained that on March 12th, when he first told me I would have my privileges restored, it was my intention to take legal action against the doctors who had framed me, but that now, two months later, I had spent an additional $25,000 on legal fees in my fight against the hospital. I said I could have used that money to sue my adversaries had my privileges been restored back in March. Dr. Browne said that the following Friday he would bring up the issue of Dr. Paytons calling my patients in parliament.

I mailed my letter to Dr. Paytons and left the Island for a much-needed vacation. I asked Mrs. Remond, my friend, to keep the newspapers for me and to watch for any article about my fight with the hospital. When I returned a week later Mrs. Remond, who religiously read the local paper every day, told me nothing regarding my case had appeared.

On June 2nd, a month after our meeting, Dr. Browne asked if my privileges had been restored yet. I replied that they had not. He seemed as surprised as I. He gave me the phone number of a reporter from one of the local newspapers and suggested I call. I took the number, but did not call because my case was being heard and I felt that my talking to a reporter would not advance it. On June 16th, Dr. Browne again asked about my privileges. He also inquired as to whether I had spoken to the reporter and I replied that I had not. Then he said, "We should watch the case in court with interest."

One June 19th Dr. Burke, the Board member who had said he could help "by another venue," phoned to tell me he still had not heard from the health minister.

A few days later, Mr. Bascon, the health minister and a black Bermudian, phoned me because one of my patients had complained to him about her insurance company. I had prescribed an MRI of the head as the patient had been having severe headaches, but the insurance company would not allow her to travel abroad for an MRI. My patient, a young woman, was especially worried because two of her family members, both young, had recently died from ruptured aneurysms in the head; both had gone to the hospital with headaches and had been sent home without proper testing. The minister and I spoke at length about my patient and why she required an MRI. Our conversation was courteous but the minister did not make mention of my privileges and I did not bring up the subject.

CHAPTER FORTY-SEVEN

The Court Hearing

When we finished working on the documents, Mr. Song told me he had never worked so hard on producing an affidavit. He said our affidavits obliterated those of the other doctors on which the hospital's defence rested and predicted that our opponents would have a hard time responding to the facts we presented.

My first indication that Mr. Song was right was when a friend called to inform me that the law firm acting for the hospital had called a senior attorney out of retirement to "water down" the case so that at least the hospital would not have to compensate me for any loss of income.

My second indication was a letter I received from Dr. Cooperson. Dated June 9th, 1999, the letter said: "I have been advised to inform you that I have received a letter from Mr. S.L. and it may be that she is going to make a complaint against you." The letter suggested that my privileges at the hospital might be restored and Dr. Cooperson was building up complaints against me to discourage me from returning. It is interesting that, of all my patients, Mrs. S.L was the one who Dr. Cooperson and his group had found to complain about me. Mrs. S.L was a forty-four-year-old black Bermudian who had first undergone surgery locally in 1996. The surgeon mistakenly removed two discs from her back instead of the one abnormal herniated disc she presented. Mrs. S.L.'s back pain worsened after the surgery and her surgeon asked me to see her when he could not control her post-operative pain. For six months I conservatively treated Mrs. S.L. I finally operated after this treatment failed. She did so well after the second surgery that she attended almost every cricket match in Bermuda. She once invited me to her lodge to attend a three-day international tournament (I declined).

Mrs. S.L often travelled to the Caribbean to support the Bermuda cricket team. The last time she came to me, she had just returned from Trinidad. She told me she had danced for three nights during the carnival there. Mrs. S.L. was one of the patients who had written to the Board on my behalf (Website: www.theonlywaytoeternallife.com, Letter 15). She wrote: "In closing, I would like to add that I am very grateful to Dr. Bah for giving me my life back. In the last two years that I have been under his care I have found him to be very professional. He has always been there for me whenever I have called on him." In response to Dr. Cooperson's letter I could have produced a dozen letters from patients who had complained about him, but I chose not to.

The court hearing was scheduled for July 26th, 27th and 28th. Mr. Diels advised me that it was not necessary for me to attend. He said he would call me and keep me updated on the proceedings.

On Thursday, July 29th, I phoned Mr. Diels' office, as he had not called to inform about the hearing. His secretary told me he was in court and would call me as soon he returned. Later that afternoon I phoned again. The secretary informed me that the hearing had been postponed and that Mr. Diels was busy and would call me on Monday. I immediately went to his office in order to arrive before it closed for the day. I told the staff that I wanted to see Mr. Diels and sat in the waiting room. I met with him fifteen minutes later.

Mr. Diels apologized for not phoning earlier and said he had been very busy. At his request, he explained, the court hearing had been postponed from the first day. On the first morning of the hearing the other party had dumped on the court a binder of material that represented its new arguments. Mr. Diels showed me the binder and explained that what the other party had done was legal. He said he had asked the court to postpone the hearing until he reviewed the new material, as it would be unfair for him to argue my case without acquainting himself with it. Mr. Diels proposed that he review the material over the weekend and meet with me Monday to discuss our response to the new arguments.

On Monday, August 2nd, Mr. Diels and I met in his office once again and he summarized the hospital's three new arguments: that it had followed to the letter the rules and regulations of the Board in conducting the review of my practice; that the independent review on which they had based their decision to withdraw my privileges could not and should not be reviewed in court; and that my patients' letters should not be admitted as evidence. Mr. Diels said he sensed the hospital believed they had a weak case, which was why they did not want the court to hear the independent review, the basis for the withdrawal of my privileges and the backbone of their defence.

Mr. Diels smiled and said that before the next hearing he would have to prepare a new submission in response to the hospital's new allegations. I knew exactly why he was smiling and asked how much this would cost me. "$7,000," he replied. I objected to this figure and reminded Mr. Diels that I had already paid him $22,000 in legal expenses in the short time we had worked together. I also reminded him that the first time we met he told me that the $28,000 Mr. Richardson had billed me was excessive. He then suggested a figure of $6,000, and I accepted. As soon I got back to my office I composed a letter to Mr. Diels summarizing our monetary agreement and enclosing a cheque for $6,000, for he had said I would have to pay him before he started working on the new submission.

The following week Mr. Diels prepared a twelve-page response to the hospital's new arguments. He summarized the submission as follows:

"It is respectfully submitted that it is not necessary to delve deeply into the authorities concerning Judicial review to ascertain that the Board either itself or through the activities of its Committee or reviewers (independent or otherwise) have broken almost every single rule of natural justice known. Some examples:

1. Acting without jurisdiction – the Credentials Committee – wrong committee.

2. Refusing to allow Dr. Rah legal representation. Note had it been in front of the correct Committee Dr. Bah would have been entitled to representation.

3. Removing Dr, Bah from the proceedings while allowing Dr. Cooperson, the complainant, to remain.

4. Failing to identity the complainants.

5. Flagrant misrepresentations in the conduct of the Brookson report.

6. Failing to provide a list of reviewers as agreed.

7. Failing to provide any opportunity to prepare his case when faced at

7.00 p.m. the night before with a list of sixty-two patients for review. See pages 189–199 of Supperstone on Judicial Review. There cannot be, it is submitted, a shadow of a doubt that at the very least there is an arguable case that the Hospital has acted in breach of these rules. The time lines and unrelenting procession of poorly arranged hearings or reviews all suggest strongly that Dr. Bah was the subject of a witch hunt to have him removed and the Hospital was prepared to go to any lengths at the expense of Dr. Bah's rights to have this accomplished...

That is reviewable, the submission that Dr. Sonby/Voraks not under a power or duty, i.e. in that they could decline the appointment is incorrect. They in fact had a power of enquiry, which was in essence assigned to them from the Board. Any member of any Committee can say no to their appointment but once appointed their job is reviewable particularly as it involves Dr. Bah's future. See comments of Denning in Re Godden...

It has been submitted that there is no evidence of orchestration by Doctors Cooperson and Fascioni. That is an extraordinary submission.

Dr. Cooperson

(a) Actively filed a complaint:

(b) Made no secret" that he had done so.

(c) Got Dr. Brookson to do a Report on Dr. Bah.

(d) Objected when Dr. Bah was reinstated.

(e) Assisted with the second review with the Chief of Staff.

Dr. Fascioni

(a) Also made no secret of his attitude to Dr. Bah.

There can be no doubt the Hospital was trying to get rid of Dr. Bah. Why? Not his patients. See the letters (interestingly called irrelevant by Counsel) of his patients."

Mr. Diels suggested we concentrate our efforts in court on fighting for compensation for loss of income instead of for restoration of my privileges. He strongly advised me not to return to the hospital, as the environment there was not a healthy one in which to work, and to leave the Island once the case was over. I accepted his recommendation and agreed that he argue in court for the hospital to compensate me for loss of income.

The hearing was rescheduled for September 9th and 10th. Two days before it was to commence, Dr. Browne, the transport minister and my landlord, asked me about the particulars of the hearing because he wanted to attend. When I gave him the dates he said he would be unable to attend because he had office hours on the 9th and had to be in parliament on the 10th. Dr. Browne is the sort of man who always looks a person in the eye when he speaks. For the first time since I had known him, he seemed uneasy, looking down at the floor as he spoke. He asked if I knew that Mr. Diels was also working for the hospital. I replied that I did not. Then he informed me that the hospital had recently hired Mr. Diels to negotiate the leasing of an MRI. I knew the implications of what Dr. Browne had just told me. There was no need for either of us to comment further.

The ACB law firm, which represented the hospital, was one of the largest in Bermuda, with more than three dozen attorneys. There were more attorneys on the Island than members of any other trade except taxi drivers. For the hospital to suddenly hire my attorney meant only one thing: it would go to any length to win the case, just as Mr. Talbots, the former chairman of the Board, had warned. The fact that the hospital bought off my attorney at the last minute when they realized they were about to lose the case did not surprise me. It was typical of Bermuda. What did surprise me was that Mr. Dills, the gentleman who had told Dr. Klein he was disgusted over the old Board's handling of my case, was the chairman of the new Board that had hired Mr. Diels.

The same day that I spoke to Dr. Browne, Dr. MacLean, the Canadian who had conducted the review on my behalf, dropped by my office. It was Dr. MacLean who had recommended Mr. Diels to me. He was one of the few individuals in Bermuda who had advised me not to give up, because, he said, under the new government the court system might be independent of the political apparatus. Like Dr. Browne, Dr. MacLean had come to inquire about the particulars of the hearing, as he wished to attend. I told him what Dr. Browne had related to me about Mr. Diels being on the hospital's payroll. Dr. MacLean was stunned. He said, "Oh well! If that is the case I don't have to attend the hearing." Now that the hospital had bought off my attorney, I had a good idea what the outcome of my case would be, but I was curious about how an attorney representing the hospital would argue against an attorney bought by the hospital.

I asked Dr. MacLean how he thought Mr. Diels would behave in court.

He said that Mr. Diels would argue my case, as he should, like an actor in a play. Dr. MacLean and I reached the conclusion that we would not attend a masquerade, a kangaroo court.

My case against the King Edward VII Memorial Hospital was heard as scheduled on September 9th and 10th. On the afternoon of the 10th I phoned Mr. Diels. He said things had gone relatively well and the case was in "the hands of the gods." He said he expected to hear from the court within three weeks and would immediately advise me of the verdict.

A month later, I still had not heard from Mr. Diels so I telephoned him. He said he had not heard and we should not press the court. He said I would be the first to know once a decision had been reached.

CHAPTER FORTY-EIGHT

Licence to Harm

In May 1999, I wrote to Dr. Paytons asking him not to phone my patients. He replied that the Board had mandated him to call patients of mine who had had complications arising from their surgeries, "to help or diminish the suffering of the patients." He suggested that I had harmed my patients and reminded me that the golden rule of medicine was "primum non nocere" – first, do no harm.

During my years in Bermuda Drs. Cooperson and Fascioni accused me of harming my patients so often that there were times I wondered if I really was as unskilled as they claimed and had indeed harmed my patients. But then I would see patients of theirs and realize that I was no more unskilled than my accusers. Now, with Dr. Paytons also accusing me of harming my patients, I wondered anew. Around the time I received his letter, however, I became aware of the case of two young patients who had died in the hospital, which confirmed that I was no less skilled than the other orthopaedic surgeons at the King Edward VII Memorial Hospital.

A woman came to my office suffering from back pain. She said she had gone to the hospital complaining of low-back pain with sciatica and the orthopaedic surgeon who saw her suggested knee surgery. The woman told me she had no pain in her knees, but did have sciatica, then began to cry. She said she was crying because her nephew had died in the hospital a few days earlier. A healthy man in his thirties, he had died during surgery to remove a wire from his kneecap. The woman and other family members had met with Dr. Paytons, who told them nothing could have been done for the man and his death had been inevitable. The most painful aspect of the experience, she said, was that the family would never understand why he had died and would never see justice done.

Then I became aware of a second death of a young patient in the orthopaedic division. This time, Dr. Paytons and the hospital were able to suppress the news of the death only up to a point. The death occurred in June but did not become public until October, and then only because of the family's perseverance. On October 14th, a story about the death appeared in a local newspaper:

> "A nurse yesterday gave damning evidence against doctors during an inquest into the death of American visitor Mia Warren.
>
> Registered nurse at King Edward VII Memorial Hospital Anita Lewry told a four-man, four-woman jury doctors refused to treat or even examine Ms Warren while she was disoriented and held down by restraints.
>
> The 21-year-old waitress, who traveled to the Island for her aunt's wedding, was admitted to the hospital in the early hours of May 28, having complained of back pain.
>
> An autopsy revealed that Ms Warren's death, on June 4, was caused by staphylococcal meningitis, a condition brought on by bacterial infection of the outer portion of the brain...
>
> Yesterday in her statement and in answering questions from the Warren family's lawyer Michael Smith, Ms Lewry said: "When I consulted with the doctor he simply asked me it I had any bright ideas."
>
> Ms Lewry described how she decided to call St. Brendan's so that a psychiatrist could come and examine Ms Warren himself.
>
> "When Dr. (Gareth) Smith arrived in the patient's room he immediately said he could smell the illness in the room and 'this is not a psychiatric case'," she said. "When I tried to get Dr. Trott to do something he refused to see the patient. I wouldn't let him off the phone until he agreed to get someone to see her though."
>
> "All of us nurses were extremely concerned.
>
> "Dr. Smith could tell there was something seriously wrong medically and we couldn't get any doctors to come and see her."
>
> Specialist in internal medicine at the hospital, Wilbert Warner, also gave evidence yesterday...
>
> Dr. Warner admitted that C.A.T. scans revealing the abscess had not been performed until several days after Ms Warren had been admitted.
>
> And he also revealed that vital blood tests showing her high white blood cell

count were not performed until that point either…

Prompted by questions from Mr. Smith, Dr. Warner stated: "If tests had been done sooner, it is possible that the infection would have been revealed."

The specialist said meningitis is curable if discovered early enough.

In this case, however, detection came too late and the intravenous antibiotics Dr. Warner treated Ms Warren with were not enough to save her life…

The inquest continues today in Magistrates' Court…"1

Another article, titled "Doctor: Victim Did Not Display Infection Signs," appeared the next day:

"…Coroner William Francis ordered an adjournment after the surgeon in charge of Mia Warren's hospital case, Dr. S. Trott, decided he needed to consult with and be represented by an attorney…

The doctor returned for the afternoon session represented by lawyer David Kessaram.

The hearing, now in its fourth day, has been looking into the circumstances surrounding the death of the 21-year-old Ms Warren at King Edward VII Memorial Hospital in June 1997.

Ms Warren, who traveled to the Island from Memphis, Tennessee, for her aunt's wedding, visited the hospital on May 28 complaining of back pain…

She had been involved in a car accident two years earlier and, during subsequent surgery, had two metal supports, called Harrington Rods, and fitted into her back to support her spine.

Ms Warren's condition gradually deteriorated after being admitted and she died in the early hours of June 5.

An autopsy revealed that death was caused by staphylococcal meningitis, a bacterial infection of the outer portion of the brain, which had been caused by the rupture of an abscess that had formed around one of the rods.

Dr. Trott explained that his working diagnosis during Ms Warren's first few days at the hospital had been "mechanical back pain".

But prompted by questions from Mr. Smith, Dr. Trott admitted that such pain could have been caused by infection…

Dr. Trott continued with his account of events.

"I prescribed drugs for her treatment on my working diagnosis and she was hooked up to a P.C.A. (Patient Controlled Analgesic)," he said.

He described how Ms Warren's condition seemed to progressively improve until the afternoon of June 2, when she "became disoriented and began to engage in in-appropriate behaviour."

The four-man, four-woman jury heard how Dr. Trouts had mistakenly diagnosed this behaviour to be caused by a "drug induced psychosis."

Later examinations by St. Brendan's psychiatrist Dr. Gareth Smith and internal medicine specialist Dr. Wilbert Warner – who was consulted some four days after Ms Warren was admitted and then ordered CT scans and blood tests which revealed she was suffering from meningitis- revealed that the "inappropriate behaviour" was not caused by narcotics, but by the pain from the swelling of Ms Warren's brain due to bacterial infection...

The orthopaedic surgeon's version of events also came into conflict with Dr. Smith's testimony, in regards to the description of the Posey Jacket that was being used to restrain Ms Warren.

While Dr. Smith had explained on Tuesday that he had seen the patient "spread-eagled about" in a kind of "junior straitjacket," Dr. Trott described the Posey Jacket to be a "cotton vest that holds the patient face down on the bed, but leaves the arms free."[2]

The following day, the newspaper published a story titled "Policeman Is Praised at Inquest":

A Police officer was yesterday commended for doing a "sterling job" in heading up an investigation into the circumstances surrounding the death of an American visitor...

Coroner's officer Sgt. Phil Taylor called the Policeman to the stand yesterday as the last witness of the inquiry which has, since Monday, been detailing the last few days of Ms Warren's life to a four man jury.

The evidence P.c. Welch was about to give was discarded, however, after Mr. Francis ruled that it did not seem right "that a Policeman should be giving an opinion about the actions of doctors." "If this was an incident involving a road accident, it would be different," Mr. Francis said. "However, I think that P.c. Welch's testimony in this matter could only serve to unfairly influence the jury."...

Thursday's session, in which the orthopaedic surgeon in charge of Ms Warren's case [Dr. Trouts] gave testimony brought evidence to light that the Memphis, Tennessee resident had been admitted to hospital under the mistaken working diagnosis of "mechanical back pain."

It was not until her fourth day in hospital that her infection was discovered and, despite being administered intravenous antibiotics, she died on June 5…

Deciding that this case deserved "a special amount of time and attention," Mr. Francis adjourned it until Monday morning when he will read out a final summary of evidence to the jury and they will retire to decide the verdict.[3]

Six days later, in an article titled "Mia Warren: A Life That Ended Too Soon," the newspaper reported on the outcome of the inquest:

"According to her mother, Jody Lynn Hays, she expressed early her ambition to become a school teacher.

"Mia just loved kids," she recalled. "I was always trying to talk her out of being a teacher, telling her how they don't make very much. But you could see that's what she really wanted to do…

After surgery, and the insertion of the two back supports, Mia made massive improvements…

Mia began a job as a waitress at a Memphis restaurant and started to save up for the day when she would, hopefully, go to the University of Memphis and study to be a teacher…

But just when things were beginning to "go smoothly" again, the family made the fateful trip to Bermuda for an uncle's wedding…

"We had no idea that it was life threatening. When we got the news that they were drilling holes in her back it was bad enough. When we heard she had died it was a horrible shock."…

Mia's impact on those around her was clear after her death.

"The entire community was devastated," Mrs. Hays, said. "At her funeral there were at least 600 people. When I talked to them, they all seemed to think of Mia as their best friend. That's the kind of girl she was."

On Monday a five-day inquest ended into the 21-year-old's death during which a Coroner's jury heard evidence from doctors, nurses, family members and friends. Coroner William Francis ruled that it was not for the jury to decide if anyone bore responsibility for the death. The jury recorded the simple facts of where Ms Warren died, on what date and of what cause. An autopsy had revealed Ms Warren was the victim of staphylococcal meningitis, or a bacterial infection to the outer portion of the brain. The family is now seeking legal action against the hospital and a doctor." [4]

What really happened to this young woman? As reported in the newspaper, she had travelled to Bermuda to attend the wedding of an aunt and began to have back pain after arriving. She went to the emergency room of the hospital where the physician on duty gave her some pain medication and discharged her. She went to the emergency room again because of severe back pain. A second physician saw her, gave her some pain medication and sent her home with a prescription. She went to the pharmacy to have her prescription filled, but was too ill to wait for the medication. She returned to the emergency room and was seen by a third physician, Dr. Mackintosh, a Jamaican. Dr. Mackintosh ordered back x-rays and phoned me at home.

Before I was able to explain to Dr. Mackintosh that I was not on duty, he related to me the details of the case. He said the young woman was in severe pain that was localized in the upper back. The x-rays showed a loosening of a rod and hook at the upper end of the back, which was consistent with the pain she was experiencing. I said that loosening was not uncommon with the type of rods that had been inserted in this patient's back. Then I told Dr. Mackintosh that I was not on duty. He explained that Dr. Trouts, my associate, was on duty and that was why he had called me. Dr. Mackintosh and some other emergency room physicians often phoned me when patients presented with back pain or complex orthopaedic trauma while Dr. Trouts was on duty. In the past I had gladly gone to the emergency room to attend these patients, but since Dr. Trouts refused to pay me I decided I would not cover for him any more; I would let him manage his own cases and would consult on his patients only if he requested me to do so. I told Dr. Mackintosh he would have to phone Dr. Trouts.

Dr. Trouts saw the patient, gave her a prescription for back pain and sent her home. He was the third physician to release her from the hospital. According to Dr. Mackintosh, he confronted Dr. Trouts and urged him to keep the patient in hospital for at least a few hours. Dr. Trouts yielded to the pressure. He admitted the young woman and put her on intravenous morphine to manage her pain. A few hours later she became very confused and agitated. As reported in the newspaper, the treating physician assumed she was confused because of the morphine he had prescribed and ordered her to be tied to her bed. With her condition worsening and the treating physician refusing to see her, the nurse in charge took it upon herself to call in a psychiatrist. Upon entering the patient's room, the psychiatrist could see that her illness was serious and that she did not have drug-induced disorientation as had been assumed by the treating physician. The psychiatrist consulted an internist, who ordered blood tests and a CT scan and performed a spinal tap. The results showed that the patient had an infection in her upper back in the exact area where Dr. Mackintosh suspected the problem lay. The patient was given intravenous antibiotics and plans were made to transport her to the United States by air ambulance, but she expired before the transfer could be carried out.

The last I had heard of this case was when Dr. Mackintosh had phoned me about it. A week later, I noticed that Dr. Trouts was in a sombre mood. A few days after that a resident physician presented the case at the surgical meeting. The presentation was brief, evasive and less than two minutes in duration. The resident said that the patient had been admitted for back pain and had died because of an infection in her back. Then Dr. Joneson, the chief of surgery, said she had taken the patient's chart home over the weekend in order to review it and had found nothing unusual about the treatment administered. She said nothing should have been done differently from how Dr. Trouts and the other physicians had treated the patient. That was the conclusion on the death of this young woman. Everyone remained silent. None of the other physicians present commented on the case and the resident proceeded to talk about other patients who had died and in whose case nothing could have been done differently. At the Canadian hospitals where I trained and worked, all physicians were required to occasionally present their complications, for all physicians do have complications. At the hospital where I worked in Montreal, the case of the deceased young woman would have been presented differently. In the process of preparing to present a case at complications rounds, the treating physician or the resident would have discovered if any mistake had been made during the patient's treatment. In the process of preparing for the meeting, the physician would have learned what he might do in the future to avoid or minimize the risk of a similar complication. At the meeting, the presenting physician would honestly convey his findings to his colleagues for the purpose of sharing knowledge, educating each other and serving the interests of the patients. At the end of the presentation, the audience would question the treating physician or comment on the treatment administered, in the interests of other patients rather than for the purpose of chastising the treating physician.

If the case of the young woman had been presented in this way, we would have learned that Dr. Mackintosh had made a partial diagnosis of rod loosening. We would have learned that whenever a diagnosis of rod loosening is entertained the diagnosis of infection must be considered as well, because more often than not the two are associated. We would have learned that, accordingly, a blood test should have been ordered upon admission. We would have learned that once a back infection is discovered the only way to save the patient's life is to operate and clean up the infection, and not to transport the patient abroad. We would have learned many other lessons, which ultimately would have served the interests of all future patients at the hospital.

Instead, the case of the deceased young woman and all the other complications that occurred in the department of surgery at the King Edward VII Memorial Hospital were presented with the purpose of sweeping them under the rug and moving on. In this case, the hospital authorities tried to find a scapegoat in the person of Dr. Mackintosh, a black man and a foreigner. Dr. Jameson, the chief of staff, attacked Dr. Mackintosh for not ordering a blood test when he saw the young woman in the emergency room. Dr. Mackintosh – one of the most competent emergency physicians I have had occasion to work with – pointed out that two other emergency physicians (both of whom were white) had sent her home before he pressured Dr. Trouts, a white Bermudian, to admit her. He also pointed out that Dr. Trouts, a specialist, did not order a blood test even after the patient, who was under his care, was in hospital for five days. Only when they realized that Dr. Mackintosh would not be a willing scapegoat did Dr. Jameson and the authorities try to sweep the case under the rug. Had it not been for her family's perseverance, the young woman's case would never have been the subject of an inquest.

After the inquest the family sought to take legal action against the hospital and the treating physician, but could find no attorney in Bermuda willing to take on the case. One attorney was willing to do so, but only if they paid him $40,000 in advance. The family refused because they believed they would be investing in a losing proposition.

The cases of this young woman and the man in his thirties made me realize that it was unacceptable for my patients to have residual pain after surgery, but acceptable for the patients of other surgeons to die. These two cases also made me realize that Mr. Talbots, former chairman of the Board, had been right when he said, "the hospital never loses in court." The hospital may never lose in court, but it loses patients all the time.

---

[1] Ben Greening, "Inquest into US woman's death hears damning evidence' against hospital" *The Royal Gazette,* October 14th, 1999, p. 2.

[2] Ben Greening, *The Royal Gazette,* October 15th, 1999, p. 2.

[3] Ibid., October 16th, 1999, p.2.

[4] Ibid., October 22nd, 1999, p. 6–7.

CHAPTER FORTY-NINE

To London!

At the beginning of October 1999, while my case against the hospital was in legal limbo, I decided to deal with the matter of the money owed to me by my former associate, Dr. Trouts. I called the office of Mr. Dunkin, the attorney who was handling that case, and asked in vain for an appointment. Then I faxed him a letter explaining that I had been unable to secure an appointment by phone. Finally, on October 22nd, I met with him in his office. I showed Mr. Dunkin the figures indicating how much Dr. Trouts owed me. He said the figures would have to be reviewed and approved by an accountant before he wrote to Dr. Trouts requesting payment. Mr. Dunkin asked who my accountant was. I replied that it was Mrs. Lewis and asked if I should have her verify the figures or if he had another accountant in mind. Instead of saying that Mrs. Lewis was his accountant – something that I would learn later – Mr. Dunkin told me that I should continue working with her because she was white and would have more leverage in a Bermudian court. He said I would have to follow his advice if I wanted to win the case. I knew exactly what he meant and told him I would contact Mrs. Lewis at once.

After leaving Mr. Dunkin's office, I phoned Mrs. Lewis. She said she was scheduled to fly to New York later that day, but could see me the following Friday. In order to calculate how much Dr. Trouts owed me, Mrs. Lewis said, she would need to examine the ledgers for the years 1996 and 1997, when I worked with him. I had the ledger for 1997 in my possession and Mr. Dunkin's office had the ledger for 1996. The first time I had consulted with Mr. Dunkin's associate he suggested it would be safer to leave the ledger in his office, which I did. Therefore, at the end of my meeting with

Mr. Dunkin I asked his secretary to find the ledger for 1996. The secretary advised me to return to the office on Monday to pick it up.

On Monday, October 27th, I called the secretary and asked if she had found the ledger. She said the staff had been looking for it since Friday and suggested I call back at the end of the day. At the end of the day I called, but was told that she had left the office. Three days later the staff still had not found my ledger. The secretary told me they had just moved their office to the current location and most of the documents were still in boxes. On Thursday morning, I went to the office and told them I was not going to leave until they found the ledger. After four hours sitting in the waiting room I gave up and returned to my office, as I had work to do.

Before I left, the staff assured me they would find the ledger in time for my meeting with the accountant the next day. Towards the end of the day I called, but they had not found it. Finally, on Friday, the day of my meeting with the accountant, Mr. Dunkin's secretary called me to tell me they had found the ledger; all the while it had been sitting on a shelf near the front desk. I immediately drove in to town to pick it up.

On Friday evening, I met with Mrs. Lewis and handed her the two ledgers. She reviewed them and determined that Dr. Trouts still owed me $424,000 US for the years 1996 and 1997. She presented the figures, along with her calculations, to Mr. Dunkin.

At our last meeting Mr. Dunkin had advised me to obtain letters from Dr. Trouts' former staff confirming that he had altered figures in the ledger to his advantage and my detriment. Mrs. Douglas, a Christian woman, was the first person I approached for this purpose. Mrs. Douglas had worked for Dr. Trouts for one year before resigning. She had recently moved back to Canada. On November 10th, 1999, she wrote the following:

"I, D. Douglas, worked for Orthopaedics & Sports Medicine of Bermuda. Ltd from October 1996 to December 1997.

On March 6th, 1997, I witnessed Dr. S. Trouts and Mrs. S. Trouts ask the bookkeeper M. Robbins to change the accurate numbers of the accounting ledger of Dr. C. Bah to reflect inadequate accounts receivable figures to a lesser amount.

If you have any questions or need further assistance, please do not hesitate to contact me at the above number."

On December 10th, I met with Mr. Dunkin. He perused the above letter and another from Mrs. Lewis, then drafted a letter to Dr. Trouts, which read in part:

> "Our client has secured the services of a local accountant who has reviewed the accounts from your business covering the period he worked. Based upon those figures, we are instructed that you owe our client a total sum of $424,77.10.
>
> Based on the unimpeachable accounting material our client was supplied with by your former bookkeeper and secretary's admission to our client that you and your wife altered the figures in your accounts to the detriment of our client, our client now seeks the sum of $424,777.10 in full and final settlement of this claim within fourteen (14) days of the date of this letter, failing which our client will have no option, but to issue Court proceedings to recover the same."

Mr. Dunkin asked me if Mr. Robbins, Dr. Trouts' former bookkeeper, would be willing to act as a witness on my behalf. I replied that I was not sure and that in any event Mr. Robbins had moved back to the United Kingdom three months earlier. Mr. Dunkin strongly advised me to obtain a letter from him. This meant that I had to first locate Mr. Robbins and then possibly travel to the United Kingdom to meet with him. At first I was hesitant, but it did not take me long to see that my travel expenses would be in the order of $4,000, considerably less than one day's court appearance for Mr. Dunkin, so I told him I would try to track down Mr. Robbins. Mr. Dunkin asked how I was going to proceed. I said I would first try the Internet and then hire a private detective. He suggested I hire a private detective off the Island, for a detective in Bermuda might belong to the same private clubs as Dr. Trouts and tell him we were looking for his former bookkeeper.

In December 1999, I started searching the Internet for the London address of Mr. Robbins, because I knew that before moving to Bermuda he had lived in London. My search generated a list of a thousand Robbins living in London. I called a few of the phone numbers on the list, but without success. Then I remembered that a year earlier Mr. Robbins had told he was looking to sell his apartment in London. I realized that M. Robbins could be anywhere in the United Kingdom so I broadened my search, and came up with more Robbins than I could phone in a year. I contacted a private detective in the United Kingdom, but was told I would need more personal information on Mr. Robbins and his wife. Then I remembered the day Mr. Robbins had celebrated his birthday when we worked together three years earlier, so I tried to find out his wife's birthday as well, and her middle name. I gave this information to a friend in Bermuda who came up with the Robbins' forwarding address in Coventry. I phoned the private detective again and gave him the additional information. The detective said he would try to locate the Robbins, but since they had just moved to the United Kingdom they had not yet generated much information. I would have to give him my credit card number and authorize him to withdraw the sum of £595, or $1,000, in the event he located them. Four days after I instructed the detective to locate the Robbins he sent me a fax notifying me that he had done so; he gave me an address and phone number in Coventry.

I could have phoned Mr. Robbins with my request, but I believed that the chances of his agreeing to it were greater if I were to meet him in person. I therefore purchased an airline ticket and made plans to travel to the United Kingdom in February 2000. I tried to book a room in Coventry through the Web and by phone, but all the hotels in and around the city were booked. After two hours on the phone I was ready to give up, but decided to call one last hotel. The clerk there told me he had a room. I immediately made a reservation and asked for a confirmation number.

My wife had told me she did not want to hear any more about my fights in Bermuda once the year 2000 arrived (not that I spoke to her about my fights or professional matters). However, I convinced her that she needed a vacation and asked her to accompany me to the United Kingdom. She accepted my invitation and on Sunday, February 6th, 2000, we flew to London. Our plane landed at Heathrow on Monday morning and we took a bus to downtown Coventry, two hours northwest of London. We arrived at our hotel towards mid-afternoon, unloaded our luggage from the taxi that had taken us to the hotel from downtown, and went to the front desk. I introduced myself to the clerk and said I had a reservation. The clerk looked for my name on the computer, but could not find it. She told me they were fully booked and there was not a single room available there or at any other hotel in town because a festival was taking place. I gave her my confirmation number and the name of the person who had taken my reservation. She said the name I gave her was that of the night porter, who was new at the job and was not allowed to make reservations.

I told the clerk a mistake had been made. I had a reservation number and they had to provide me with a room. She said she would confer with her manager and went into the back room. While my wife and I were waiting for her to come back, other people, who had been driving around Coventry in search of accommodations, arrived at the desk looking for room. A few minutes later the clerk appeared and said they would find a room for us towards the end of the afternoon. She advised us to leave our luggage with her and go to the restaurant for a late lunch. I thanked her and asked that the night porter who had made the mistake and given me the reservation not be reprimanded or fired.

At five o'clock my wife and I went back to the hotel and were given a room as promised. We went to our room, took a shower and rested. At seven o'clock I decided to go looking for Mr. Robbins because I had only three working days to find him and have him prepare a letter and have it notarized. We were scheduled to fly to Montreal the following Monday. We asked the desk clerk to order us a cab. When the cab arrived I gave the driver the address that the detective had provided for Mr. Robbins. The driver looked at the paper and said he did not know the street. He called his dispatcher and read out the address. After what seemed an eternity, the dispatcher said the street did not exist. My wife looked at me and asked if the detective agency had misled me by giving me a wrong address and we had travelled all that distance for nothing. I told my wife and the driver that the address had to exist. Before leaving for the United Kingdom, I said, I had verified it on the Web and had purposely picked a hotel not too far from it. Finally the driver decided to look in his book. A few minutes later he told us he had found the street.

The drive from the hotel to the Robbins' address took less than ten minutes. The streets around the apartment complex were not lit, but we were able to locate the Robbins' dwelling on the first floor. The driver said the area was unsafe at night and suggested that my wife wait in the car while I checked to see if the Robbins were home. When I reached their unit I could not see any light in the window nobody seemed to be home. I decided to knock on the door anyway. After a while the light came on and a woman looked out the window. I immediately recognized Mrs. Robbins and told her it was I. She was surprised to see me and opened the door. We greeted each other before I went to get my wife. The Robbins had a two-year-old baby girl and Mrs. Robbins was pregnant and due to deliver in ten days. We talked for an hour and she never once asked why we were in the United Kingdom. She told us her husband was working part-time for the telephone company through an agency; he still had not found a permanent job. She expected him home at ten o'clock and suggested we wait for him. We declined to stay because she was pregnant and said she needed rest. Before my wife and I left, Mrs. Robbins reached her husband on the phone at work and I was able to speak with him. He said he was free the next morning and he and his wife would come to our hotel to have breakfast with us. Mrs. Robbins called us a cab and we returned to our hotel.

At ten o'clock the next morning, Tuesday, the Robbins came to our hotel and we went together to a nearby restaurant for breakfast. After we talked for a while, Mr. Robbins, who was in his mid-thirties, said he was happy to see us, but did not think we had come so far just to visit him. I told Mr. Robbins I needed him to testify that in 1997 Dr. Trouts and Mrs. Trouts had ordered him to alter the figures in the ledgers. I said that Mrs. Douglas, Dr. Trouts' other former employee, had agreed to testify on my behalf. I explained that there was a legal way of circumventing his having to travel to Bermuda to appear in court. In any event, I said, the case might not have to go to court if he agreed to serve as a witness, as Dr. Trouts would think twice before having two people testify that he had ordered an employee to alter the figures in a ledger. When I finished speaking Mr. Robbins blushed and began to perspire. He said he always knew that the issue of the tampered ledger would come back to haunt him. He said he had taken notes and made a copy of the ledger in the event he would one day have to testify in court, but did not remember where he had placed them. I said I had made copies of the alterations and had brought it with me for him to review. All I needed from him, I explained, was a brief letter stating that Dr. Trouts and Mrs. Trouts had ordered him to alter the figures in the ledger, to my detriment, and have the letter notarized. I showed him the letter that Mrs. Douglas had written and said I needed a similar one from him. Mr. Robbins agreed to write the letter. He said he would have a friend in London who was an attorney prepare the letter and he could travel with us to London on our way back to the airport in order to sign it. Meanwhile, the Robbins scheduled to have dinner with us on Wednesday and Mr. Robbins offered to take us to Stratford on Thursday.

The next day the desk clerk gave me a note to call Mr. Robbins. When I reached him later that afternoon he said he had discussed the matter with his wife and had changed his mind about writing the letter. His current situation, he said, was not favourable to his getting involved in a legal case. He explained that he did not have a full-time job, his financial situation was precarious and his wife was due to deliver within days. I tried in vain to convince him to write the letter. I said he had altered the figures knowing that it was wrong and now he had an opportunity to undo the wrong. Mr. Robbins said it did not bother him to have altered the figures. I asked if he had no remorse about doing so. He replied that he had no conscience and slept well. Mr. Robbins and I parted on that note.

My wife told me I should not give up after having travelled so far. She said I might have a better chance of convincing Mr. Robbins if I met him in person. So I phoned and asked him to meet me. He agreed to meet me the next day.

On Thursday morning, Mr. Robbins came to our hotel room. He returned all the papers I had given him. I tried again to convince him to write the letter. I told him he did not have to fear Dr. Trouts because at that point Dr. Trouts could do nothing against him (Dr. Trouts had often threatened to fire Mr. Robbins, have his work permit revoked and have him deported). Mr. Robbins said he had left Bermuda because of Dr. Trouts and he and Dr. Trouts were not the best of friends anyway. He told me again that his financial and family situation precluded his becoming involved in a legal battle. He said he had discussed the whole matter with his wife before coming to the hotel and they agreed he would not get involved. He said he might help me in the future once his job situation was stable. I tried to tell him the Bible teaches that God might help us in another way if we help others (Galatians 6:7). He interrupted me the moment I said "God," saying he knew I believed in God, but he did not believe in that sort of thing. I thanked Mr. Robbins for coming and escorted him to the door. After he left my wife said I had not tried hard enough to change his mind. I told her I preferred not to deal with anyone who has openly told me he does not have a conscience and does not believe in God.

I then called Mr. Dunkin and told him Mr. Robbins would not be testifying and we would have to go to court without him on our side. The only good news, I said, was that Mr. Robbins had told me he would not take Dr. Trouts' side either. Mr. Dunkin suggested we hire an attorney friend of his in London and subpoena Mr. Robbins to give a deposition. I told him I did not think it was a good idea to subpoena a person who did not wish to get involved in a case. I said that if we were to subpoena Mr. Robbins he might lie and say he did not alter the figures or could not remember because it was so long ago. The whole idea of having Mr. Robbins testify on my behalf, I explained, was to force Dr. Trouts to settle out of court, and in any event the figures that Mr. Robbins had altered represented only a fraction of what Dr. Trouts owed me. Mr. Dunkin agreed with me and said he would correct the draft letter that he had written to Dr. Trouts and send it off before I returned to Bermuda.

My wife and I decided to make the best of our time in the United Kingdom. We visited the countryside and London before heading home.

CHAPTER FIFTY

The Network

A few days after I left the United Kingdom I was back working in Bermuda. On Saturday, February 19th, I was in the office catching up when an acquaintance phoned to ask if I could see her. The woman, who was in her thirties, said she was in a lot of pain. I agreed to see her immediately, but she said she would prefer to come on Sunday because she was a Seventh Day Adventist. I set up an appointment for the next afternoon after my church service.

On Sunday afternoon Mrs. L.W., a white woman from the United Kingdom, came as scheduled. Her right arm was immobilized in a sling and she seemed to be in pain. She proceeded to tell me her story. She had fallen in her kitchen on January 14th and experienced severe pain in her right shoulder. She went to the emergency room the same day and was seen by Dr. Mackintosh, the physician on duty. Dr. Mackintosh examined her and ordered x-rays of her shoulder, which showed a dislocation. He gave her some medication and performed a reduction on her shoulder. She felt better until February 3rd, when she slipped on the stairs and experienced the same severe pain. She went to the emergency room and saw Dr. Schmaltz, the chief emergency physician, who happened to be on duty. Dr. Schmaltz ordered x-rays and a CT scan of her shoulder, which he then reviewed and told her she had not have a dislocation. He sent her home with a referral to the orthopaedic clinic.

Mrs. L.W. said she saw Dr. Cooperson four days later in the orthopaedic clinic. He told her that her shoulder was fine and prescribed physiotherapy. When she told Dr. Cooperson she was in a lot of pain, he advised her to start the physiotherapy immediately. Mrs. L.W. said she started the physiotherapy three days later, but the sessions were excruciatingly painful and the physiotherapist was unable to move her shoulder, which seemed to be "stocked." After a few sessions the physiotherapist stopped the treatment and referred Mrs. L.W. to her family physician, who saw her and said everything must be all right if Dr. Cooperson had said so. Mrs. L.W. said she had not had a full night's sleep since her second fall because she was unable to lie down and sat on the sofa all night long. A white-collar worker, she had managed to work by writing with her left hand, but was exhausted and drowsy because of the lack of sleep and because of the codeine she was taking on a regular basis to relieve the pain.

When Mrs. L.W. finished telling me her story, her husband and I removed the sling and her blouse. First, I noticed that the ball of her shoulder was out of the joint and her right shoulder was protruding further to the front than her left. The morphology of the shoulder was so unusual that I decided to review Mrs. L.W's x-rays instead of moving her shoulder and hurting her. Even a quick glance at the x-rays revealed that the shoulder was dislocated. I looked at them from different angles and reached the same conclusion each time. Next, I tried to examine the shoulder and found that the head of the shoulder was complete out the joint and that her shoulder was immobile, locked in one position. I informed the couple that the shoulder was dislocated and needed to be treated under general anaesthesia because it had been dislocated for more than two weeks. I suggested Mrs. L.W. go to the emergency room.

I phoned the emergency room, hoping that Dr. Mackintosh, the physician who had seen Mrs. L.W. in January, would be on duty. The secretary told me that a female physician from Canada with whom I had a good working relationship was on duty. I told this doctor about Mrs. L.W's shoulder and advised her that the dislocation needed to be treated surgically. She agreed to see Mrs. L.W. and asked me to send her to the emergency room at once.

By the time Mrs. L.W. got to the emergency room, after being screened and completing the paper work, the physician I had spoken to had finished her shift and left. The doctor presently on duty happened to be Dr. Schmaltz, the physician who had seen Mrs. L.W. after her second fall and told her the shoulder was fine. Dr. Schmaltz saw Mrs. L.W. again.

He examined her shoulder, reviewed her x-rays and told her the shoulder was not dislocated. When Mrs. L.W. insisted that she was in severe pain and her shoulder did not feel right, Dr. Schmaltz called Dr. Fascioni, the orthopaedic surgeon on duty. Mrs. L.W. said Dr. Fascioni examined her shoulder, reviewed her x-rays and told her the shoulder was "fine" and there was "nothing to be done." He had seen hundreds of people with a similar condition, he said, and her shoulder would get better with time. Mrs. L.W and her husband were very upset and told Dr. Fascioni that Dr. Bah had told them the shoulder was dislocated. Dr. Fascioni said, "Forget Dr. Bah, he's no good," but then compromised and said the shoulder was subluxed (partially out of the joint) though not dislocated (completely out of the joint). Even then, however, he tried to reassure Mrs. L.W. that it would heal with time and did not require treatment.

Mrs. L.W. and her husband left the emergency room and went home, with Mrs. L.W still in pain.

Later in the afternoon Mrs. L.W's husband phoned to inform me of his wife's encounter with Drs. Schmaltz and Fascioni. I asked him if he had kept his wife's x-rays. When he said no, I suggested he go back to the emergency room and get them because x- rays tended to mysteriously disappear at that hospital. Mr. L.W. told me he and his wife were tired and he would pick them up early Monday morning.

On Monday Mr. L.W. went back to the hospital to get the x-rays. He went to the emergency room and was told that they had been sent to the radiology department. He went to the radiology department and was told they had been sent to Dr. Fascioni's office. He rushed to the office of Drs. Fascioni and Cooperson and was told they must be in the emergency room. Mr. L.W. spent more than half a day running between the emergency room, the radiology department and Dr. Fascioni's office looking for the   x-rays. But he would not give up; he was determined to find them. Finally, in the afternoon, Dr. Fascioni told Mr. L.W. that he had the x-rays and would release them only after Mrs. L.W. came to see him in his office.

The next day Mrs. L.W. and her husband went to see Dr. Fascioni in his office. He examined Mrs. L.W. again and told her, "The shoulder is slightly out of the joint; there is nothing that needs to be done and it will get better within six weeks." Mrs. L.W. said she reminded Dr. Fascioni that her shoulder was already dislocated for more than three weeks and was not getting any better. Dr. Fascioni released the x-rays to Mrs. L.W. only after she paid his consultation fee for seeing her in his office.

That afternoon Mrs. L.W. and her husband came to my office with the x-rays. Mrs. L.W. asked me the same question over and over – whether her shoulder was dislocated. I answered yes each time. She asked me why the other doctors were telling her otherwise. To reassure Mrs. L.W that her shoulder was dislocated and that the excruciating pain she was suffering was not the product of her imagination, I proposed taking x-rays of her shoulder from different angles. Dr. Browne's x-ray technician took these and before sending Mrs. L.W. back to my office he told her she had a dislocation of the shoulder. Even after the new x-rays showed a dislocation, Mrs. L.W. was still wondering why three doctors at the hospital were telling her that her shoulder was fine and I was telling her otherwise. I therefore suggested we get a second opinion. I asked Dr. Browne, who was seeing a patient in an adjacent examining room, to review her x-rays. I briefly related Mrs. L.W.'s story to Dr. Browne without mentioning the name of the doctors who had seen her. Dr. Browne glanced at the x-rays, in the presence of Mrs. L.W. and her husband, and walked away without saying anything. Mrs. L.W. asked me what Dr. Browne thought of her x-rays. I said, "If I am not mistaken, Dr. Browne agrees with me that your shoulder is dislocated." She then asked me why he had not said anything. "After all," she said, "he is a doctor at the hospital and a minister in the government." I said that in May 1999, Dr. Browne had written to Dr. Paytons, the chief of staff, citing the "horrendous problems" at the hospital and suggesting solutions. Instead of dealing with the allegations, I explained, Dr. Paytons accused Dr. Browne of leaking the hospital's problems to the media.

When Mrs. L.W. and her husband left my office, Dr. Browne came and asked me which orthopaedic surgeon she had seen. I replied that she had seen both Drs. Cooperson and Fascioni. He said that this was not an isolated case. He asked me what I was going to do about Mrs. L.W. I said I would try to refer her abroad. He said, "Please do that."

Mrs. L.W. told me she met Dr. Browne in town the next day. She cornered him and asked what he thought about her shoulder. He responded that her shoulder was dislocated and advised her to leave the Island and get treatment.

Mrs. L.W. and I then tried to convince her insurance company that she needed to go abroad to have open surgery on her shoulder because after more than three weeks of dislocation it would be impossible to put the shoulder back in place by means of manipulation only. I wrote to the company describing the case in detail and the type of surgery required. Mrs. L.W. delivered my letter to the company. The company told her she did not have to go abroad, that Drs. Cooperson and Fascioni could treat her adequately.

Mrs. L.W. asked her insurance agent how the doctors on the Island could treat her if they did not agree that her shoulder was dislocated and suggested it would heal with time. (I had made the proper diagnosis and would have treated her had I not lost my privileges because the two doctors who failed to diagnose the dislocation complained that I was incompetent.) She said that the more she spoke with people about her case the more she heard of patients who were told by the doctors that their condition would improve, but then got worse. She gave as an example Dr. Browne's office cleaning lady who Dr. Fascioni had treated for three years for an apparent tendinitis of the shoulder only to have another doctor recently discover, after doing a simple x-ray of the shoulder, that she had a malignant tumour. The woman was currently abroad having the tumour treated. Mrs. L.W. also cited the case of a young boy who had been told by the local doctors that his shoulder dislocation would get better; after one year, the shoulder dislocation did not get better, but got worse and the boy's parents had to take out a second mortgage on their house in order to raise the $100,000 it cost to have the shoulder treated in the United States. In the short time she had been sick, Mrs. L.W. had discovered that most of the wealthy people on the Island travelled abroad for medical treatment. She asked the insurance agent why Dr. Cooperson's own brother-in-law had recently gone to the United States to have an arthroscopy of the knee, the simplest orthopaedic procedure, if the local doctors were so competent. Even after hearing the above arguments, the insurance agent told Mrs. L.W. that the company would not pay for her to go abroad to have her surgery, because she would be "out of the network" and the local doctors could perform the surgery. Mrs. L.W. phoned, wrote letters, sent e-mails, went to the insurance company on several occasions and spoke to the vice-president of the insurance company. After two weeks, the company finally agreed to pay eighty percent of her total medical bill.

More than six weeks after presenting in the emergency room, Mrs. L.W. went to Canada to have open reduction of her shoulder. The surgeon found that she had severe damage to the cartilage in her shoulder and might require more surgery in future because of arthritis. The surgeon also predicted that in the short term Mrs. L.W. could have other complications because the shoulder had been dislocated for so long. Mrs. L.W's surgery was uneventful and she had little post-operative pain. Five days after the procedure she was back in Bermuda and working.

While Mrs. L.W. was abroad, her father-in-law died at the King Edward VII Memorial Hospital. He had been admitted a few days earlier for a minor stroke. A nurse had taken him to the toilet and apparently forgot about him. A few hours later the man's wife found him dead in the bathroom. He had fallen and hit his head on the floor.

When it came time to pay Mrs. L.W's medical and travel expenses, totalling $18,000, the Imperial Insurance Company paid only sixty percent instead of the eighty percent it had agreed to. Mrs. L.W. and her husband felt that it was not fair they should have to pay the remainder. They also felt they should be compensated for the loss of income they incurred and for Mrs. L.W's suffering. Mr. L.W., a black Bermudian businessman, had taken a lot a time off work to look after his wife and their children. The couple believed that the local doctors had lied to them and therefore should compensate them. Mrs. L.W. sought the advice of an attorney. The attorney advised her to write to the doctors requesting compensation. She wrote the following letter to Drs. Cooperson and Fascioni:

> "...On February 3rd, I fell again and was in so much pain that I went back to the hospital... I saw Dr. Cooperson the following week and when he saw the x-rays he also said it was not dislocated. When I said that I was in a terrible amount of pain with it and could not sleep or work, he proceeded to give me a week of sick leave...
>
> After several attempts to get help because I could not sleep, work or move my arm at all, I went back to the hospital, once again, to beg them to put it back in place... Dr. Schulte was on duty and told me that it was not dislocated. At this point, he called Dr. Fascioni who came in, examined me,

looked at the x-rays and said it my shoulder was subluxed. I also saw him in his office. I told him that my arm was completely numb, I couldn't move it and that I was in terrible pain. He proceeded to tell me that it would get better by itself...

At this stage, I was so extremely discouraged that I did not know where to turn. I would never have believed that this would have happened to me, although clearly I have known many cases of medical malpractice. The feeling of hopelessness was overwhelming.

As a last resort, I decided to go overseas to get a second opinion. As both opinions were the same, and I was still in tremendous pain, I proceeded with the surgery. What a relief to have my shoulder back in place and to start feeling better within days of the surgery!

Attached is the report of the hospital and the surgeon who operated on me. I was more upset when I received this report because I know that I have some irreparable damage that will not be cured. This is due to not being acted on or listened to...

Due to the above, I feel that it is only fair that I receive some compensation. The operation was expensive, part of which I have had to pay myself. In addition as a business owner I have lost many weeks of income, as has my husband and I have irreparable damage.

The amount that I am requesting is as follows: -

Surgery (portion not covered by insurance)	5,050.00
Loss of income	5,000.00
Permanent damage	5,000.00
Total	$15,050.00

Although the compensation is relatively small, I believe that there is a larger principle at stake that needs to be fought for. The principle is that everybody should receive proper care from a professional and not be left to feel so hopeless and helpless. Therefore, I will be proceeding with this through the legal system if necessary.

I look forward to your response.

Yours sincerely,

L. W."

The couple's monetary demands were very conservative under the circumstances. Even though Mrs. L.W., who was an accountant, had managed to work most of the time she had the dislocation, she still lost some income when she travelled abroad for surgery. Furthermore, her overseas surgeon indicated that she might develop arthritis in her shoulder in the future, which would require more treatment and probably cost significantly more than the $5,000 she was demanding for permanent damage.

A few days after Mrs. L.W. wrote to the doctors her employer notified her that they no longer required her services. She had been working as a financial controller for the largest travel agency in Bermuda. Mrs. L.W. said her employer gave her no reason for suddenly dismissing her, but she knew it had to do with the letter. She knew that the "network" her insurance company spoke of had a strong grip on Bermuda, but she did not think her letter asking for compensation would cost her job.

A few days after her employee fired her, Mrs. L.W.'s attorney advised her that he could no longer represent her against the two doctors. He said he was now working for the hospital and suggested she find another attorney. Mrs. L.W. told him she was seeking legal compensation not against the hospital, but against the two doctors, who, she believed, had mistreated and misled her. Still, the attorney indicated he could not continue to represent her. Mrs. L.W. said that if she happened to find another attorney who dared take on her case she would end up paying a hefty legal fee, to no avail. Therefore, she dropped all attempts to obtain compensation from the two doctors.

Mrs. L.W., who is a fighter, did not give up everything. She decided to open her own travel agency and is now in competition with the agency that fired her.

CHAPTER FIFTY-ONE

Leaving Bermuda

Sunday, February 27th, 2000, was the day I had been praying for and waiting for, the day I would be leaving Bermuda. In the morning I went to church to thank and said goodbye to some of the people who had given me moral support over the previous four years. Mrs. E. Simmons, a church member and friend who had helped me in many ways, said she was sad that my stay in Bermuda had turned out the way it had. I told her I was one of the happiest men around. I said that, by the grace of God, I had been able to do what I did and God would see to the rest.

Mr. and Mrs. Remond drove me to the airport. For the preceding two years the Remonds had been my family. We had grown used to each other's daily routine and I was sad to leave them behind. The Remonds were also sad to see me leave, but they said they were happy for me because they knew what I had been through. They were in the process of selling their house and moving back to France. I wished them well and said I hoped our next meeting would be in France or Canada.

The flight from Bermuda to Toronto was as routine as the more than two dozens similar flights I had made over the years. When I reached Toronto my blood pressure went from 200 mm Hg to 120. At the airport a friendly customs and immigration officer asked where I was coming from. When I answered Bermuda she said I was lucky. I smiled and said nothing. Then she asked the purpose of my trip to Canada. I replied that I was moving back to Canada to join my family. The officer said, "From Bermuda?" I answered, "Yes, from Bermuda." She asked if was crazy. I smiled again and said I was fine. I always find it interesting when people assume an individual is lucky, even enviable, without having a clue about that individual's life experiences.

We talked about other things for a while and then she let me through.

Two other Canadian physicians left Bermuda at the same time as I. Dr. Sale, a cardiologist from southern Ontario whom I had befriended, had moved to the Island eighteen months earlier. He was in his early fifties. Dr. Sale told me he had gone to Bermuda to work for few years in order to "cushion my retirement." He said he had billed more than $1 million a year in Canada, but felt this was not enough to build up a comfortable retirement. He spent $0.25 million annually on office expenses (salaries, rent, office equipment, etc.). He paid his wife a yearly salary of a $100,000 to supervise the office and another $100,000 for household expenses, even though their house was paid for. After paying $325,000 in income tax, he said, he was left with only $225,000 a year for travel, miscellaneous expenses and retirement.

Dr. Sale told me that a Bermudian family physician, an acquaintance of his, said that if Dr. Sale moved to Bermuda he could bill $1 million US a year. Dr. Sale said he figured that with a tax imposition of twelve percent in Bermuda, even if his wife were to spend more than $200,000 a year he could still manage to save enough for a comfortable retirement.

Before pulling up stakes, Dr. Sale travelled to Bermuda to "test the waters." During his visit he met Dr. Jameson, the former chief of staff of the King Edward VII Memorial Hospital, and Mrs. Anderson, the executive director. Dr. Jameson told him that a cardiologist was needed in Bermuda and he would be welcome there, but Mrs. Anderson warned him that the only other local cardiologist, a Portuguese Bermudian, might give him a hard time. Dr. Sale said he made the move thinking that everything would be fine if he worked from his office, as the other cardiologist worked only from the hospital. As soon as he arrived, however, the other cardiologist summoned all the white internists, including the new chief of staff, Dr. Paytons, to a meeting. Dr. Little, a young Bermudian who attended, told Dr. Sale that the purpose of the meeting was to exclude him from the hospital by every means possible. She said she disagreed with this agenda, but had no choice but to go along with it. Dr. Sale wondered if Dr. Little expected to comfort him by telling him about the scheme and that she disagreed with it, but had no choice but to go with the majority. I explained to him that in Bermuda it is unthinkable to go against the establishment, and anyone who dares to do so must suffer the consequences.

After the meeting Dr. Paytons and the Bermudian cardiologist began questioning Dr. Sale's judgement and treatment methods. Dr. Sale said he felt insulted by this because he had treated more heart patients than all the internists in Bermuda combined. With time he discovered that Dr. Paytons and the internists were willing to go so far as to harm his patients in order to undermine his reputation. Dr. Jameson denied ever having said Dr. Sale would be welcome on the Island and refused to come to his defence, although Dr. Browne, the transport minister, backed him and urged him to stay. Dr. Sale decided to leave because it was not a healthy environment in which to work. In addition to dealing with the situation at the hospital, he had to pay $12,000 a month for rent and so-called managerial fee to the Bermudian family physician that had sponsored him. Instead of making the promised $1 million a year, he lost money every day he stayed in Bermuda. Two days before I left Dr. Sale dropped in to my office on his way to the bank to pay a $200,000 loan that his Bermudian adventure had cost him. He was returning to Canada realizing how fortunate he had been there. His stay in Bermuda had made him see that money was not everything. He said he was going to cut his wife's salary and spending allowances and his own spending. Fortunately for Dr. Sale, he had only taken a sabbatical from the Canadian hospital, where he sat on the Board. He had also somehow managed to keep his office in Canada running by hiring a locum doctor.

The second Canadian doctor who left Bermuda at the same time as I was Dr. Lee, an endocrinologist and university professor. Some time earlier, a Canadian businessman residing in Bermuda, a mutual friend of ours, had invited me to his home to meet Dr. Lee and advise him whether he should move to Bermuda. Dr. Lee's reason for considering the move was similar to Dr. Sale's: he wished to cushion his retirement. I neither encouraged nor discouraged Dr. Lee. I told him that his status in Bermuda would be different from mine since it was the white doctors, the establishment, who had invited him to come. Dr. Paytons and the other white internists needed Dr. Lee because the incidence of diabetes in Bermuda is much higher than in Canada and the United States and there was no endocrinologist there. Dr. Lee, who was in his early fifties, moved to Bermuda a year before I left. Once he arrived, he found that the white doctors who had wanted him to set up practice to Bermuda refused to refer their patients to him, jealously holding on to them for financial reasons. I was told that after one year in Bermuda Dr. Lee had lost in the vicinity of $50,000 US. He decided it was time to cut his losses and leave.

CHAPTER FIFTY-TWO

Witnessing

"And he [Jesus] said unto them, Go ye into all the world, and preach the gospel to every creature (Mark 16:15)."

"Look unto me, and be ye saved, all the ends of the earth: for I [am] God, and [there is] none else (Isaiah 45:22)."

There are a lot of thing I like about being Christian. Besides having eternal life, I particularly like the way I now pray to God as a Christian. To pray to God I do not need to look for the moon, sunset or sunrise or wait for a specific time as I did in the past. I do not have to dress in a particular way, nor to wash or purify myself, nor to bend or sit in an uncomfortable position. I do not have to repeat a sequence of words that I do not understand nor to speak out aloud or hum. I do not have to burn candles, count beads and do the countless things I did in the past. Now that I am a Christian, I can pray to God any time and anywhere. I pray when I am standing, walking, sitting, lying down, kneeling or driving my car. However, most often I pray in a kneeling position in the same quiet place. I kneel, bow my head in respect, close my eyes in order to better concentrate, and speak to God in a non-repetitive way that originates from my heart and my soul. As a new Christian, I spent more time praying for my own needs. With time I realized that I was somewhat ungrateful and did not spend enough time praising God and praying for others. I also realized that God knew what was in my heart and took care of my needs anyway. There were times when He granted me things even before I prayed for them. Now my prayers are less centred on myself, on my needs, and I spend more time praising God and praying for others. At one point I made a list of the things I needed to pray for, because my mind was always wandering during my prayers. Then one day I did away with the list because it was too repetitive and went back to praying from my heart. When I stumble during my prayers because of my wandering mind, I pause for a few seconds, gather my thoughts and continue where I left off. I am sure God does not mind. Now, although I prefer to pray from my heart, I occasionally use a prayer list to pray for others, a list that I update regularly. I am constantly learning how to pray to God and asking God to help me with the way I pray.

If there are a lot of things I like about being Christian, there is one thing that at first I did not enjoy. The Bible teaches that every believer is a worker and an ambassador of Christ (*John 20:21; Acts 26:16–18; Ephesians 6:20; II Corinthians 3:6; 5:20; 6:1*), that it is the duty of every Christian to go into the world and preach the gospel to the lost people (*Matthew 10:5,6; 28:19; Mark 13:10; 16:15; Luke 14:21–23; 24:47,48; John 15:16; 20:21; Acts 1:8; Romans 10:14,15, 18; 16:26; 15:20,21; Ephesians 2:17; Colossians 1:6,23; I John 4:14; Revelation 14:6*), that it is the duty of every believer to tell every lost soul that accepting Jesus Christ as Saviour will lead to eternal life and that rejecting Jesus Christ as Saviour will lead to damnation and hell (*Isaiah 45:22; Matthew 18:11; Mark 16:16; Luke 19:10; John 1:12; 3:15,16,36; 5:24; 6:40,47; 10:28–30; 11:25,26; 12:44–46; 17:2,3; 20:31; Acts 8:37; 13:41; 16:30,31; Romans 5:1,2, 21; 6:22,23; 10:9–14; I Corinthians 1:18; II Corinthians 4:3; Galatians 2:16,20; Hebrews 7:25 10:39; I John 2:25; 5:1,11–13,20*). It is not that I did not enjoy talking about Christ, quite the contrary, but I disliked the reception I received when I talked to people about God. People felt uneasy and looked at me as if I were crazy. I noticed that in general people listen attentively to others only when they should not or when they think there is some money to be made effortlessly. However, in the end I started witnessing to people for four reasons: I realized that God holds believers accountable for every lost soul they did not tell there is a way to avoid the horrendous destiny of hell (*Genesis 9:5; Ezekiel 3:18–19; 34:10; Luke 13:3,5; Acts 20:26,27*); because the Bible teaches that if we deny Jesus Christ before men, He will deny us before God (*I Samuel 2:30; Psalms 119:46; Matthew 10:32,33; Luke 9:26; 12:8,9; John 9:22; Romans 10:9,10; I Timothy 6:12,13; II Timothy 1:8; 2:12; I John 2:23; 4:15; Revelation 2:13; 3:5*); because I realized that witnessing to others serves my own spiritual growth (*II Corinthians 9:8; Ephesians 2:10; II Timothy 2:21; 3:16–17; Titus 2:14 3:1*); and because Jesus, if He wished, could return to earth Himself and win souls for God (*John 4:1–30; Acts 9:3–20*).

Finally, I started talking to others about Jesus because I was grateful that someone else, Florence, had taken the time to talk to me about Him and because I wished to share with others my love for them.

Before going out into the world to witness to others as the Bible urges believers to do, I decided to witness to my family and friends. The first family member I spoke to about Jesus Christ and invited to church was a non-practising Muslim. He briefly listened, then interrupted and said he believed in something, a force, that created humankind and everything in the universe. My relative would not go so far as to use the word "God." I told him that what he referred to as "something" and "a force" was God. I asked him if he believed in electricity. This person, who was very knowledgeable about electricity, smiled and started talking enthusiastically about atoms, nuclei, electrons, protons and the workings of electricity. I asked him if he has seen or touched electrons or protons. He answered that he had not seen them, but knew they existed; he saw them manifested in light bulbs, for example.

I told my relative that I had not seen God, but believed in His existence. Like the person who believes that electricity is the manifestation of electrons and protons, I believed the Bible, which teaches that the heavens (galaxies, stars, planets, the sky), earth, the sea and the animals are God's creations and are the manifestation of God's existence (*Genesis 1:6–25; Exodus 20:11; Psalms 8:3; 19:1; 33:6–9; 50:9–12; 115:16; 146:5,6; 148:3,4; 150:1,2; Isaiah 40:22–26,28; 44:24; 45:6,7,12; Jeremiah 10:11,12; 32:17; Daniel 12:3; Acts 7:48–50; 14:15; 17:24; Romans 1:19, 20*). My relative asked, "How many religions are there in the world?" I said there are apparently close to ten thousand, but the important thing is not the number of religions and gods there are, but to know the true God, to be saved, to worship and serve God the right way. Then he asked, "Who is the true God?" I said the true God is the God of Abraham, of Isaac, of Jacob (Israel). My relative interrupted me as soon as I said God of Jacob (Israel) and said I was biased. I said I was not biased, but was merely answering his question about which I believed to be the true God. I continued and said the true God is the God of Israel, Ishmael, Moses, the God and father of Jesus Christ and the God of all who worship him as such. My relative asked me on what basis was I affirming that there is only one God and he is the father of Jesus of Christ. I said I was affirming this based on my reading and limited understanding of the Bible. I said that the Bible is not only the best work of literature in existence, but also a mysterious and prophetic book that allows one to commune with God. My relative asked for an example of the mysterious and prophetic nature of the Bible. I said that when I first read the Bible I learned that God told Abraham, who was seventy-five years old, that he would bless him and give him an heir with whom God would establish a covenant (*Genesis 12:1,2*), and that God fulfilled this promise with the birth of Isaac when Abraham was a hundred years old and his wife, Sarah, was ninety (*Genesis 17:19, 21; Genesis 21:5*). In the subsequent chapters of the Bible, I said, the prophet wrote that God tested Abraham's faith by asking him to sacrifice his eight-year-old son, Isaac (*Genesis 22:1,2*). The Bible teaches that Abraham obeyed God and at the last moment God provided a ram as a substitute for Isaac (*Genesis 22:3–13*). I said that at first I could not understand why God had asked Abraham to sacrifice his son for the sake of testing him, since God had tested Abraham on many occasions in the past and he had always obeyed, but then I saw the parallel between God asking Abraham to sacrifice his son and God sacrificing His own Son, Jesus Christ (*Romans 8:3; I Corinthians 5:7; Ephesians 5:2; Hebrew 9:28; 10:10,12*). I said I understood that God asking Abraham to sacrifice Isaac was not only a test of faith for Abraham, but also a prophecy, to show that some day God would sacrifice His own Son for the sins of all humankind (*John 3:16; Romans 8:32; Hebrews 10:10; 11:17*). I told my relative that the parallel between Abraham and Isaac and God and Jesus Christ is only one of the many mysteries and prophecies of the Bible; God does things for reasons that we do not always understand and accept.

Then my relative asked why, if there is only one God, there are so many religions? I said the Bible teaches that God is not the author of confusion (*I Corinthians 14:33*). My relative asked if God is not the author of confusion, then who is misleading the people about God? I said the Bible teaches that the "god of this world," the devil, is the author of confusion (*John 12:31,40; 14:40; 16:11; Acts 26:18; I Corinthians 10:20; II Corinthians 4:4; Ephesians*

2:2; 6:12; *Revelation 20:2,3*). He looked at me as if I were out my mind and said he believed in God all right, but not in the devil. I did not mind that he did not believe in the devil, for at least now I could talk to him about salvation, since he said he believed in God.

My relative said he thought he would go to heaven anyway because he gave to the poor and tried to be good. I said the Bible teaches that God does not suggest we give to the poor, but commands us to (*Exodus 23:11; Leviticus 19:10; 23:22; Deuteronomy 15:7; 15:11; Job 29:12,16; 30:25; 31:16,19; Psalms 82:3; 113:7; 146:7; Isaiah 58:7; Matthew 19:21; 26:11; Mark 10:21; 14:7; Luke 18:22; 19:8; John 12:8; Acts 4:34–35; II Corinthians 9:9; Galatians 2:10; I Timothy 6:17–18*). However, the Bible teaches that even though God wants us to do good, our righteousness, which always has some hidden, personal motive, will not get us into heaven (*Genesis 6:12; Jobs 15:16; Psalms 12:1,2; 25:7; 51:5; Proverbs 20:6; Ecclesiastes 8:1; 9:3; Isaiah 1:21; 57:1; 59:1–13; Jeremiah 3:25; 5:1; 17:9; Micah 7:1,2,4; Matthew 15:19*). I told my relative that even though he tried to do good, he had sinned against God countless times and would continue to do so. I explained that in our society some crimes are punishable by a fine, some by a reprimand, some by imprisonment and some (in certain countries) by death, but that the Bible teaches that in God's court of law the wages of all sin is death and the sentence is hell and eternal punishment (*Ezekiel 18:4,20; Romans 5:12; 6:23; I Corinthians 6:9,10; Galatians 6:7; James 1:15; Revelation 21:8*). I told him that, accordingly, all humankind is condemned to die, go to hell and suffer forever, because we all have sinned against God and that salvation is the only way to avoid this sad fate.

I described, in detail, the path to salvation. I told my relative that once he was saved, the only changes he would have to make in his life were to read the Bible, the most rational work of literature, tell people about Jesus Christ, attend church regularly to praise God as a gesture of gratitude for everything God has done for him and lead a Christian life (*Proverbs 11:1; 16:11; 20:7; Isaiah 26:7; Romans 12:9–21; 13:12–13; I Corinthians 13:1–13; Galatians 5:22; Ephesians 4:17–5:20; Philippians 4:4–9; Colossians 3:5–17; I Thessalonians 5:1–22; Titus 2:11–14; James 1:21; 3:17; I Peter 1:13–22; 2:1,9; 4:7–9*). I told him that if the Bible and the prophets were right about eternal life and hell – and I was sure they were – he would thank

God when he died, but if it turned out that the Bible and the prophets were wrong and there was no eternal life or hell, but only a complete void, he would not even be conscious of it to reproach me for advising him to read the Bible, lead a Christian life and waste his time in church. After I finished speaking my relative remained quite for a while. Then he changed the subject and talked about something completely unrelated to God.

For the next few months my relative refused to let me talk to him about God. He spoke about the world economy and socio-politics and I listened. Meanwhile I prayed to God and waited patiently for an opportunity to witness to my relative. After six months of listening to him talk about everything except God, I finally had that opportunity.

One day my relative expounded about politics. "The poor are getting poorer and the rich richer," he said. "In the developed countries the large corporations hardly pay taxes, while the middle-class workers pay most of their income in taxes. The wealthy countries speak of helping the poor countries, but what they do is take the raw materials from the poor countries, transform them in their own countries and export the waste to the poor countries." When the poor countries receive money from the developed countries it is publicized as aid, but is usually a loan, he said, adding that most of the money that the rich countries lend to the poor countries never reaches the people who need it the most; part of it goes to the highly paid consultants and others who manage the money in the rich countries and in that sense never even leaves the rich countries.

The greedy rulers of the poor countries who have been installed or kept in power by the rich countries, he continued, divert the little money that reaches their countries for their own personal use; in fact, most of it goes into their bank accounts in the rich countries. He said the leaders use some of the money to buy weapons from the rich countries to finance their armies, and the armies in turn oppress the people who the money was intended for. My relative said that when, against all odds, the struggling people of developing countries produce goods, they cannot sell these goods in their own countries or in the rich countries because the corporations, which are heavily subsidized, can sell their own products at a lower price. As if this were not enough, he said, the rich countries send their huge fishing fleets to over-fish the coasts of poor countries. The leaders of the rich countries talk about democracy and economic advancement for the poor countries, he complained, but are interested only in maintaining a stable and friendly environment in those countries for the benefit of huge corporations and their own electorates.

My relative said that although humankind is more technologically advanced than it was centuries ago, socially we have not evolved at all. He said that humankind resolves its differences through war, just as it did thousands of years ago. While centuries ago men fought with spears and daggers, now we use weapons that can eradicate all life forms from the face of the planet. He said he wished humankind had not developed some of the weapons we have in our possession.

My relative talked about other problems that face humankind such as the dissolution of the family, the ever-increasing crime rate, substance abuse and despair. He said there was no solution in sight and things would only get worse. He concluded by saying he was glad he would not be around to face the world's growing problems and pitied future generations.

I told my relative that he was right in his assessment of the world situation. I said Jesus and the prophets prophesied about the present day. They called it the last days before the return of Jesus Christ and prophesied that "**men shall be lovers of their own selves** [selfish], **covetous** [lovers of money, never content, always desiring what others have], **boasters, proud, blasphemers** [speaking evil of God and His name], **disobedient to parents, unthankful, unholy** [wicked], **without natural affection, trucebreakers, false accusers, incontinent** [lacking self-control], **fierce** [cruel, lacking gentleness], **despisers of those that are good, traitors, heady** [reckless, inconsiderate], **highminded** [arrogant, conceited], **lovers of pleasures more than lovers of God, having a form of godliness** [baptized as Christians ,but making a show of religion], **but denying the power thereof: from such turn away,...they which creep into houses, and lead captive silly women laden with sins** [mislead and abuse weak women], **led away with divers lusts** [seduced by prostitution and lust], **ever learning, and never able to come to the knowledge of the truth** [God]" (*II Timothy 3:1–7*).

I said the prophets also wrote that in the last days "**some shall depart from the faith** [from the doctrine of faith in Christ as the only foundation of hope], **giving heed to seducing spirits, and doctrines of devils** [worshipping and praying to images and relying on external connections and observances for salvation]; **Speaking lies in hypocrisy; having their conscience seared with a hot iron** [professing to honour Jesus Christ but with souls branded with the marks of sin]; **Forbidding to marry** [vows of celibacy], **and commanding to abstain from meats, which God hath created to be received with thanksgiving of them which believe and know the truth"** (*I Timothy 4:1–3*). Jesus and the prophets also prophesied that in the last days **"nation shall rise against nation, and kingdom against kingdom: and there shall be earthquakes in divers places, and there shall be famines, pestilences and fearful sights and great signs and troubles"** (*Matthew 24:3–22; Mark 13:5–37; Luke 21:10,11*). The Bible teaches that there will arise in the last days many "false prophets which come in sheep's clothing but inwardly are ravening wolves," "false teachers" seducing by their language and deceiving many, including Christians, by showing wonders and promising peace (*Isaiah 9:15,16; Jeremiah 14:14–16 23:13–16; 28:15–17; 29:21,32; Ezekiel 13:16,22; Micah 3:5–7,11; Matthew 7:15–21; 24:11; 24:4,5, 11, 24,25; Mark 13:22, 23; Luke 6:26; II Corinthians 11:14; II Peter 2:1–3; I John 4:1; Revelation 19:20*). The Bible teaches that there will be justice and peace in the world only when Jesus comes back to judge and reign over all nations (*Psalms 72:1–20; Isaiah 2:4; 11:1–13; 32:1,17; Jeremiah 33:15; Zechariah 8:1–23; Revelation 19:11; 20:1–6*) (*Daniel 7:13–27; Matthew 24:30; 25:31; 26:64; Mark 13:26; 14:62; Luke 21:27; John 14:3; Acts 1:11; I Thessalonians 1:10; 4:16; II Thessalonians 1:7–10; Hebrews 9:28; Revelation 1:6,7; 5:10; 20:6*).

I asked my relative, who had told me he was glad he would not be around to face the world's growing problems, where he would be. He said he would probably be in heaven. I asked him why he thought so. He said because he had tried to do good and had not killed anybody. I asked him on what basis he could say he had done good. I asked him if he knew the Ten Commandments and all the other commandments by which God judges whether we are righteous. He did not answer. Even if he knew all the commandments, I said, he would not be able to obey all of them all of the time. I said the Bible teaches that all those who have not accepted Jesus Christ as their Saviour will end up in hell (*Revelation 19:20; 20:10–15*). My relative said he did not believe in hell – it was a device to scare people. I asked him where killers end up, since, according to him, those who have not killed end up in heaven. He considered this for a while, but did not answer. Whether he believed it or not, I said, the Bible teaches that hell exists and any individual, even a killer, who repents and accepts Jesus as his or her personal Saviour is saved from hell, but that any individual who will not do so ends up in hell (*Exodus 2:12–14; Matthew 17:3; Mark 9:4; Luke 9:30*).

The Bible teaches that if we talk to people about God and Jesus Christ and they do not listen, we should leave them alone (*Matthew 10:12–14; Mark 6:11; Luke 9:5; 10:10,11; Acts 13:48–51; 18:5,6; 19: 8,9*), so this is exactly what I did with my relative. However, I gave him a Bible in the hope that he would read it. To my great joy, he began reading it enthusiastically. A few days later, he said he found the Bible repetitive. I said that forty men of God wrote the sixty-six chapters of the Bible as inspired by God. The seeming repetitiveness of the Bible, I explained, shows the consistency of God. What God told the prophets four thousand years ago was the same as what He told them two thousand years ago. Moreover, in discussing a topic more than once the Bible makes it clear and helps us to understand what God wants from us. I said that what God expected of us four thousand years ago was the same as what He expected of us two thousand years ago, and what He expects of us today.

A few days later, he told me he found the Bible to be a violent book with a lot of killing. I said I had some hypothetical questions for him. Suppose he had a family, I said, and suppose he told his children to love one another and gave them rules to live by. And suppose a few days later he finds that his children have broken every one of those rules. They are lying, stealing and killing each other. His sons are having sex with their mother, raping their sisters and molesting their children. His children are committing adultery and having sex with animals. My relative gestured for me to stop – he had heard enough. I asked him what he would do. He did not answer. I said suppose his children continually refused to respect him, cursed his name and referred to strangers as their father. They are killing their unborn and their newborn and sacrificing their children to idols. Instead of loving each other as he had instructed them to do, they hate and discriminate against each other, constantly war against and kill each other. My relative interrupted me and said angrily, "I would kill them all! I would cut them with an ax." I said that at the time when the Bible was written, the people were doing all of those things (*Leviticus 18:1–30*), and we are still doing all of those things, and more. I told my relative that instead of killing all humankind, as we deserve and as he would have done to his children, God gave Jesus Christ, His Son, as an offering to redeem all of us from our sins (*Isaiah 53:4–12; Daniel 9:24; Matthew 20:28; Romans 3:25; 4:25; 5:6–9; 8:3,32; I Corinthians 15:3,4; II Corinthians 5:21; Galatians 1:4; 3:13; Ephesians 5:2; I Thessalonians 1:10; Titus 2:14; Hebrews 1:3; 2:17; 9:28; I Peter 1:18,19; 2:24; 3:18; I John 1:7; 2:2; 4:9,10; Revelation 1:5; 5:9*).

My relative said the Bible was a very complex book and it would take a lifetime to understand it. I said the Bible teaches that some of the mysteries it contains cannot be understood in this lifetime (*Job 38:4–41:34; Psalms 25:14; Isaiah 64:4; 65:17; Matthew 4:11; 11:25; 13:11; 24:36; Luke 8:10; John 1:14,18; 3:4; 14:9; 16:25; I Corinthians 2:7–14; 15:51; Ephesians 1:9,18; 3:3–9; 5:32; 6:19; I Timothy 3:16; Revelation 10:7; 17:5–7*). We are unable to comprehend most of what is written in the Bible, I said, because there are prophesies that have not been fulfilled yet and because we have not seen anything like it (*Exodus 34:29,30; Matthew 17:2; 28:2; John 17:2; Acts 26:13–15; Romans 8:29,30; I Corinthians 15:42–54; II Corinthians 3:18; Ephesians 1:5,11; Philippians 3:21; I John 3:2; Revelation 1:13–16; 10:1*).

I told my relative that the idea was not to understand the whole Bible, but to understand enough to acknowledge that he was a sinner and that his good deeds could not save him from his sins. Once he understood that much and opened his heart to God, I explained, God would give him the faith to see that only the death and resurrection of Jesus could take away his sins and save him from eternal damnation. I said that millions of adults and children who can barely read, let alone understand the whole Bible, have opened their hearts to God and received the gift of faith from God in order to be saved. I told my relative that I would answer to the best of my knowledge any queries he might have while reading the Bible. Some weeks later I noticed that he was devouring another book, which he offered to lend me once he had finished. I asked him what had happened to his Bible reading. He said he had given up reading the Bible. My relative had given up reading the Bible and would not accept Jesus as his Saviour, but his favourite quotation was from Jesus: "**He that is without sin among you, let him**

first cast a stone" (*John 8:7*). I asked my relative why he used Jesus' words whenever it was convenient for him to do so and reject the rest of Jesus' teachings. He said, "Humankind is complex and full of contradictions" (which I thought was a polite way of saying humankind is foolish).

The second family member I witnessed to was a non-practising Catholic whom I had seen in church only twice, once for a wedding and once for a baptism. The moment I started to talk to him about God and invited him to my church, he interrupted and said I was not to talk to him about religion or politics. He said I could talk to him about sports or any other subject under the sun, but not religion or politics. J.M., a pastor for Sahalis Washington State, once said that he became irritated when people told him they did not want to discuss religion or politics. He said that religion and politics have ruled people's lives since the beginning of time, and that for a person to say that he or she does not want to discuss these subjects is analogous to an ostrich hiding its head in the sand. The pastor said that as much as he disliked talking to people who did not wish to discuss religion or politics, one has to find ingenious ways to engage these people and witness to them. He was right, for the Bible teaches that Christians are not to dissociate completely with non-Christians, but to be in the world among the unsaved for the purpose of winning souls for Christ (*Proverbs 11:30; Isaiah 66:19; Matthew 28:19–20; Mark 2:17; 16:15; Luke 15:2-7; 19:7,10; John 13:14,15; Acts 16:17; Romans 1:14; 15:2,3; I Corinthians 2:15; 9:19–22; 10:24; 10:33; Galatians 5:13; I Thessalonians 5:9; II Timothy 2:3,10*). However, the Bible teaches that Christians should not be in the world with the aim of doing the ungodly things that unsaved people do (*Psalms 26:4,5; Proverbs 1:15; 4:14; 9:16; I Corinthians 5:9–11; 10:20,21; II Corinthians 6:14–17; Ephesians 5:7, 11; I Timothy 5:22; I John 1:6,7; Revelation 18:4*). With this in mind, I discussed sports with my relative. Meanwhile, I prayed and waited patiently for an opportunity to witness to him.

Some months later my relative was admitted to hospital with a serious illness. I visited him in hospital and told him I had been praying for him. He said he knew I had been praying for him, thanked me and asked me to continue. Then he informed me that the chaplain had given him communion a few minutes earlier. I told him I was glad the priest had visited and asked if the priest had said anything. My relative said he had not. I told him it was not written anywhere in the Bible that receiving communion would lead to salvation and eternal life. I asked my relative if he remembered the story of the two malefactors who were crucified with Jesus. He nodded. I said he probably remembered that one of the malefactors mocked Jesus.

I said the second malefactor reprimanded the first and asked him if he did not fear God. He said further: **"We indeed justly...receive the due reward for our deed: but this man [Jesus] has done nothing amiss. And he said unto Jesus, Lord, remember me when thou comest into thy Kingdom"** (*Luke 23:39–42*). In his speech, I explained, the malefactor did three things: acknowledged that he was a sinner and deserved to die; acknowledged that Jesus was not a sinner and did not deserve to die; and acknowledged that Jesus was the Lord and asked Jesus to save him. Jesus said to the malefactor, **"Verily I say unto thee, to day shalt thou be with me in paradise"** (*Luke 23:43*). I told my relative that the second malefactor who was crucified did not receive Communion, yet the Bible teaches that he is heaven with Jesus today. I told him that the Bible teaches:

> **"That if thou shalt confess with thy mouth the Lord Jesus, and shalt believe in thine heart that God hath raised him from the dead, thou shalt be saved."** (Romans 10:9)

I told my relative that attaining salvation was as simple as the above sentence suggests. To my great astonishment, he listened attentively to my talk about God and salvation. He said he understood everything, but would not accept the Lord Jesus Christ. He would not accept the Lord Jesus even though an hour earlier he had received communion; I suspected he did not understand the significance of this and had taken communion for the sake of tradition.

A few days later, I returned to the hospital to see my sick relative. He was feeling better, sitting up in bed reading the sports section of the newspaper. Some weeks later, he left the hospital doing relatively well. He does not want me to talk to him about religion and politics any more. The irony is that while he will not allow me to talk to him about God, he asked me to pray for him when he had to fly in an airplane. He wants to hear about Christ only in times of crisis. So, unfortunately, I have to wait until my relative gets sick to the point of dying before I can talk to him about God.

The third relative who I talked to about Jesus Christ was a non-practising Muslim with whom I used to spend hours discussing philosophy. I spoke to him about Jesus Christ and he listened attentively without interrupting. When I finished, my relative, an idealistic person with numerous post-graduate degrees, said he had been trying for years to distance himself from Islam, an Eastern religion that his parents had imposed on him from birth. Now that he could finally claim he had succeeded in distancing himself from Islam, he said, I was trying to impose Christianity, a Western religion, on him. He said that for thousands of years our ancestors who lived along the Nile had their own religions[1] and were doing fine before Islam was imposed on them, then they, in turn, imposed Islam on the people they came in contact with during their migration to West Africa; the rest of the Africans who were fortunate not to come in contact with Islam had their own religions and were doing fine before the European colonizers imposed Christianity on them.

My relative said an individual or nation should never impose their religious beliefs on other individuals or nations. Instead of copying others, he said, Africans should go back to the religions of their ancestors and to worshipping their African gods. He was all pumped up when he talked, then sighed and relaxed when he finished.

I told my relative I agreed with him that an individual or nation should not impose their religious beliefs on other individuals or nations, but I had one question. I asked him if it was God Who created humankind, or the other way around? Without hesitation, he said it was God who created humankind. In that case, I said, could every individual or nation create its own god and worship that god? Could the Orientals create their own god and say they did not want to worship the god of the Europeans? Why could the French not say they did not want to worship the god of the English, the Bantu not say they did not want to worship the gods of the Zulu, the Koreans not say they did not want to worship the god of the Japanese, and so on? What right do we have to question the judgement of God, the creator of the universe and of humankind? I would have gladly listened to the gospel had God sent a European or an Oriental to preach it. Instead, God sent His own Son in the person of Jesus Christ, a Mediterranean Jew, to bring salvation to humankind, and I am glad to accept Him (*Isaiah 11:1,10; 53:2; Jeremiah 23:5,6; Matthew 1:1–23*). Moreover, I said, we miss the point when we dwell on the human nature of Jesus Christ and fail to see that God is a spirit and those who worship Him must worship Him in spirit and in truth (*John 4:21–24; Romans 8:2; II Corinthians 3:17; Philippians 3:3; I Timothy 1:17*). Finally, I told him that Christianity is not a Western religion, that the first Christians were Jews (*Acts 11:22,26; 13:1; 15:22; 18:2,22,26; I Corinthians 16:19*).

After I finished speaking, my relative said I was fundamentalist and narrow-minded. I told him he was not the first to call me fundamentalist; I had been mocked and called worse names by other relatives who had heard me speak about Jesus. I told him that if I were to say 1 = 1 he would say of course. If I were to go to him the next day and say 1 = 2, and the third day 1 = 3 and so forth up to 1 = 10,000 he would say that is not true and probably add that I was out of my mind. Yet when I told him that there was only one God and one way to worship that God, and not ten thousand different and contradictory ways to worship the only true God, he called me names. I told him that it was God, Jesus and the prophets, and not I, who said there was only one God and one way to worship that God (*Isaiah 45:5; John 14:6*); therefore if he had any complaints he should address them to God and the prophets. My relative said if there is only one God, as I suggested, why the God of the Bible? I told him I had the same reaction when I first learned that Jesus said there is only one God and he, Jesus, was the only "way" to God; that the first few times I read the Bible I hoped to find contradictions in it to nullify the notion of only "one way" to God and validate my previously held belief that there are many ways to God. But instead of finding contradictions, I said, I found consistency throughout the Bible. I found the writings in the Bible structured and I found agreement between the first and last chapters. My relative said he understood everything I said about God, Jesus and salvation and would consider it in his search for the truth. I told him I would pray for him to find the truth.

Two weeks later my relative phoned me. He was excited and said a student of his had talked to him about Jesus. He was amazed because his student had told him exactly the things about Jesus I had told him. However, he was confused about one thing. His student had told him that dancing in nightclubs and listening to certain types of music was of the devil. His student gave him the impression that only classical music was of God. My relative, who knew that I liked Reggae music, asked me if I still listened to Reggae. I said God gave the commandments and the law to Moses to show the nation of Israel how to love God, love their neighbour and live a holy life (*Exodus 20:1–17; Leviticus 1:1–17:16*). When Jesus came into this world he reproached the religious leaders of the time for performing rituals, for misleading the people into observing man-made traditions instead of God's word. Jesus reproached the religious leaders for minding insignificant details while ignoring what is important - justice, faith and mercy, and for appearing saintly outside while remaining hypocritical, greedy and corrupt inside (*Matthew 23:1–39; Mark 12:38–40; Luke 20:45–47*). Jesus told the religious leaders and the people to cleanse their hearts first and the rest of them would be clean (*Isaiah 55:7; Jeremiah 4:14; 13:27; Ezekiel 18:31; Matthew 12:33; 23:26; Luke 6:45; II Corinthians 7:1; Hebrews 10:22; James 4:8*). He exhorted the religious leaders to follow the two greatest commandments, to love God with all one's heart, soul and mind, and to love one's neighbour as oneself (*Matthew 22:37–40; John 13:34; 15:12*). I told my relative that the first thing he had to acknowledge was that he was a sinner, repent and accept Jesus Christ as his personal Saviour. I said once he was saved, I would advise him on fulfilling God's two greatest commandments. If he loved God and obeyed God's commandments, I said, the spirit of God would abide within him (*John 14:23,26; I John 2:27; 4:16*) and guide his life regarding what type of music he should listen to.

A few weeks later my relative phoned to inform me that he had accepted his student's invitation to attend a service at his church. He liked the church, the pastor and the message preached by the pastor, but would not be going back because he was busy with his work. Since then he has asked me on a few occasions to pray for him when he has had problems. Each time I have told him I would pray for him, but advised him to accept the Lord Jesus Christ as his personal Saviour so that he could pray for himself, for others and for me.

The next person I told I was Christian and invited to my church was a practising Muslim. This friend said he did not understand me because many well-known people have converted from Christianity to Islam while I did the opposite. I said I did not do things for the sake of following the majority, but because I thought and knew them to be right. He asked me how

I could become Christian when I knew that it was Christians who brought Africans to America and used them as slaves. I said the slave trade of Africans by Europeans and the ensuing slavery of Africans in America is one of the greatest tragedies in the history of humankind. But slavery existed in the Arab and Muslim world long before it did in America, and continued long after it was abolished in America.[2] Besides, I said, no nation can boast of not having oppressed another nation or its own citizens at some time in its history; even as we speak, people of all faiths and virtually all nations are involved in human trading and exploitation of some sort.

The friend said his religion was the fastest-growing religion in the world, with more than a billion worshippers, which proves that it is a good religion. I said it is not a numbers game and Jesus said the following in relation to the difference between what the multitude do and the way to eternal to life: **"Enter ye in at the strait gate: for wide *is* the gate, and broad *is* the way, that leadeth to destruction, and many there be which go in thereat: Because strait *is* the gate, and narrow *is* the way, which leadeth unto life, and few there be that find it"** (*Matthew 7:13,14*).

I tried to explain to my friend what Jesus Christ meant by these words, but he interrupted me and said his was a "good" religion because many countries that espouse it have oil and are wealthy. I said there are people who worship the sun as their god and are extremely wealthy. Furthermore, Jesus said, **"Verily I say unto you, that a rich man shall hardly enter into the kingdom of heaven. And again I say unto you, It is easier for a camel to go through the eye of a needle, than for a rich man to enter into the kingdom of God"** (*Matthew 19:23,24*). The Bible teaches that most often a rich man will care more about his riches than about the things of God and trust his riches instead of God (*Proverbs 10:15; 18:11; 23:4,5; 28:11; Mark 10:24,25; Luke 12:16–21; 18:25; I Timothy 6:17*).

Then my friend asked me to explain why I felt my religion was a good religion. I told him it was not so much about a good or bad religion, but about the way to salvation and eternal life. I started talking to him about the way to salvation. With the exception of Jesus Christ, all men and women who walk on this earth are sinners. My friend said I was wrong, that the prophets never sinned, although they might have appeared to sin. I said the Bible says that Abraham lied (*Genesis 12:11–13*), Jacob (Israel) stole his brother's blessing and misled his father (*Genesis 27:1–40*), Moses killed a man (*Exodus 2:12*) and David killed a man and stole the man's wife (*II Samuel 11:2–27*). The Bible shows that the prophets sinned to teach us that we too could fall into temptation and sin, if the prophets, men of God, did so. I explained to my friend that the Bible says the prophets sinned to teach us that when we sin our sins are against the Lord and it gives His enemy an opportunity to blaspheme the name of the Lord (*II Samuel 12:14; Psalms 32:5; 41:4; 51:1–4; 74:10; Isaiah 52:5; Ezekiel 36:20–23; Romans 2:23,24*). The life of the prophets also teaches us, I said, that sin separates us from the Lord, affecting our lives and those of our children and our children's children (*Deuteronomy 31:17,18; 32:20; Ezekiel 39:23,24,29; Micah 3:4*), (*Exodus 20:5; 34:7; Leviticus 20:5; 26:29,39,40; Numbers 14:18,33; I Samuel 15:2,3; II Samuel 21:1–6; I Kings 21:29; II Kings 23:26; Jobs 5:4; 21:19; Psalms 79:8; 109:14; Isaiah 14:20,21; 65:6,7; Jeremiah 2:9; 32:18; Matthew 23:34–36*). But mostly, I said, the stories of the prophets and their sins teach us that if we genuinely repent God will forgive us, because He is merciful and just (*Leviticus 26:40–42; I Kings 8:47–50; II Chronicles 6:37–39; Nehemiah 1:6–9; 9:2–37 Job 33:27,28; Psalms 32:5; 51:2–5; Proverbs 28:13; Daniel 9:4–20; Matthew 3:6; Mark 1:5; Acts 19:18; I John 1:9*).

My friend said I was blaspheming and repeated again that the prophets never sinned. He listened to me speak about salvation until I said that Jesus Christ was the Son of God. For a few instants he appeared to be having a petit mal seizure. When he was himself again he spoke for five minutes in his native language, citing the Koran. Finally, he said I could steal, cheat and do all sorts of wicked things and God would forgive me, but God would never forgive me for saying He had a son. We continued our discussion with me being able to say one word for every twenty my friend spoke.

The next time the friend spoke to me about faith, he asked me if I drank alcohol. I said I had occasionally in the past, but did not drink any more, for health and personal reasons, the personal reason being that I would rather be in control of my senses than let alcohol dictate my behaviour. He asked me to explain why his holy book forbids the use of alcohol while the Bible allows it. I said that the Bible teaches various things about alcohol consumption. Although it refers to the adverse effects of wine and liquor consumption (*Genesis 9:21–23; 19:31–36; I Samuel 25:37,38; Proverbs 20:1; 21:17;*

23:20,21, 29–35; Isaiah 5:11,22; 24:9; 28:3,7,8; Hosea 4:11; Habakkuk 2:5,15,16; Luke 21:34; I Corinthians 6:10; Galatians 5:21; I Thessalonians 5:6–9), it also refers to the benefits of wine (*Numbers 15:5,7,10; Judges 9:13; Psalms 104:15; Proverbs 31:6; Ecclesiastes 10:19; I Timothy 5:23*). The Bible teaches that God warned the priests that drinking wine or alcoholic beverages would affect their senses, their judgement and their ability to teach (*Isaiah 28:7*); that God forbade the Levites (the priests) from consuming alcohol and going to the shrine in His presence (*Leviticus 10:9; Numbers 6:3; Ezekiel 44:21; I Timothy 3:8; Titus 1:7*); that God warned the priests that they could die if they disobeyed this commandment (*Leviticus 10:1,2,9*); that kings and princes (rulers) were to abstain from drinking wine and strong drink (intoxicating liquor) because it could affect their memory and pervert their judgement (*Proverbs 31:4,5; Ecclesiastes 10:17*); and that God commanded the Nazarite (a man or woman chosen by God or any man or woman who wished to devote their life to God) to abstain from drinking wine or strong drink (*Numbers 6:2,3; Judges 13:4,5,7,14; I Samuel 1:15; Jeremiah 35:6–8; Daniel 1:8; Luke 1:15; 7:33*). As for the believer, I said, the Bible strongly exhorts the believer to remain sober and not be deceived by wine (*Proverbs 20:1; Luke 21:34; Ephesians 5:18; I Thessalonians 5:6,8; I Timothy 3:2,11; I Peter 1:13; 4:7; 5:8*). The Bible teaches that the believer will suffer the many consequences of excessive drinking if he or she chooses to ignore the teachings of the Bible about alcohol. The Bible teaches that a drunkard will not inherit of the Kingdom of heaven (*I Corinthians 6:9; Galatians 5:21*). I told my friend that this is how the God of the Bible works; the God of the Bible wants men and women to think freely, to do things that are good for them and that are in accordance with the will of God, because they love God, who loved them first. I said the God of the Bible created men and women not to enslave them, but to have them join in fellowship with Him (*Genesis 3:8–9; I Corinthians 3:9; Ephesians 3:9; Philippians 1:5; I John 1:3,6,7*).

My friend said his religion has only one holy book, which has been unaltered since it was first written, which proves that his holy book is the word of God. He said that the Bible, on the other hand, has been altered so many times that it cannot be the word of God. I proposed that I explain to him another time why there are many translations and versions of the Bible. When we met a few days later he eagerly listened to me explain why the Bible is the word of God, hoping I would fumble. I told him the Bible teaches that God said the gospel would be preached throughout the world, in all nations, before the end of time (*Psalms 19:4; 98:3; Matthew 4:23,24; 9:35; 11:1,5; 24:14; 26:13; 28:18; Mark 1:32–39; 6:6,56; 13:10; 14:9; 16:15; Luke 4:43,44; 13:22; Romans 1:8; 10:18; 15:19–21; 16:25,26; II Corinthians 10:14,16 Colossians 1:6,23; Revelation 14:6*). God wished to give all humankind the opportunity to hear His word and wished that all would accept it and be saved (*Lamentations 3:33; Ezekiel 18:23, 32; 33:11; Hosea 11:8; Romans 11:26; I Corinthians 9:19,22; 10:33; I Timothy 2:4; II Peter 3:9; Revelation 2:21*). However, God knew that some would hear His word and accept it while others would hear His word and reject it (*Matthew 10:40; Mark 16:16; John 1:12; Acts 2:38; 16:33; Romans 8:14; Ephesians 1:13; Colossians 2:6; I Thessalonians 2:13*) (*Job 21:14; Psalms 10:4; 119:155; Proverbs 1:7; Isaiah 6:10; John 3:18; 12:40,47; Romans 3:11; II Corinthians 4:4; Ephesians 6:12; Revelation 20:3*), but no individuals would be able to claim some day that the gospel of Christ has not been preached to them. This is the reason, I said, why the Bible has been translated into many languages. (As of January 1st, 2000, the entire Bible had been made available in 371 languages and dialects, and portions of it in 1,862 other languages and dialects.[3])

I told my friend I would give him an illustration to explain why there are many versions of the Bible. I produced an American $20 bill and asked him if he recognized it. He said of course. I asked him if he was aware that other countries besides the United States name their currency the dollar. He answered of course and mentioned the Canadian dollar. I said that other countries, including Liberia, Australia and New Zealand, also call their currency the dollar. I said the dollars of all these countries are legal, but not at par with the US dollar. I said it is the same with the Bible. I said that if one compares several versions of the Bible word for word one will find some slight differences because of the difficulty of translating the original manuscripts into the languages we speak today. Nonetheless, these versions of the Bible still reflect the word of God. Then I asked him if he had heard of counterfeit US bills. He said he had heard of them, but had never seen one. I said that when you have something as valuable as the US dollar, it is only natural that thieves will want to forge it and profit from it. It is the same thing with the Bible, I said. When you have something as valuable as the Bible, which has sold billions of copies, it is only natural that there will be people who want to publish their own Bible for the purpose of making money. (In 1934 it was estimated that two billion Scriptures had been published since the invention of printing.[4]) God foretold that false prophets would change His word and deceive many (*Deuteronomy 4:2; Proverbs 30:6; Jeremiah 8:8; 29:8; Matthew 15:6; 24:4, 5,11, 23–25; Mark 7:9, 13; 13:5,6,21–23; Luke 21:8; Acts 20:30; I Corinthians 15:33; II Corinthians 11:3,13–15; Galatians 3:15; Ephesians 5:6; Colossians 2:4,8,18; II Thessalonians 2:3,9–11;II Timothy 3:13; Titus 1:10,11; I John 2:18; 4:1; II John 1:7; Revelation 12:9; 22:18–19*).

After I finished answering my friend's question about the existence of more than one version of the Bible, I offered to give him a Bible. He said he would accept the Bible only if I agreed to watch a videotaped lecture by a Muslim scholar. He said the scholar talks about which version of the Bible is good. He said he would accept my Bible and read it if it was the same Bible that the scholar refers to in his lecture. My friend brought me the videotape. In the lecture, presented at the University of Louisiana, the South African Muslim scholar Ahmed Didat compares Islam and Christianity. Mr. Didat talks about racism, pornography, homosexuality, fornication, alcoholism, child abuse and the increased number of single women in the United States, all of which he attributes to Christianity. He proposes that the number of single women be decreased by allowing polygamy. He also discusses what he calls the "J syndrome" in the West. He says words in the Bible with Aramaic origin such as Yoshua and Yahweh have been changed in the Bible to words such as Joshua and Jehovah. Dr. Didat suggests that the word "Comforter" as found in the Bible refers to Mohamed, the prophet of Islam. I watched the two-hour tape and gave it back to my friend.

He asked me if I enjoyed watching the tape. I said yes and did not expand for I was not in the mood to argue. He asked me again if I liked Mr. Didat's lecture. I answered yes again without commenting. He pressed me again and again to comment on the tape. Finally I told him that Mr. Didat was very knowledgeable about the Bible and also seemed to know Hebrew and Greek, the languages in which some of the early manuscripts of the

Bible were written. I said, however, that Mr. Didat was able to come to the West and openly discuss and even criticize the Bible because of the tolerance brought about by the Bible. I said I doubted that a Christian scholar would be able to openly criticize the Koran in Muslim countries, which Mr. Didat said he visited before coming to the United States. Regarding the social problems (racism, discrimination, child abuse, homosexuality, fornication, alcoholism, pornography, prostitution) Mr. Didat discusses, I said, these are not exclusive to the United States, but exist to varying degrees all over the world; these practices are widely condemned in the Bible and are not products of Christianity, but the result of humankind's disregard of God's word (*Genesis 19:5; 35:22; 38:18,19,26; 49:4; Exodus 22:19; Leviticus 18:1–30; 20:11–23; Deuteronomy 4:1,2,40; 12:31,32; 18:9–12; 20:18; 22:30; 23:18; 25:16; 27:15,20,22,23; Judges 19:22; II Samuel 13:11–14; 16:21,22; I Kings 14:24; II Kings 16:3; 21:2; Psalms 7:4; 35:13,14; 105:44,45; Proverbs 19:17; 22:9; 25:21,22; 26:24–26; Jeremiah 44:4; Ezekiel 22:10,11; Amos 2:7; Malachi 3:5; Matthew 5:27; 15:18–20; Mark 7:10–23; Luke 6:27,28,34,35; 8:15; 11:28; 23:34; John 14:15,21–23; 15:14; Acts 7:60; 15:20; Romans 1:26,27; 2:22; 12:14,20,21; I Corinthians 3:17; 4:12,13; 5:1; 6:9; 13:4–8; Galatians 3:26–28; 5:19; Ephesians 5:8; Colossians 3:21; I Timothy 1:10; Hebrews 13:4; I Peter 2:23; 3:9; I John 2:9,11; 3:10–15; 4:7–11; Jude 1:7*).

Finally, I told my friend that Mr. Didat seems to be quoting from the KJV (King James Bible), the Bible I used. I said that other than complaining about the letter "Y" in the Aramaic language being changed to the letter "J" in the KJV, he does not say anything about the KJV being corrupt. I asked my friend if he would take my Bible as per our agreement, since I had watched the videotape. He accepted my Bible and said he would read it.

The next time I met my friend he was not satisfied with my earlier comments about Mr. Didat's lecture. He wanted to know if Mr. Didat had convinced me to change my faith. I told him that Mr. Didat had not, for the simple reason that the apostle Paul said "**But though we, or an angel from heaven, preach any other gospel unto you than that which we have preached unto you, let him be accursed. As we said before, so say I now again, If any** *man* **preach any other gospel unto you than that ye have received, let him be accursed**" (*Galatians 1:8–9*). I said that Jesus, the Apostles and Paul preached that all humankind have sinned and come short of the glory of God (*Romans 3:23*). They preached that salvation is a gift from God through faith in Jesus Christ alone (*Ephesians 2:8–10*) and can be attained only by believing in the death and resurrection of Jesus Christ for our sins, and not by obeying the Law, doing good deeds, belonging to a particular church, being baptized, offering sacrifices, receiving a sacrament or performing many of the other rituals that humankind continues to do in vain (*Romans 1:16; 3:24–26; 4:24,25; 6:4–6; 8:3,4; 14:9; Galatians 1:1,4; 2:20; 3:13; 6:14; Ephesians 5:2; Colossians 2:11–14; I Peter 1:18–21; 3:18; Revelation 1:5,18; 2:8), (Deuteronomy 11:26–28; 27:26; Psalms 119:126,139; Jeremiah 8:8; 11:3; Hosea 4:6; Malachi 1:10; 2:7–9; Matthew 15:3,6; Mark 7: 8,9,13; Luke 18:9–13; Romans 3:19,20,31; 4:15; 7:9–13; 8:7; Galatians 2:16; 3:10; Hebrews 10:4,6,8*). They preached that once we are freed from sin by the blood of Jesus, we are adopted into the family of God and can call God our father (*Galatians 4:2–7*). I said that the Apostles and Paul preached that once we are saved we should live a holy life because Christ has freed us from sin (*Galatians 5:1–26*). I told my friend that this is the gospel that Jesus, the Apostles and Paul preached and Mr. Didat had not convinced because he was preaching a different gospel.

I asked my friend if he had started reading the Bible I gave him. He replied that he did not need to read the Bible because it was old and elementary. I said that sometimes it is necessary to read the old in order to comprehend the new. Besides, I said, the Koran teaches that the Law of Moses and the Gospel of Jesus are "a guide to mankind" and "criterion of judgement between right and wrong" (*Sura 3:3*). It was in his interest, I said, to know the criterion by which God would judge him. I asked him about our agreement: that he would read my Bible if I watched his videotape. He said it was never his intention to read the Bible; it was just a ploy to get me to watch the videotape and maybe convert to his religion.

In the end my friend and I agreed that he had failed to convert me to his religion and I had failed to win him over to Christ. We agreed to disagree on the way to salvation. We agreed to remain on good terms and talk about other matters. We agreed that we were fortunate to live in Canada, a country where we could openly talk about each other's faith and freely practise our faith. He said he would pray for me. I said I would do likewise for him.

The next person I invited to church and told about Jesus was a friend of the Sikh faith. He said I was arrogant to think and say there was only one way to God. After some discussion he agreed with me that more than likely there is only one God who created the complex, harmonious universe and all humankind on earth. He agreed that it was not rational to have ten thousand diametrically opposed ways to worship that one God. I said that therefore it was important for us, indeed for all humankind, to find the true way to worship the one God. I said that when it comes to the God of the Bible, the Bible teaches that "he is a jealous God" and does not tolerate his children worshipping or glorifying false gods (*Exodus 20:5; 23:24; 34:14; Deuteronomy 4:24; 5:7,9; 6:4,15; 32:21; Joshua 23:7; 24:20; Psalms 81:9; Jeremiah 25:6; 35:15; I Corinthians 10:22*).

I said that the God of the Bible is very precise about how His followers should worship him (*Leviticus 9:24; 10:1–3; 16:1; Numbers 3:3,4; 4:15,19,20; 16:32,33,49; 26:61; Deuteronomy 4:1,2; 12:32; 17:11,20; 28:14; Joshua 1:7; 23:6; I Samuel 6:19; II Samuel 6:7; I Kings 18:21; II Kings 1:10,12; I Chronicles 13:10; 15:2,13; 24:2; Psalms 125:5; Proverbs 4:27; Matthew 6:24; Acts 5:4,10; Romans 6:16–22; I Corinthians 10:21,22; II Corinthians 6:14–16; Revelation 3:15,16*). My friend asked why I was certain that the God of the Bible was the true God. I asked him if he did right all of the time. He said he tried to do right most of the time. I reminded him that I had not asked if he *tried* to do right, but if he *had* done right *all of the time*. He answered that he had not. I said he had answered correctly for it is impossible to do right all of the time. I said that, with one exception, all the religions of the world teach that humankind is good by nature and a person who tries to be good will go to heaven when he dies. The Bible is the only holy book, I said, to say that humankind drinks iniquity like water and the imagination of the human heart is evil from youth (*Genesis 6:5; 8:21; 13:13; 18:20,21; Deuteronomy 29:19; Job 4:19; 14:4; 15:14–16; 42:6; Psalms 14:1–4; 51:5; 53:2,3; 58:3; Proverbs 6:18; 20:9; Ecclesiastes 7:20,29; 9:3; Isaiah 47:12,15; 48:8; 53:6 Jeremiah 8:6; 17:9; 18:12; Matthew 15:19; John 3:6; Romans 1:28–30; 3:9–19; Titus 3:3*). I told my friend that the Bible is the only holy book to say that one can never attain salvation by virtue of one's good deeds. I said that Jesus, Who was sinless, bore the sins of all humankind so that we could become righteous in the eyes of God. In the end my friend said that everything I told him made sense. He said that a Christian colleague of his had already told him everything I said about Jesus and salvation. He said that unfortunately his religion, the Sikh religion, was part of his culture.

I told my friend I was not asking him to change his culture (although I would argue that the world tends to be of one culture, the culture of money, image and instant gratification), but showing him the way to salvation and eternal life. I told him that although God commands us to love our father, mother, wife and children, He commands us to love Him first (*Exodus 20:12; 21:15,17; Leviticus 19:3; Deuteronomy 6:5; I Samuel 20:30–34; Proverbs 1:8,9; 15:5; 20:20; 22:6; 23:25; 28:24; 30:17; Matthew 15:4–6; 22:37; Mark 12:30,33; Luke 10:27; 18:20; Ephesians 5:21,22–29; 6:4; Colossians 3:19–21*). I told him that Jesus Christ said, "**He that love father or mother more than me is not worthy of me: and he that loveth son or daughter more than me is not worthy of me. And he that taketh not his cross, and followeth after me, is not worthy of me**" (*Matthew 10:37–38; Luke 14:26*). My friend thought for a while about what I had said and I sensed he was torn between his culture and the way to salvation. He chose his culture.

I could not be accused of being a chauvinist for witnessing only to male family members and friends for I also witnessed to many female family members and friends. But only one was receptive to hearing about Jesus. I told this friend about Jesus and salvation. This friend said, "In any event we are all children of God." I said, "This was not the case." I said "The Bible teaches that God made humankind in His image, but sin entered into the world when Adam sinned and death was passed upon all humankind, for we all have sinned" (*Genesis 2:17; 3:19, 22-24; Romans 5:12; I Corinthians 15:21*). I said, "The Bible teaches that the moment sin entered into the world, it separated us from God because He hates sin and we became the children of disobedience, of wrath and of the devil" (*Genesis 3:23,24; Deuteronomy 32:19; Psalms 104:29; Proverbs 15:29; Isaiah 50:1; 59:2; Jeremiah 5:25), (Ephesians 2:2,3; 5:6; Colossians 3:6; II Peter 2:14; I John 3:10*). I said, "On the other hand, the Bible teaches that any person who accepts Jesus Christ as their Saviour receives the spirit of adoption, becomes the children of God by faith and could again call God their father" (*Luke 11:2; Romans 8:15,16;*

I Corinthians 2:12; Galatians 3:26; 4:5,6,7; Ephesians 1:5).

This friend told me she had already accepted Jesus Christ as her Saviour. Then, I invited the sister to the church. She said she did not need to attend church and could pray by herself to God at her house. I told the sister that the Bible teaches that once we accept Jesus as our Saviour we are not anymore ours but have been redeemed, bought with a price, by the blood of Jesus. Therefore, we belong to God (*Luke 1:68; I Corinthians 6:20; 7:23; Galatians 3:13; I Peter 1:18*). I said, "The Bible teaches that once we accept Jesus as our Saviour, the spirit of God dwells in us, our body is the temple of God and we could no longer do anything we desire" (*I Corinthians 3:16,17; II Corinthians 6:16; Ephesians 2:13; Hebrews 10:19; 13:12; I John 1:7; Revelation 1:5; 3:12*). I said, "Although the Bible exhorts the believer to constantly pray alone everywhere, including home, the Bible also commends the believer to meet regularly with other believers to worship God" (*Matthew 14:23; 26:36; Mark 1:35; 6:46; Luke 3:21; 5:16; 6:12; 23:46; John 6:15) (I Samuel 12:23; Luke 18:1; 21:36; Romans 12:12; Ephesians 6:18; Colossians 4:2; I Thessalonians 5:17; I Peter 4:7*).

I said, "Besides, a church is not a building, but the whole body of the redeemed, believers, who meet to worship God" (*Psalms 89:7; 111:1; Matthew 16:18; 18:20; Acts 13:1; 20:28; Romans 16:5; I Corinthians 1:2; 15:9; Galatians 1:13; Ephesians 1:22; 5:23,25,27,29,32; Colossians 1:24; I Timothy 3:5; Philemon 1:2; Hebrews 12:23*). I said, "The Bible teaches that every believer is an essential member to the proper functioning of the church, just as an eye, a hand, and a foot are essential members of the body" (*Romans 12:4,5; I Corinthians 10:17; 12:12-27; Ephesians 1:23; 2:16; 4:4,12; 5:23,30; Colossians 1:18,24; 3:15; Hebrews 13:3*). Finally, I told the sister that the Bible teaches we grieve the spirit of God in us and we show our ingratitude toward Jesus Christ who died for us when we neglect to read our Bible, witness to the unsaved and meet with others believers to worship God (*Acts 7:51; Ephesians 4:30; I Thessalonians 5:19; Hebrews 3:10*). I said, The Bible teaches that the Holy Spirit withdraws from the believer, does not make intercession for the believer and God does not answer the prayers of the believer if he or she grieves the spirit of God by failing do to what God commands us to do" (*Job 27:8,9; 35:12; 42:8; Psalms 18:41 34:15; 66:18-20; Proverbs 1:28,29; 15:29; 21:13; 28:9; Isaiah 1:15; 58:9; Jeremiah 11:11;*

14:12; Ezekiel 8:18; Micah 3:4; Zechariah 7:13; John 9:31; Hebrews 10:7; James 5:15,16; I Peter 3:12; Revelation 2:15; 3:16). The sister told me she would find a church in her neighbourhood to attend.

One of the last friends I invited to church and talked to about Jesus was a colleague who had been raised in a Roman Catholic environment. The friend told me that he was an atheist. I told him the Bible teaches that one day God will judge all, including atheists, and whoever had not accepted Jesus as his Saviour while on earth will end up first in hell and then in a lake of fire (*Psalms 9:7,8; 28:4; 50:3–6; 62:12; 96:13; 98:9; Proverbs 24:12,29; Ecclesiastes 11:9; 12:14; Jeremiah 17:10; 32:19; Daniel 7:10; Matthew 11:27; 16:25–27; 25:31–46; 28:18; John 3:35; 5:22–29; 17:2; Acts 10:42; 17:31; Romans 2:1–16; 14:9–12; I Corinthians 4:5; II Corinthians 5:10; II Thessalonians 1:7–10; II Timothy 4:1,8; I Peter 4:5; Revelation 1:7; 2:23; 12:12,13; 20:11–15; 22:12) (Job 3:5; 10:22; 11:8; 24:19; 34:22; 38:17; Psalms 9:17; 11:6; 16:10; 21:9; 31:17; 49:15; 86:13; 139; 8; Proverbs 5:5; 7:26, 27; 9:18; 15:24; 21:6; 30:15,16 Isaiah 14:9,15; 33:14; 38:10; Jeremiah 13:16; Ezekiel 31:15–17; Daniel 3:6,15–17; Amos 9:2,3; Matthew 3:12; 5:22,29; 8:12; 11:23; 13:41–42; 18:8, 9; 22:13; 23:33; 25:30,31,41; Mark 9:43–49; Luke 10:15; 16:23,24; I Corinthians 15:55; Ephesians 2:1; II Thessalonians 1:8,9; II Peter 2:4,17; Jude 1:6,13; Revelation 1:18; 14:10; 19:20; 20:10,13,14,15; 21:8*).

My friend said he would end up in heaven, if there were a heaven, because patients of his who were nuns told him they would pray for him. I said his patients had told him the truth if they said they would pray for him to be saved (*Isaiah 45:22; Ezekiel 18:23,32; Luke 14:23; Acts 2:47; I Corinthians 10:32–33; I Timothy 2:1–4*), but had misled him if they told him they would pray for him to go to heaven, for the Bible teaches no such thing.

Even though my friend did not believe in God and Christ, he cursed the name of Jesus Christ at least once every five sentences. I told him the Bible teaches that we should not use the name of God in vain and especially not curse the name of God (*Matthew 5:33–37; 23:16–22; James 5:12*). He said he was not swearing, but using slang, as many people do. I said that, whatever the reason, I would prefer he did not use the name of Christ in vain in my company (I find it curious that people who say they do not believe in God swear using the name of Jesus instead of using the name of a more spectacular and colourful person like Alexander the Great, Napoleon or Hitler). My friend promised not to swear and especially not to use the name of God in vain in my presence. He kept his promise for one week and then went back to swearing using the name of Jesus Christ. I continued to remind him now and then that he was not to use the name of God in vain. He continued to tell me he was an atheist.

Then, one evening, my friend phoned me. To my great astonishment and joy he started talking about Christ. He said he resented having to confess to a priest when he was young. My friend said that he and his parents never rejected Christ, but they rejected organized religion. I told him that when the Bible says, **"Confess *your* faults one to another, and pray one for another, that ye may be healed"** (*James 5:16*) it does not mean for us to confess our faults to a priest, but is referring to reciprocal confession, or the mutual forgiveness of offences (*Matthew 18:15–17*). With regard to being saved, as in achieving eternal life, I explained to my friend, the Bible says,

> **"That if thou shalt confess with thy mouth the Lord Jesus, and shalt believe in thine heart that God hath raised him from the dead, thou shalt be saved"** (Romans 10:9).

He said he understood what I was saying and that was why he resented having to confess to a priest.

I told my friend the Bible teaches that whosoever is angry with another person without cause has sinned (*Matthew 5:22*) and that a man has sinned if he looks at a woman with lust (*Matthew 5:28*). I reminded my friend of the days when, as young doctors, we would glance at the derriere of nurses who wore transparent uniforms. My friend laughed. According to the Bible, I said, he and I were big sinners. He laughed again. I told him that if our righteous deeds were to be weighed against the sins we had committed the scale would tilt on the sin side and break. My friend agreed with me. I told him that, according to the Bible, he and I did not stand a chance of attaining eternal life. I explained that Jesus took away the sins of all humankind and now God sees as righteous whoever accepts Jesus as his personal Saviour and bestows eternal life on that person.

My friend said everything I told him about Jesus and salvation made sense. It was not only a matter of understanding, I said, but also a matter of accepting Jesus Christ as one's personal Saviour. He said he accepted Jesus as his personal Saviour. I asked him if he acknowledged that he was a sinner, repented, understood that Jesus Christ died for his sins and accepted Jesus as his personal Saviour. My friend said yes. I could not believe what I was hearing. I put the question to him again, and he answered with a definite yes. I asked him a third time and he said, "Yes, I am a sinner. I understand that Jesus died for us and I accept Jesus as my personal Saviour." I was overwhelmed with a sense of joy. I was happy for my friend and understood that all the credit for his salvation belonged to God. I said that according to the Bible he had been saved if he genuinely meant what he had just told me. "This is it?" he asked. "Yes," I said. The best thing about salvation, I explained, is not the fact that it is as simple as saying yes, not the fact that it is a gift from God and not something we deserve (*Romans 3:24,27; 4:16; 5:15,17; 6:23; 11:6; I Corinthians 15:10; II Corinthians 9:15; Galatians 2:21; Ephesians 2:4–9; Philippians 3:9; II Timothy 1:9; Titus 3:5; I John 4:9,10; 5:11*), but the fact that God assures of eternal life the moment we accept Jesus as our personal Saviour (*John 3:36; 5:24; 6:47; 10:28; Romans 4:7,8,11; II Corinthians 1:22; 5:19; Ephesians 1:13,14; 4:30; II Timothy 2:19; I John 3:14,15; 5:10–13; Revelation 2:17; 7:2; 9:4*).

I asked my friend and brother in Christ to come to church with me now that he was saved. He asked me why. In order to show his gratitude to God for sending His Son, Jesus Christ, to die for his sins, I replied, and also to learn from the Bible about God and about how best to worship, serve and please God. He said, "Oh no, not me. It's one thing to accept Jesus, but quite another to be out there and vocal." He said he did not want to be eccentric like some Christians he saw. I said the Bible exhorts Christians to be humble, but to love God with all their hearts, souls and minds (*Numbers 12:3; Psalms 22:26; 25:9; 69:32; 131:1; 147:6; 149:4; Isaiah 11:4; 29:19; 42:1–4; 61:1; Zephaniah 2:3; Zechariah 9:9; Matthew 5:5; 11:29; 12:19,20; 21:5 Galatians 5:23; Ephesians 4:2, 22; Colossians 3:12; Philippians 2:3; I Timothy 6:11; II Timothy 2:25; Titus 3:2; James 1:21; 3:13; I Peter 3:4,15*).

My friend and brother in Christ said he thought I had told him earlier that he had been assured of eternal life once he accepted Jesus Christ as his personal Saviour. I said he was correct and I had not changed my mind.

He then asked why he had to attend church. I said the Bible teaches that in heaven God has reserved a most excellent reward for the believers who served him, preached the gospel and remained faithful to the end (*Genesis 15:1; Ruth 2:12; Psalms 62:12; Proverbs 11:18; 19:17; Ecclesiastes 11:1,6; Daniel 12:3; Matthew 5: 46; 6:1,2,5; 10:41,42; 16:27; Luke 6:35,38; 14:14; 19:16–26; John 4:36–38; Romans 2:6,7; 4:4,5; I Corinthians 3:8,11–15; 4:5 9:17,18; 15:58; II Corinthians 9:6–12; Galatians 6:7–9; Ephesians 6:8; Colossians 2:18; 3:23–25; Hebrews 6:10; 10:35; 11:6; I Peter 5:4; II John 1:8; Revelation 2:23; 22:12*). I told him that the Bible teaches that in heaven the faithful believer will receive a crown of glory and reign with Christ (*Psalms 49:14; Proverbs 4:9; Daniel 7:22,25–27; Matthew 19:28; Luke 22:29,30; I Corinthians 6:2–4; 9:25; II Timothy 2:5; 4:8; James 1:12; I Peter 1:4; 5:4; Revelation 2:10,26,27; 3:11,21; 4:4,10; 5:10; 20:6; 22:5*). My friend and brother in Christ said he was not interested in a crown.

At this stage my friend and brother in Christ and I had been on the phone for more than ninety minutes. This was a friend who usually did not talk on the phone for more than three minutes. After he said he was not interested in a crown, I explained that the Bible teaches that in heaven God has treasures that are inestimable and beyond humankind's comprehension for those who love Him (*Psalms 31:9; Isaiah 64:4; Matthew 19:21; 25:34; Luke 12:33; John 14:3; I Corinthians 2:9,10; Hebrews 11:16; I John 3:2; Revelation 21:1–4,22–24; 22:1–5*). I said I did not want to miss out on the treasures and the chance to have communion with the Lord. My friend seemed to have a change of heart. He asked me which church I attended. I told him I attended a Baptist Church. My friend, a Canadian of European extraction, was shocked. He said he thought Baptists were white suprema-cists. I said that was not the case. Many Baptists were loving Christians, I said, and there were Baptist churches even in Africa. My friend said he had been under the impression that Baptists were intolerant people. I said this was not the case although in my short life as a Christian I had come across a few Baptists whose views on the diversity of humankind were very odd.

Two years after I had been saved I heard two Christian brothers, in a Baptist church I was attending, discuss some books one of them had just bought. They spoke highly of the books. I thought (mistakenly) I had read too much of the Bible and needed to read other books about God, so I asked one of the brothers to order the books for me. When I received the books I start flipping through them. Instead of learning about God, I learned about the author's negative views of the United Nations Educational, Scientific and Cultural Organization, the Peace Corps, the National Association for the Advancement of Colored People, the American Civil Liberties Union and the Equal Rights Amendment.[5] The author, a preacher and Bible scholar, wrote: "What this amounts to is the evolutionary theory that man (by his own effort through education), can bring in a perfect peace on earth by levelling all distinctions. This is done by making men like women, making women like men, making white people like black people, by taking money from the rich and giving to the poor, by making Occidentals Orientals, by making Catholics Protestants and Protestants Catholics, and, in the end, you wind up making God like the devil and the devil like God."[6] Then he resorts to name calling: "Now the way the Pentecostal Charismatic heresy gets so screwed up on the Bible is by simply refusing to finish the sentence."[7]

It was a shock for me to look through the books of this preacher because I had been under the impression that Christians who read such a perfect book as the Bible tried to emulate and be as loving as Jesus Christ (*Psalms 19:7–10; 119:96–105; Romans 7:12; James 1:25*) (*Genesis 6:9; 17:1; Leviticus 11:44; 19:2; 20:26; Deuteronomy 18:13; II Chronicles 19:9; Job 1:1,8; 17:9; Psalms 37:37; 72:17–19; Proverbs 4:18; 8:13; 16:6; Matthew 5:16,45,48; 18:3; Luke 6:36,40; John 17:23; Acts 9:31; 23:1; 24:16; I Corinthians 2:6; 14:20; II Corinthians 7:1; 13:9,11; Ephesians 4:12,13; 5:1,2; Philippians 1:9,10; 3:12–15; Colossians 1:28; 4:12; I Thessalonians 3:12,13; 4:1,7,9,10; 5:23; II Thessalonians 1:3; Hebrews 12:23,28; James 1:4; I Peter 1:15,16,22; 5:10; Revelation 3:2*). I was also under the impression that the Bible does not teach Christians to insult others and alienate God, but tells them to **"live peaceably with all men"** (*Nehemiah 9:17; Psalms 15:3; 50:20; 101:5; Proverbs 10:18,19; 13:3; 14:17,29; 15:2,18; 16:32; 17:14,27; 18:13,21; 19:11,19; 21:23; 25:28; Ecclesiastes 5:2,3; 7:8,9; 10:12; Matthew 5:22; 12:36; Luke 4:22; Romans 14:19; I Corinthians 15:33; II Corinthians 13:11; Galatians 5:20,21; Ephesians 4:3,26,29–31; Colossians 3:8,15; 4:6; I Thessalonians 15:13; Hebrews 12:14; James 1:19,20; 3:1,2*) (*Romans 12:18; Colossians 3:15*).

The Bible also teaches the believer to help and not despise the poor (*Leviticus 25:35; Deuteronomy 15:11,17; Job 29:16; 30:25; 31:16; Proverbs 22:16; Matthew 25:35–45 26:11; Mark 14:7; Luke 19:8; John 12:8; Romans 15:26; James 2:6*). It commands Christians to preach the gospel to all humankind without distinction as to nation or class so that everyone will be saved (*Isaiah 45:22; 49:6; 52:10; 60:1–3; Mark 16:15; Acts 1:8; Romans 10:18; 16:26; Colossians 1:23; Revelation 14:6*). Jesus underscored this point when he said "**They that are whole have no need of the physician, but they that are sick: I came not to call the righteous, but sinners to repentance**" (*Matthew 9:12; Mark 2:17; Luke 5:31*). While it is true that Jesus rebuked the religious leaders of His day for pretending to be righteous and religious while stealing and misleading the people, He did not insult the people to whom God had sent him to preach (*Matthew 12:33–37; 23:4–38; Mark 12:38–40; Luke 11:37–51; 20:46–47*).

The Bible exhorts the believer not to speak or judge others without due consideration. Since the Bible also teaches that we are to respect men of God (*Genesis 21:9; II King 2:23–24; II Chronicles 36:16; Job 19:8; 30:1,8,9; Psalms 35:15; Isaiah 57:3,4; Galatians 4:29*), I thought I should look at other writings by the preacher in order to understand him better and not misjudge him.

In another of his books I learned about his negative opinions of Janet Reno, Albert Einstein, Bertrand Russell, Nelson Mandela, Bob Jones III, Michael Jordan, blacks, homosexuals, "females," Catholics, "Democratic Presidents – Lincoln, FDR, JFK, Clinton," "Catholic countries of Europe," "Catholic dictatorships in South America," "Italian American Roman Catholics," Muslims, Hispanics, Buddhists, the PLO and *The Color Purple*.[8] Perhaps what bothered me the most about the preacher's writings was that they were mostly random, opinionated and unsubstantiated. After expounding negatively about almost everybody and everything, he writes: "I am a Bible-believing, white, straight adult, male Protestant. As an ordained Southern Baptist minister, I pastor a local, Bible-believing Baptist Church. I hold five earned degrees, I am not a 'UFO buff.' I am neither a chemist, a physicist, nor a scientist, and I certainly was never a biologist or a geneticist."[9]

The preacher forgot to say he was a sinner like everyone else. His attitude reminded me of the parable of the publican (tax collector) who went to pray at the temple. Jesus said: "**The Pharisee stood and prayed thus with himself, God, I thank thee, that I am not as other men** *are*, **extortioners, unjust, adulterers, or even as this publican. I fast twice in the week, I give tithes of all that I possess. And the publican, standing afar off, would not lift up so much as** *his* **eyes unto heaven, but smote upon his breast, saying, God be merciful to me a sinner. I tell you, this man went down to his house justified** *rather* **than the other: for every one that exalteth himself shall be abased; and he that humbleth himself shall be exalted**" (*Luke 18:9–14*).

The Southern Baptist minister failed to remember that the apostle Paul exhorts believers not to be "**puffed up, one against another**," for everything good and perfect we have is a gift of God by his grace and not something we deserve (*I Corinthians 4:6,7, 18,19; 8:1; 12:7–9*).

In boasting about himself, the preacher forgot that the Bible teaches the believer to glory not in himself, but in God (*I Chronicles 16:10,35; Psalms 49:6; 105:3; Isaiah 10:15; 41:16; 45:25; Jeremiah 9:23,24; Romans 3:19,27; 4:2; 15:17; I Corinthians 1:12–17, 29,31; 3:4–7; 4:6,7; 5:6; 10:31; II Corinthians 10:17; Galatians 6:13,14; Philippians 3:3*) and teaches that if we have to boast at all, we should boast in our afflictions and sufferings for Christ, for otherwise we are as fools (*II Corinthians 11:30–12:6*).

The Southern Baptist minister concludes his book with a list of events that he believes have contributed to the demise of the United States as a nation. At the top of the list is the institution of the women's vote in 1920. Second is the abolition of slavery. I searched through the Bible to see if he was right, to see what the Bible lists as the causes of a nation's demise, assuming that nation is a Godly one. The Bible teaches that the demise of the Godly nation of Israel began when the people rejected God as their leader, preferring to be ruled by humankind (*Exodus 16:8; Deuteronomy 17:14–20; I Samuel 8:4–9; 10:19; 12:17–19; I Kings 10:21; 11:1–4; 15:5*), when kings started to rule Israel and not when prophets such as Deborah judged Israel (*Judges 4:1–5:31*), when Israel started to worship other gods instead of worshipping God (*Exodus 32:4; I Kings 12:28; 18:21; II Kings 17:16; Hosea 8:4–7*), and when Israel chose to reject God's commandments and live by man-made laws (*Deuteronomy 17:18–20; 29:24–28; I Kings*

14:8–16; Psalms 52:5; 81:12; Isaiah 40:24; Hosea 9:11,12,16,17).

After I finished looking through the pastor's books, I had a pretty good idea of who I was dealing with. Now, I wanted to know why the two Christian brothers had spoken so highly of him. I asked one of the brothers if I had misunderstood the preacher. He said the preacher's books were a collection of his messages. He tried to explain to me that the preacher provoked people in the hope that they would learn about God. Then the brother, who was white, said he agreed with the preacher on many points. He said, for example, that people of different origins should not mix. He said that God separated humankind at Babel because He did not want people to mix and that we should remain separated.

I said that God separated Noah's descendants and confounded their language because they decided to stay together and, in effect, disobey God's earlier commandment that they "**multiply and replenish the earth**" (*Genesis 1:28; 9:1*), because they built a monument to their achievement instead of honouring God (*Genesis 11:1–9*), because they challenged the supremacy of God when they said, "**let us build a city and a tower whose top may reach unto heaven**" (*Genesis 11:4*), and because of their presumptuous declarations when they said, "**let us make us a name**" (*Genesis 11:4*) (I would not be surprised if God made humankind of different complexions and features at the same time he confounded their language because He knew that humankind are so vile and prejudiced that they would not work together any more).

I told the Christian brother that the Bible teaches that God made all humankind of one blood (*Genesis 1:26,27; 3:20; Malachi 2:10; Acts 17:26; Romans 5:18; I Corinthians 15:22*), something that took humankind thousands of years, and billions of dollars spent on genome science, to discover.

I told him that the Bible teaches that once we are saved we are all the children of God (*Matthew 5:9; Romans 8:15; Galatians 3:23–29; 4:3–7; I John 4:4*). The Christian Brother said that spiritually, Christians might be brothers and sisters, but physically they should remain separate. I asked him what criterion he would use to separate the people. Without hesitation, he said race. I told him that when the Bible speaks about the diversities of humankind it uses the word "nation", not race. He argued that the Bible refers to people by their race. I said that the King James Bible uses the word "race" when it speaks about people running a race and uses the word "nation" when it speaks about diversity. In the King James Bible, I said, God spoke of Jacob (Israel) and Esau, two twin brothers, as "two nations, and two manners of people" (*Genesis 25:23*). I told the Christian brother that the NIV, NASB, Living Bible and other Newer Bible Versions mistranslated Greek and Hebrew words such as "seed," "brethren" and "generation" in the original manuscripts as the word "race," as in the colour of one's skin.[10] I felt that the Christian brother, who was usually fond of the King James Bible, would have liked to discard that Bible and quote from the newer versions that were more in tune with his race-segregation theory. At this stage I put an end to the conversation .The irony is that when this brother was ill he proudly told any colleague of mine whom he met that he knew me. Of course, I assisted him as much as I could when he asked for my help.

Still curious as to how a Christian preacher could publish such hate literature, I asked another Christian brother, a former student of the Southern Baptist minister, what he thought of the books. This brother, a white assistant pastor, said his former professor was right in suggesting that people of different colours should not interact because studies have shown that African-American children learn better in an environment separate from white American children. I asked him if the researchers had given any explanation for their findings. He said he did not remember. I asked him if the findings were that African-American children learn better in environments that are welcoming and conducive to learning. He said he did remember the details of the studies and suggested I speak with the pastor of our church, who was also a former student of the Southern Baptist minister and who was more knowledgeable about the studies. I said, "I think I have got the picture, but I have one last question for you." I asked him if African-American children learn better in an environment composed exclusively of African-American children, as the studies suggested, then would I, a Canadian of African extraction, learn better in a church composed exclusively of Canadians of African extraction? The brother blushed and did not answer.

The Bible teaches that we are to forgive others even if they do not ask for our forgiveness (*Luke 23:34; Acts 7:60*). It teaches that if we do not forgive others, God will not forgive us for our sins (*Proverbs 21:13; Matthew 6:12,14–15; 7:2; 18:21–35; Mark 11:25,26; Ephesians 4:32; Colossians*

3:13). Forgiving was one of the things I had never been able to do in the past. However, now that I was a Christian and trying to lead a Christian life, I sincerely forgave and prayed for the two Christian brothers.

A Christian sister, who, like I, felt very uncomfortable in the environment where these two Christians brothers worshipped, told me that sometimes one has to take the good things from people and ignore the bad. She said it is like eating chicken: "One eats the meat and spits out the bones." I said that as a physician I have seen patients who almost died from swallowing chicken bones. That is why I prefer to eat my chicken boneless. The Bible teaches me to forgive others, but the Bible also teaches me not to be around people who do not love me, people who hate others and disobey the commandments of God (*Romans 16:17; II Thessalonians 3:6, 14; I Timothy 6:3–5; II Timothy 3:5; Titus 3:10; II John 1:10*).

I prayed for God to find a church for the children and me where the people not only preached the Bible, but also obeyed the word of God.

A few days after my conversation with the two Christian brothers and before I left the environment where they worshipped, I had a conversation with a Christian sister about the Southern Baptist minister. I asked her where she had been on vacation. She told me she had travelled to Florida to hear the Southern Baptist minister whose books I had skimmed. I asked what topic he had preached on. She said Martin Luther King Jr. She told me she learned from the Southern Baptist minister that Martin Luther King Jr. was a communist and more of a troublemaker than a peacemaker.

I told the sister that I knew only a little about Martin Luther King Jr. and knew more about Nelson Mandela: I said that years ago people said Nelson Mandela was a communist and a troublemaker and now we know he was not a communist and was far from being a troublemaker. I said all Nelson Mandela wanted, and probably all Martin Luther King Jr. wanted, was dignity for his people.

I made the mistake of asking the Christian sister if she agreed with the Southern Baptist minister's message about Martin Luther King Jr. and with his race theory. She said she did not agree with the violent method used by some white supremacist groups, but did agree with the minister's race theory. To prove her point, the sister said that when she was in Florida, the African-American kids were the "rowdiest" people on the beach. I told her

I lived in an environment where the majority of the people were first and second generation Canadians of European extraction and some of them sounded the horn of their car to announce their arrival instead of ringing the doorbell and some of the kids listened to rap and hip hop music, but instead of calling the people rowdy I greeted everybody and witnessed to whomever I had an occasion to witness.

My comment did not change the Christian sister's feelings towards people of African descent. I asked her to give me a biblical reason or reasons to justify her negative feelings towards people of African descent. She said that Ham, the youngest son of Noah, slept with his father. She said that Noah cursed Ham and said he would be the servant of his older brothers, Shem and Japheth. She said that slavery is justified because of this. I told the sister that she had misquoted and misinterpreted the Bible. I said the Bible says, **"Ham, the father of Canaan, saw the nakedness of his father"** (*Genesis 9:22*). I said when Joseph was governor of Egypt he told his brother, who went to get food in Egypt, **"Ye are spies; to see the nakedness of the land ye are come"** (*Genesis 42:9,12*). I said that Joseph did not mean to tell his brother that they slept with the land. I explained that the Bible uses the words "uncover the nakedness" to refer to one individual sleeping with another (*Leviticus 18:6,7–19*). Thus Ham saw Noah naked, but did not sleep with his father. I related to the Christian sister the facts regarding Noah and his sons, as follows: God saved the lives of Noah his family from the flood because He was merciful (*Genesis 6:1–8:22*). God blessed Noah and his sons (*Genesis 9:1–17*). Noah planted a vineyard and instead of offering the first fruits of his labour to God, as he should have done, he made wine and got drunk just as had the people God had allowed to die in the flood (*Genesis 4:3,4; 9:20,21; Deuteronomy 26:2; Numbers 18:12; Proverbs 3:9*). Ham, Noah's younger son, saw his father naked and told his two brothers (*Genesis 9:22*). Noah cursed Canaan and prophesied that some day Canaan, Ham's fourth son, would serve Shem (*Genesis 9:26*). I pointed out that the Bible says Noah cursed Canaan, but not Ham's other siblings (Cush, Mizram and Phut). I told the Christian sister this prophesy would be fulfilled eight hundred years later when Israel would subdue the Canaanites and put them to tribute (*Joshua 1:6–11:23; Judges 1:28,30,33,35*).

I said the Bible teaches that God does not accept people because of their outward appearance or because they belong to a certain nation – whether Jews or Gentiles – or because of their economic status. I said the Bible teaches that God accepts people of all nations and classes if they fear him and strive towards righteousness (*Deuteronomy 10:17; Job 28:28; Psalms 19:9; 85:9; 111:10; Proverbs 1:7; 2:5; 3:7; 16:6; Ecclesiastes 12:13; Matthew 22:16; Luke 10:21; Acts 9:31; 10:2,34,35; Romans 2:11, 13, 25–29; 3:22,29,30; 10:12,13; I Corinthians 12:13; II Corinthians 7:1; Galatians 2:6; Ephesians 5:21; 6:9; Colossians 3:11,25; James 2:4,9; I Peter 1:17; I John 2:29*). I said that while Noah cursed Canaan, the Bible says that God allowed David, Solomon and His Son, Jesus, to come through the lineage of Thamar, a "righteous" Canaanite woman (*Genesis 38:26–29*). I said that Thamar, a Canaanite woman, Rachab, another Canaanite woman, and Ruth, a Moabite woman, are mentioned in the genealogy of Jesus with the same rank as Mary, the mother of Jesus (*Matthew 1:1–17*). I told the Christian sister if the Southern Baptist minister and his race theory were correct one could say that Jesus, Who was of Canaanite descent, should have been a slave. She interrupted me and said the seed comes from the man and not from the woman. I said I was taught in medicine that a baby receives half (twenty-three) of its chromosomes from its father and half from its mother. I said the Bible teaches that the seed comes from both the man and the woman. The sister said this was not true. I showed her the passages of the Bible that say the seed comes from both the male and the female (*Genesis 3:15; 4:25; 7:3; Isaiah 7:14; Jeremiah 31:22; Micah 5:3; Matthew 1:23,25; Luke 1:31–35*).

Then the Christian sister said that God did not want the Israelites to intermingle with the Canaanites. I said that God did not want the Israelites to intermarry with the Canaanites not because He was racist, but because He knew that the Canaanites, who worshipped other gods, would turn the Israelites against worshipping the true God (*Exodus 34:15,16; Deuteronomy 7:3,4; Joshua 23:12,13; Judges 3:6,7; I Kings 11:1–13; Ezra 9:1,2; Nehemiah 13:23–27*), just as Paul advised a believer not to intimately bond with an unbeliever because he feared the latter would keep the believer from worshipping God (*II Corinthians 6:14–17, I John 1:6,7*). God and the patriarchs were not racist and full of hatred, I said, as humankind is. Joseph married Asenath, an Egyptian (*Genesis 41:45*), and Manasseh and

Ephraim, Joseph and Asenath's children, were equal heirs in Israel (*Joshua 13:1–24:33*). Moses first married a Midiniate (*Exodus 2:21*) and later an Ethiopian (*Numbers 12:1*). God rebuked Aaron and punished Miriam for challenging Moses' authority and speaking against Moses and his Ethiopian wife (*Numbers 12:1–15*).

I tried to impress upon the Christian sister that no individual should be the slave of another. God made humankind to serve and worship only God, not as slaves, but as beloved servants of God and friends of Jesus Christ (*Exodus 3:9; 22:21; 23:6–9; Leviticus 19:15; 25:17; Deuteronomy 16:18–20; 23:16; 25:1; II Samuel 23:3; Job 29:7–17; Psalms 72:2–4; Jeremiah 5:28; 9:24; 21:12; 22:3; Micah 3:11; Zechariah 7:9–11; II Corinthians 11:20*) (*Genesis 3:8, 9; Exodus 3:12,18; 4:22,23; 5:1; 8:1,20; 9:1,13; 10:3,26; Deuteronomy 5:9; 6:13; 10:20; 11:13; Joshua 24:15,18,21,22,24; I Samuel 12:14,20; II Chronicles 33:16; 34:33; Job 21:15; Psalms 2:11; 72:11; 100:2; Isaiah 41:8; 56:6; Jeremiah 27:7; 30:9; Daniel 7:14,27; Zephaniah 3:9; Matthew 4:10; 6:24; 9:11; 20:13; 22:12; 26:50; Mark 10:42; Luke 4:8; 12:4; 7:34; 15:2; 16:13; 19:7; 22:25; John 12:26; 15:14,15; Acts 27:23; Colossians 3:24; I Thessalonians 1:9; II Timothy 1:3; Hebrews 9:14; 12:28; James 2:23; Revelation 7:15; 22:3*).

The sister was not convinced by my arguments, so I reminded her that the Bible teaches that we are to love our neighbour (all humankind) as we love ourselves (Leviticus *19:18; Matthew 19:19; 22:39; Mark 12:31; Luke 10:27–37; Romans 13:9,10; 15:2; Galatians 5:14; 6:10; James 2:1–26*) and that God will know that we love Him and He will love us if we love one another (*John 14:21,23; 15:9,10; 16:27; 17:23*). She apparently remained unmoved, so I also reminded her that the Bible teaches that a man does not speak the truth if he says he loves God, Whom he has not seen, and hates his brother, whom he has seen (*I John 2:4; 3:17; 4:12,20*).

The Christian sister basically told me that she and I were not brother and sister. She indicated to me that the divisions brotherhood and sisterhood among humankind remained frozen in time since the time of Noah and his three children. I tried to impress upon the white Christian sister, who was not all white, that the North African half of her heritage, which she despised, was Hamite. But she refused to listen. She had been indoctrinated by the environment she attended church, an environment where some worshipped the Southern Baptist minister from Florida.

I felt like reminding the Christian sister that the Bible says, "**Whosoever hateth his brother is a murderer: and ye know that no murderer hath eternal life abiding in him**" (*I John 3:15*). But I did not. Ignorance is not good, but neither is too much knowledge, especially of the type I was gaining from the not-so-white Christian sister. So I decided I had learned enough from her and put an end to our conversation.

Another Christian sister, who had been in an adjacent room and overheard our conversation, said she felt sorry for me. I said she should feel sorry not for me, but for other girl and all the people who thought as she did, because the Bible teaches that God will judge all nations (*Matthew 25:31–46*), all humankind (*Hebrews 9:27*), small and great (*Revelation 20:12*), righteous and wicked (*Ecclesiastes 3:17*), believers (*Romans 14:10–12; I Corinthians 3:13,14; II Corinthians 5:9–10; James 2:12*) and non-believers (*Romans 2:12–16*). God will judge every man according to his thoughts, words and deeds (*Ecclesiastes 12:14; I Corinthians 4:5*), (*Matthew 12:36,37; Jude 1:15*) (*Ecclesiastes 11:9; 12:14; Revelation 20:13*).

I had heard more hatred from the Christian sister and the two Christian brothers than I had heard in my entire life, and this from people who read a Bible that says:

> "**Therefore all things whatsoever ye would that men should do to you, do ye even so to them: for this is the law and the prophets**"(*Matthew 7:12*).

The writings of the Southern Baptist minister and my conversations with the Christian sister and brothers gave me some understanding of what African Americans have put up with for centuries. It also gave me some indication of why many of them have been lured away from the truth and from Christianity for the people who know the truth are not necessarily charitable, tolerant and loving. As for myself, I was glad that many years earlier I had ignored the attitudes and the many atrocities committed by Christians and looked to Jesus for Who He was. Now that I was a Christian and had read and heard all these slurs coming from Christians, I decided to concentrate not on what Christians said or did, but on what I could do to please God, because I know that one-day I would stand before God to give account for myself alone.

God answered my prayer and found, for the children and me, two Baptist churches whose members did not adhere to the race theory of the Southern Baptist minister and seemed to practise what the Bible teaches. What I had told my friend to whom I had been witnessing earlier seemed to be true: most Baptists are loving people.

I also came across Baptists who disagreed with and distanced themselves from the Southern Baptist minister, proving that this man and his ilk are not representative of Baptists. In his book "*What About Ruckman?*", David W. Cloud, an American Baptist minister and Christian scholar, writes: "I reject Dr. Ruckman's mean-spirited, fleshy name calling. Some of the names Ruckman calls men who disagree with him are 'jackass,' 'poor, dumb, stupid "red legs,"' 'silly asses,' 'apostolic succession of bloated egotists,' 'two-bit junkie,' 'two-face, tin-horned punk,' 'some incredible idiot,' 'this bunk of egotistical jack legs,' 'conservative asses whose brains have gone to seed,' 'cheap two-bit punks,' 'jacklegs,' 'stupid little Bible-rejecting apostates'."[11] Cloud continues, "Ruckman is fighting for a holy Book in an unholy manner. It is confusion...Ruckman's spirit and language is not that of the Bible."[12] In response to Ruckman's calling him "little rascal...lying little hypocrite...ole son...buttery, smooth, slick, mush mouthed sissy...smooth, slick, little, fluctuating compromiser... A puffed-up, conceited ass,"[13] Cloud reminds us of what the Bible says:

"There is that speaketh like the piercings of a sword: but the tongue of the wise *is* **health"** (*Proverbs 12:8*).

"Make no friendship with an angry man; and with a furious man thou shalt not go. Lest thou learn his ways, and get a snare to thy soul" (*Proverbs 22:24–25*).

"And the servant of the Lord must not strive; but be gentle unto all *men*, **apt to teach, patient, in meekness instructing those that oppose themselves; if God peradventure will give them repentance to the acknowledging of the truth"** (*II Timothy 2:24–25*).

"But if ye have bitter envying and strife in your hearts, glory not, and lie not against the truth. This wisdom descendeth not from above, but *is* **earthly, sensual, devilish. For where envying and strife** *is*, **there** *is* **confusion and every evil work. But the wisdom that is from above is first pure, then peaceable, gentle,** *and* **easy to be intreated, full of mercy**

and good fruits, without partiality, and without hypocrisy. And the fruit of righteousness is sown in peace of them that make peace" (*James 3:14–18*).

As for my witnessing, I would not qualify as someone who wins over many people to Jesus Christ, but I have the consolation of knowing that I have not failed, for the only failure in witnessing is the failure to witness (*Ezekiel 3:18–19*). For a while I put a halt to witnessing while I was helping to clean the church and doing other tasks. I was soon reminded, however, that doing other things for Christ's sake is no substitute for witnessing (*I Corinthians 9:16–17*). I also remembered that the Bible warns all believers that they are accountable to God if they fail to witness (*Isaiah 6:5; Luke 9:62; I Corinthians 9:16; Colossians 4:17*). So I went back to inviting people to church and talking about Jesus. I no longer mind the odd look or comment I get when I witness, because I know I am not the first person to be treated like a fool for talking about Jesus and God (*II Kings 9:11; John 7:20; 8:52; 10:20; Acts 26:24–25*) and because Jesus Christ will some day deny us if we deny Him in front of men; if some day we are to reign with Jesus Christ, we must suffer rejection as He did (*II Timothy 2:12*).

[1] Aboubacry Moussa Lam, *De L'origine Egyptienne des Peuls* (Gif-sur-Yvette and Paris: Khepera and Présence Africaine.

[2] Murray Gordon, *Slavery in the Arab World* (New York: New Amsterdam Books, 1989).

[3] Bruce M. Metzger, *The Bible in Translation: Ancient and English Versions* (Grand Rapids, MI: Baker Academic, 2001), p. 9.

[4] David W. Cloud, *Rome and the Bible: The History of the Bible Through the Centuries and Rome's Persecutions Against It* (Port Huron, MI: Way of Life Literature, 1966/2001), p. 276; Olaf Morgan Norlie, *The Translated Bible 1534–1934: Commemorating the Fourth Anniversary of the Translation of the Bible by Martin Luther* (Philadelphia: United Lutheran Publication House, 1934), p. 203.

[5] Peter S. Ruckman, *Theological Studies* (Pensacola, FL: Bible Baptist Bookstore, 1998), p. 159, 414.

[6] Ibid., p. 415.

[7] Ibid., p. 611.

[8] Peter S. Ruckman, *Black Is Beautiful* (Pensacola, FL: Bible Baptist Bookstore, 1996), p. xii, 5, 17, 19, 211, 233, 265.

[9] Ibid., p. 320.

[10] G.A. Riplinger, *New Age Bible Versions* (Ararat, Virginia: A. V. publications, 1993), p. 588.

[11] David W. Cloud, *What About Ruckman?* (Oak Harbor, WA: Way of Life Literature, 1994/2000), p. 13.

[12] Ibid., p. 14.

[13] Ibid., p. 43.

CHAPTER FIFTY-THREE

"Many patients against you."

"These things I have spoken unto you, that in me ye might have peace. In the world ye shall have tribulation be of good cheer; I have overcome the world" (John 16:33).

"I will extol thee, O LORD; for thou hast lifted me up, and hast not made my foes [enemies] to rejoice over me" (Psalms 30:1).

"For a just [man] falleth seven times, and riseth up again: but the wicked shall fall into mischief" (Proverbs 24:16).

Before becoming ill and moving to Bermuda, I had no difficulties in my life that I considered serious enough to confide to people. Of course, like most people I would whine about everything and nothing. Now that I had issues serious enough to confide to people I realized that most people have their own problems and are not keen to listen to those of others. However, I was fortunate to have a few friends who cared enough to listen to my problems. Dr. Mackintosh, a physician from the West Indies, was such a friend. He and I would meet occasionally for lunch at a Jamaican restaurant in downtown Hamilton, to talk about and even laugh about our misadventures. When it came to my adventures, Dr. Mackintosh would mockingly call me his "freedom-fighting friend" and suggest that I was still in Bermuda because I liked fighting. I would tell him I did not like fighting at all. One day Dr. Mackintosh, who was a physician in the emergency room, asked why I was all pumped up and cheerful to the staff at the hospital if I did not like fighting. I told him I did not want my problems to affect others negatively. I also said that if I allowed myself to become depressed my adversaries would eat me alive. Dr. Mackintosh shook his head and asked why I was putting myself through so much. I told him not to worry about me; I would be fine because God is good. Then he asked why I had to go through so much if God is good.

Initially, I felt the same as Dr. Macintosh. I thought that all of my problems would be over since I had found the truth (Jesus Christ), was doing what God wanted me to do and was praying to God. It took me a while to understand why men of God, like Moses and Paul, suffered more when they walked with God than when God was not in their lives. It took me a while to understand why the believer suffers.

Suffering is not evidence of Christianity and of course not everyone who suffers can claim they are being tried because they are Christians. A person who is undergoing a trial must search his or her heart to see if he or she is a child of God by faith and is suffering for the sake of Christ. The Bible teaches that all those who live godly lives will suffer tribulations (*II Timothy 3:12*), that once an individual accepts Jesus as his or her Saviour and walks with God, he or she becomes the enemy and target of the gods of this world (*Job 2:7*), and that the believer can to expect to have tribulations in a world that is not of his or her making (*John 16:33*).

The Bible teaches that in addition to the gods of this world persecuting the believer, God will scourge every believer whom He receives and loves (*II Samuel 7:14; Psalms 119:71,75; Proverbs 3:12; 13:24; Hebrews 12:6,7,8; Revelation 3:19*). God allows the believer to suffer and scourges him in order to remove sins from the believer's life; God wants to purify and shape the believer to the image of Jesus Christ (*Romans 8:29*); God purges the believer so he will yield fruit, just as a farmer prunes a tree so it will produce more fruit (*John 15:1,2*); God scourges the believer in order to prepare him for a holy life in heaven in the presence of God, who is holy (*Exodus 19:6; 22:31; Leviticus 11:44; 19:2; 20:7,26; 22:32; Amos 3:3; Acts 1:5,8; I Peter 1:15,16; 3:11*).

A person who is wealthy has many friends. But if that person has the misfortune of losing their wealth, they can tell their real friends from those who were their friends only because of their wealth. The Bible says it well:

"Wealth maketh many friends; but the poor is separated from his neighbour" (Proverbs 19:4).

"All the brethren of the poor do hate him: how much more do his

friends go far from him? he pursueth [them with] words, [yet] they [are] wanting [to him]" (Proverbs 19:7).

How an individual reacts to persecution, to people who are facing persecution and to people of different social positions says much about that individual's character and integrity (*Psalms 38:11; 88:8,18; Proverbs 19:7; Ecclesiastes 9:15,16; Luke 10:30–37; James 2:1–6*). The Bible teaches that sometimes God sends trouble to the believer to test his or her character, to see if the believer maintains his or her integrity or curses God in time of trouble, if she remains faithful to Christ or forsakes God for the world (*Genesis 19:26; Judges 9:8–20; Job 2:3,9; 27:5; 31:6; Matthew 13:3–8; Mark 4:3–20; Luke 8:5–15; 17:10–19; II Timothy 4:10*). God seeks people who are charitable, faithful, honest and consistent (*Philippians 1:1–13*).

The Bible teaches that the human heart is sinful, selfish and deceitful (*Jeremiah 17:9*) and that a human being's worst enemy is himself because he cannot resist the smallest temptation (*Genesis 6:5 8:21; Job 15:14–16; Psalms 51:5; 53:1–3; Proverbs 28:26; Ecclesiastes 9:3; Matthew 15:19; Mark 7:21,22; Hebrews 3:12; James 1:14,15*); thus a believer may suffer because he or she has become lukewarm to God and because sin has driven him or her away from God into darkness (*Genesis 3:1–24; 4:8–14; 6:5; 8:21; Joshua 7:21–24; I Samuel 2:23–35; II Samuel 11:2,3; I Kings 21:2–4; Job 31:9,27; Psalms 55:9–11; Proverbs 4:23; Isaiah 44:20; Hosea 13:9; Matthew 5:28; 15:18,20; Mark 7:21,22; Romans 1:18–32; 2:1–16; 7:11,13; Ephesians 4:22; Hebrews 3:13; James 1:13–15; I John 3:1–10*).

Instead of resenting the scourging and suffering, says the Bible, the believer should use the opportunity to become humble, become a better person and grow closer to God (*Hebrews 12:1–13; James 1:1–18*), should endure trials and relate to Jesus Christ, Who suffered to deliver the believer from sin (*Isaiah 53:1–12; Matthew 8:17; Galatians 3:13; Hebrews 9:28; I Peter 2:24; 3:18; I John 2:2*). Instead of withdrawing into himself the scourged believer should relate to the suffering of other believers as well as that of non-believers, have pity on them and help them (*Genesis 18:2–8; 19:1–3; 40:4–8; I King 17:10–16; Proverbs 3:9,10; 11:24,25; 14:21,31; 19:17; 22:9; Matthew 25:35–45; Luke 23:40–42; Acts 16:15; 22–34; Romans 12:13; II Corinthians 1:4,5; 7:6,7; 8:1–5; Philippians 1:14; I Thessalonians 4:18; II Thessalonians 2:16,17; I Timothy 5:10; Hebrews 13:1–3; I Peter 4:9; III John*

1:5–8).

At times the believer may suffer so that the glory of God might be manifest in the believer (*Matthew 11:5; John 9:1–3; 11:4,40; 14:11–13; Acts 4:21).* While the believer should pray for God to ease his suffering according to God's will, he should spend more time praying that God will give him the grace to endure the trials and that the work of God will be manifest through his suffering (*Psalms 4:1–7:17; Matthew 26:42,44; Mark 14:36; Luke 22:40–46; II Corinthians 8:1–5; 12:7–11; Ephesians 6:18).*

How the believer endures his trials is a great witness to the non-believers (*II Corinthians 8:1–5).* Thus the Bible teaches that the believer is to endure trials patiently and do the work of an evangelist as a good soldier of Jesus Christ so that non-believers might be saved (*I Corinthians 13:7; II Corinthians 1:6; II Timothy 1:8; 2:3,10; 3:10–12; 4:5; Hebrews 6:15; 10:32; 11:27; 12:2,3; James 1:12).* It teaches that only those who suffered and endured tribulations will be glorified and reign with Jesus (*Romans 8:17; II Timothy 2:12; Revelation 3:21; 21:7).*

Believers should not only endure their trials patiently, but take pleasure and glory in them, because they are suffering for the love of Christ (*Matthew 5:10–12; Luke 6:22,23; Acts 5:41; Romans 5:3; 8:35–37; II Corinthians 11:23–30; 12:9,10; Ephesians 3:13 Philippians 1:29; 2:17,18; Colossians 1:24; I Thessalonians 3:8,9; James 1:2,3,12; I Peter 3:14; 4:16–19)* and because Jesus Christ partakes in their suffering (*II Corinthians 4:8–11; Philippians 2:1).* They should rejoice in their tribulations, because God, the Creator of the universe and everything in it, is their strength and shield (*Genesis 15:1; Psalms 18:1,2 19:14; 28:7,8; 84:11; 91:4; Isaiah 12:2; 45:24; Ephesians 6:10)* and because God has promised He will never leave nor abandon a faithful believer (*Genesis 28:15; Deuteronomy 31:6,8; Joshua 1:5; I Samuel 12:22; I Chronicles 28:20; Psalms 37:25,28; 56:2,3; Proverbs 14:26; 18:10; Isaiah 41:10,17; John 14:16–18,26; 15:26; 16:7–15; I Corinthians 9:10,23; II Corinthians 1:5, 8–10; 6:4; 7:5,6; 11:23–30; II Timothy 1:8).* Believers should glory in their tribulations because they have the comfort of knowing that, no "**tribulation or distress, or persecution, or famine, or nakedness, or peril, or sword...neither death, nor life, nor angels, nor principalities, nor powers, nor things present, nor things to come, nor height, nor depth, nor any other creature shall be able to separate**

us from the love of God, which is in Christ Jesus" (*Romans 8:35–39*), because they know that even though outwardly they are suffering inwardly they are being renewed (*Job 19:26,27; Psalms 51:10; 73:26; Proverbs 30:12; Isaiah 40:31; 57:1,2; Jeremiah 4:14; Matthew 5:29,30; 12:33; John 3:30; Luke 16:16; Romans 6:3–11; 7:22; 12:2; II Corinthians 2:15; 4:16; 12:10; Galatians 2:20; 5:24; Ephesians 3:16; 4:23; Philippians 1:20,21; Colossians 3:10; II Timothy 2:11,12; Titus 3:5; James 4:8*), and because they know that in all things they are "**more than conquerors through him [Jesus Christ] that loved us**" (*Romans 8:37*). The Bible teaches further that believers should rejoice in their tribulations because they have the assurance that the trials they face in this world are nothing compared to the blessings they will receive in heaven (*Romans 8:18; Colossians 3:4; II Thessalonians 1:7–12; 2:14; I Peter 1:13; 4:13; 5:1; I John 3:2*). The Bible gives many other reasons why believers should rejoice in their tribulations.

If the Bible exhorts the believer to rejoice in his or her tribulations, it teaches that the believer should not envy the ungodly, who might appear prosperous and free of worldly trials and tribulations (*Psalms 73:1–28*). It teaches that the joy of the ungodly is momentary, their prosperity fleeting and uncertain, their end a sudden, terrible destruction, while the believer will enjoy peace and everlasting prosperity (*Job 20:5; 27:8; Palms 37:38; 58:9; 73:17; Ecclesiastes 8:12,13; Isaiah 30:13; Jeremiah 5:31; Luke 12:16–21; 16:22,23; I Thessalonians 5:3; Revelation 18:1–10*) (*Psalms 37:37; Job 42:12–17; Proverbs 14:32; Isaiah 32:17; 33:6; 57:2; Matthew 6:20; 19:21; Luke 2:25–29; 12:33; 18:22; Acts 7:59,60; I Timothy 6:17; II Timothy 4:6–8; Hebrews 10:34; 11:26; James 2:5; I Peter 1:4; II Peter 1:14; Revelation 2:9*).

I could have answered Dr. Mackintosh's question as to why I was going through so much if God was good by explaining to him the reasons why believers suffer, but he would not have listened for he was very sceptical of anybody who held any faith. Dr. Mackintosh said he had seen too many religious people backslide. So, instead of answering his question, I just told him again not to worry about me; I would be fine, I said.

During one of our regular get-togethers Dr. Mackintosh suggested I was fighting solely for financial reasons. He advised me to leave Bermuda and forget the money that Dr. Trouts owed me. I replied that he was mistaken, that I was not fighting solely for financial reasons. Then he said, "Out of curiosity, how much does Dr. Trouts owe you?" When I told him how much, he said, "Wow, where I come from you could buy two houses with that kind of money." Then Dr. Mackintosh advised me to return to Montreal to be with my family and try to recuperate the money Dr. Trouts owed me from abroad – that way, at least I would not have to deal with the hospital. I told him that leaving Bermuda would not necessarily end my problems with the hospital and my adversaries. On many occasions my adversaries had tried to undermine my reputation by urging patients to complain about me or even to take legal action against me. I explained that Dr. Jameson, the former chief of staff, had once told me that if I stayed in Bermuda he would find patients to complain about me. My adversaries would continue the practice of getting patients to complain about me, I said, if I went back to Montreal without honourably defending myself. Dr. Mackintosh nodded his approval and I think he understood some of the reasons why I continued to fight from Bermuda.

My prediction about my adversaries' intention to find patients willing to take legal action against me turned out to be correct.

A thirty-two-year-old black Bermudian was one such patient. In 1996, Mrs. M.D., a chambermaid at one of Bermuda's largest hotels, developed neck pain, weakness on the right side of her body, with difficulty walking and taking care of herself, after she slipped and fell on a wet floor at work. After her fall, Mrs. M.D. went to the United States to have an MRI and to see a neurosurgeon. The MRI revealed one the largest and most unusual herniated discs I have ever seen in my practice or in a textbook. The disc fragment was so large that it was located completely behind the vertebrae and compressed more than sixty percent of the spinal cord. According to Mrs. M.D., the neurosurgeon in the United States offered to operate and told her that it would take eight hours to complete the surgery with a fifty-percent risk of paralysis. She refused to have the surgery because of the risk.

I first saw Mrs. M.D. in July 1996, a few weeks after her return from the United States. My evaluation showed that she presented with a herniated disc with a "central cord syndrome," which is described in the medical literature as follows:

"Complete motor paralysis...with small [a] amount of sensation around the sacral area [anus]… These patients have [a] 50% chance of recovery enough muscle power and sensation to be independently ambulatory [able to walk]… Therefore, the typical patient with a Central Cord Syndrome regains bowel and bladder control [the ability to urinate] and is able to walk with a spastic gait but has fine poor recovery…of the upper extremities [hands].”[1]

Mrs. M.D.'s pathology was so complex and difficult to correct that I was disinclined to operate on her at the hospital in Bermuda, but referred her to a spine surgeon abroad. The spine surgeon saw Mrs. M.D. and told her he had operated on one similar case with success, but there was definitively some risk of paralysis. She again refused to have the surgery.

Three months later Mrs. M.D. came back to me and asked me to conduct the surgery on her neck because her symptoms had worsened to the point where she was barely able to walk and needed her husband's help to go to the bathroom. I agreed to perform the surgery because of the worsening symptoms. I described the procedure to her, which would consist of removing the vertebrae body in order to get to the offending disc that was compressing her spinal cord, removing the herniated disc, replacing the vertebrae body with a bone taken from her hip, and stabilizing the neck with a plate and screws. I repeated to Mrs. M.D. what the other two surgeons had told her about the risk of paralysis. She said she trusted me and urged me to operate.

It took three hours to complete the surgery and things went relatively well. The only problem I encountered during the surgery was with the insertion of the screws and plate. The routine x-ray taken at the end of the operation showed that two bottom screws were not in optimal condition and were touching the bottom disc. Normally, I would need only to change the angulation of the two screws, a procedure that would require only five minutes of additional surgery. I proceeded to verify that I had the proper screws to correct the problem. To my great surprise, I found that I did not. A few days before the surgery I had spoken to the pharmaceutical representative overseas requesting that the surgical trays be completed. The representative had sent all the necessary implants in order to complete the tray and faxed me a letter to that effect. In addition, I had verified the surgical trays the night before the surgery and found that no implants were missing. When I inquired, I was told that the screws had been lost between my verification and the sterilization process. Therefore, I decided not to replace the bottom screws that were not in an optimal position since I did not have the proper screws and because in the short term this would not be detrimental to the patient. Mrs. M.D. woke up from the surgery moving her hands and legs. I advised her that the screws would be removed once her neck healed, and this was done.

Amazingly, Mrs. M.D. recovered one hundred percent of the weakness in her legs and arms. I would often see her walking to the bus stop and to the grocery store. She came to my office regularly for her routine follow-up and for me to prepare medical reports for her and her attorney. Mrs. M.D. was seeking compensation from her employer for the work-related injury. She never paid my fee. She promised to pay me once her legal matter was settled, but somehow I knew that she never would. In addition, Mrs. M.D. came to my office on two occasions complaining that her husband had thrown her out of the house and that she and her children had nothing to eat. She asked me to lend her money for groceries, which I did.

One day Mrs. M.D. told me that her attorney, who was a member of the Bermuda Hospitals Board, had urged her to take legal action against me on the grounds that she still had pain. She also informed me that Dr. Paytons, the chief of staff, had called and urged her to lodge a complaint against me. She even wrote a letter to the Board on my behalf indicating that Dr. Paytons had phoned her. Mrs. M.D., who did not take any pain medication except for a few days in the immediate post-operative period, told me I did not have to worry about her loyalty. She said I was dealing with wicked people and told me to "hang it there and fight them."

In August 2000, a few months after I left Bermuda, Mrs. M.D.'s attorney sent me a letter informing me that Mrs. M.D. was initiating proceedings against me in the Supreme Court of Bermuda in relation to damages she sustained during her operation. The letter stated:

> "Since the operation Mrs. M.D. has encountered a series of worsening of symptoms including, but not limited to dizziness often culminating in blackouts, severely impeded movement and use of her limbs, severe pain in the area of her neck, back and extremities, memory loss, etc…a series of physical and physiological challenges that are likely to affect her for the remainder of her life."

Mrs. M.D. was one of the patients who had expressed gratitude for what I had done for her. When I was experiencing difficulties with the hospital, she wrote to the Board on my behalf. Her letter stated:

> "I write this letter to say thanks to Dr. Bah for the operation he did on my back. Before the operation I suffered so much with headaches, swelling in my neck and dizziness that I could not hold my head up on my pillow. I also needed the assistance of my husband when I went to the bathroom and could not take a shower without the help of my husband. But with the professionalism, understanding and knowledge that Dr. Bah has in his field as a spine surgeon, he has made me feel ameliorated [sic].
>
> Dr. Bah is a very good surgeon and I am not just speaking for myself, but a lot of people that I have spoken to say nothing but commendable things about him. Before I had my surgery done, he took the time and explained the procedures, the risks and rehabilitation to me meticulously.
>
> In closing, I would just like to again say thank you to Dr. Bah for everything he has done for me.
>
> Thank You.
>
> M.D."

My attorney in Bermuda wrote to Mrs. M.D.'s attorney indicating that we did not accept his client's allegations that her current symptoms were the result of the surgery I had performed. He also sent him a copy of the letter Mrs. M.D. had written to the Board on my behalf.

Mrs. M.D. was one of the many people who encouraged me to fight the hospital and who would leave my office saying, "God bless you." Initially I liked this and thought that God would bless me even more with a lot of people offering this wish. With time, however, I realized that many people use the term "God bless you" loosely and that they did not really mean it. I realized that, by protecting me against people like Mrs. M.D. and my adversaries, God had blessed me every day of my life, in innumerable ways; that God had helped me out of trouble long before I even knew I was in trouble; that what I had been attributing to luck was not coincidence or luck, but God's blessings. I no longer use the term "luck" when I speak about good things happening to me, and I do not like it when people say "God bless you," for I know that God blesses me every instant of my life in spite of others and myself.

M.M., a thirteen-year-old white Bermudian boy, was the second patient my adversaries recruited to take legal action against me. In February 1999, while I was still in Bermuda fighting the hospital, an attorney sent me a letter stating that he was acting on behalf of M.M. in respect to injuries the boy sustained as a result of treatment I had administered. I referred the matter to my insurance company.

In March the boy's attorney sent a letter and his client's medical records to my attorney stating that the documents "clearly establish" my negligence. The attorney threatened to issue proceedings against me if we did not review the documents, "admit liability...and discuss settlement."

After receiving a few more threatening letters, my attorney responded as follows:

> "In none of your letters have you set out in clear and concise statements what your client alleges against Dr. Bah... Rather, you have provided us with a stack of documents over an inch thick and have contented yourself with the dismissive statement that "the said documents clearly establish the negligence of your client."

> In your letter of 8th April you state that you are loathe to issue proceedings against a professional man unless there is no alternative and you repeat your request that our client admit liability.

> A professional man should be entitled to expect that those who accuse him of negligence will state clearly what it is alleged he did which he ought not to have done and that which he failed to do which he ought to have done. A professional man is entitled to expect that his accusers will do more than simply present him with a bundle of documents with the request that he find out for himself what it is alleged he did wrong.

> In the circumstances, unless and until your client provides proper particulars of the allegation of negligence, our client can only reply that he does not accept that his treatment of your client was in any way negligent."

The attorney replied that M.M.'s records clearly demonstrated that I had been negligent in failing to diagnose symptoms of infection, which resulted in his client's developing osteomyelitis (an infection of the bone). He again strongly urged us to admit guilt and negotiate a settlement.

My attorney answered a second time:

> "We note that the substance of your client's allegation of negligence against Dr. Bah is a failure to do something, i.e., diagnose and treat an infection, rather than his positive treatment of your client for the initial complaint... To this extent, it would appear that your letter suggesting that the damages Mr. M. sustained were as a result of our client's treatment of him does not

properly characterize your client's claim…

Our client does not accept that the manner in which he dealt with your client was negligent.

Should your client be minded to institute proceedings against Dr. Bah, we have instructions to accept service of the same."

After this exchange of letters in early 1999 I heard nothing more about the case until March 2002, two years after I had left Bermuda, when my attorney sent me a copy of a claim deposited on behalf of M.M. and his father in the supreme court. The claim stated that I had neglected to diagnose and appropriately treat an infection and had discharged M.M. from hospital when he was "exhibiting classic symptoms of infection, namely great pain…fever, vomiting…and reluctance to ambulate" and in fact developed a bone infection. They were seeking $276,243 in damages, which they said was the amount the insurance company had to pay for M.M. to have treatment abroad.

My attorney asked me to explain why I had not been negligent in failing to diagnose and treat the infection. I wrote that I first saw the thirteen-year-old boy on December 6th, 1996, after he had sustained a severe injury to his right leg while playing basketball. The injury consisted of a fracture dislocation of the distal right femur. I saw him in the emergency room and operated on his leg less than two hours after he had sustained the injury. The surgery consisted of repairing the fracture with two wires and I was able to achieve anatomical reduction (setting the leg as it should have been). As is customary, the boy received antibiotics pre- and post-operatively to prevent infection. I saw him daily and supervised the dressing of the surgical wound until he was discharged home on December 12th. M.M. was afebrile and the wound was clean when he left the hospital.

On December 14th I saw M.M. in my clinic. He was not running a fever and the surgical wound showed no sign of infection. I saw him again on December 16th and 20th and he was not running a fever and was doing well.

On the evening of December 24th, the boy's mother called me (his father had gone to Colorado for the holidays) to inform me that he was having leg pain. I saw M.M. in the emergency room. I proposed removing the cast to look at his leg, but he was crying and would not let me get close to his leg. My other option was to have him anaesthetized in the operating room, remove the cast and look at the surgical wound. I could not do this because he had eaten a large pizza before coming to the hospital, so I proposed to his mother that he remain in hospital and undergo surgery the next day. She suggested taking her son home because it was Christmas and bringing him back to the hospital the next morning.

On December 25th, the mother brought the boy to the hospital as agreed. I took him to the operating room, removed the cast and the dressing, and noticed an infection of the wound. I cleaned the wound and left it open, as is advisable in such cases, and admitted M.M. to hospital for intravenous antibiotics and daily dressing of the wound.

Four days later I discovered that M.M. had an infected toenail on the right foot, the same side that he had been operated on. His mother said the infected toenail had been oozing pus intermittently for a year. I learned that he had sustained an injury and an ensuing infection to his toenail when a truck had run over his foot a year earlier. His mother informed me that she had proposed taking him to his doctor for the infected toenail on many occasions, but he had refused to go.

I believed that the right infected toenail had probably been the source of the infection to his right leg. I also believed the leg infection would never heal properly unless the chronic infected toenail was treated at the same time. I discussed this with the mother and proposed to have a general surgeon see and surgically treat the toenail. (In Montreal I would have surgically treated the infected toenail without seeking the opinion of another surgeon, but it was the policy of the King Edward VII Memorial Hospital that general surgeons treated infected toenails.) A general surgeon saw the boy and wrote in his chart that the toenail did not require immediate treatment. The infected toenail was not treated surgically.

M.M. received three weeks of intravenous antibiotics and the leg wound almost completely healed. He was walking with crutches, eating junk food and doing well. I suggested to the parents that he be kept in hospital for another three weeks of intravenous antibiotic treatment to allow the leg to heal completely. On January 15th, 1997, they ignored my advice and took him home because his birthday was the next day.

Three weeks later M.M.'s grandfather brought him to my clinic for follow up (the parents were vacationing in Europe). As I had predicted, the infected toenail was oozing pus, as was the surgical leg wound, which had almost healed before the parents had taken him home. I told the grandfather to phone the parents in Europe and urge them to return to Bermuda to authorize treatment for their son.

A few days later the boy's parents came back from Europe and brought him to the hospital. I explained to them that the infected toenail needed to be treated surgically and that the leg wound needed further debridement (cleaning to remove the pus and dead tissue). They signed the consent form allowing me to treat the infected toenail only, indicating that "no other procedure" could be performed on the leg. M.M. was anaesthetized and I operated on the infected toenail. After the surgery both the boy's pediatrician and I recommended that he stay in hospital and receive a long course of intravenous antibiotics to allow healing of the leg wound. The parents rejected our advice and took him home, because, as the pediatrician wrote in the chart, the boy was "angry and upset at being in the hospital."

Two weeks later, I saw M.M. in the orthopaedic clinic for follow up and, as I had predicted, the surgical wound was oozing pus; it was worse than when he had left the hospital fifteen days earlier. My impression was that the infection to the skin and muscle had progressed deeper, into the bone. I explained to the parents that M.M. needed leg surgery, which would consist of debridement of the wound and treatment of the infected underlying bone. They refused again and said I could clean the wound superficially, but not touch the bone. At this stage I transferred M.M. to another surgeon and withdrew from his treatment.

The surgeon tried to treat the leg infection, which had spread to the bone, but with the same limitations the parents had imposed on me. Eventually M.M. was transferred to the United States for further treatment. Apparently he underwent eleven operations to his leg before the infection, which had progressed to the bone, healed and with the right leg being one and a half centimetres shorter than the left.

If I had felt in any way responsible for the complications M.M. suffered, I would have admitted it and apologized to the family. But I believed that the boy and his parents were responsible for the complications. In response to the accusations of M.M. and his father, I wrote that the parents had removed him from the hospital for his birthday, against my advice. I pointed out that the pediatrician had written in the chart that they had removed him from the hospital against medical advice when he was doing well and responding to treatment. I cited the resident physician's notes in the chart indicating that M.M. had had a toenail infection for one year for which he refused to seek medical treatment and the parents had complied with the wishes of the child. I cited the nurses' notes indicating that M.M. was not running a fever, not vomiting, but eating junk food and walking alone before the parents took him home, against my advice, the first time. I cited the radiology report indicating that the leg was healing well and showed no signs of infection to the bone before the parents removed him from the hospital, against my advice, for his birthday. I cited the nurses' notes indicating that the boy and his parents were noncompliant not only with my advice, but also with the advice of the nurses and the pediatrician. For example, the pediatrician had prescribed a diet, since M.M. was significantly overweight. On a few occasions the nurses wrote that the parents brought him ice cream, pizza and other junk food against the advice of the pediatrician.

I responded to many other accusations in the claim, which were completely unfounded and contradictory to what was written in the chart. I wrote that the osteomyelitis developed because M.M.'s parents removed him from the hospital a second time on February 14th, against my advice and that of the pediatrician, because he was "angry and upset at being in the hospital." I wrote that for these reasons and many others, which I expanded upon, M.M. and his father did not merit the award they were seeking.

My attorney asked if I would be available to attend a court hearing. I responded that in many jurisdictions we would have had a good chance of winning such a case, because on two occasions the parents refused the recommended medical treatment, which would have allowed the leg to heal without complications, and because the pediatrician had written in the chart that the parents refused medical advice. But I had lived in Bermuda long enough and had dealt with its legal and political system enough to know that I would not have a fair hearing. I was at a disadvantage for three reasons. First, the boy was a white Bermudian while I was of African extraction and a foreigner. Second, I had lost my privileges at the hospital – even though I still maintained this was an unjustified move. Third, the boy suffered visible complications such as the leg shortening and a surgical scar that were impressive enough for the court to sympathize with him. I therefore concluded that it would be futile to spend at least a week in a Bermuda courtroom arguing my case. I suggested that my attorney settle out of court. My attorney and the insurance company took my advice and did so.

Ms. P.H., a Portuguese Bermudian in her early forties, was the third and last patient my adversaries were able to recruit to take legal action against me. Ms. P.H. presented with severe neck and arm pain following a ski accident in 1994. A MRI done abroad showed that she had two herniated discs in her neck, which were compressing her spinal cord.

Dr. Trouts and a doctor acting as a locum for him operated on Ms. P.H. The surgery was so successful that three days later the patient said she had no neck or arm pain and just three months later was able to return to her secretarial job three days a week. Ms. P.H.'s employer, a Portuguese Bermudian like the patient and social services minister in the UBP government, fired Ms. P.H. because he did not want her to work three days a week and progressively reintegrate into her job.

After this, Ms. P.H. came to my office complaining of recurrent neck pain and complaining that her sister, who was married to a wealthy man, would not share some of her wealth with Ms. P.H. One year after the surgery she was still complaining of neck pain. X-rays showed complete postoperative healing with slight angulations of the bone where the surgery had been performed, caused partly by the patient's refusal to wear the brace she had been prescribed after the surgery. The operating surgeon believed that the angulations were too minimal to cause her any discomfort. However, I gave Ms. P.H. the benefit of the doubt and offered to repeat the surgery with a view to correcting the slight angulations of the bone in the hope that this would improve her reported residual neck pain. In retrospect this was an error on my part because it gave Ms. P.H. the impression that the first surgery had been a failure, which it had not been.

I repeated the surgery on Ms. P.H. and was able to completely correct the slight angulations. Post-operative x-rays showed that the surgery was a total success with no compression of the spinal cord and nerve. Three months after the second procedure Ms. P.H's neck was healed and she presented only minor neck pain for which she occasionally took pain medication.

A few months before I left Bermuda I met Ms. P.H. in a store. She informed me that she was being seen by Dr. Cooperson. She said the first surgeon who operated on her, Dr. Trouts, and I had promised her that we would use a plate and screw and that the first surgery had been unsuccessful because a plate had not been used, as I had done in the second surgery. She said her problem was entirely my fault. In the type of surgery that Ms. P.H. had undergone, the decision to not use a plate is as technically sound as the decision to use one and the two options are chosen equally among spine surgeons. Ms. P.H. was so verbally abusive in front of the other customers in the store that I left without completing my purchase.

In January 2002, two years after I moved back to Montreal, I received a letter from an attorney informing me that he had filed a writ against Dr. Trouts and me on behalf of Ms. P.H. The letter did not state the grounds on which the writ was filed. I referred the matter to my insurance company.

[1] The Cervical Spine Research Society, *The Cervical Spine: Second Edition* (Philadelphia, Pennsylvania: J.B. Lippincott Company, 1989, p.521.)

CHAPTER FIFTY-FOUR

Conclusion

"Let us hear the conclusion of the whole matter: Fear God, and keep his commandments: for this [is] the whole [duty] of man.

For God shall bring every work into judgment, with every secret thing, whether [it be] good, or whether [it be] evil" (Ecclesiastes 12:13–14).

"Beware lest any man spoil you through philosophy and vain deceit, after the tradition of men, after the rudiments of the world, and not after Christ" (Colossians 2:8).

After the court hearing in September 1999, Mr. Diels, my attorney, told me the court should take four weeks to render a verdict in my case against the hospital and he would advise me of the decision. Four weeks later I called and asked if he had heard anything. He said he had not and it would be unwise to pressure the court. He told me I would be the first to be informed of the verdict.

On November 10th, Mr. Diels' secretary phoned to tell me that I owed their office $5,000 in legal fees. I told her I had paid in full and would write Mr. Diels to that effect. At the end of our conversation I asked if the court had reached a decision in my case. She checked with the junior partner and then said that they had not heard from the court.

I wrote to Mr. Diels enclosing copies of our previous correspondence, which summarized our agreement with regard to the legal fees I was to pay. I also enclosed copies of cheques totalling $28,000 US that I had paid to his office, which proved I had honoured our agreement. In order to avoid any future misunderstanding, I wrote, I would appreciate obtaining a note of confirmation from him, his accounts department or his secretary. Mr. Diels did not acknowledge my letter.

On February 21st, 2000, five months after the court hearing, I faxed a letter to Mr. Diels requesting a copy of a particular document that he had in my personal file in his office. Three days later Mr. Song, his junior partner, replied as follows:

> "Thank you for your fax dated 21st February, 2000. After conferring with our Mr. Diels who is currently off the Island, it was decided that we would release a copy of your affidavit as per your request if you pay $5,000.00 in full and final settlement of your $11,201.68 outstanding fee."

I immediately phoned Mr. Song to discuss the matter. I asked him why Mr. Diels had not acknowledged my November 1999 letter proving that I owed him nothing, and why he had not called or written me in November to explain why I owed him another $5,000, a figure that had now ballooned to more than $11,000. Mr. Song said he could not speak for Mr. Diels, but the fact that they had not replied to my letter did not represent an admission on their part that I owed them nothing. I then asked him to justify the fee of $39,000 ($28,000 already paid plus $11,000 outstanding). I explained that I had met with Mr. Diels briefly on three occasions and had spoken to him on the phone twice, for less than five minutes each time. Mr. Song retorted that I had also paid $28,000 in legal fees to Mr. Richardson, my previous attorney. I said that this was so, but at my first meeting with Mr. Diels he had told me that Mr. Richardson's fee was high and he would not bill me nearly as much. In addition, I said, Mr. Richardson never withheld any documents from me. I spent half an hour on the phone with Mr. Song trying to convince him that I did not owe his firm any money and to send me a copy of the document I had requested. Mr. Song remained firm. He said his instruction was to not release any documents to me unless I paid $5,000 of the $11,000 outstanding. I did not ask him about the outcome of my court case and he did not volunteer the information. That was my last contact with Mr. Diels' office.

Out of curiosity I reviewed the invoices Mr. Diels had sent me. I noticed that he had billed me for work he had never done. For instance, with regard to the first court hearing scheduled for July 1999, Mr. Diels told me he had been in court less than half an hour and had asked for a postponement of the hearing in order to study the new documents the other party had presented. His invoice dated July 30th, 1999, with regard to that hearing read as follows:

07/21/1999	Preparation for hearing	3 hours	$975.00
07/22/1999	Preparation for hearing	4 hours	$1,300.00
07/23/1999	Perusal	0.3 hours	$82.50
07/23/1999	Conference	0.5 hours	$137.00
07/23/1999	Preparation for hearing	3.5 hours	$1,137.50
07/26/1999	Court attendance	7 hours	$2,275.00
07/27/1999	Court attendance	5 hours	$1,625.00
Total		23.30 hours	$7,532.50

The invoice shows that Mr. Diels billed $3,900 for twelve hours in court while in reality he had spent less than thirty minutes in court. I found that he had over billed me similarly for the second court hearing, in September. In another instance Mr. Diels billed me for reading a newspaper article in which my name was mentioned once. On August 11th, 1999, the *Bermuda Sun* ran excerpts from an interview with Dr. Brock, the African-American vascular surgeon[1], after the hospital had erroneously declared one of his patients dead and notified the family of the death. In the interview, Dr. Brock speaks about the many problems at the hospital and mentions my case as an example of the ongoing injustice. Mr. Diels billed me for buying and reading the newspaper. In the end, for obvious reasons, I decided not to pay Mr. Diels one penny of the $11,000 he claimed I owed him.

When, in September 1999, Dr. Browne told me the hospital had placed Mr. Diels on its payroll I had a good idea of how my case against the hospital would turn out. I was still curious, nevertheless, to know the details of what transpired. On December 16th, I went to see Dr. Browne and asked if he had any idea of what had happened with my case. He said he had no idea and his government was not involved in the matter. He mumbled something and I thought I heard, "The governor general and the chief justice are responsible for the courts and the justice system."

In the past I would not have believed Dr. Browne if he told me he did not know what had happened with my case. I would have said, "Yes, the governor general and the chief justice are responsible for the courts, but it is unlikely they hired my attorney to work for the hospital in the middle of a court case involving the hospital." I would have reminded him that it was the new Board that had bought off Mr. Diels, that it was his government that had appointed Mr. Dills chairman of the Board and had appointed the other Board members, and that it was Mr. Dills who had bought off my attorney. I would have said that in a democracy the judicial system is concerned only with fairness and does not bend to political pressure. I would have pointed out to Dr. Browne that the leader of his party, the prime minister, had said in one of her speeches, "We are a society with a firm belief in God and in the principles of the Bible [justice]."[2]

Now that I had been saved and knew a little about the Bible, I believed Dr. Browne when he said he did not know what had happened with my court case. Previously when Christians in Bermuda said I was involved in a spiritual battle and advised me to seek strength in the Lord, I would become irritated because I could not see the relationship between my spiritual path and my dispute with the hospital. I saw the Christians as fatalists. Now that I had fought long and hard, had dealt with the different networks in Bermuda and knew a little about the Bible, I realized that I had been wrong about who my opponents were. Now I saw that the Christian brothers and sisters were right and were not fatalists. They understood the words of Paul:

> **"Finally, my brethren, be strong in the Lord, and in the power of his might. Put on the whole armour of God, that ye may be able to stand against the wiles of the devil. For we wrestle not against flesh and blood, but against principalities, against powers, against the rulers of the darkness of this world, against spiritual wickedness in high places"** (Ephesians 6:10–12).

Fortunately the Bible does not reveal the believer's enemies to him and then leave him stranded. It gives the believer hope and ways to confront his enemies. It teaches that the believer does not stand a chance against his enemy on his own, but must depend on God (*Ephesians 6:14–18*). It commands the believer to resist his enemies by donning a whole suit of "armour of God." As an analogy, the Bible teaches that, just as the Roman soldier wore a suit of armour when engaging in warfare, so must the believer, who is also involved in a kind of warfare.

As for the first piece of "armour of God," the Bible exhorts the believer to stand and have his "**loins** [hip] **girt about with truth**" (*Ephesians 6:14*), which means that he must continually read the gospel of truth, the Bible (*I Thessalonians 4:11; II Timothy 2:15*). The Bible teaches not only that the believer should know the truth, the Bible, but that his whole life and emotions should be governed by it. The believer must be gentle, meek, peaceable, loving, honest, sincere and truthful (*Joshua 24:14; I Corinthians 2:4,5,13; 5:8; 15:10; II Corinthians 1:12,17; 4:2; 10:2–4; 12:15–19; Philippians 1:10; I Timothy 1:5,19; Titus 2:7; James 3:13–18; 4:6*). I follow the advice of the apostle Paul and read my Bible daily. I occasionally read it when I have some free time in my office. When the enemy puts a thorn in my flesh preventing me from reading the Bible, I listen to recorded readings from the Bible.

The second piece of armour is the **"breastplate of righteousness"** (*Ephesians 6:14*), which means that the believer must be armed with faith and must strive to be Christ-like.

As a third piece of armour, the believer must shod his feet in **"preparation of the gospel of peace"** (*Ephesians 6:15*), which means that the believer must have complete knowledge of the gospel, abide by the gospel and be ready to preach the gospel even in the most trying of times.

The fourth piece of armour is **"the shield of faith"** (*Ephesians 6:16*), which means that the believer must put his or her faith in God and trust that God will provide and protect him or her (*Genesis 15:1, I Kings 3:11–13; 17:13–16; II Chronicles 1:7–12; Psalms 84:11; 91:2; 115:9–11; 144:2; Proverbs 30:5; Matthew 6:33; Luke 12:31; John 6:27*).

The fifth piece of armour is the **"helmet of salvation"** (*Ephesians 6:17*), which means that the believer must be certain that Jesus Christ alone is his or her personal Saviour. The believer who confesses to Jesus Christ and still puts his or her trust in works, saints, angels or any other like figures for salvation is not wearing the "helmet of salvation."

The sixth piece of armour is **"the sword of the Spirit, which is the word of God"** (*Ephesians 6:17*): the believer should not only study the Bible, but memorize the word of God, write it in his or her heart and be ready to use it when under attack by the devil (*Job 22:22; Psalms 1:2; 37:31; 40:8; 119:11, 97; Proverbs 2:1,10,11; Isaiah 51:7; Jeremiah 15:16; Matthew 4:4,7,10; Colossians 3:16; Hebrews 4:12*). I keep a verse of the Bible on a business card displayed on the dashboard of my car – to memorize when I am stuck in a traffic jam.

As the seventh and final piece of armour, the Bible exhorts the believer to pray – **"always with all prayer and supplication in the Spirit, and watching thereunto with all perseverance and supplication for all saints"** (*Ephesians 6:18*).

Unlike the Roman soldier, who could remove his armour at night or when not engaged in battle, the believer must wear the complete suit of armour at all times, day and night, because the devil is **"as a roaring lion"** walking about **"seeking whom he may devour"** (*I Peter 5:8; Job 1:7*).

As regards my case against Dr. Trouts, on February 11th, 2000, I spoke to Mr. Dunkin, my attorney handling the matter. Mr. Dunkin said he would amend a letter he had written to Dr. Trouts advising that if he failed to pay what he owed we would initiate proceedings against him.

On February 25th, Mr. Dunkin told me he had amended the letter and given it to his secretary to type. Four days later, I spoke to his secretary and asked if she had had time to type it. The secretary, who was very sweet, said her boss had not given her any letter to type regarding my case. On March 8th, finally, Mr. Dunkin faxed me a copy of the letter he was about to send to Dr. Trouts advising that if we did not hear from him within two weeks we would have no choice, but to initiate proceedings to recover the money.

By April 24th we still had heard nothing so Mr. Dunkin sent a second letter to Dr. Trouts' attorney notifying him that we would commence legal proceedings within seven days if we did not hear from them.

On April 28th Dr. Trouts and his attorney responded as follows:

> "Whilst we regret the delay in responding to your letter of March 7, 2000, we ask that it be noted that the delay was caused by your client's failure to respond to the matters which were set out in our letter of 11 September 1997 to you."

They had not responded to our letters, they said, because I had not accepted the guidelines Dr. Trouts had set for my accountant and me three years earlier to review the ledgers. They repeated that we had to agree to these guidelines before we could access the ledgers to determine how much money Dr. Trouts owed me. They again sent us the guidelines, which indicated that the records were "strictly confidential"; we were not to "disclose their contents to any person [my attorney] or entity [a court of law]" nor to "make copies of the confidential records," and that at the end of the audit we were to return to Dr. Trouts "all the confidential records, any copies of the same, together with all papers, documents, studies, reports, brochures, analyses, compilations, forecasts studies or other documents prepared."

These guidelines were as unacceptable to me then as they had been back in April 2000. I instructed Mr. Dunkin to commence the court procee-dings.

One month later I still had not heard from Mr. Dunkin. I wrote to him inquiring if he had made any progress in the case. He sent me the following few lines:

"I apologize for not getting back to you sooner.

I am happy to do your case and intend to conduct your case with due dispatch.

The situation we must confront now is that Dr. Trouts has renewed his offer for your accountant to review his books with the threat that failure to do so may make us vulnerable to paying indemnity legal costs whatever the outcome of the legal proceedings...

On a more pragmatic note, it appears that Dr. Trouts acknowledges he may owe you some money – the issue is how much…".

He suggested that one way to get around the situation of being liable for Dr. Trouts' legal costs was to have my accountant review the figures in the pre-altered ledgers and write a letter supporting her audit. I once again gave my accountant the ledgers, along with the records of Dr. Trouts' office expenses and his salary payments to me. My accountant conducted a second review and composed a letter to be presented to the court if necessary.

On August 16th, Mr. Dunkin forwarded a copy of my accountant's let-ter to Dr. Trouts' attorney. In his accompanying letter, Mr. Dunkin invited Dr. Trouts to make an offer of settlement, which should reflect the sum of $424,777.10 that my accountant determined he owed me.

Mrs. Remond, my friend, had been following my case with interest. She asked me why, if he admitted to owing me money, Dr. Trouts would not pay me. She asked me if I had done something to him to justify his withholding the money. I replied that I had not knowingly said or done anything to Dr. Trouts to justify his actions. I explained that he never paid Dr. Morais, who covered for him for while he was on vacation, and that he also owed money to Ortho-Conception, a brace and prosthesis company in

Canada. The company made braces for my patients and those of Dr. Trouts and billed the insurance companies. The insurance companies paid for the braces in full, sending the cheques to Dr. Trouts' office. Dr. Trouts cashed the cheques, but never paid Ortho-Conception. Mr. Blain, the president of Ortho-Conception, wrote to him many times requesting reimbursement. Dr. Trouts never acknowledged the letters. I told Mrs. Remond the irony with Dr. Trouts was that while he was reluctant to pay other people he would not exonerate people who owed him money, no matter how minuscule the amount. He would see American patients in the emergency room with his credit card machine and have them pay before he performed emergency surgery. He referred all outstanding accounts to the collection agency, even as little as $5 owed by patients who had paid him thousands in medical fees. For accounts of less than $5, which the collection agency would not handle, he would keep sending reminders to the patient. I told her about the case of a patient who had an outstanding account of $1.18. Mr. Robbins, the bookkeeper, asked Dr. Trouts' wife, who was also the office manager, if he should send a reminder for such a negligible amount. Mrs. Trouts told him to do so. Mr. Robbins determined that it would cost more to send a reminder (ten minutes of his time plus the cost of the stationery and the stamp) than the amount owed. He therefore checked with Dr. Trouts, who told him to go ahead. I did not follow up to see if the patient paid the $1.18 or if Dr. Trouts' office sent second and third reminders. I told Mrs. Remond that since she was older than I, and understood more about human nature, perhaps she could explain to me why Dr. Trouts refused to give me my money.

By November 2000, I still had not heard from Mr. Dunkin. I wrote and asked him if Dr. Trouts and his attorney had replied to our letter of August 16th offering to settle out of court. When I failed to get hold of Mr. Dunkin, I informed my accountant of the little progress we had made in the case and asked her to pressure Mr. Dunkin into working on it. In January 2001, my accountant wrote to say that she had pressured Mr. Dunkin, but to no avail. She described the situation as "pathetic", but said that of all the attorneys on the Island Mr. Dunkin represented my best and perhaps only hope of winning the case. She said she would speak with his associate to try to determine the problem.

If I had essentially given up on my attorney, my accountant was determined not to. She wrote:

> "I have been on to Mr. Dunkin on the phone and by email without avail. However, I did bump into him in the street the other day and asked him outright what was happening with your case. He said he was afraid of it being "struck out." I said, "Now Mr. Dunkin, I am not a lawyer, but to me this is a straightforward case, the man owes the money. It can't be any easier, we have it straight from Dr. Trouts' own records and his own contract."
>
> So, Mr. Dunkin was humming and hawing, and I was 2 seconds away from saying "you've been bought." I am pregnant so definitely out of patience. It makes me sick to see the stuff that goes on here and he could see it in my face.
>
> Anyway what do you know a few days later I receive the case on my desk! I don't know whether you received one too but I will fax it to you if you want. I guess I need to hear from you what you want to do from here. I don't think you should drop it unless it causes you anxiety etc."

A few days later, Mr. Dunkin wrote to advise me that Dr. Trouts and his attorney had never replied to our letter of August 16th. He faxed me the documents he had prepared for filing the writ in court and apologized for his tardiness. I reviewed the documents and then faxed him a letter instructing him to proceed with the writ.

On December 5th, Mr. Dunkin filed the documents in court. A few days later Dr. Trouts and his attorney reminded him that because I was not a resident of Bermuda I would have to provide the amount of $17,550, which would serve as security to pay the court fees in case I were to lose. They had inflated the security costs in the hope that I would be unable to come up with the figure. Before filing the writ in court, Mr. Dunkin had spoken to me about the security costs and I had already paid them. Hence he informed Dr. Trouts and his attorney that the security costs had been deposited in trust.

One week later, on December 11th, Dr. Trouts and his attorney wrote to Mr. Dunkin asking for an extension so they could file their defence. They suggested that the dispute be resolved by arbitration pursuant to the arbitration clause in the contract Dr. Trouts and I had signed. They proposed that an accountant acceptable to both parties review the documents provided by both parties and produce a report on how much money Dr. Trouts owed me; the report would be binding.

I asked Mr. Dunkin why Dr. Trouts was suddenly willing to settle out of court after repeatedly refusing to do so in the past. He said that Dr. Trouts was probably hoping that with time I would drop the case; now that it appeared imminent the matter would go to court he wished to avoid having the whole community learn that he had "ripped off" one of his colleagues.

Even though I had instructed Mr. Dunkin to initiate court proceedings, I had always hoped the matter would not go to court, for I had no confidence in the judicial system in Bermuda, especially in light of my case against the hospital. He tried to reassure me that my case against Dr. Trouts was different from my case against the hospital, but I still preferred the arbitration route. I informed him that Dr. Trouts' proposal of arbitration was acceptable to me.

For the next few weeks Dr. Trouts and his attorney did everything in their power to delay the arbitration process. First they claimed that I owed him $30,000 at eight-and-a-half-percent interest per annum on a loan to buy a car upon my arrival in Bermuda. I produced documents, prepared by Dr. Trouts, showing that I had paid him in full plus interest. Next, Dr. Trouts alleged that I owed him $10,739.71. The ensuing correspondence cost me more money and benefited only the attorneys and Dr. Trouts, who was still hoping I would drop the case. Tired of the arguments, I wrote Mr. Dunkin that the whole discussion of my owing Dr. Trouts a few thousand dollars was semantic since he owed me more than $400,000 plus interest, and that he should supply the records to corroborate his allegations to the arbitrator – or, if he had changed his mind about the arbitrator, to the court.

Finally, in March 2001, the process of selecting the arbitrator began. Dr. Trouts and his attorney proposed an accountant from a large accounting firm. Mr. Dunkin rejected this accountant because he said he was likely a member of one of the all-white private clubs that Dr. Trouts belonged to (Dr. Trouts was a member of Bermuda's four most prominent and exclusive, essentially all-white, clubs). Mr. Dunkin proposed instead two accountants from another large firm, a foreigner and a black Bermudian, neither of whom, he said, were members of the private clubs Dr. Trouts belonged to.

In June, finally, Dr. Trouts and his attorney indicated that they accepted one of the proposed accountants as arbitrator. For the next few weeks the two attorneys negotiated the terms of reference and conditions of the review.

One year later, in July 2002, Mr. Dunkin wrote the designated accountant informing him that he could contact each party and start the review. A senior accountant in the same firm wrote to say that the designated accountant had left Bermuda. He offered to conduct the review.

In September Dr. Trouts and his attorney informed us that the new accountant was an acceptable replacement. Over the next two months the two attorneys and the designated accountant discussed by phone, in person and in correspondence the terms of engagement of the accountant and the nature and scope of the review. Finally, in November, everything was in place for the accountant to review the documentation presented by both parties and start the arbitration process.

Mr. Dunkin's secretary phoned and asked me to send her the ledger and copies of all the relevant documents for the review. I wrote to Mr. Dunkin indicating that I had left the ledger and all the relevant documents with his office; I enclosed a copy of a letter his secretary had signed indicating that she had received all of these.

Five months later, in March 2003, Mr. Dunkin and his staff were still looking for the ledger. In June the secretary informed me that they had found the ledger and the relevant documents.

I had been so busy fighting the hospital and copying my patients' hospital records that I had not taken the time to make extra copies of the ledger and the other documents before leaving them with Mr. Dunkin.

On October 31st, 2003, Mr. Dunkin forwarded me a copy of a letter he had sent to an accountant employed by the same firm as the two accountants who had previously been proposed as arbitrators. The letter indicated that he was again seeking a qualified accountant to conduct the review and act as arbitrator. As I had predicted, the second designated arbitrator had left the firm, and the Island, by the time Mr. Dunkin's office had found all the necessary documents.

A year later, on November 2nd, 2004, Mr. Dunkin wrote to suggest that we have an accountant conduct the review "in view of the difficulties we are facing in bringing" the matter to a resolution. He gave me the name of an accountant and added that he urgently awaited my response. I accepted his proposal only to realize later that this accountant happened to be the very one suggested by Dr. Trouts in 2002. Back then, Mr. Dunkin had advised me to reject Dr. Trouts' proposal because the accountant might be a member of one of the many exclusive clubs that Dr. Trouts belonged to. The letter-writing between the attorneys and the accountant started all over again. At press time there has been no resolution of the matter, and I doubt that it ever will be resolved.

The irony is that this whole story started with a call for help from Dr. Trouts. However, Dr. Trouts was not the first person to ask me to join him in Bermuda. In 1990, four years before Dr. Trouts had reappeared on the scene, Dr. Jameson, the black Bermudian chief of staff at the King Edward VII Memorial Hospital, had asked me to work with him there. Dr. Fowler, my program director, had referred me to Dr. Jameson, saying that he needed the services of a black orthopaedic surgeon. At the time I wondered why. When I arrived on the Island in 1995 I began to discover why. Sixty percent of the Bermudian population is black, and in general black people, who have been oppressed by the white oligarchy for more than three centuries, prefer to be treated by a black physician – or any physician, black, white or oriental, who has no close ties with the oligarchy. Dr. Jameson understood this situation well and had been looking to hire a black orthopaedic surgeon for financial reasons, not because he cared for the black population. In fact, Dr. Jameson, who had been rejected by the oligarchy upon returning to Bermuda in the 1960s after being trained in Canada, had gradually joined the oligarchy. As they say in Bermuda, he had sold birthright just like Esau sold his birthright to Jacob.

The oppression of the black population by the white oligarchy in Bermuda was such that a large segment of the black population sees every problem on the Island as black versus white and sometimes good versus evil. Because of its enclosed space, its prosperity, and its small population of Christians and non-Christians from all corners of the globe, Bermuda taught me a lot about the human character. My dealings with the people, whom I have referred to throughout this book as Asian, black or white, showed me that not all white is evil and certainly that not all black is good, and that women are not better than men and vice versa. My dealings with the people showed me that the Bible is right when it teaches that:

> **"Lo, this only have I found, that God hath made man upright; but they have sought out many inventions"** (Ecclesiastes 7:29).

> **"All we like sheep have gone astray. We have turned every one to his own way"** (Isaiah 53:6).

> **"There is none that understandeth, there is none that seeketh after God.**

> **They are all gone out of the way, they are together become unprofitable; there is none that doeth good, no, not one.**

> **Their throat** *is* **an open sepulchre; with their tongues they have used deceit; the poison of asps** *is* **under their lips.**

> **Whose mouth** *is* **full of cursing and bitterness.**

> **Their feet** *are* **swift to shed blood:**

> **Destruction and misery** *are* **in their ways:**

> **And the way of peace have they not known:**

> **There is no fear of God before their eyes"** (Romans 3:12–18).

> **"For there is not a just man upon earth, that doeth good, and sinneth not"** (Ecclesiastes 7:20).

> **"There is none righteous, no, not one"** (Romans 3:10).

> **"There is none good but one, [that is], God"** (Mark 10:18).

My dealings with the people taught me that human beings come together by virtue of nationality, religious belief, financial or other common interests and oppress or exclude any individual who is different or does not belong to their group on the grounds of nationality, religious belief, skin colour, social status or one of the many other discriminatory barriers that exist in the world. I understood that in fact the main and perhaps only reason for oppression and exclusion in our society is greed. As the Bible so aptly puts it **"the love of money is the root of all evil"** (*I Timothy 6:10*).

As for Christians, one of whom by the grace of God I am, I came across some of the warmest and most loving, caring and honest people I have ever met. I also met very cold, self-centred, unloving and non-Christ like Christians. Fortunately, not all is gloomy in this world, for there are believers who fear God and non-believers who have a conscience and try to do good. And fortunately we have hope in God.

Mrs. Austin, Dr. Browne's office manager, was one of the first persons in Bermuda I informed about my decision to leave the Island. I had become very close to Mrs. Austin, an expatriate African American. She told me that when she informed Dr. Browne, the transport minister and my landlord, of my decision, he was apparently saddened and said, "They always do that." By this he meant that the establishment always pushes aside any person who does not abide by their rules. If the person fights back, they starve him financially and let the court case linger until the person gives up and leaves. This tactic is commonly referred to in Bermuda as "giving somebody a monkey ride." Mrs. Austin left Bermuda two weeks after I did.

A few days after my conversation with Mrs. Austin, I met Dr. Browne and told him I was definitely leaving. He asked me if the fact that my hospital privileges had not been restored would affect my chances of securing employment abroad. I told him I would be all right. He offered to speak to Mr. Dills, the chairman of the Bermuda Hospitals Board, about restoring my privileges on paper so that my file would indicate this. I asked him not to speak to Mr. Dills and said that everything would be fine. I knew that everything would be fine because during my four years in Bermuda I had learned that if I prayed to God every morning when I got up, did my best according to God's will, put my faith in God, remained patient and thanked God every night before I went to bed, everything would be fine. Dr. Browne and I settled all of our business matters in a friendly way in just ten minutes. Before I left his office he said that if, on the plane to Montreal, I dictated everything that had happened to me in Bermuda and then sent him the tape, he would pass it on to a Bermudian journalist who would write a newspaper account of my story. I said I had enough material to write a book and was thinking of doing so. Dr. Browne said that Bermudians prefer to read the newspaper and that would be a better medium. I thanked Dr. Browne for his help. We shook hands and embraced and I left his office.

A few of my patients learned that I might write a book about my experiences in Bermuda. One such patient, a Christian woman, said, "I hope you won't destroy my Island." I told her the Bible teaches that only God has the power to make and destroy things, people and nations (*Genesis 1:1–31; 2:1,2; 6:7; 7:4; 18:14; Deuteronomy 9:4; Jeremiah 12:17; Zephaniah 2:5;*

Luke 20:16; John 10:18; 19:11; I Corinthians 3:17; James 4:12; Revelation 11:18).

Another patient, a well-spoken black Bermudian, tried at length to dissuade me from writing a book because it could destroy people's lives. He advised me to examine myself, for I might have unresolved personal problems and my adversaries might not be at fault at all. I told my interlocutor that even though I was not an impartial judge of myself I did not believe I had any unresolved personal problems. I told him not to worry about my adversaries: I had dealt with them long enough to know that they cared mostly about their pockets and I did not think my book would in any way affect their earnings.

My interlocutor said that my intention was to avenge myself. I said I was aware of the Bible's teachings that we must not avenge ourselves and that **"vengeance and recompense belongeth"** to God (*Deuteronomy 32:35; Psalms 94:1; Romans 12:19*). I said I was also aware of the Bible's teaching that **"The heart** [of humankind] **is deceitful above all things and desperately wicked"** (*Genesis 6:5; 8:21; Psalms 53:2–4; Ecclesiastes 9:3; Jeremiah 17:9; Matthew 15:19; Mark 7: 21–23*). I said I was the first to admit the latter truth and that was why I prayed constantly for God to help me with the thoughts in my heart and to guide me.

My interlocutor repeated that my book could destroy people's lives. I said that even though my adversaries tried to do just that, my intentions were to write about injustice and the truth that God encourages. I said I did not hate the other doctors and never felt any hatred for them throughout the experience. I said that even now I still prayed for them. I said I would be lying if I said I loved them, for I was not able to do that yet. At the beginning and throughout the experience, I thought I was right and my adversaries were wrong. I thought I was in control. But now, I explained, I realized that we have little or no control over events, and that was why I tried not to lose sleep over things, but to spend more time praying and doing. I said that in time I also realized that my fight was not really about who was right or wrong, but about fearing God. I told my interlocutor that any book I wrote would be not so much about the doctors as about me seeking the truth, being chastised, humbled, finding God – or, rather, being found by God – fearing God, loving God and doing the will of God. For reasons unknown to me, Bermuda just happened to be the stage for the story.

The gentleman said again that my intention was to avenge myself and that my talk about God was a metaphor. I asked him if he believed in God. He said he was spiritual, but did not attend church because he did not believe in organized religion. I remembered a time when I had thought I was spiritual, but in truth had been as far from God as east is from west. I felt like telling the gentleman that there are many varieties of churches and he could find one to attend to if he really wanted to. But I did not.

Next, the gentleman informed me that he too would write a book some day. I asked him what it would be about. He said his book would be about "black people," who, unlike other people, he said, do not help each other, but go to great lengths to hinder each other. That was not first time I had heard this rhetoric. I said that while it may be true in the West, it was not the case in the Africa where I grew up. (In the Africa where I grew up a man would give his bed to a foreigner and sleep on the floor, a mother would starve in order to feed her children, a working parent would willingly support more than ten immediate and distant family members – which is both an asset and a liability to Africa: an asset because many people, especially the elderly, suffer in times of high unemployment and some irresponsible government; a liability because it tends to suffocate initiative.) I asked the gentleman when he planned to write his book. He said when he retired and left Bermuda.

The gentleman was not consistent. On one hand he was begging me not to write the book because it might negatively affect the reputation of a few individuals. On the other hand he was planning to write a book that could negatively affect millions of "black people" when he retired and his own career and livelihood would not be affected. But the most paradoxical aspect of his attitude was that he seemed to be part of the so-called problem of black people not helping each other, for he had told me earlier he would never fight for any "black person or black cause" even though part of his job was to fight injustice.

In the end, the gentleman told me I should forgo writing my book and do what I did best – treat sick people. I felt like telling him that saving people's souls is as important, if not more so, than healing them. But I did not. Instead, I put an end to our conversation.

Not all my patients who learned that I might write a book about my experiences in Bermuda were so defensive. A few were encouraging. Mrs. A. Bean, a Christian woman in her seventies who had been told by other doctors that she was too old to have surgery and on whom I had successfully operated, phoned me every few months to encourage me to tell my story. She sent me every book published in Bermuda in recent years that she thought might be useful to me in writing this one.

But perhaps the most encouraging conversation I had throughout this story was one I had with a patient a few weeks before I left Bermuda. The patient, a Christian woman in her fifties, came to my office complaining of neck and arm pain with numbness in her hands. X-rays showed damage to three discs in her neck. I asked her how she had sustained the neck injuries. She said two of her female colleagues had beaten her and pushed her down some stairs. The woman, who worked as a taxi dispatcher, said her colleagues had beaten her because she would not participate in a money making scheme they had devised. She said her dispatcher colleagues would preferentially assign calls to the taxi driver who gave them money.

The woman said she refused to participate in the scheme because she was already getting paid for the work she did and felt that as a Christian it was immoral for her to collect any additional money from taxi drivers. She said she assigned each call to the nearest available driver, which angered her colleagues, who then beat her.

I told my patient I knew a woman in her seventies who, like her, worked as a taxi dispatcher. This woman, who was very friendly, had befriended my wife when we first arrived in Bermuda. When I told my patient the name of my wife's friend, she said that woman was one of the colleagues who had beaten her. I was shocked. "But she is a Christian," I said. "She travels abroad with Christians and is involved in a lot of Christian activities." My patient said, "There are a lot of people who wear their Christianity on their sleeve." She added, "You know, there are a lot of wicked people in this place." I said, "There are a lot of wicked people all over the world." She said, "You're probably right, but this place is called Devil's Island."

My patient changed the subject and inquired about my court case. I said everything was fine. She said she commended me for fighting the hospital the way I had and she regretted not having sued the two colleagues who had harmed her. I told her she did not have to regret anything, for the worthiest battle in our life is to find Jesus. The Bible says that once we have found Jesus we have won all the battles in the world, because Jesus Christ has conquered the world for us (John 16:33; I John 4:4; 5:4). She said, "You know, God is a good God." I nodded my approval. She said, "God is good to those who love Him." I smiled and said, "Amen."

[1] Ayo Johnson, "Doctor Lifts Lid on Problems at King Edward Hospital. Surgeon Cites Problems of Communications, Management, Even Racism. Hospital Challenges Allegations," *Bermuda Sun,* August 11th, 1999, p. 3.
[2] Meredith Ebbin, "The final push: Messages from the party leaders," *Bermuda Sun,* November 6th, 1988, p. 1.

Appendix

Letter 1

February 28, 1998,

S.B.

Dear Board Members,

My name is S. B. and I am a 26-year-old woman who has suffered with back pain for the majority of my life. When I reached my early teens, my back began to hurt and often prevented me from participating in physical education at school and other 'normal' activities. The pain became more intense when I was physically active. I began to get 'shocks' down my right leg and it often felt numb. My mother became worried and took me to doctors to investigate the problem.

One of the first specialists that I saw was from overseas; he told me that part of my problem was due to some curvature in my spine. I was asked to have x-rays taken of my back. When I went back to the doctor, he had left the island. Dr. Chess, another doctor from overseas had arrived on the island and I made an appointment to see him. Dr. Chess agreed on the diagnosis of scoliosis, but after examining me, he became concerned about the lower part of my spine. I was asked to have x-rays taken of my lower back. When I called to make another appointment, I was told that Dr. Chess was no longer on the island and that I would have to see Dr. Cooperson.

My visit with Dr. Cooperson was the most humiliating and infuriating experience that I have ever had with a doctor to date. Dr. Cooperson was not warm and he spoke to me in a demeaning manner. He asked me to bend over and touch my toes. I did so successfully and once I was erect, he told my mother that there was "nothing wrong with her back and do not return to waste my time." My mother attempted to inform Dr. Cooperson of Dr. Chess's concerns about my lower spine; he replied, "I'm not Dr. Chess". I never saw Dr. Cooperson again after that visit.

The problems with my back continued, but I felt that no assistance was available on the island. Pain management consisted of taking several hundred milligrams of Ibuprofen at a time and resting. At one point, I was sent home from preparatory school in Maine because I could not manage my pain.

My next major 'back attack' was at the completion of my second degree. When I returned home, I was barely able to walk and was in extreme pain. A friend recommended that I see Dr. Bernius (a chiropractor). At that point, I was willing to try anything. I started going to Dr. Bernius three times a week for a month and then my visits were reduced to twice a week, then once a week and eventually once every two weeks. I saw Dr. Bernius over a period of seven months. I terminated the visits with him because I [sic] continued feel pain and noticed no improvement. I went to my General Practitioner, Dr. Gordon Campbell, because I was in a lot of pain. Dr Campbell was very concerned because my right leg was not responding to reflex tests. He referred me to Dr. Bah.

Dr. Bah listened intently to my concerns about my back pain, looked at the x-rays that I was asked to get by Dr. Bernius and immediately recognized a problem with the lower part of my spine. Dr. Bah asked me to have a CT-scan. When I returned to Dr. Bah's office he looked at the CT-scan, [sic] informed me of the name of my condition, and gave me two options. One was to have physiotherapy and the other was to have surgery. I choose to have surgery because I wanted the pain to end and did not want to go through any more physical manipulation.

I had the surgery on June 24, 1996. Dr. Bah followed me very carefully and my recuperation went very smoothly. My lower back has not given me any problems since I had the surgery and I am happy with my decision.

I feel that Dr. Bah has saved my life. I trust him fully, value his experience and I am willing to travel to any part of the world in order to receive his expertise. I have relied on the so-called "specialist" available on the island for years and I am disgusted with the care that I had received before meeting Dr. Bah. I feel that Bermuda would be losing a saviour for back sufferers if he were forced to leave the island. I fully support Dr. Bah in his effort to stay in Bermuda because there are no other options.

Respectfully,

S. J.B. B.

J. B. (mother)

Letter 2

February 10, 1998

S. P.

My name is S. P. I am a patient of Dr. Bah. I would like to give a history of the injuries and subsequent treatment I received because of an accident almost a 1 ½ years ago.

On November 12, 1996 1 reported for work at the Bank of. ...I walked into the ladies restroom and immediately slipped on a wet tiled floor. I fell in a twisted position to avoid hitting a wall. My upper body twisted in a clockwise manner. As I fell, my left arm hit the sharp corner of a metal box causing a laceration and I felt my right knee twist at the time. Upon hitting the floor, I landed squarely on my backside.... I then noticed my arm was bleeding profusely so I tried to get straight up. At this time, I also felt pain in my knee and in the middle of my back. After I got up, I could hardly breathe and felt lightheaded. I made my way out the restroom door and asked to be taken to the hospital. At this time, I was in shock and did not realize the seriousness of my injuries. My main concern was to get to the hospital. A fellow staff member transported me to the hospital in her private car. Whenever she made turns in her car, I felt pain in the right side of my back.

Upon reaching the Emergency Department, I informed the receptionist that my injuries consisted of my arm, knee and back. Dr. E. Schulte examined me in the Emergency Department. He put 13 sutures in my arm and sent me for x-rays of my knee and back. After viewing the first set of x-rays, Dr. Schulte felt it necessary to send me back for another x-ray of my back. Dr. Schulte felt it was possible I may have suffered a compressed disk because of my fall, but that was not something that shows up easily on an x-ray. An appointment was then made for me to see Dr. Fascioni at the Fracture Clinic on November 18, 1996.

During the early days of my injuries, my knee felt worse than my back. When I saw Dr. Fascioni at the Fracture Clinic, he asked what I was there for. I told him about my fall at work and that my knees and back hurt. He asked me which was hurting me the most. I told him my knees hurt the most but my back also hurt. He looked at the x-rays of the knee and my back and told me he did not see anything significantly wrong. He felt I probably had pulled a muscle in my back.

He also said that I was overweight and that if I lost weight it would help my back. He then ordered me to attend physiotherapy for my knee injury. He did not prescribe any treatment for my back.

I attended a number of physiotherapy sessions for my knee during the next two weeks. During this period my back was feeling progressively worse even wearing a bra was painful. The back pain was radiating around my right side to the front. I was experiencing muscle spasms quite often. I asked the physiotherapist if she could do treatment on my back, but she told me I would have to make another appointment with Dr. Fascioni, which I did.

On December 2, 1996, I had my second appointment with Dr. Fascioni. I told him I was having severe pain from the middle of the back around my right side and to the front. I also told him about the muscle spasms. Once again, he looked at the x-rays and concluded I had pulled a muscle and mentioned my being overweight. He then ordered physiotherapy for my back.

At this time, I would like to make a comment about Dr. Fascioni. During my two visits with him, I found him to be quite abrupt and arrogant. I felt insulted, humiliated, and discriminated against when he kept dwelling on my being overweight. A person knows his or her own body best. I knew that my back injury was more serious than a pulled muscle and my being overweight was irrelevant to the injury. Later the same day, I saw my family doctor, V. Jamieson to obtain a medical certificate to be off from work till December 12th. When I was there, she phoned Dr. Fascioni to discuss my case. They discussed my weight during this call. Dr. Jameson weighed me and we discussed a diet. I continued my physiotherapy visits for my back as the treatments for my knees had been stopped. The pain was getting even worse day by day in my hack. I was having spasms on a regular basis and pain with movement of my arms.

On December 12th, I went back to see Dr. Jamieson because the pain in my back was getting worse. I was sore to the touch and was having great difficulty in sleeping due to the pain. She then referred me to Dr. C.R., a sport medicine doctor for treatment and told me not to tell Dr. Fascioni [Dr. C.R. is a sport medicine doctor from Ireland who came to Bermuda in 1995 to take over the practice of Dr. M. Dr. M. had been forced to leave the Island because Dr. Cooperson and Fascioni had complained that he was seeing too many patients].

On December 16, 1996, I went to the office of Dr. R. He found that I was in too much pain and having too many spasms to manipulate me. I even had spasms in his office. He gave me an injection for pain in a muscle in my back. I went back to Dr. R. on December 23rd. At that time, he performed acupuncture on me. One of the acupuncture needles that were placed near the most painful area of my back quivered rapidly. On this day, he ordered a bone scan of my back. The next day when I went for the bone scan at the hospital they were unable to find a vein to make an injection so another bone scan appointment had to be made for December 31st.

On December 31, after the bone scan was taken, the radiologist told me I have a "hot spot" on number 9 and 10 disks of my spine and told me to go back and see Dr. R. Later that day I went back to see Dr. R. He told me because the "hot spot" could be compression or some other type of injury, I may have to go overseas for a MRI in the future. He also gave me instructions to attend physiotherapy for my back.

I saw Dr. R. again on January 9th, January 23rd, and February 6th 1997. Between these visits, I continued to receive physiotherapy at the hospital, which consisted mainly of ultrasound to my back. During my visits to Dr. R., he prescribed Diazepam, Amitriptyline and Distalgesic Co-Proximal for me. During my final visit to Dr. R., he informed me that as a sport medicine doctor, he could not do anything for me anymore. He recommended I see an Orthopaedic and Spine Surgeon, Dr. Bah.

My first visit to Dr. Bah was on February 25th, 1997. He greeted me in a warm and friendly way and proceeded to examine my x-rays and bone scan. He felt my back and asked me to try and bend certain ways. After reviewing the x-rays and bone scan, he ordered a CAT scan for me. He told me the bone scan showed there was a problem but it was not clear what it was. On March 4th, I went back to Dr. Bah to learn the results of the CAT scan. He showed it to me and told me there was some shadowing on the 9th and 10th vertebrae. He then ordered a MRI for me in Boston, Massachusetts on March 11th, 1997. He instructed me to ensure I brought the MRI images back with me to ensure a quick analysis.

On March 20th, my mother accompanied me to see Dr. Bah. At this time, I gave him the MRI images. After he looked at them, he did not comment on them. He asked my mother and I to look at them to see if we could see anything wrong. Even with my untrained eye, it was obvious for me to pick out that one disk in my spine was damaged. Dr. Bah then commented that I was right and explained that I had a herniated disc. He then ordered physiotherapy for six weeks. He told me that sometimes physiotherapy could work for this type of injury but also mentioned that mine being a mid-back injury would be the most difficult to treat.

On April 29th, I saw Dr. Bah again. There was no change in the way I was feeling. The pain was still very severe and I was still taking medications. At this time, we discussed surgery. He told me the decision was mine whether to have the surgery or to go on with the way things were in the hope my back would eventually get better. I then made the decision to go ahead with surgery because I was in severe pain. A date was set for July 16th 1997, but I was to continue with physiotherapy with the hope it would improve. I was finding that everything I did with my arms and general movement caused me great pain.

On July 16th, 1997, Dr. Bah performed surgery on me at the King Edward Hospital. He repaired the disc by removing a rib and using it for bone grafting. He also had to insert a metal rod in my back. After the surgery, I was in the ICU for three days and on a general ward for 11 days. While in the hospital, Dr. Bah visited me everyday and kept my family and I fully updated about my condition. About 2 weeks after returning home, I saw Dr. Bah at the Fracture Clinic. He examined my surgical incision and arranged for a district nurse to visit me regularly until my incision healed. About 2 weeks later Dr. Bah examined my incision again and was pleased with the healing. I saw Dr. Bah at the Fracture Clinic on October 3rd. This time he took x-rays and was pleased with the progress of my back. On January 9th 1998, I saw Dr, Bah at the Fracture Clinic, again when he had another X-ray taken he was once again pleased with the healing.

At present, seven months after surgery, I am feeling a lot better and I hope to be back to normal soon. I no longer have the same pain I had prior to surgery. I am very happy that I had the surgery as I am starting to perform tasks, which I have not been able to do since the accident occurred.

Dr. Bah assures me I should be able to return to work, which is something that I might not have been able to do without the surgery as I was in such severe pain.

I would like to say that it is because of the concern, understanding and most of all professionalism of Dr. Bah that I am well on the road to recovery. I am truly grateful to have had him as my doctor. He took the time to research what was wrong with me rather than write it off as being a "pulled muscle", "all in my mind", or "weight related" as Dr. Fascioni did.

Bermuda is privileged to have a surgeon of Dr. Bah's ability here. Hopefully he will remain with us for many years to come.

Yours sincerely,

S.P.

Letter 3

February 17, 1998

C.G.

My name is C.G. and it has been sometime since Dr. Bah performed my surgery and I am pleased that Dr. Bah was my surgeon. I do not have any back or leg pains anymore. Thanks to Dr. Bah and the mighty God, I am completely as active as I use to be.

I hope others will be able to benefit from Dr. Bah and his professionalism as I did.

God Bless and Keep you,

C.G.

Letter 4

February 18, 1998.

Mrs. J.B.L

Re: In defense of Dr. C. Bah.

Without prejudice,

When I first became aware of the attempt to discredit Dr. Bah, I was, to say the least, appalled! What could possibly be said against a man of such unquestionable ability and integrity? I then read paragraph (e) of the [Brookson' report] correspondence doing just that, where I am described as 'obese' and realized that given such an inaccuracy, those responsible deserve no respect whatsoever!

Upon closer scrutiny of the infamous paragraph (e), the contents of which is almost laughable, I discovered such a wealth of misinformation, there is no way under the sun to validate any of what was written.

I derived the distinct impression that 'any old professional' can come into Bermuda, and so long as they uphold the status quo', everything is fine. But woe betides anyone who does otherwise.

Dr. Bah was fully aware of my entire medical history and would in no way endanger my well being. To insinuate that use of the OR (operating room) at KEMH (King Edward Memorial Hospital) was in breech of hospital policy or any other concocted idea is ludicrous!

To prove my point: At the time of my back problems, I was suffering from blood clots, diabetic and definitely [sic]not overweight. My weight at this time is probably more than desirable because of inactivity. Dr. Bah's colleague (at that time) said that a MRI was needed and only then could an accurate assessment of my condition be made. I had the MRI in Boston Ma. (March 97) and was operated upon within a month. Given the long recovery time, I was told that back pain would continue for quite some time. Leg pains due to blood clots were an entirely separate issue.

No sooner had I become adjusted to my recovery routine, than it became necessary to operate again (in July) on an entirely different site on my spine. To date, barring pains from clots, I am doing quite well. My medication serves its purpose and there only remains the element of time. Bermuda undoubtedly needs doctors of Dr. Bah's caliber and a MRI unit. To hinder either is obscene.

Sincerely,

J.D. (B) L. (Mrs.)

c.c. The Editor The Royal Gazette

Bibliography

Abdul-Haqq Abdiyah Akbar. *Sharing Your Faith with a Muslim.*
Minneapolis: Bethany House, 1980.

Al-Biruni Dar. *The Holy Qur'an: Meanings in English.* Beirut, Lebanon:
Dar An-Nafaés, 1998.

Barnes New Testament Notes. Online Bible Millennium Ed. Winterbourne,
ON: Timnathserah, 1987/2002.

Compton Reference. Carlsbad, CA: Compton's New Media, 1995.

Encyclopaedia Britannica. CD-ROM. Encyclopaedia Britannica,
1994/2002.

Flavius Josephus. *The New Complete Works of Josephus* (trans. by William
Whiston). Grand Rapids, MI: Kregel, 1999.

Harries-Hunter, Barbara. *The People of Bermuda: Beyond the Crossroads.*
Toronto: Gagné-Best, 1993.

Hodgson, Eva. *Second Class Citizens; First Class Men,* 3rd Ed. Hamilton,
Bermuda: Writers' Machine, 1997.

The Holy Bible: King James Version. Nashville, TN: Thomas Nelson, 1990.

The Holy Bible: King James Version Read by Alexander Scourby. Anderson,
SC: Alpha Omega Marketing Inc., 1996/2000.

Life Application Study Bible: King James Version. Wheaton, IL: Tyndale
House, 1988/1989.

Martin, Walter. *The Kingdom of the Cults.* Minneapolis: Bethany House,
1928/1989.

Mason, Steve. *Josephus and the New Testament.* Peabody, MA:
Hendrickson, 1957/1992.

Matthew Henry Commentary. Online Bible Millennium Ed.
Winterbourne, ON: Timnathserah, 1987/2002.

Matthew Poole's Commentary of the Bible. Online Bible Millennium Ed.
Winterbourne, ON: Timnathserah, 1987/2002.

Microsoft Encarta Encyclopaedia 2002. Microsoft Corp., 1993/2001.

Morey, Robert. *The Islamic Invasion: Confronting the World's Fastest*

Growing Religion. Eugene, OR: Harvest House, 1992.

Olsen, Viggo, with Jeannette Lockerbie. *Daktar: Diplomat in Bangladesh.* Grand Rapids, MI: Kregel, 1996.

Online Bible. Millennium Ed. Winterbourne, ON: Timnathserah, 1987/2002.

Rice, E. M. *A Child's History of Bermuda* (illus. by Bobbe Cauchi). Hamilton, Bermuda: Island Press, 1964/1988.

La Sainte Bible, Version Martin 1855. Dallas: International Bible Association, 1980/1995.

Walton, Robert. *Charts of Church History.* Grand Rapids, MI: Zondervan, 1986.

Williams, J. Randolph. *Lois: Bermuda's Grande Dame of Politics.* Hamilton, Bermuda: Camden, 1956.

Wilson Ross, Nancy. *Buddhism: A Way of Life and Thought.* New York: Knopf, 1980.

ISBN 1-41206399-X